# Foundations of Entrepreneurship and Economic Development

'Entrepreneurial activity is the key to growth and prosperity. This volume provides a detailed analysis of the role of the entrepreneur and the conditions necessary for the unleashing of its creative potential.'

James Gwartney, Professor of Economics, Florida State University

'*Foundations of Entrepreneurship* offers a careful and scholarly look at the connections between economic freedom, entrepreneurship, and economic growth. Serious policy-makers could learn a lot from its in-depth analysis.'

David Boaz, author of *Libertarianism: A Primer*

Entrepreneurship is the key factor in economic development. It determines how quickly and accurately an economic system identifies and responds to the profit opportunities inherent in disequilibrium situations. Thus, it both generates greater coordination of economic activities at a point in time and increases the growth rate of the economy over time.

This book brings to light entrepreneurship in all its aspects for the first time within a unified framework. It considers the economic, psychological, political, legal and cultural dimensions of entrepreneurship from a market-process perspective. It examines the environmental conditions most conducive to a blossoming of the entrepreneurial drive. David Harper has produced a volume that analyses why some people are quicker than others in discovering profit opportunities. Importantly, the book also covers the issue of how cultural value systems orient entrepreneurial vision and, in contrast to conventional wisdom, the book argues that individualist cultural values are not categorically superior to group-oriented values in terms of their consequences for entrepreneurial discovery.

This stimulating and original book will be of great interest to development and market economists as well as their students. The implications for economic policies and institutions also make the book important reading for those working in the public sector.

**David A. Harper** is Associate Clinical Professor in the Department of Economics, New York University, USA.

# Foundations of the market economy
Edited by Mario J. Rizzo and Lawrence H. White
*New York University and University of Georgia*

A central theme in this series is the importance of understanding and assessing the market economy from a perspective broader than the static economics of perfect competition and Pareto optimality. Such a perspective sees markets as causal processes generated by the preferences, expectations and beliefs of economic agents. The creative acts of entrepreneurship that uncover new information about preferences, prices and technology are central to these processes with respect to their ability to promote the discovery and use of knowledge in society.

The market economy consists of a set of institutions that facilitate voluntary cooperation and exchange among individuals. These institutions include the legal and ethical framework as well as more narrowly 'economic' patterns of social interaction. Thus the law, legal institutions and cultural and ethical norms, as well as ordinary business practices and monetary phenomena, fall within the analytical domain of the economist. Other titles in the series:

# Foundations of Entrepreneurship and Economic Development

David A. Harper

Routledge
Taylor & Francis Group

LONDON AND NEW YORK

First published 2003
by Routledge
2 Park Square, Milton Park, Abingdon, Oxon, OX14 4RN

Simultaneously published in the USA and Canada
by Routledge
270 Madison Ave, New York NY 10016

*Routledge is an imprint of the Taylor & Francis Group*

Transferred to Digital Printing 2007

Typeset in Garamond by Taylor & Francis Books Ltd

*British Library Cataloguing in Publication Data*
A catalogue record for this book is available from the British Library

*Library of Congress Cataloging-in-Publication Data*
Harper, David A.
Foundations of entrepreneurship and economic development /
David A. Harper
(Foundations of the market economy)
Includes bibliographical references and index.
1. Entrepreneurship. 2. New business enterprises.
3. Economic development. I. Title
II. Foundations of the market economy series.

HB615 .H337 2003
338'.04-dc21200203314

ISBN10: 0–415–15342–5 (hbk)
ISBN10: 0–415–45920–6 (pbk)

ISBN13: 978–0–415–15342–3 (hbk)
ISBN13: 978–0–415–45920–4 (pbk)

To my mother, Eunice

# Contents

# Illustrations

## Figures

## Tables

# Preface

This book focuses upon the phenomenon of entrepreneurial alertness and its determinants. Alertness, of course, has been the central theme of Israel Kirzner's path-breaking work on entrepreneurship and the character of competitive market processes. Kirzner focuses mainly upon the economic function of alert entrepreneurs and places less emphasis upon the environmental conditions that are most conducive to the generation of entrepreneurial talent. That is the subject of this book.

My study applies Kirzner's theory of entrepreneurship and delves into the psychological, cultural, political and institutional contexts that frame entrepreneurial discoveries of unexploited gains from trade. It invokes psychological and cultural explanatory principles in its account of entrepreneurial behaviour. It is concerned with the process and not just the outcome of entrepreneurial cognition. With its emphasis upon the extralogical forces that affect entrepreneurship, this book is an important complement to my previous work, *Entrepreneurship and the Market Process*. That book sought to investigate the latent structure of rationality behind entrepreneurs' problem-solving efforts. It provided a predominantly logical skeleton of the growth-of-knowledge process inherent in the operation of markets.

The present work is an elaboration of ideas first sketched out in my monograph *Wellsprings of Enterprise*, published by the New Zealand Institute of Economic Research (NZIER) in 1994. The NZ Treasury commissioned the research project that resulted in that monograph. I am grateful to NZIER for permission to use passages from that earlier work.

I am also grateful for permission to publish material on money and alertness, which first appeared in *Journal des Economistes et des Etudes Humaines*.

The writing of this book would not have been possible without the generous support and financial assistance of the following individuals and organisations: Mrs Sally Somers von Behren, Mrs Ethelmae Humphreys (J.P. Humphreys Foundation), David B. Kennedy (Earhart Foundation), Richard M. Larry (Sarah Scaife Foundation) and Robert Reinwald (Österreichische Nationalbank).

I have benefited from extensive feedback from my colleagues at New York University, particularly Israel Kirzner and Mario Rizzo, and other members of the Austrian Economics Colloquium at NYU, especially Bill Butos and Chidem Kurdas. (I would also like to thank Mario Rizzo, as series co-editor, for his insistence that I be 'a little less cautious' and more 'American' in talking up the merits of my contribution!) I also appreciated suggestions on specific chapters from Peter Boettke, Roger Garrison, Steven Horwitz and the late Don Lavoie. In addition, valuable comments have been received at workshops of the Annual Conference of the Society for the Development of Austrian Economics and the J.M. Kaplan Workshop in Politics, Philosophy and Economics at George Mason University.

I would like to acknowledge the patience and guidance of my editors at Routledge over the years – Alan Jarvis, Alison Kirk and Robert Langham.

Any remaining errors of course are my own.

David A. Harper
New York City
July 2002

# 1   Introduction

A prominent feature of a competitive enterprise economy is the ability of people continually to seek out and seize opportunities for profitable new activities in local and world markets. Encouraging and releasing people's entrepreneurial energies is an essential key to the achievement of greater economic prosperity in a country and to the continuing regeneration of its economy over time. Indeed, the economics of entrepreneurial discovery should be the hub of the economics of growth and development.

Economic development is essentially an evolutionary learning process that involves the growth and restructuring of knowledge and the overthrow of old ideas and organisations. It is a discovery process propelled by competition among alert entrepreneurs who, lured by the scent of profit, locate pockets of market ignorance and then exploit hitherto untapped opportunities for specialisation and trade in the network of economic transactions. The entrepreneurially driven process of economic development thus mobilises hidden and fragmented bits of knowledge in the economy that would otherwise lie dormant and unutilised.

Entrepreneurship is critical to enhancing the innovativeness and responsiveness of businesses, to boosting productivity and to improving cost structures and trade performance. The entrepreneurial spirit may manifest itself in the development of new markets, new products, new methods of production and management, the discovery of new inputs and the establishment of new businesses and even new organisational forms. Entrepreneurship is pertinent to the analysis of how new ideas or 'recipes' for reconfiguring objects in the material and social world can be harnessed to enhance a nation's wealth.

In the longer term, a country's economic progress depends on its ability to increase the value of what it produces with its resource base (people, land and capital). The point cannot be emphasised too strongly, however, that neither the ends to which these resources are put nor the means for achieving these ends (i.e. the set of resources and how they are used) are given or fixed. They are the result of entrepreneurial choices and are open to entrepreneurial initiative. Individual entrepreneurs and entrepreneurial teams bring to light the resources, technologies and trading opportunities that make economic development possible. Indeed, whenever entrepreneurs are the first to discover the availability and potential economic value of new resources, they are in effect bringing those resources into existence in economic terms (Kirzner 1989). The process of economic development is the overall, unintended outcome of a complex myriad individual acts of entrepreneurial discovery. It entails much more than the efficient allocation of given and known means among people's given and known ends.

As a result, entrepreneurship (within an appropriate institutional framework) may in effect override resource endowments and scarcity as the prime determinant of economic performance.[1] As Romer (1993) has pointed out in another connection, ideas are not scarce, they are almost limitless. 'The world, in Romer's view, isn't defined by scarcity and the limits on growth. Instead, it's a playground of nearly unbounded opportunity, where new ideas beget new products, new markets, and new possibilities to create wealth' (Kelly 1996: 148). Moreover, entrepreneurship itself often generates more entrepreneurship, so that economic development is a process that can be kept in motion by endogenous economic forces rather than exogenous shocks (say, in resource availabilities). Every entrepreneurial act of discovery generates at least some unintended consequences, including the creation of new value scales (i.e. unexpected changes in consumer tastes) and new technologies, so that each entrepreneurial action has the potential to create new markets for new goods and services.

Seen in this light, the development process and the growth of our knowledge do not converge towards an end state but remain open-ended: 'We never know what real possibilities remain to be discovered; we never know what the real limits are to the elasticity of the resource constraints that circumscribe our existence' (Kirzner 1984a: 43). Of course, recognising the primacy of entrepreneurship in economic development does not mean that resource constraints do not matter at all. Indeed, a thorough explanation of economic development requires an understanding of how entrepreneurship interacts with the discovery and amelioration of resource constraints (Irigoin 1990: 204). Entrepreneurs find out what the relevant constraints are and develop innovative ways to alleviate them, thereby enhancing the range of effective options available to people.

Recognition of the pivotal role of entrepreneurship in development leads us to emphasise the importance of institutions that engender processes of entrepreneurial discovery. It motivates us to enquire into the institutional conditions that are highly conducive to entrepreneurship and to investigate the institutional changes necessary in moving towards a more market-oriented economy. Indeed, differences in the nature of institutions and in the structure of incentives they create for entrepreneurship explain much of the variation in the wealth of nations.

A better appreciation of entrepreneurship is required if we are to be able to understand market processes and to explain how economies, individual markets and business organisations adjust to new circumstances. Such knowledge is needed to account for the coherence of market-based economic systems and for the continuous tendency towards economic balance and coordination of economic plans.

Although entrepreneurship is the main mechanism that creates wealth, explanations of economic growth and development often ignore (or fail to acknowledge explicitly) the entrepreneurial forces of change and adaptation that underlie economic performance.[2] Surprisingly, the role of entrepreneurship in economic development has attracted less professional interest than the role of other factors, such as the accumulation of physical capital, expansion of the labour force, R&D, technological progress and education. Entrepreneurship is something we ignore at our peril.

## The distinctive approach in this book

This book is intended to reassert the role of entrepreneurship as the 'prime mover' in the process of economic growth and development. It is the first book to deal with entrepreneurship in all its aspects within a unified analytical framework. It considers the economic, psychological, political, legal and cultural dimensions of entrepreneurship from a market-process (or entrepreneurial-discovery) perspective.

The entrepreneurial-discovery approach argues that what is important for economic development is how an economic system identifies and responds to disequilibrium (i.e. a breakdown in the coordination of economic plans). Unlike most contributions to the economics of development, the entrepreneurial-discovery approach is a disequilibrium, process-oriented approach that depicts entrepreneurship as the real engine of economic transformation. Entrepreneurship is a process of discovering profit opportunities inherent in disequilibrium situations. The specific 'talent' that entrepreneurs possess is an acute alertness to as yet unexploited opportunities for mutually beneficial exchange.

The upshot is that we should judge the performance of an economic system not only by the degree of efficiency with which it allocates available and already known resources but also, and more importantly, by the speed with which the system discovers and reduces the excesses and discoordination of economic disequilibria over time. Consequently, the book's focus is upon the potential of different types of institutions to evoke entrepreneurial discovery of genuine market error (i.e. hitherto unsuspected profit opportunities).

Unlike many economics contributions to the field, this book analyses the antecedents of entrepreneurship more so than its consequences. It explains the causal mechanisms that generate entrepreneurial discovery. In particular, it examines the causal paths from culture, institutions and individual psychology to entrepreneurial alertness. Although most economists concede that social, cultural and high-level institutional factors are more far reaching in their effects than regulatory and tax policies, they usually assume that these factors are intractable and not amenable to economic analysis.

Another distinguishing characteristic is that the approach is highly cognitive. The analysis of the antecedent conditions of entrepreneurship makes use of a simple but important psychological conjecture about the cognitive determinants of entrepreneurship. It argues that our expectations about the causes of what happens to us are the fundamental drivers that switch on entrepreneurial alertness. These cognitive representations of cause–effect relations are referred to as 'personal agency beliefs or judgements'. They are a core element in our understanding of the world and how we live in it. They are not personality traits: the perception of personal agency is a cognitive process. (Alertness too, of course, is a perceptual and cognitive phenomenon.) To form their judgements about the causal sources and controllability of what happens to them, people must integrate their perceptions of the contingency of events upon action with their perceptions of their competence to carry out those very actions. Individuals who have a strong sense of their own causal power over events will be the persons whose alertness is the most highly developed.

This psychological insight is used to investigate the environmental conditions that are most conducive to a robust sense of personal agency and a blossoming of the entrepreneurial drive. The approach requires us to identify the fundamental, institutional principles that define the basic structure of people's rights in a society and to identify the general character of the political and legal system. It spurs us to examine how institutions mould people's expectations of action–reward sequences. The approach considers how constitutional, legal, economic, political and ethical rules of the game affect people's perceived causal capabilities, the degree of their alertness and the directions in which their entrepreneurial energies are channelled.

Unlike the new institutional economics and economic theories of entrepreneurship, this book delves into the most fundamental levels of social analysis in its examination of the antecedents of entrepreneurship. In addition to higher-order institutions that frame market processes, such as constitutions and property rules, this book also examines the cultural dimension of entrepreneurship. More specifically, it investigates the cultural lenses that orient entrepreneurial vision. It explains how different cultural value systems affect the profile of the discoverer of profit opportunities and the types of opportunities to which people are most attuned.

The approach rejects aggregate notions of national culture that depict a culture as inherently pro- or anti-entrepreneurship. In contrast to the conventional wisdom, the book argues that individualist cultural values are not categorically superior to group-oriented values in terms of their consequences for entrepreneurial discovery. Rather, we can expect some group-oriented cultures to exhibit considerable entrepreneurial talent. The book also rejects the received view that group-oriented cultures inevitably converge towards a uniform set of individualist values as they develop economically.

This is a work in applied economics, not pure economic theory. Although this book is not intended to deliver a detailed policy statement, the analysis has important practical and policy implications for the design of institutions that stimulate (or at least release) entrepreneurship. It is the first book to flesh out fully a uniquely market-process perspective for developing public policy. Instead of listing specific policy prescriptions or laissez-faire rules of thumb, the approach identifies the key assumptions and specific rules for doing policy analysis. It supplies general instructions on how market-process economists should go about identifying and defining policy problems and choosing the most appropriate analytical methods for informing their policy analyses.

The emphasis of this book is upon a broad coverage of issues rather than a narrow concentration. The analysis is wide ranging in the intellectual wells that it draws from. The approach involves a comprehensive synthesis of ideas derived from the theory of market processes, new institutional economics, social learning theory, legal scholarship, cross-cultural psychology and the field of 'entrepreneurship studies' in business administration.

## Analytical conception of entrepreneurship

> Entrepreneurship is connected with change, but there are many kinds of change, and correspondingly many concepts of the entrepreneurial function.
>
> (Loasby 1982b: 244)

Standard economic theory has developed along lines that virtually exclude the entrepreneurial role. This has largely been a result of the tendency to exclude all elements of unexpected change, to focus attention almost exclusively on equilibrium states of affairs, and to treat individual decisions as immune from the hazards of error. Taken together, these features mean that mainstream (neoclassical) economics provides a very distorted picture of the competitive market process and of the process of economic adjustment. Economic decision-makers are assumed to respond mechanistically and automatically to the signals of the market. There is no spotting a gap in the market, no exercise of initiative. Entrepreneurial characteristics are specifically excluded from the model.

If it were appropriate to examine only equilibrium (market-clearing) levels of prices and output, we would not need a theory of entrepreneurship. But if we want to explain the disequilibrium process by which prices and outputs adjust in markets, then we must have a theory of the entrepreneur. The market process cannot function, even within the market for a single commodity, if all market participants are assumed to be non-entrepreneurial maximisers who react mechanically to changes enforced upon them by external circumstances over which they have no control (Kirzner 1962). A theory of entrepreneurship is a prerequisite to any theory of the dynamics of the market process.

The absence of a neoclassical theory of the entrepreneur has been investigated at length within the economics literature and need not be discussed in detail here.[3] At this juncture, it is sufficient to mention that the standard economic theory of competition cannot explain market processes – the way in which market forces bring about adjustments in prices, quantities and qualities and the introduction of new products and processes. At best, neoclassical theory describes the conditions for competitive equilibrium (economic balance), without explaining adequately if or how equilibrium may be reached. (For an exception, see Fisher 1983; 1987.)

Economic theories of entrepreneurship, of course, do exist but there is little consensus as to what constitutes entrepreneurship and the entrepreneurial function. There is no uniform treatment of the role that entrepreneurship plays in the operation of the market system. In the economic literature, the entrepreneur is portrayed, among others, as a heroic innovator who carries out 'new combinations' and initiates discontinuous change (Schumpeter 1934), as an economic leader who directs novel, non-routine activities of business organisations (Baumol 1993; 2002), as the person who takes highly uncertain decisions associated with unique business situations (Knight 1921), as a specialist who takes judgemental decisions about the allocation of scarce resources (Casson 1982), as a Popperian-style decision-maker who formulates conjectures and then tests them in the market environment (Harper 1996), as a 'gap filler' and 'input completer' who creatively responds to 'X-inefficiency' by plugging up holes in markets for the resources required to carry out a venture (Leibenstein 1968).

## Entrepreneurial alertness and discovery

For the purposes of this book, the emphasis is upon Kirzner's conception of entrepreneurial *discovery* and the market process. The key concept in Kirzner's theory is *alertness*. 'The idea of alertness forms the basis of a radically different outlook on the market: one that eschews the equilibrium-always formulation of neoclassical economics' (Rizzo 2002: 3).

Alertness to profit opportunities is the essence of entrepreneurship. Alertness is the entrepreneurial element in economic decision-making. It is a human propensity. What entrepreneurs do is identify opportunities for gain that others (and even they themselves) have earlier overlooked. The entrepreneur recognises something that others have failed to recognise: that there is an opportunity waiting to be snapped up. Often located between different markets, alert arbitragers are the individuals who first sense emerging trends and find 'ten dollar bills lying on the sidewalk'. More specifically, entrepreneurship involves the discovery of opportunities to buy one thing (e.g. a resource) at a low price in order to sell it (or its resulting output) at a high price. The price discrepancy occurs because many market participants simply overlook opportunities for mutually beneficial exchange.

Alertness is to be distinguished from the standard optimising behaviour of decision-makers in mainstream economic models. The latter is the allocation of *given* means to achieve a set of *given* ends. It does not involve the discovery of previously unperceived opportunities. In contrast, alertness involves the identification of which (new) ends to pursue and the discovery of which (new) means are available. It is not limited to optimisation within a presupposed ends–means framework. Entrepreneurial alertness involves the discovery or perception of the ends–means framework within which allocation and optimising are to take place.

A simple example can serve to clarify the difference between entrepreneurial alertness and optimisation. Consider R&D in a private firm. Optimisation is concerned with how a research manager allocates the R&D budget among competing given research projects. But entrepreneurial alertness is concerned with how a particular research manager identifies before others that a project idea is worth putting on the research agenda.

The propensity to be alert manifests itself in spontaneous discovery of profit opportunities and arbitrage activity. Arbitrage is one of three classes of entrepreneurship – the other two being speculation and innovation.[4] In Kirzner's system, speculation and innovation are analytically equivalent to arbitrage. *Pure arbitrage* involves the simultaneous coordination of transactions in different parts of the market within a single time period. No uncertainty is implied by arbitrage: the arbitrager captures profits arising from *existing interlocal price differences*. *Speculation* (or intertemporal arbitrage) involves discovering and exploiting perceived opportunities created by different market transactions entered into at different dates. Speculators plan to make gains from *intertemporal price differences* that arise from forces over which they have no control (such as shifts in demand or exogenous supply shocks). *Innovation* concerns the introduction of new goods and services, new methods of production, new ways of organising transactions and new forms of industrial organisation. These of course are the activities performed by the Schumpeterian innovator.[5] The innovator hopes to capture profits from the introduction of a new product (or process). Profits are made if the innovator is able to sell the new product over a future time period at a price–quantity configuration that brings revenue greater than the sum of production and transaction costs. Innovation entails making gains from *intertemporal revenue–cost differences* but, unlike speculation, innovation implies bringing about the revenue–cost differential by means of the entrepreneur's own actions.

For Kirzner, each of these kinds of entrepreneurship tends to coordinate decisions towards a more favourable pattern of resource allocation:

> Pure arbitrage tends to ensure the exploitation of all available opportunities for mutually profitable exchange; intertemporal arbitrage tends to avoid 'wasteful' intertemporal allocation (and thus, where warranted, to build up towards the optimal capital structure); the entrepreneurship

exercised in innovative production tends to generate technological progress.

(Kirzner 1992: 50)

Chapter 2 examines the theory of entrepreneurial discovery and the concept of alertness in more detail. It also looks more closely at the issue of whether the entrepreneurial market process generates superior coordination of economic plans and tends towards equilibrium.

## Analytical distinctions between the entrepreneur and other economic decision-makers

It is important to distil the most salient features that specifically distinguish the entrepreneurial function from other functions and that are also relevant for institutional analysis and public policy.

The unit of analysis throughout most of this book is the individual entrepreneur, not the entrepreneurial team or firm (nor is it the entrepreneurial event or transaction).[6] It must be noted that the individual entrepreneur is the personification or embodiment of a particular economic function, type of act or market role:[7]

> Economics, in speaking of entrepreneurs, has in view not men, but a definite function. This function ... is inherent in every action and burdens every actor. In embodying this function in an imaginary figure, we resort to a methodological makeshift.
>
> (Mises 1966: 252–253)

The individual entrepreneur is thus a special device that is introduced to simplify the framework and to develop a line of analysis.

As we shall see in Chapter 6, the unit of analysis that one selects for one's enquiry is also to some extent culture bound. For example, a specification of entrepreneurship in terms of heroic individuals is more appropriate for individualistic societies such as the USA, whereas a conception of entrepreneurship in terms of interdependent members of entrepreneurial teams is more applicable to group-oriented societies, such as Japan. How the entrepreneurial function is conceived can have important implications for institutional analysis and the design of public policy.

It is clear, of course, that in the real world a single physical person often embodies more than one function. Each economic agent acts in an integrated manner, which we (as economists) artificially analyse as separate functions. The real-world entrepreneur is a single composite personality who is also a manager, leader, capitalist, coordinator and organiser. Thus, although entrepreneurial, managerial and capitalist *functions* are conceptually distinguishable, in the real world the activities are invariably intertwined. Owing to transaction costs and other factors, entrepreneurs must perform many non-entrepreneurial and managerial functions, and they must often provide some capital to facilitate the realisation of their own ideas. Transaction-cost factors inhibit the transfer of entrepreneurial knowledge and block the formation of an external market in which entrepreneurs could sell their ideas to other participants who could realise them.

## Entrepreneurship versus resource ownership

Prior ownership of resources is *not* a prerequisite to entrepreneurial alertness (Kirzner 1979: 97). However, in a world in which production is not instantaneous and investment in capital is often required, we may observe entrepreneurs as owning resources as well. For the purpose of reallocating resources in the pursuit of profit, entrepreneurs may need to acquire them. For example, in order to exploit a perceived profit opportunity, it may be necessary to purchase an asset in period $t_0$ to be sold for a higher price in the later period $t_1$. What is decisive, however, is that at the time of the initial entrepreneurial insight, the entrepreneur does not necessarily have any resources at all to contribute to the productive process. The original entrepreneurial hunch responsible for the venture precedes the act of purchasing the asset. Consequently, entrepreneurship is not to be treated as a factor of production.

In the real world, we are likely to observe market participants exercising entrepreneurial alertness as well as being resource-owners at the same time. For analytical purposes, however, Kirzner believes it justifiable to consider an individual who performs both functions to be two separate decision-makers. If, as a result of earlier entrepreneurial decisions, an entrepreneur becomes a resource-owner, the entrepreneur can be conceived as purchasing these inputs from him- or herself.

Both Kirzner and Schumpeter are quite definite that entrepreneurship does not include the control, accumulation or provision of capital. It is 'essential to note that the entrepreneurial function, though facilitated by the ownership of means, is not identical with that of the capitalist' (Schumpeter 1947: 151). A pure entrepreneur owns no capital. Institutions that facilitate the separation of ownership and control give rise to capitalists who are not entrepreneurs and to entrepreneurs who are not capitalists. And since pure entrepreneurship does not include the provision of capital (or any resources for that matter), it must necessarily follow that it does not include risk bearing either, because the risks are borne by the capitalists who lend funds to the entrepreneur. (In fact Schumpeter (1954) strongly criticised attempts to include risk bearing within entrepreneurship.) It is the capitalists who lose their money in the event of business failure. Entrepreneurs only bear risk to the extent that they may also act as their own capitalists, as they often do when they invest their own personal funds at the seed financing stage of commercial ventures. (Entrepreneurs may also supply 'reputation capital' to themselves and this too may be at stake.) Consequently, one should not expect entrepreneurs to exhibit special risk-taking propensities. Another important implication of this definition of entrepreneurship is that profit is a reward for superior perception or alertness; it is not a reward for risk taking or uncertainty bearing.

### Entrepreneurship versus invention

Although the entrepreneur may also be an inventor, there is no necessary connection between entrepreneurship and invention. The inventor produces new scientific and technical ideas, whereas the entrepreneur may perceive the opportunity to apply such new ideas commercially. The entrepreneur is alert to changes in technology that create profit opportunities. Entrepreneurial alertness is required to ensure that new methods of production will be introduced. The entrepreneur is thus *not* an inventor, but may be someone who decides to allocate resources to the exploitation of an invention. Entrepreneurship is 'exploiting the new opportunities that inventions provide, more in the form of marketing and developing them for widespread use in the economy than developing the knowledge itself' (Rosen 1983: 307). Entrepreneurial activity may, but need not, embody an element of scientific novelty.

The alertness needed to spot profitable opportunities for trading a new product can be separated from the creativity involved in the invention of that very product. Although one has to be technically proficient in order to invent a digital camera, one does not have to be technically oriented to perceive a lucrative market for digital cameras and to notice that the sum of input prices is less than what the market is willing to pay for the digital cameras that those inputs can produce. A flesh-and-blood individual might possess both technical creativity and entrepreneurial alertness, but only the second attribute is necessary to qualify as an entrepreneur.

### Entrepreneurship versus the formation of new firms

Scholarly enquiry into entrepreneurship in business schools (subsumed under the rubric 'entrepreneurial studies') often lacks rigorous theoretical foundations and precise analytical concepts. The field typically equates entrepreneurship with the creation of new firms. 'The common assumption is that most entrepreneurial activity occurs through *de novo* startups' (Shane and Venkataraman 2000: 224). The focus of enquiry is frequently upon explaining the relative performance of new businesses over time rather than the emergence, discovery and exploitation of entrepreneurial opportunities. In his early work, Schumpeter too identified entrepreneurship with the creation of new production functions by new firms rather than the ongoing management of established firms. 'Only someone who establishes a new business to produce a new product, or to make an old product in a new way, is to be called an entrepreneur' (Loasby 1982b: 240).

The economic theory of entrepreneurial discovery can provide a sound intellectual framework for entrepreneurial studies and can also broaden the scope of its enquiry. From a market-process perspective, it must be emphasised that entrepreneurship may merely entail separate one-off arbitrage transactions that do not involve the founding of new business ventures. Entrepreneurial activity can occur without the involvement of firms. *The creation of new firms is neither necessary nor sufficient for entrepreneurship.* Buying ten units of a good at a low price in one part of the market and selling them at a higher price in another part constitutes a transitory act of entrepreneurship, but it does not require the entrepreneur to establish a hierarchical governance structure (i.e. a firm) in order to discover and seize the profit opportunity and to administer the relevant transactions. Of course, entrepreneurship might include the creation of new business organisations (including the merger of existing organisations), but this is not a defining or essential characteristic of this phenomenon.

Launching a new firm and keeping it going may involve few entrepreneurial decisions, and the management of the business may even be quite routine. However, entrepreneurship can occur within the boundaries of existing firms. Indeed, the Austrian theory of the firm sees the firm as 'an entity that organizes localized discovery procedures in the context of a structure of incomplete contracts and supporting shared mental constructs' (Foss 1997: 194). Sautet's (2000) notion of the 'complex firm' captures the idea that economic knowledge and the locus of entrepreneurial discoveries are not centralised within modern business enterprises. Rather, individual employees, who themselves display entrepreneurial qualities and have localised knowledge not shared by others, are alert to opportunities that they discover and exploit within a system of rules imposed by the hierarchical structure. The complex firm is set up by the entrepreneur–promoter as a semi-planned coordinative framework to govern productive activity in line with his or her original entrepreneurial insight. But the evolutionary growth of the firm is influenced by spontaneous entrepreneurial discoveries and indeterminate elements that were not planned or expected by anyone. Sautet evocatively refers to the 'complex firm' as a 'nesting of entrepreneurs'.

### Entrepreneurship versus management

Because the management function is more readily observable than the entrepreneurial function, the latter is often subsumed within the former. However, the management function is actually narrower in scope than entrepreneurship. The manager is the agent who supervises the ongoing efficiency of the firm's processes of production and exchange. The manager's role is to work out how to reach the firm's production possibility loci; that is, to improve its efficiency within the limits of known technology. The standard neoclassical theory of the firm adequately describes the managerial function and the routine optimising decisions that managers make. The manager is the individual who equates marginal costs to marginal benefits in a routine (though not necessarily static) manner.

As already mentioned, flesh-and-blood business people may embody entrepreneurial, managerial and other functions and may shift from one role to the other. Thus, real-world entrepreneurs must undertake many non-entrepreneurial, managerial activities because of transaction cost difficulties that impede the transfer of entrepreneurial knowledge. Consequently, the entrepreneur's managerial skills can have a significant impact on the outcome of a venture. Efficient organisation and management may be essential for entrepreneurial success. If entrepreneurial profit equals total revenue minus the sum of production and transaction costs, and if superior management is required to keep down costs, then whether a venture makes a profit or a loss may depend in part at least upon the entrepreneur's ability to manage the enterprise.

### Entrepreneurship versus rent seeking

Following Ricketts (1987; 1992), I will define rent seeking as an attempt to challenge coercively the established structure of property rights held by people at a point in time (the 'status quo'). More specifically, in the pursuit of personal gain, the rent-seeker challenges the *initially given* delineation and assignment of economic rights to the attributes of assets. The essential characteristic of rent seeking is that it involves *uncompensated* transfers of property rights from unwilling parties. Rent seeking is value decreasing *relative to (i.e. from the perspective of) the initially given property rights structure.* Examples include theft, piracy, bribing judges or lobbying politicians to use the coercive powers of the state to modify the rights structure in a way that is favourable to the rent seeker. Thus, rent seeking and challenges to the status quo are not necessarily unlawful: people have a constitutional right to attempt to change the given initial set of property rights by legitimate means through the political process.

The distinction between rent seeking and entrepreneurship receives a relatively brief treatment in Kirzner's work, largely because he does not emphasise property rights issues. In Kirzner's theory of market processes, the structure of property rights is assumed to be a datum, as something given to the entrepreneur. Individuals *qua* entrepreneurs do not regard the property rights framework in which they act as an object of choice. In fact, according to Kirzner, the emergence of markets and the phenomenon of market entrepreneurship presuppose the existence of well-defined private property rights and other extra-market institutions. Kirznerian entrepreneurs can only operate within a given rights structure. They are alert to opportunities and gains from *voluntary* market exchanges that are implicit in the anterior backdrop of given property rights. Unlike rent-seekers, they pursue personal gain by trading property rights in resources through non-coercive means, and they implicitly accept the status quo framework of property rules (and prevailing definitions of what it means to own something).

The status quo, of course, is not a brute objective fact but a 'subjective' state of affairs that depends upon people's rival interpretations of entitlements. People do not necessarily share the same knowledge and expectations about property rights. If entitlements are not clearly defined and agreed upon, distinguishing rent seeking from entrepreneurship is highly problematic. For example, it is difficult to determine whether an attempt to establish private rights in a resource is rent seeking or entrepreneurship when some people in a community regard that resource as an open access or communal resource while others regard the same asset as previously unowned and ripe for appropriation (Ricketts 1992: 76–77).

The issues are complex and subtle. Kirzner's stipulation that entrepreneurship can take place *only* within an initially given set of property rules may be too restrictive and generally not necessary analytically for my purposes. All market entrepreneurship involves the creation of new ends–means frameworks. Using new means to achieve new ends can make it necessary to redefine property rights vis-à-vis other existing means. New ways of using resources create new conflicts of interest. Technological developments and the innovative ventures to which they give rise may require extending property rights to new objects or shifting existing rights. The bolder and more path breaking the innovation, the more likely this may be. Chapter 4 revisits this subject.

## Organisation of the book

Chapter 2 provides a more detailed account of Kirzner's entrepreneurial-discovery approach. It first investigates the intellectual precursors of Kirzner's theory and how his approach draws upon Mises's image of the market as an entrepreneurial process and Hayek's vision of the role of knowledge and learning in competitive markets.

The chapter supplies important building blocks for the examination of the psychological, institutional and cultural foundations of entrepreneurship in later chapters. It focuses upon the implications of Kirzner's approach for the causal factors that provide scope for entrepreneurship. It also examines the unique, often subtle and sometimes counterintuitive, characteristics of entrepreneurial alertness (such as its non-deployable and tacit quality) that distinguish it from conventional productive resources.

With its emphasis upon the abstract entrepreneurial *function*, Kirzner's approach deliberately neglects the concrete *person* who actually does the perceiving of entrepreneurial opportunities in real-world markets. In fact, according to Kirzner, investigating the psychological determinants of entrepreneurship is outside the bounds of economic science. Chapter 3 rectifies this deficit by examining the role that cognitive variables play in switching on and intensifying people's alertness to entrepreneurial opportunities. Building upon earlier research by Gilad (1982a; 1982b), the discussion addresses the question of why some people and not others discover particular profit opportunities in particular contexts.

Chapter 3 argues that there is a strong causal connection between people's propensity to be alert and their own sense of *personal agency*. Perceived personal agency represents a person's belief about the extent to which they can exert causal power over what happens in their life. It comprises two cognitive elements – beliefs in *locus of control* (or contingency expectations) and beliefs in *self-efficacy* (or competence expectations). (The former derives from Rotter's social learning theory, the latter from Bandura's.) The thesis is that the more confident individuals are that desired economic outcomes in particular contexts are contingent upon actions rather than outside forces such as luck (i.e. the more internal their locus of control), and the more certain they are that they have the personal capabilities to carry out success-fully the relevant actions (i.e. the greater their perceived self-efficacy), the more alert they are likely to be to opportunities.

The chapter presents a simple conceptual model that synthesises what we have learnt about the psychological determinants of individual differences in entrepreneurial alertness (see Figure 3.1). According to this model, internal locus of control and high self-efficacy are each necessary conditions and together they are sufficient for acute and sustained alertness.

In order to explain entrepreneurship, of course, we need to examine more than just the psychological characteristics of certain types of people. We need to look at the *interaction* between the individual and the intricacies of his or her situation. This leads us to consider the institutions that shape the situational contexts people encounter and that affect the availability of entrepreneurial talent.

Accordingly, Chapters 4 and 5 examine the economic and political insti-tutions that are required for entrepreneurship and a thriving market economy. These chapters identify the institutional matrix that is most likely to evoke a robust sense of internal control, self-efficacy and personal agency and thus a heightened level of alertness to business opportunities. The assumption is that people's psychological and cognitive properties (especially their personal agency beliefs and attentiveness) are not exogenous to the institutional and cultural context in which they find themselves. Indeed, institutions matter because they shape people's experiences of action–outcome sequences, and they thereby affect their beliefs about the causal structure of the world in which they live. In this way, institutions not only affect how alert people are but also influence how and where entrepreneurial alertness is directed in a society.

Chapter 4 argues that freedom (in the sense of absence of constraint) is the overarching institutional principle for promoting entrepreneurship. The argument is that a constitutional and institutional framework that maximises individual freedom (subject to equal freedom for all) is most conducive to the development of a deep-seated sense of personal agency and is therefore most likely to produce highly alert, entre-preneurial individuals. The freer people are, the more control they feel they have over events in their life, and the more alert to opportunities they become.

Chapter 4 explains how maximal freedom and acute and sustained entrepreneurial alertness are most likely to be provided in a society based on the rule of law, a spontaneous legal order that embodies this rule, tangible liberties that frame entrepreneurial choice, a system of private property rights and contracts, and decentralisation of economic and political decision-making. The chapter examines each of these institutional features in terms of how they mould and determine people's perceptions of agency and the degree of their alertness.

Chapter 5 continues the institutional analysis of the preceding chapter. It argues that the phenomenon of money plays an important role in cultivating entrepreneurial alertness. The emergence of money and a system of money prices enhances entrepreneurs' perceived self-efficacy by improving their capacity to acquire the relevant knowledge needed to plan rationally. It can also strengthen entrepreneurs' perceptions of the contingency of economic rewards upon entrepreneurial actions by removing problems arising from a lack of coincidence of wants and the indivisibility of commodities. The chapter briefly considers how discretionary interventions by central banks can dampen entrepreneurs' perceptions of agency and their alertness to market opportunities.

After examining the phenomenon of money, Chapter 5 moves on to consider how the political order can affect the development of agency beliefs and encourage or constrain the generation of entrepreneurial alertness. Following Weingast (1995), it is argued that the rule of law, well-defined property rights and the freedom of contract are not enough to secure vigorous, entrepreneurially driven market processes. What is needed in addition is a self-enforcing political infrastructure, such as 'market-preserving federalism', that credibly commits to protecting economic freedom of private decision-makers.

Shifting attention from the political to the legal order, Chapter 5 then discusses decentralisation of the legal process and its implications for entrepreneurial alertness. It is argued that a decentralised law-making process, such as the common law, that evolves spontaneously and gradually is more likely than a centralised and codified legal system to generate the certain, general and equal legal rules conducive to entrepreneurship.

Revisiting themes first raised in the previous chapter, Chapter 5 then delves further into exploring the unique character of freedom of entrepreneurial choice and how it can be embedded in concrete economic liberties that assure a private sphere of unimpeded entrepreneurial action. The chapter concludes with a review of empirical research into the relation-ship between economic freedom (and changes in it over time) and processes of economic growth. There is mounting evidence that an institutional framework supportive of economic freedom is a major determinant of higher rates of economic growth.

Chapter 6 examines the cultural dimension of entrepreneurship – a sadly neglected area of research in economic theorising about entrepreneurship. Two hypotheses advanced in the literature help frame the discussion. Following Weber, the conventional belief in the social and organisational sciences is that individualist cultures are inherently more entrepreneurial than are group-oriented cultures (what I term 'the cornerstone hypothesis'). The second widely held hypothesis is that as countries advance economically, their predominant cultural values will converge towards individualism ('the convergence hypothesis').

Chapter 6 makes a case for rejecting both hypotheses. The chapter examines how crucial aspects of culture might steer entrepreneurial alertness in particular directions and influence how alertness is manifested. It elaborates a non-individualist model of the cognitive determinants of entrepreneurial alertness and shows that individualism is neither a necessary nor a sufficient condition for entrepreneurial alertness. Indeed, the chapter suggests that some group-oriented cultures have the potential to be highly entrepreneurial. In addition, the chapter argues that higher-order cultural values are relatively stable and that group-oriented values are likely to persist.

In order to explain how culture affects entrepreneurial alertness, Chapter 6 examines how people in individualist and group-oriented cultural groups perceive and experience their personhood (see Table 6.1). Such cultural conceptions of the self determine the most common locus of alertness within a cultural group. They determine the nature of the entity that discovers profit opportunities, whether it is a self-contained and autonomous entrepreneur (an 'independent self') or an interdependent member of an entrepreneurial team (an 'interdependent self'). How the self is conceived will also determine the nature of the opportunities that serve the self and to which the self is alert and sensitised (see Table 6.3). In addition, cultural conceptions of the self have an effect on the structure, content and perhaps even the strength of people's agency beliefs – the cognitive drivers of entrepreneurial alertness (see Table 6.2).

Chapter 7 is in the spirit of Vaughn's (1998) challenge to Austrian economists that they pay more attention to real-world events and policies and do more applied work. Accordingly, it develops the implications of the entrepreneurial-discovery perspective for public policy analysis. The chapter distils some general principles that a market-process economist can adopt when working as a policy adviser, particularly when developing or evaluating policy towards entrepreneurship.

To organise the discussion, Chapter 7 elaborates what is referred to as the 'Austrian market-process policy programme' (the MPP). The MPP describes *how* a market-process economist should conduct policy analysis. It is a set of hard-core ideas and rules (or heuristics) for guiding policy analysis that is grounded in Austrian market-process theory. The heuristics of the MPP require the economist to examine the full range of effects of government interventions and to pay particular attention to the unintended consequences of policies for entrepreneurial discovery processes, such as the unanticipated creation of barriers to new market entry. The MPP also supplies a unique appraisal criterion for comparative assessments of institutional arrangements that emphasises the dynamic aspects of economic coordination.

The remainder of Chapter 7 is largely devoted to comparing the MPP with two other policy programmes that are prevalent in the economics profession: namely, the 'perfect-markets' policy programme and the 'market-failure' policy programme. The chapter explains how the three programmes differ in their perspective on the operation of markets and in the policy prescriptions that their proponents are likely to recommend (see Tables 7.3 and 7.4).

Chapter 8 addresses four issues that relate to the limitations of the analysis and the agenda for future research. First, it outlines potential empirical tests of the hypothesis that entrepreneurs in less regulated industries have a higher degree of internal locus of control, a greater sense of personal efficacy and a stronger belief in their personal agency.

Second, Chapter 8 examines whether the institutional rules of the game described in Chapters 4 and 5 are applicable to group-oriented societies. It asserts that economic freedom, the rule of law, a sound monetary framework and the institutions of private property and contract are as essential for economic prosperity in group-oriented societies as they are in individualistic ones.

Third, Chapter 8 deals explicitly with the issue of reciprocal causation. In general, the analysis in this book has depicted institutions and cultural values as antecedent conditions that affect people's cognitive processes and alertness. Causation has been in one direction. It has not investigated the possible feedback loops that might exist when personal agency beliefs and entrepreneurial activity affect the nature of culture and institutions.

Fourth, the chapter provides suggestions for future research on public policy analysis based on a market-process perspective. Among other things, it recommends that further work be conducted to examine the relationship between the goal of enhancing entrepreneurship in a society and other policy goals and that work be done to flesh out the implications of the market-process approach for the mix, design and sequencing of public policy reforms.

By way of conclusion, Chapter 9 reiterates the key causal role of entrepreneurship in the economic development process, and it provides some final thoughts on how the book enhances our understanding of the institutional and cultural contexts in which entrepreneurial processes are embedded.

# 2 The theory of entrepreneurial discovery

The theory of entrepreneurial discovery is the most widely accepted conception of entrepreneurship among market-process theorists. In line with the broader research programme within which it is embedded, this approach is distinguished by its focus upon the nature of competitive processes, market disequilibria, the role of knowledge, expectations and learning in the operation of markets, the nature and significance of entrepreneurial discovery, and the comparative effectiveness of alternative institutional frameworks for evoking entrepreneurship.

Kirzner's scientific contributions on the entrepreneurial function and the institutional conditions for economic development are central to a more sophisticated understanding of entrepreneurial capitalism and the dynamic adjustment processes that coordinate economic activities in market economies.[1] His entrepreneurial theory of market processes supplies the 'disequilibrium foundations of economic analysis' (Boettke and Rizzo 1995: xiv). It can also be argued that Kirzner's concept of entrepreneurial alertness is a common thread that runs through many of the diverse notions of the entrepreneurial function offered in the economics literature.

The scope of influence of Kirzner's theory of entrepreneurship is not limited to the disciplinary boundaries of economics. Some business administration scholars have employed his theory (in conjunction with other approaches) to construct a robust conceptual framework for the field of 'entrepreneurial studies' and to isolate the field's distinctive contribution, which they identify as the investigation of the existence, discovery and exploitation of entrepreneurial opportunities (Shane and Venkataraman 2000). There is also an emerging stream of empirical research in entrepreneurial studies that applies Kirzner's notion of entrepreneurial alertness and tests for differences in the informational cues and learning strategies used by entrepreneurs and managers in spotting profit opportunities (Kaish and Gilad 1991; Busenitz 1996).

The marketing and business strategy literatures have also drawn insights from Kirzner's theory of entrepreneurial discovery (e.g. Jacobsson 1992). In particular, the strategic management literature on firms' capabilities emphasises themes, such as knowledge problems, learning processes and entrepreneurship, which have a Kirznerian and Hayekian flavour. Similarly, recent contributions to the incipient Austrian market-process theory of the firm also draw on Hayek's seminal work and Kirzner's notion of entrepreneurial behaviour in order to explain why firms exist and to shed light on the boundaries and internal organisational structure of businesses.[2]

This chapter fleshes out the key implications of Kirzner's theory of entrepreneurship for how and why markets work. It sets out the fundamental ideas on the entrepreneurial function that are required for subsequent chapters on the psychological determinants of entrepreneurship and its institutional and cultural foundations. Of particular interest are the causal factors that provide scope for entrepreneurship. The emphasis here is on the role of imperfect coordination between market transactions that arises because of a lack of mutual awareness among buyers and sellers. The chapter pays close attention to the non-deployable and tacit quality of entrepreneurial alertness and its other distinctive characteristics. We need to appreciate its nature fully if we are to be able to explain the effects of different institutional rules and economic policies on entrepreneurship.

The closing section considers in more detail Kirzner's conception of the market process and his claim that markets have systematic equilibrative tendencies. Finally, it presents an alternative vision of the market process that rejects the notion that competitive markets tend to generate improved coordination of economic plans.

## Antecedents to the entrepreneurial-discovery approach

The modern Austrian theory of entrepreneurship has its origins in the works of Mises and of Hayek. 'From Mises the modern Austrians learned to see the market as an *entrepreneurially* driven *process*. From Hayek they learned to appreciate the role of *knowledge* and its enhancement through market interaction, for the equilibrative process' (Kirzner 2000: 11; emphasis added).

Mises emphasised the dynamic and entrepreneurial character of the market process. He saw the market process as generated by the actions of profit-seeking entrepreneurs who operate in a radically uncertain world:

> The driving force of the market process is provided neither by the consumers nor by the owners of the means of production – land, capital goods, and labour – but by the promoting and speculating entrepreneurs. These are people intent upon profiting by taking advantage of differences in prices. Quicker of apprehension and farther-sighted than other men, they look around for sources of profit. ... Profit-seeking speculation is the driving force of the market as it is the driving force of production.
>
> (Mises 1966: 328–329)

In his *magnum opus*, *Human Action*, Mises analyses market *processes* rather than equilibrium *states*. Entrepreneurial activity plays a crucial role in the former, but there is no scope left for it in the latter. Nonetheless, the equilibrating properties of the market process depend vitally upon the activities of entrepreneurs. Entrepreneurs see opportunities for profit in the conditions of disequilibrium. Competition among profit-seeking entrepreneurs is the agency which would bring the market prices of all goods and services to their equilibrium levels if no further changes in market data were to take place. Indeed, Mises considers entrepreneurship to be analytically insepa-rable from the process of competition.

In contrast, Hayek did not focus explicitly upon the role of entrepreneur-ship in explaining the market process. Rather, he emphasised the role of knowledge and mutual learning. He examined how, in the course of the market process, market participants come to obtain more accurate knowl-edge of each other's plans.

Indeed, Hayek (1978) conceived of the competitive market process as a discovery procedure. In his seminal articles, he referred to the competitive process as a procedure for the discovery of particular 'facts' that are useful for achieving specific, transitory purposes.[3] Hayek was not so much concerned with major discoveries, such as technological advances, but with rather minor discoveries about individual wants at particular times and places. More specifically, competition is a spontaneous process that leads to the discovery of previously unsatisfied 'wishes and desires of the consumers, including the goods and services which they demand and the prices they are willing to pay' (Hayek 1948: 96). It also leads to the discovery of lower-cost techniques for producing existing commodities and new methods of indus-trial organisation.

Moreover, these discoveries are localised so that different people have access to different information. This point brings us to a pivotal idea in Hayek's thought – the so-called 'knowledge problem'. This problem consists in the dispersed character of available knowledge in a society:

> The peculiar character of the problem of a rational economic order is determined precisely by the fact that the knowledge of the circum-stances of which we must make use never exists in concentrated or integrated form but solely as the dispersed bits of incomplete and frequently contradictory knowledge which all the separate individuals possess. The economic problem of society is thus not merely a problem of how to allocate 'given' resources – if 'given' is taken to mean given to a single mind which deliberately solves the problem set by these 'data'. It is rather a problem of how to secure the best use of resources known to any of the members of society, for ends whose relative importance only these individuals know. Or, to put it briefly, *it is a problem of the utilization of knowledge which is not given to anyone in its totality*.
>
> (Hayek 1948: 77–78; emphasis added)

Hayek highlighted the central role of the price mechanism in mobilising local knowledge of resources, technology and preferences. Each individual possesses unique and often tacit knowledge of the particular circumstances of time and place. It is only by utilising such knowledge in conjunction with the price mechanism that rational economic decisions are able to be made. 'The most significant fact about this [price] system is the economy of knowledge with which it operates, or how little the individual participants need to know in order to be able to take the right action' (Hayek 1948: 86). Only a competitive market system with decentralised decision-making is capable of addressing (if not dissolving) the Hayekian knowledge problem.

Building upon Mises' work, Hayek developed the implications of these insights into a devastating critique of socialism. In particular, he argued that the knowledge problem implies the impossibility of rational economic calculation under central planning. The reason is that, in the absence of a price mechanism, the socialist planner is unable to access the economic knowledge necessary to coordinate economic activity (see Lavoie 1985a).

Both Mises and Hayek were instrumental in creating a distinct modern market-process approach that is separate from mainstream neoclassical economics. Although there are differences between Mises' and Hayek's conceptions of the market process, their two perspectives are highly complementary and mutually reinforcing:[4]

> It is true that Mises did not draw special attention to the mutual learning that must occur during the entrepreneurially-driven process of equilibration. Nor did Hayek emphasise the speculative, entrepreneurial character of the market process. But ... these two ways of articulating a theory of market process turn out to be two sides of the same coin.
>
> (Kirzner 1997b: 18)

Kirzner's theory of entrepreneurial discovery is based upon the complementarity between Mises' and Hayek's insights into the market process.

## Kirzner's theory of entrepreneurial discovery

In common with much of mainstream economics, Hayek's analysis suffers from one serious problem: it assumes that all market participants are price-takers. The question remains: how are prices (and other elements of the marketing mix) determined and how do they move towards their equilibrium levels?

Kirzner bridges the theoretical deficit left by Hayek by providing a theory of entrepreneurial price adjustment that develops the work of Mises. In Kirzner's theory, the price-adjuster is the entrepreneur. Entrepreneurs perceive changes in economic circumstances, discover imperfect coordination between individual decisions and adjust prices to new market conditions.

Kirzner's perspective on entrepreneurship thus seeks to explain the process of economic coordination in modern market economies.

## Kirzner's single-period model of entrepreneurial alertness

In Kirzner's original and simplest formulation of his theory (1973; 1979), entrepreneurship is defined exclusively in terms of a market for a single good within a single period. Kirzner appropriately describes this theory of entrepreneurship as an *arbitrage* theory (in fact Kirzner never distinguishes between arbitrage and entrepreneurship). The entrepreneur in a single-period market is an arbitrager who discovers inconsistency between transactions in different parts of *today's* market. The inconsistency manifests itself in a multiplicity of prices for the same good. Market participants who sold for low prices did not coordinate their plans with those who have bought for higher prices.

The entrepreneur discovers existing *interlocal* price differences for the same commodity in the same market (i.e. where buyers have been paying too much and where sellers have been receiving too little). The price discrepancy represents an opportunity for pure entrepreneurial profit. The entrepreneur knows exactly what to do: the entrepreneur bridges the gap by offering to buy for a little more and to sell for a little less. 'The pure entrepreneurial function consists in buying cheap and selling dear – that is, in the discovery that the market has undervalued something so that its true market value has up to now not been generally realised' (Kirzner 1997b: 34).

The price movements arising from entrepreneurial actions gradually communicate increasingly accurate information to more and more market participants. The actions of pioneering entrepreneurs confront less alert entrepreneurs and imitators with information that they themselves were not sufficiently alert to discover. Thus, the process of capturing entrepreneurial profits is at the same time a process of correcting market ignorance.

Entrepreneurial alertness not only drives the prices of a given commodity towards equality throughout the market, however. It also continually redirects resources from lower-valued uses (as indicated by the prices consumers are willing to pay) to higher-valued uses. It thereby accounts for the market forces responsible for the allocative efficiency of market economies: 'It is the law of a single price which, working through the process of entrepreneurial discovery, powerfully redirects the pattern of capitalist production into more, rather than less, allocatively efficient channels' (Kirzner 1997b: 43).[5]

Kirzner extends this simple analysis to include arbitrage opportunities arising from imperfect coordination between transactions in resource markets and those in product markets. The imperfect coordination expresses itself in a divergence between the price of inputs in factor markets and the price of outputs in product markets. More precisely, the divergence represents the difference between the sum of prices in factor markets of a bundle of resources required to make a product and the price of that commodity in the product market. This discrepancy in prices is generated by pure error on the part of market participants: 'some market participants have undervalued these resources relative to the future eagerness of consumers to acquire the product in question when it can be produced' (Kirzner 1997b: 41). Thus, entrepreneurship includes alertness to price differences in factor and product markets for what is essentially the same good.[6]

Indeed, one of the most 'crucial junctures' where entrepreneurial alertness is likely to be required is the interface between the factor market and the product market because many of the unnoticed opportunities comprise possibilities for improved coordination between transactions in factor markets and product markets (Kirzner 1973: 44). This then can also be expected to be the major locus of entrepreneurial activity. The entrepreneur can thus be conceived as a type of linking pin or middle person connecting external factor and product markets: 'The essence of entrepreneurial activity ... involves simultaneous participation in more than one "market" – in fact, this activity consists of linking up different markets' (Kirzner 1973: 124). Indeed, regulatory reform of markets for key inputs (such as finance, energy, transport, telecommunications and labour) can give a spur to entrepreneurial activity between factor and product markets.

### *Kirzner's multi-period model*

The single-period arbitrage theory is limited to the more or less instantaneous discovery and exploitation of *interlocal* price differences. In the generalisation of this theory, Kirzner uses single-period alertness as an analogy for speculative entrepreneurship in a multi-period context: that is, for a theory of the discovery and exploitation of *intertemporal* (rather than interlocal) price differences in the same commodity market or between factor and product markets. It is assumed that alertness to imperfect coordination between different parts of today's market is the same as recognising imperfect coordination between transactions today and transactions in the next period's market. In short, the coordination of markets across space (i.e. arbitrage) is regarded as essentially the same as the coordination of markets across time (i.e. speculation). Furthermore, the overall function of entrepreneurship in a multi-period context is argued not to change from that in the single-period case:

> It is still the case ... that the entrepreneurial function is that of bringing about a tendency for transactions in different parts of the market (conceived broadly now as including transactions entered into at different times) to be made in greater mutual consistency.
>
> (Kirzner 1982c: 154)

In the single-period case, the entrepreneur equilibrates the present market by promoting convergence towards a uniform market price. Correspondingly, in the multi-period case, the entrepreneur coordinates present transactions with future transactions. Kirzner also extends the arbitrage analogy to include the introduction of new productive processes, new products and new forms of organisation.

### Ignorance as the source of entrepreneurial opportunities

As mentioned above, according to Kirzner's theory, scope for entrepreneurial activity is provided by imperfect coordination between transactions in different parts of the market. The imperfect coordination in turn arises from ignorance. (In a situation of perfect knowledge and no ignorance, one would expect the law of one price to prevail.) Indeed, the particular type of ignorance that Kirzner argues is important for providing scope for entrepreneurial alertness is the inexplicable 'failure to utilise a resource available and ready to hand', the failure of market participants to perceive opportunities 'staring them in the face' (Kirzner 1979: 130). The term 'ignorance' means that market participants are unaware of and overlook superior opportunities available to them.

This ignorance takes the form of over-pessimism, and Kirzner refers to the mistakes to which it gives rise as *errors of over-pessimism*. Over-pessimism arises from underestimating the willingness of sellers or buyers to trade in a commodity. Buyers pay 'too high' a price for a good because they are simply unaware that potential sellers exist who would sell to them at more favourable terms. Sellers accept 'too low' a price because they are unaware that potential buyers exist who would buy from them at higher prices. Opportunities for mutually beneficial exchange between buyers and sellers are not noticed and fail to be exploited. 'We notice immediately that where the conditions for exchange in fact exist but are not exploited owing to ignorance there now exists scope for profitable entrepreneurship' (Kirzner 1973: 216).

According to Kirzner, knowledge of a profit opportunity simply involves entrepreneurs opening their eyes and discovering economic facts that had previously been overlooked by all other market participants. The entrepreneur simply perceives an exogenous change that has already taken place in consumer tastes, technological knowledge or resource availability.

It should be noted that imperfect coordination between decisions (i.e. market disequilibrium) and the resultant opportunities for entrepreneurship cannot be wholly explained in terms of high positive transaction and information costs. For even in a market with zero transaction costs, mutually beneficial exchanges might still fail to take place (and hence scope for entrepreneurial alertness may still arise). The implication is that public policies to reduce transaction costs may not necessarily increase entrepreneurial activity. If the members of a society are not alert, profitable exchanges will fail to occur even under ideal conditions of zero transaction costs. This point is discussed further in the next section.

A final point is that there is another type of ignorance that takes the form of *over-optimism*. Excessive optimism arises from believing that buyers and sellers are more eager than they really are, as, for example, when potential buyers mistakenly expect to purchase a good at a price so low that it is not available at that price, or when sellers plan to sell a good at a price so high that no buyer is willing to pay that price. These errors generate a disequilibrium price for a commodity that is either too low or too high to clear the market.

Errors of over-optimism are likely to be discovered faster than those stemming from over-pessimism, because over-optimistic errors lead to a distinct disappointment of market participants' plans (which is observed directly in the form of shortages and surpluses) and they tend to require less intense alertness for their correction. 'Such disappointment can be expected to alert entrepreneurs to the true temper of the market' (Kirzner 1997b: 45). When shortages exist, entrepreneurs nudge prices higher and expand supply through production or arbitrage. When surpluses exist, they nudge prices lower.

## Characteristics of entrepreneurial alertness

> Boldness, impulse, hunch are the raw materials of entrepreneurial success (and failure).
>
> (Kirzner 1997b: 39)

It is important to examine the unique characteristics of entrepreneurial alertness if we are to appreciate this elusive concept and to understand the types of institutions and economic policies that are likely to be conducive to it. A general point is that entrepreneurship is *not* a factor of production, not even a special kind of productive factor (Kirzner 1979: 180–181). The characteristics of entrepreneurial alertness which distinguish it sharply from conventional economic resources can be summarised as follows:

1   entrepreneurial alertness does not represent the mere possession of superior knowledge of market opportunities;
2   entrepreneurial alertness is non-deployable and tacit;
3   no market exists for hiring entrepreneurial services, and entrepreneurship cannot be treated in terms of demand and supply curves;
4   entrepreneurship is costless.

### *Entrepreneurial alertness does not represent the mere possession of superior knowledge*

Entrepreneurial alertness is 'the knowledge of where to obtain information (or other resources) and how to deploy it' (Kirzner 1979: 8). Entrepreneurial alertness is a kind of prior knowledge or foreknowledge. In this connection Kirzner is echoing the distinction between two types of knowledge recognised by Samuel Johnson: 'Knowledge is of two kinds. We know a subject ourselves, or we know where we can find information about it.' Entrepreneurial alertness refers to the latter kind of knowledge. More specifically, entrepreneurial alertness is defined as the knowledge of where to find market data rather than the knowledge of substantive market information per se.

An important implication of this definition is that alertness does not represent the possession of superior knowledge concerning market opportunities. The entrepreneur is not necessarily privy to specific or localised information that other agents do not possess. 'What the entrepreneur possesses rather is a sense for discovering what is around the corner' (Kirzner 1984b: 3). Alertness does not involve simply knowing more than others do where inputs can be purchased most cheaply or where outputs can be sold at the highest prices.

Hence, entrepreneurship is *alertness* to the opportunities presented by new and existing information rather than the possession of information by itself. This distinction may be clarified by considering the example of an entrepreneur who hires a marketing manager. It is granted that the marketing manager may possess superior knowledge concerning market conditions – for example, by having specific or localised information on changes in the marketing environment, including changes in the problems faced by particular market segments. However, since the manager cannot see how his or her knowledge can be successfully employed (if the manager had done, he or she would have acted as his or her own employer), it is the entrepreneur who exhibits the higher level of alertness in perceiving the opportunity presented by the information possessed by the manager. '[T]he alertness of the entrepreneur is the abstract, very general and rarefied kind of knowledge which we must ultimately credit with discovering and exploiting the opportunities specifically unearthed by those whom [the entrepreneur] has been wise enough to hire, directly and indirectly' (Kirzner 1973: 69).

If entrepreneurship were conceivable in terms of superior knowledge, there would exist a factor market in which the services of people who possess such entrepreneurial knowledge could be hired. However, no such market exists (see below).

Hence, public policy proposals to increase the supply of market information and technical information (e.g. trade commissioner services, information bureaux and statistical data) cannot be considered to increase entrepreneurship directly. Entrepreneurial alertness is still required to perceive any profit opportunities that may be presented by such information. Entrepreneurship can also be argued to be pushed back to an earlier stage: the stage at which public policy-makers decide on where to find relevant information and when they choose the information they consider worth

collecting in the first place. The completion of any possible mutually beneficial transactions that are suggested by publicly provided or publicly
funded information is by no means inevitable, and it is very definitely not
automatic or instantaneous. People may still not be aware of that information, even if the government were to make it available at zero cost; they
must still perceive the opportunity to learn that information (Kirzner 1973:
227).

## Entrepreneurial alertness is non-deployable and tacit

It is argued that entrepreneurial alertness differs fundamentally from
conventional economic resources, such as technical knowledge, in that,
unlike technical knowledge, it is not possible to make deliberate decisions
concerning the deployment of entrepreneurial alertness. The entrepreneur is
not able to decide whether or not to deploy it, for which competing
purposes to deploy it, and how and in what quantity to deploy it (Kirzner
1983b: 64). In the course of their decision-making, entrepreneurs do not
consider their hunches as a means (i.e. a stock of knowledge) available to
achieve given ends. Individual entrepreneurs cannot decide to allocate, say,
10 per cent of their alertness to the discovery of opportunity A, and the
remaining 90 per cent to the discovery of opportunity B. Entrepreneurial
alertness is not a resource that can be acquired deliberately like other aspects
of human capital.

A major factor which gives rise to the non-deployability of entrepreneurship is its tacit nature. An essential difference between entrepreneurial and
technical knowledge is that the entrepreneur lacks self-consciousness
concerning the former. Rather than being aware of their hunches,
entrepreneurs' actions simply reflect their hunches. A further aspect of this
tacit quality is that entrepreneurs are not able to articulate or explain their
alertness.

Kirzner's conception of entrepreneurship as non-deployable and tacit
stands in stark contrast to that in neoclassical treatments of entrepreneurial
supply, such as Baumol (1990), Casson (1982), Murphy *et al.* (1991) and
Schultz (1975). They rely on the idea of entrepreneurship as a resource
that can be allocated like any other factor of production. They contend
that the institutional context and the rules of the game (the reward structure of the economy) affect the *allocation* of entrepreneurial resources
between productivity-increasing activities, such as innovation, and largely
unproductive, redistributive activities, such as rent seeking and organised
crime.

## No market exists for hiring entrepreneurial services

The implication of the previous arguments is that no market exists for the
hire of entrepreneurial services because the market and the entrepreneur are

unaware of the need for (or the existence of) entrepreneurial alertness for any particular opportunity (Kirzner 1979: 174). Furthermore, the market does not recognise that any particular individuals possess entrepreneurial alertness. It does not identify any specific ability for discovering price discrepancies or profit opportunities, even though individuals differ in their ability to perceive entrepreneurial opportunities. Were the market to recognise entrepreneurial alertness in the sense of an available useful resource, there would be 'markets in which this factor service was hired, with its price rising to reflect its full productivity, ruling out scope for pure market profit' (Kirzner 1979: 181).

Consequently, strictly speaking, it is not possible to treat entrepreneurship in terms of demand and supply curves.[7] The market does not demand (in the ordinary sense) the services of entrepreneurs. For any instance of imperfect plan coordination about which market participants are supposed to be ignorant, it is not possible for these same market participants then to demand a service that is supposed to discover that very maladjustment. It should be noted that to hire 'an entrepreneur' is to be an entrepreneur. (On the other hand, if they are aware of a particular opportunity, then they do not need to hire alert entrepreneurs to discover it.) Market entrepreneurship reveals to market participants imperfect coordination and opportunities that they did not realise existed and that they did not recognise as needing correction.

The implication for public policy-makers is that identifying entrepreneurs *ex ante* is very problematic. Furthermore, if public policy-makers subjectively believe that they can discover opportunities to improve the existing structure of the economy, then they are also trying to act as entrepreneurs by spotting possibilities for better coordination.

### Entrepreneurship is costless

An essential characteristic of entrepreneurial knowledge is that it is spontaneously learnt, spontaneous in the sense that it is acquired entirely without being planned. Entrepreneurial alertness is the ability to discover unexploited profit opportunities *without deliberate search* for information:

> What distinguishes *discovery* (relevant to hitherto unknown profit opportunities) from *successful search* (relevant to the deliberate production of information which one knew one had lacked) is that the former (unlike the latter) involves that *surprise* which accompanies the realization that one had overlooked something in fact readily available. ('It was under my very nose!')
>
> (Kirzner 2000: 18; emphasis added)

When entrepreneurs make surprising discoveries, their discoveries are not the result of any prior deliberate search for a missing piece of information –

they do not know beforehand how much information they lack, the value of the missing information or the cost of obtaining it. Alertness may, however, include the discovery of previously unrecognised opportunities for deliberate search (e.g. market research), but this initial discovery is itself not the product of deliberate search activity by the entrepreneur. (For further discussion on the differences between deliberate search and entrepreneurial alertness, see Reekie 1984: 93–100.)

The cost of using technical knowledge is measured in terms of opportunity cost: the cost of using technical knowledge for a particular purpose is the value of the best forgone alternative. In contrast, entrepreneurial alertness does not involve opportunity costs because hunches are learnt spontaneously. No resource inputs are involved in acquiring them since no deliberate act of learning or of search is undertaken.

However, in describing entrepreneurial knowledge as costless, Kirzner provides clarification to avoid potential misunderstanding: 'To be sure, the spontaneous learner has incurred no cost or sacrifice through his learning. But this is not so much because the knowledge was costlessly available as because the knowledge was simply not deliberately sought' (Kirzner 1979: 143).

Klein (1999) develops a similar line of thought. He writes that, rather than regard the cost of an entrepreneurial hunch as zero, it is better to regard the concept of cost as not applicable to pure entrepreneurship (at least not to the 'deep level of mind' where Klein argues entrepreneurial 'epiphanies' occur). Opportunity cost relates to choice, and in Kirzner's eyes, entrepreneurial discovery is not an object of choice. 'Kirznerian entrepreneurship is costless in the sense that sound is weightless – not that sound weighs zero pounds, but that the concept of weight does not apply to sound' (Klein 1999: 54).

Demsetz (1983) does not agree that entrepreneurship is costless (though he does concede that in many cases the costs of alertness might not be significantly different from zero). First, Demsetz regards the time and mental energy that an entrepreneur devotes to considering a prospect and judging its potential as a *cost of maintaining alertness*, because the entrepreneur's mind is diverted from other tasks. Second, *costly prior acquisition of knowledge* may be necessary in order to discover opportunities.

This latter viewpoint appears to be supported by a recent empirical study. In the first phase of a three-part investigation, Shane (2000) undertook an in-depth field study of eight sets of entrepreneurs who exploited a single MIT invention (a three-dimensional printing process). The range of ventures included ceramic casting, drug manufacture, the manufacture of ceramic filters and orthopaedic applications. He tested hypotheses to do with whether entrepreneurs discover those opportunities that are related to the information that they already possess. In particular, he examined the effects of entrepreneurs' prior knowledge of markets, of ways to serve markets, and of customer problems, on the process of entrepreneurial discovery. His results showed not only that prior knowledge influences the discovery of opportunity,[8] but also that much of the prior knowledge is developed through costly and idiosyncratic education, research and work experiences. For example, in one venture to manufacture ceramic filters for the power generation market, the education and work experience in ceramic engineering of the entrepreneurial team enabled them to see how the MIT invention would solve problems with filter geometry and could make uniform-porosity ceramics.

The results of Shane's field study do, however, indicate that the entrepreneurial-discovery process is one of recognition rather than a search for information. None of the eight entrepreneurs believed that their respective opportunity was obvious from information about the MIT invention alone. Nor did any of the entrepreneurs believe that they were searching for the opportunity prior to its discovery. As one entrepreneur in the study put it: 'For whatever reason ... I just intuitively saw the opportunity in chronopharmacology. I certainly wasn't searching for the opportunity.'

It should also be noted that not all theorists who emphasise superior perception as the defining characteristic of entrepreneurship are in agreement with Kirzner's exclusion of search activity from the entrepreneurial function. In contrast to Kirzner, for instance, Casson (1982) includes the search for information within the entrepreneurial function and emphasises that entrepreneurial search does not just involve the extensive collection of facts. A synthesis of information is also required in identifying opportunities for coordination. Furthermore, Casson regards the *judgemental* decision-making of the entrepreneur as having a positive opportunity cost.

## Kirzner's conception of the market process

Up to now, we have talked about the market process in very general terms. It is now timely to define precisely what Kirzner means by 'market process' and to examine the properties of this phenomenon. I finish this section by considering criticisms of Kirzner's version of the market process.

### Defining the market process

The second chapter of Kirzner's 1992 book, *The Meaning of Market Process*, sets out to clarify the most important aspects of his conception of the market process.[9] His analysis distinguishes between two sets of variables. On the one hand, we have *underlying variables* (UVs), which by convention are defined as consumer preferences, population, resource availabilities and technological possibilities. To this list of UVs within Kirzner's model, I would also add institutions, legal rules and property rights. On the other hand, we have *induced variables* (IVs), which include prices, production processes, output quantities and qualities. These are the variables that market participants set and adjust under the effects of the UVs.

Changes in these two types of variables comprise two distinct sets of forces for economic change. Changes in UVs are exogenous and disequilibrating; changes in IVs are endogenous and equilibrative. The latter are endogenous in that market forces systematically generate them.

In mainstream microeconomics, changes in UVs are at all times fully and instantaneously reflected in observed changes in IVs. 'Equilibrium economics postulates that at each and every instant the actual market values of the IVs are those equilibrium values predetermined by the relevant values of the UVs' (Kirzner 1992: 42). In contrast, by emphasising the role of knowledge and learning in processes of equilibration, Kirzner sees the impact on IVs of changing UVs as far less mechanical and deterministic: 'The former retain a degree of freedom with respect to the latter' (Kirzner 1992: 42). However, movements of IVs in the market are not completely divorced from changes in underlying market data. Thus, the sequence of values of IVs is neither fully determined by, nor entirely independent of, the values of UVs.

Kirzner's theory defines the market process *exclusively* in terms of the second set of changes – changes in IVs. More specifically, *the market process refers to the endogenous changes in IVs that occur as entrepreneurs discover price differentials and exploit opportunities for pure profit inherent in disequilibrium market conditions.* 'The market process, then, consists of those changes that express the sequence of discoveries that follow the initial ignorance that constituted the disequilibrium state' (Kirzner 1992: 44). In its purest analytical form, the market process comprises that sequence of changing IV values that would occur even if we were to isolate IVs artificially from the effects of exogenous changes in underlying data. If such changes in UVs could be suspended, the market process would continue until all gaps in awareness (of what other participants are planning to do) were eventually filled.

## Do entrepreneurial market processes generate better coordination of economic activities?

In Kirzner's view, the market possesses a *systematic tendency* towards the diffusion of knowledge and equilibrium: 'The entrepreneurial process … is a process tending toward better mutual awareness among market participants. … Enhanced mutual awareness, via the entrepreneurial discovery process, is the source of the market's equilibrative properties' (Kirzner 2000: 19). That a strong tendency towards enhanced mutual knowledge and equilibrium exists in all markets at each moment, implies that individuals are tending to revise their plans in a manner that makes them more coordinated over time (O'Driscoll 1978: 129). The significance of this systematic equilibrating tendency is that it accounts for the degree of allocative efficiency and growth potential of market economies.

Although acknowledging the possibility for entrepreneurial discoveries to be mistaken and disequilibrating, Kirzner nevertheless maintains that there is a systematic tendency for entrepreneurs in general to make genuinely corrective discoveries rather than spurious error-enhancing ones. Moreover, there is a tendency for earlier entrepreneurial errors (which themselves create profit opportunities) to be replaced by profit-making entrepreneurial corrections. 'The market process view sees the market as displaying, at all times, the effects of powerful forces encouraging genuine and valuable discovery' (Kirzner 1992: 46).

But the existence of a systematic equilibrating tendency does not imply that this tendency actually proceeds to full completion. In the real world, market processes never succeed in achieving equilibrium because they are continually interrupted by new exogenous developments in consumer preferences, resource availabilities and technical possibilities (i.e. changes in UVs). These changes in turn set in motion new market processes which may collide with, interrupt or reinforce other market processes initiated at different points in time:

> The market process that we have outlined offers a systematic tendency, rather than a sure-fire machine-like trajectory. Moreover, the assurance that we feel concerning the overall tendency of the market process is clearly dependent upon the rate at which unanticipated changes in UVs impinge on the market. Were these changes to be so drastic in their volatility and rate of occurrence as to swamp the discovery potential inherent in entrepreneurial alertness, we could hardly expect the market process to manifest itself, in the real world, in a manner able to generate order in the face of apparent chaos. The market agitation thus generated by chaotic change in UVs could thus fail to display the underlying tendencies towards orderliness which entrepreneurial processes under less extreme conditions set into motion.
>
> (Kirzner 1992: 51)

Kirzner (1992: 35) acknowledges that such circumstances are not just a theoretical possibility. There may well be instances in capitalist history where the 'power of the coordinative market process' has been overwhelmed by the volatility of change in underlying market data and by the high rate of entrepreneurial errors.

Thus, such considerations may be especially important in the context of economic development and transition. During radical structural changes and rapid processes of liberalisation and transition, changes in UVs may be so extremely volatile, frequent and unpredictable that entrepreneurial activity does not generate greater social coordination (i.e. better mutual awareness and better consistency of plans). If political institutions, legal rules and property rights, for instance, are changing rapidly and erratically, the strength of disequilibrating forces might well overwhelm equilibrating forces so that market activity exhibits little tendency towards order. However, other things being equal, the more freedom entrepreneurs have in such circumstances to respond to perceived disequilibria and changes in underlying variables, the greater the likelihood that the market process will be able to engender some degree of orderliness. Conversely, the greater the institutional constraints on entrepreneurial adjustment in such a situation, the more severe and prolonged the instability and disorder that is likely to ensue.

## An alternative vision of the market process

Kirzner's assertion that, in the absence of extreme conditions, the market possesses a systematic equilibrative tendency is not without its critics. In particular, Lachmann (1986) and his followers have emphasised the radical uncertainty inherent in human action and its implications for the possibility of equilibration and coordination. According to this view, at each instant under even normal economic conditions, there is no assurance that equilibrative forces outweigh disequilibrating forces, with the result that we can never be sure that the market process, on balance, tends towards equilibrium. In Lachmann's system, there is apparently no systematic tendency towards improved coordination (in the conventional sense of *ex ante* consistency among participants' plans). Indeed, the entrepreneurial character of the market process itself engenders some *dis*coordination of existing patterns:

> In a competitive game there are winners and losers. By the same token, competitive market forces will cause discoordination as well as coordination of agents' plans. *In fact they cannot do the latter without doing the former.* No agent can enter a market, or extend his range of activity within one by making offers to other agents, without disrupting some market relationship presently existing between them and others. This fact is of course of the very essence of competition.
>
> (Lachmann 1986: 5; emphasis added)

Lachmann (1976) uses Shackle's (1972) notion of a 'kaleidic society' to emphasise that we cannot even speak of the market process as tending to generate greater mutual awareness among market participants. Unlike Kirzner's model, there is no reason to expect that entrepreneurs in Lachmann's system will tend to proceed in the right direction to correct previous errors.[10] Indeed, the inevitability of continual disequilibrating changes makes it impossible for entrepreneurs to make the right decisions and to determine what adjustment in prices and output is necessary to bring about movement towards equilibrium. 'Nobody can take his equilibrium bearings if he does not know how others will act. ... The beacon that had been designed to keep entrepreneurs from straying from the narrow path of convergent expectations turns out, on most nights, to be rather dim' (Lachmann 1994: 204–205).

Following Lachmann, many market-process economists recognise the significance of disequilibrating tendencies in markets. They regard entrepreneurial error and disequilibration as an inevitable and essential element of the market process. Endogenous adjustment in IVs is thus both an equilibrating and a disequilibrating force:

> These [disequilibrating] tendencies are not simply the result of changes in the exogenous data but emanate from the source of equilibrating behavior, that is, the indeterminate or creative response to perceived profit opportunities. 'The same active mental processes which are taken to adjust to change once it has occurred, will also originate change' (High, 1986, p. 115). *The very process of adjustment – or rather attempted adjustment – will produce errors that undermine equilibration.* If this were not the case and if only systematic equilibrating tendencies existed, then money and, more generally, market institutions would tend to disappear.
>
> (Rizzo 1996: xvii–xviii; emphasis added)

That concludes the summary of Kirzner's theory of entrepreneurial discovery and its implications for the market process. As an exercise in pure economic theory, Kirzner avoids delving into the psychological context of the entrepreneurial function. The task of the next chapter is to apply his theory in conjunction with other approaches in order to examine the psychological determinants of entrepreneurship and, in particular, the cognitive underpinnings of the economic construct of entrepreneurial alertness. In subsequent chapters, Kirzner's approach serves as a highly effective analytical tool for understanding the impact of institutions and culture on entrepreneurship.

# 3 Psychological determinants of entrepreneurial alertness

> Opportunities rarely present themselves in neat packages. They almost always have to be discovered and packaged. Thus, *the nexus of opportunity and enterprising individual is critical to understanding entrepreneurship*. ... [P]eople are different and these differences matter. These differences give rise to many of the interesting questions in entrepreneurship.
>
> (Venkataraman 1997: 123; emphasis added)[1]

Hypotheses about the principal determinants of entrepreneurship are strongly conditioned by the particular set of disciplinary spectacles through which one looks. By and large, economists have tended to concentrate on the nature of the entrepreneurial function, neglecting consideration of the personal factors that might characterise the entrepreneurial type in a particular setting and instead emphasising the external causes of entrepreneurial activity. For example, many economists would argue that entrepreneurial behaviour is caused by external market forces, such as market 'imperfections', that create an opportunity for entrepreneurs to earn supernormal profits. Consequently, economic models generally do not try to explain why, when and how some people, but not others, are able to discover or create these opportunities. The sources of individual differences in alertness to economic opportunities are left largely unexplained in economic models of entrepreneurship.

And yet it seems that different people in various contexts possess vastly different degrees of entrepreneurial alertness, that is, they exhibit different abilities to learn without deliberate search. 'Some are quick to spot as yet unnoticed opportunities, others notice only the opportunities revealed by the discoveries of others. In some societies, in some climates, among some groups, it appears that entrepreneurial alertness is keener than in others' (Kirzner 1983b: 67). Entrepreneurs are those persons whose alertness is the most acute, most highly developed and most sustained.

An important line of enquiry is thus to explain the psychological determinants of individual differences in entrepreneurial alertness. What are the sources of the human propensity to be alert? Are entrepreneurs a different breed of economic decision-maker? The argument in this chapter boils down to a simple proposition about the cognitive factors that switch on entrepreneurial alertness: *individuals' agency beliefs – or more specifically, their perceptions of control and of self-efficacy – are a major determinant of their alertness.*

In this chapter, *personal agency* beliefs are defined as subjective expectations about the extent to which one can produce effects (i.e. given outcomes) and exert power over what happens in one's life.[2] These beliefs are conceptualised as a composite of two kinds of interrelated, but conceptually distinct, expectations about the self: namely, beliefs about *locus of control* (or *contingency* expectations) and beliefs about *self-efficacy* (or *competence* expectations). In short, perceptions of personal agency comprise beliefs about whether actions influence events (locus of control, LOC) and beliefs about whether one can produce the relevant actions (self-efficacy). See Table 3.1.

LOC beliefs refer to causal beliefs about how outcomes are determined. As discussed later in this chapter, according to Rotter's LOC construct, people believe that outcomes are determined either by their own actions or by external forces. That is, they perceive outcomes as being either personally determined (and thereby potentially under personal control) or as externally determined (and therefore beyond personal control). The core of the construct is thus not the perception of 'control' as such but rather the perception of *contingency* between actions and outcomes.[3]

Expectations of personal efficacy refer to the perceived ability to produce certain actions oneself. They refer to self-beliefs of what one can and cannot do. According to Bandura's concept of self-efficacy, an efficacy expectation is a judgement of how well one will be able to perform in a given situation. Thus the distinction between the two types of expectations about the self becomes clear:

> An outcome expectancy [e.g. an LOC belief or contingency expectation] is defined as a person's estimate that a given behavior will lead to certain outcomes. An efficacy expectation is the conviction that one can successfully execute the behavior required to produce the outcomes.
>
> (Bandura 1977a: 193)

*Table 3.1* The components of personal agency beliefs

| Component of personal agency beliefs | Definition | Operationalisation |
| --- | --- | --- |
| Internal LOC belief (contingency expectation) | Belief about whether economic outcomes are contingent upon certain actions | 'To what extent do target economic events depend upon doing $x$?' |
| Self-efficacy belief (competence expectation) | Belief about whether one can produce the relevant actions | 'To what extent can I do $x$?' |

The central proposition of this chapter can now be restated more precisely: *the more convinced individuals are that profit and economic rewards are largely contingent upon certain actions in a particular context (internal LOC beliefs), and the more confident they are that they have the knowledge and capabilities to successfully carry out those entrepreneurial tasks and plans in certain settings (high perceived self-efficacy), the more acute and sustained will be their alertness to opportunities.* At the end of the chapter, a conceptual model is presented which encapsulates this argument.

It should be noted that the above hypothesis refers only to *economic* LOC and self-efficacy beliefs; it does not invoke the notion of overall agency beliefs that apply to every domain of human activity. 'Economic' agency, LOC and self-efficacy expectations relate to beliefs about the causes of changes in one's income and wealth, the contingency of monetary rewards on one's behaviour and one's competence to engage in particular economic activities, respectively. These beliefs are context-dependent expectations that may even be limited to particular segments of economic reality (e.g. particular markets or industries). *References in this book to agency, LOC and efficacy beliefs should generally be read to pertain to the sphere of economic achievement only unless the context implies some other realm of agency.* (For the sake of brevity, I do not refer to beliefs in 'economic' LOC and 'economic' self-efficacy, and so on.)

The above qualification is important because expectations about contingency and competence in one sphere of one's life are *not necessarily* generalisable to other areas of one's life. People can have quite different expectations about their causal powers in different fields of endeavour. For example, one can believe that the profitability of an entrepreneurial venture is mainly contingent upon one's business acumen while simultaneously believing that success or failure at golf is in the lap of the gods. However, considerable social psychological evidence suggests that successful task experiences that enhance one's sense of self-efficacy at work can directly affect perceived efficacy in other aspects of one's life, such as political participation, leisure activities and child rearing (Bowles 1998: 97–99).

The chapter surveys psychological research with a view to seeing what light previous findings might shed on how personal agency beliefs and other psychological factors might affect entrepreneurial alertness. Much of this research is couched in terms that are most appropriate for individualist cultures. Chapter 6 modifies the conception of agency beliefs and expands the analysis to include the cognitive determinants of alertness in group-oriented cultures.

Regrettably, much of the empirical work on the psychology of entrepreneurship has not been a paragon of conceptual rigour. Studies often do not offer a theory explaining what key variables mean and why and how particular entrepreneurial traits and characteristics affect entrepreneurship. Definitions of the entrepreneur are often vague and do not correspond directly to the precise notions of entrepreneurship in economic theory. To my knowledge, no empirical psychological study has directly examined entrepreneurial alertness, arbitrage or spontaneous learning on the part of entrepreneurs.

The operational definition of who is an entrepreneur and the selection of samples also exhibit a wide degree of variation. Many studies define the entrepreneur as the founder of a firm (i.e. the unit of analysis is 'enterprisers' rather than entrepreneurs), while other studies choose to designate the owner of a business as the entrepreneur.

> Still others use more esoteric approaches to defining an entrepreneur, such as someone who received a loan from a bank to start a business ... or a small business owner who was involved in the development and pursuit of an innovative strategy or in the creation and recognition of a new market.
>
> (Ginsberg and Buchholtz 1989: 35)

The distinction between entrepreneur and manager is also often blurred.

Moreover, samples of entrepreneurs and 'non-entrepreneurs' are sometimes inappropriate and not carefully selected for testing hypotheses about particular entrepreneurial characteristics or traits (e.g. Pandey and Tewary 1979). They fail to represent accurately the kinds of individuals that the studies seek to analyse.

Furthermore, it should be said at the outset that empirical research into the psychological determinants of entrepreneurship has often led to inconclusive or inconsistent results. Empirical research into the nature of entrepreneurial talent has not determined reliably how much entrepreneurs differ from managers or other classes of business people or whether there are even specific psychological characteristics that uniquely distinguish the entrepreneurial personality. This limited success may result from the methodological inadequacies described above. There is also a growing recognition that individual traits and characteristics – when examined in isolation of situational context – might by themselves be limited in their ability to predict or to explain variation in behaviour.[4] 'Previous studies seeking answers to the question, "How are entrepreneurs different from non-entrepreneurs?" have not generated a reliable or valid list of characteristics that are clearly "entrepreneurial" across all situations' (Gartner 1989: 31).

In spite of these definitional and methodological limitations, however, there is some utility in selectively surveying psychological research in order to see what we can learn about the psychological determinants of entrepreneurial alertness.[5] I start by focusing upon LOC which is a cognitive variable that has received a great deal of attention in the literature on the psychology of the entrepreneur. I then consider the concept of self-efficacy which has gained prominence in more recent psychological research. By way of a synthesis, the chapter concludes with a conceptual model of the factors that influence entrepreneurial alertness and discovery (see Figure 3.1 on p. 52).

## LOC (contingency expectations)

As a result of the cognitive revolution in psychology, and especially since Rotter's introduction of the concept of LOC, a vast amount of research has been devoted to people's beliefs about the causal structure of the environment.[6] As discussed previously, perceptions of LOC constitute one of the two main elements that make up personal agency beliefs. According to the construct of LOC, people believe that the outcomes of events are either within or beyond their personal control – that is, people differ in the degree to which they attribute events to their own actions. Belief in *internal control* means that one perceives a series of related events to be contingent upon one's own behaviour or one's own relatively durable characteristics (Rotter 1966: 1). 'Internal' people thus believe that they have some control over events in their life and that they are, therefore, responsible for their own destiny. They expect that the environment can be controlled by their own actions. 'This is not, of course, tantamount to the naive belief that individuals can ordain the final configuration of environmental events; rather internals believe that judicious efforts can moderate external impacts' (Begley and Boyd 1987: 81).

In contrast, a belief in *external control* means that a person perceives an event 'as following some action of his own but not ... entirely contingent upon his action' (Rotter 1966: 1). 'External' people are more likely to interpret events as the result of factors outside the self that they cannot influence. They see themselves as at the mercy of forces that turn them into pawns rather than actors. They are weathervanes buffeted by the wind. There are at least five types of belief in external control: the belief that events are the result of luck and chance; the belief that events are preordained and occur because of fate; the belief that events are subject to the control of 'powerful others'; the belief that events result from strong impersonal or supernatural forces; and the belief that the causes of events are too complex for outcomes to be understood and predicted.

The LOC construct is firmly embedded within Rotter's (1954) broader theory of social learning. A basic assumption of this theory is that the unit of analysis for the study of personality is the *interaction* of the individual and his or her situation. The theory holds that behaviour is a function of beliefs and the value of rewards in a specific situation. 'Behavior in different situations will be different, although there may be a gradient of generalization from one situation to another' (Rotter 1990: 491).

LOC refers to an attitude or belief in the nature of the causal relationship between certain types of behaviour and a class of similar events or situations. This belief about the causal source of what happens to the self defines one's basic approach to how one lives in the world. The LOC construct is a measure of relatively stable individual differences, though these individual differences are not immutable, monolithic traits:

> [P]eople are not totally internals or externals. The terms are used as expressive shortcuts and are not meant to imply that perception of control is a trait or a typology. The perception of control is a process, the exercise of an expectancy regarding causation; and the terms internal and external control depict an individual's more common tendencies to expect events to be contingent or noncontingent upon their actions.
>
> (Lefcourt 1982: 186)

LOC beliefs can have an important impact on behavioural patterns in a wide range of life situations. In particular, and of relevance to my aims, there is ample evidence that differences in LOC beliefs play a significant role in determining individual differences in learning processes in different kinds of learning contexts (see the discussion below on perceptual and cognitive dimensions of LOC). It has also been suggested that differences in LOC beliefs account for differences in people's willingness to take actions that are counter to the norms of the social group to which they belong (Cole and Cole 1977). Compared with externals, internal people are more likely to be able to recombine and synthesise elements into new forms, to be independent in their thinking and to resist coercion and pressures to conform.

## The relationship between LOC and other constructs

The investigation of the role of people's beliefs about causality and personal control has a long lineage in the social sciences. For instance, although Veblen's (1899) concern was with differences among societies rather than among individuals, he suggests that a society in which people generally believe in luck and chance is likely to be inefficient and unproductive. This is akin to Rotter's (1966: 3) hypothesis at the individual level that a belief in external control is likely to be related to general apathy and passivity.

Rotter's typology also bears some resemblance to that of Riesman in his study of the changing social character in the USA. Riesman (1950) distinguishes between 'inner-directed' people and 'other-directed' people. Inner-directed people shape their own destiny in terms of a set of internalised, life-long goals that they acquire early on in their development from their parents and authorities who resemble their parents. In contrast, other-directed people are the product of their peer groups – they are controlled by external forces, especially social forces. They have a heightened self-consciousness about relations to people and consequently lack the inner-directed person's capacity to go it alone.

Rotter notes, however, that the relationship between Riesman's conception and his own construct is not straightforward:

Riesman has been concerned with whether the individual is controlled from within or from without. We are concerned, however, not with this variable at all but only with the question of whether or not an individual *believes* that his own behavior, skills, or internal dispositions determine what reinforcements [i.e. rewards] he receives. While the conformist (the opportunist, in particular) who is actively trying to learn and adjust to the rules of the society he lives in is at one end of Riesman's continuum, he is likely to be in the middle of the continuum with which we are concerned.

(Rotter 1966: 4; emphasis added)

In addition, Rotter (1966: 3) believes that LOC is connected to McClelland's (1961) notion of need for achievement (*n* Ach). In its modern formalisation, the achievement motive was originally defined in Murray's (1938) theory of personality, and McClelland's earlier work on motivation reveals Murray's influence. According to McClelland (1962), individuals with a high *n* Ach are depicted as preferring to be responsible for solving problems and for setting goals to be reached by their own efforts as well as having a strong desire to receive concrete feedback on their performance. On the basis of these demonstrated characteristics, McClelland hypothesised that entrepreneurs will have high *n* Ach because they seem to possess the same characteristics.

Rotter suggests that people who have a high *n* Ach are likely to have internal beliefs, but some qualification is necessary:

The relationship [between *n* Ach and internal LOC beliefs] is probably not linear, however, since a person high on motivation for achievement might not be equally high on a belief in internal control of reinforcement, and there may be many with a low need for achievement who still believe that their own behavior determines the kind of reinforcements they obtain.

(Rotter 1966: 3)

## Psychological studies of the relationship between LOC and entrepreneurship

There is tentative support within the empirical psychological literature for characterising entrepreneurs as holding internal beliefs. In their respective reviews of the literature on LOC among entrepreneurs, Venkatapathy (1984) and Gilad (1982b; 1986) contend that the results of empirical studies support the notion that internal LOC is an important characteristic contributing to entrepreneurship. What follows is a thumbnail sketch of the most important research.

Shapero (1975) applied Rotter's Internal–External scale to determine the LOC of entrepreneurs. He found that the mean scores of 34 Italian entrepreneurs and 101 Texan entrepreneurs were more internal than those for the general population (with the exception of Peace Corps trainees).

Shapero's finding was corroborated some years later by Brockhaus and Nord (1979) (cited in Brockhaus and Horwitz 1986: 28) and Mescon and Montanari (1981). Brockhaus and Nord also found that, on average, entrepreneurs (defined as owners of new businesses) tended to have more internal LOC beliefs than those reported by Rotter (1966) for all groups in the general population except Peace Corps volunteers. Similarly, in their study of twenty franchise entrepreneurs and thirty-one independent entrepreneurs (founders of new businesses), Mescon and Montanari found that each group scored significantly higher than the general public on Rotter's Internal–External scale. Relative to the national sample, entrepreneurs as a group exhibited extremely high internal LOC.

LOC may also distinguish entrepreneurs from managers. In their study of Irish entrepreneurs, Cromie and Johns (1983) found that a sample of established entrepreneurs ($n = 42$) in the greater Belfast area was significantly more internal than a group of middle to senior managers ($n = 41$) and that the aspiring entrepreneurs ($n = 23$) were significantly more internal than the established entrepreneurs. This result supports the contention that 'an internal locus of control is one of the key characteristics of entrepreneurs. Internals are less likely to let external events dominate their lives and will tend to be proactive rather than reactive in coping with their environments' (1983: 321). Similar results were obtained in an Australian study. Perry *et al.* (1986) found that the mean internal LOC score of a sample of highly successful Australian entrepreneurs ($n = 18$) was significantly higher than the mean scores of two groups of small business owner–managers ($n = 92, n = 73$, respectively).

There is some evidence that LOC beliefs might be related to entrepreneurial expectations of starting a company someday. Borland (1974) studied 375 business school students at the University of Texas using Levenson's (1973) instrument for measuring LOC. Borland found that, overall, students who expected to start a company someday had significantly stronger beliefs in internal control than other students. (Borland also found that the concept of internal LOC was a better predictor of intentions to launch a new business than the need for achievement.) Similarly, in a sample of twenty graduate business school students, Brockhaus (1975) found that those students who intended to become entrepreneurs held significantly more internal LOC beliefs than their classmates who did not intend to set up ventures.

The LOC concept might also hold promise for distinguishing between successful and unsuccessful entrepreneurs. In a second study, Brockhaus (1980) found that owners of new businesses that had survived the three-year period after his initial 1975 study exhibited greater internality than those owners whose businesses had failed. In other words, this longitudinal study suggests that internal beliefs might be causally connected to the degree of success of entrepreneurial ventures in a later period.

However, not all empirical studies support a significant role for LOC beliefs in entrepreneurship. In a survey of 307 University of Oregon alumni, Hull *et al.* (1980) did not find a significant relationship between LOC beliefs and the decision to start a business (unlike Borland 1974 and Brockhaus 1975).

The ability of LOC to distinguish entrepreneurs from managers is also brought into question. Begley and Boyd (1987) conducted a survey of 239 members of the Small Business Association of New England. In their sample of CEOs of small businesses, they found that both entrepreneurs (founders) and managers (non-founders) exhibited an internal LOC but the former did not exhibit significantly higher internal LOC than the latter. (Brockhaus and Nord (1979) also found that LOC beliefs did not differ significantly between entrepreneurs and managers.) Furthermore, the results of Begley and Boyd's study did not support the use of the LOC concept as a predictor of financial performance: the degree of internality of CEOs in both groups did not relate positively to the financial performance of their firms.

It is not easy to reconcile the apparent conflicts between these empirical findings or to evaluate their significance, but a broad picture emerges of entrepreneurs being highly internal, more so than the general population:

> The review, in general, suggests that internal locus of control is one of the important characteristics contributing to the making of entrepreneurs. Though a few investigations … have led to the conclusion that internality is not a prerequisite for one to become an entrepreneur, the other investigations … strongly hold that internal locus of control distinguishes entrepreneurs from the rest of the population. A pattern of results with the successful entrepreneurs showing more internal orientation exists.
>
> (Venkatapathy 1984: 99)

In any case, the empirical results are at best suggestive. The definition of entrepreneurship typically employed (i.e. the starting up or ownership of a business venture) does not operationalise neatly the Kirznerian notion of entrepreneurial alertness or discovery. An alert entrepreneur who buys cheap and sells dear may not need to set up a company in order to engage in arbitrage activity, nor need a speculator. In addition, the studies also vary greatly in terms of their samples, sampling procedures, the operationalisation of the LOC construct and the measurement instrument used to determine LOC beliefs.

Furthermore, empirical research on entrepreneurship and LOC typically fails to specify a theoretical framework explaining the causal links between LOC and entrepreneurship. In particular, the studies are not connected to the social learning theory that spawned the LOC construct, or any other theoretical approach for that matter. This deficiency has important implications: 'Elements of Rotter's [social learning] theory would demand that reinforcement value and the *intricacies of the situation* in which behavior is occurring be taken into account for the most precise prediction' (Strickland 1989: 4; emphasis added).

## Alertness and other perceptual and cognitive dimensions of LOC

There is a wealth of empirical evidence supporting a relationship between internal LOC and alertness to opportunities. Gilad (1982b; 1986) and Lefcourt (1982: 60–80) provide surveys of psychological research into the perceptual and cognitive dimensions of LOC. This research comprises numerous experimental studies of diverse populations. There is strong empirical support for the idea that internals and externals differ in their perceptions and thought patterns – a typical result being that internals exhibit superior perceptual and cognitive performance.

In general, internals tend to be: more 'cognitively alert' and 'perceptually sensitive'; more attentive to environmental cues regarding opportunities; much quicker in noticing changes in conditions; superior in their ability to extract, assimilate and use information; and capable of making decisions more efficiently.

Internal individuals appear to have greater 'perceptual sensitivity' and superior attentional processes than externals (DuCette and Wolk 1973; Wolk and DuCette 1974). They are more ready to construe a given situation as offering opportunities for personal gain (Lefcourt 1967: 377), and they are more vigilant when confronting novel and uncertain situations (Lefcourt and Wine 1969):

> Whether the focus has been on attention, deliberation, inquisitiveness, or utilization of information, internals have more often been found to be active and alert individuals than have externals. ... [A]n internal locus of control seems to be a sine qua non of being able to steer oneself more clearly and appropriately through the vagaries and confusions of different situations.
>
> (Lefcourt 1982: 72)

In contrast, external persons need to be informed that the opportunities inherent in a situation are indeed available: '[E]xternal control expectancies are maintained by their own consequences, apathy and inactivity' (Lefcourt 1967: 373). If people think that there is nothing they can do to change their situations, if they think that desirable outcomes are not within their personal control, then they will not be alert to environmental cues regarding possible opportunities for subjective gain.

In addition, internals are quicker at detecting changes in the conditions about them and have a greater readiness to cognitively adjust to change (Lefcourt *et al.* 1973). They deal more adaptively with novel environments.

Similarly, internals tend to be more active perceivers and utilisers of actual or potential information (Wolk and DuCette 1974). They are better able than externals at grasping and using strategic information to improve their interpretations of ambiguous situations (DuCette and Wolk 1973). They also make more extensive use of all potential sources of information (Lefcourt 1982).

The internals' superior perceptual sensitivity and their greater ability to synthesise potential information are also related to superior performance in *incidental learning*. This is especially significant because incidental or unintentional learning is the psychological concept that corresponds to Kirzner's concept of spontaneous learning – that is, entrepreneurial discovery without deliberate search (Gilad 1982b: 137). In particular, internals give more attention to those aspects of a situation that appear to be 'irrelevant' to any explicit and intended task. As a consequence of this heightened degree of attentiveness, internals exhibit significantly greater levels of spontaneous learning. Reporting on the results of their two studies, Wolk and DuCette (1974: 98) conclude that:

[T]he internals demonstrated higher levels of incidental learning. Incidental learning is a phenomenon dependent on the acquisition of less prominent aspects of a stimulus array, and since such acquisition has been interpreted as the product of a more attentive and organizing cognitive system, it follows that the internal differs from the external in the manner in which he organizes and uses information.

Although differences in the perceptual and cognitive behaviour of internals and externals reflect generalised cognitive structures, situational conditions do affect the extent of the performance differential between internals and externals. For example, Wolk and DuCette found that the more *competitive* the situation, the greater the superiority of internals at incidental learning.

In addition to alertness and incidental learning that appear to be correlates of internal LOC, various psychological studies have found that certain other cognitive characteristics, abilities and behaviour patterns are associated with this variable. Thus, if it is accepted that entrepreneurs are likely to be internal people, then entrepreneurs might also exhibit these characteristics. In her review of research on Rotter's construct, Strickland identifies correlates of internal LOC that are pertinent to entrepreneurship: 'Internals ... hold many of the attributes that are related to creativity, such as autonomy, seeking out information that might lead to change, independence of judgment, a willingness to take reasonable risks, self-confidence, and a creative self-image' (1989: 7).

In addition, several studies have discovered that a belief in internal LOC is associated with a more active role by individuals in shaping events and with striving to control their environment (Atkinson 1957; Brockhaus

1975; Shapero 1975). Similarly, internals are also more resilient at coping with environmentally induced stress (Anderson 1977).

Rotter's theory is not the only psychological approach to emphasise the centrality of personal agency beliefs in human endeavour. The next section examines a more recent theory that has been advanced to explain the emergence, function and effects of people's beliefs in their causal capabilities. It too has the merit of having being applied to research in the psychology of entrepreneurship.

## Self-efficacy (competence expectations)

Psychological studies of entrepreneurship are giving increasing emphasis to the role of self-efficacy beliefs – which were identified earlier as the second key component of perceptions of personal agency. 'Entrepreneurship, which is driven by the envisioned opportunities of new ventures, rests heavily on a robust sense of efficacy to sustain one through the stresses and discouragements inherent in innovative pursuits' (Bandura 1997: 455). More generally, personal efficacy is a valued orientation in a world of continuous churning because 'a strong sense of personal efficacy is vital for *successful adaptation and change*' (Bandura 1995a: 34; emphasis added). Instead of investigating stable personality traits, the examination of self-efficacy affords a more dynamic approach to explaining the cognitive processes in entrepreneurial behaviour.

The concept of self-efficacy is a key component of Bandura's (1977a; 1977b; 1997) theory of social learning.[7] 'Perceived self-efficacy refers to beliefs in one's capabilities to organize and execute the courses of action required to manage prospective situations. Efficacy beliefs influence how people think, feel, motivate themselves, and act' (Bandura 1995a: 2). They pertain to people's perceptions about their own abilities to muster the motivation, cognitive resources and target behaviours necessary for exercising control over events in their lives. The upshot is that, to be successful, people must possess not only the skills required for performing specific tasks but also a *self-belief* in their own capabilities to exercise control over events to achieve their goals.

Self-efficacy arises from the cognitive appraisal of one's capabilities. According to the theory, people evaluate and assimilate data about their capabilities, and then they choose their environments, career paths, activities and effort levels accordingly.

People's beliefs about their efficacy can be influenced in several ways. The two most effective are direct mastery experience (learning by doing) and vicarious experience (learning by seeing). Actual mastery of behaviour involves directly experiencing repeated performance successes. Through their accomplishments and experience in overcoming setbacks, people gradually acquire the skills required for performing specific tasks. Thus, they may form entrepreneurial intentions early in their careers but not act upon these intentions until the process of enactive mastery (acquired through past job experience) provides the level of confidence necessary to anticipate success in an entrepreneurial venture.

Vicarious experience (or observational learning through 'modelling') is another way to affect self-efficacy beliefs. Observers raise their judgements of their own efficacy when they watch effective role models, with abilities similar to their own, handle difficult situations and successfully overcome obstacles.

The impact of observational learning on entrepreneurial self-efficacy is supported by evidence on the development of entrepreneurial career preferences (Scherer *et al.* 1988; 1990; 1989). The presence of a parent entrepreneurial role model, especially one who is perceived to be highly successful, increases offspring's perceptions of their own abilities to start and manage a venture and raises their expectations of becoming a business founder:

> A model [i.e. an entrepreneurial parent] perceived to be a high performer apparently encourages the observer through a vicarious learning process, to consider an entrepreneurial career. Moreover, even individuals with a model perceived to be a low performer have a strong expectancy for entrepreneurial career entry. While different evaluations of the model's performance result in different levels of overall career preference, the simple presence of a model appears to be the most salient factor for expected entry.
>
> (Scherer *et al.* 1989: 66)

Self-efficacy warrants a comparison with LOC, the other key factor of human agency. As we saw, LOC is a belief-based personality variable, a 'broad construct intended to study behavior in a variety of situations' (Rotter 1990: 491). In contrast, self-efficacy is more specific than generalised LOC. Perceptions of self-efficacy are always relative to particular tasks and they reflect a person's judgement about whether and to what extent they can perform those tasks at a specific standard.

Bandura himself sees the distinction between self-efficacy and LOC as more fundamental than a difference of levels of generality: 'In point of fact, they represent entirely different phenomena' (Bandura 1997: 20). People may have a strong internal LOC in general but have doubts about their skill levels in certain areas, giving rise to low self-efficacy for performing specific tasks (Bandura 1977a). For example, individuals may believe that economic outcomes and entrepreneurial success depend entirely upon their own actions (internal LOC), but they consider themselves to be lacking the requisite skills in organisation building, marketing, innovation and financial control (low self-efficacy).

Although differences exist between the two constructs, there are obvious similarities. Both self-efficacy and LOC are cognitive and are about personal agency. Furthermore, just as self-efficacy can be affected by performance, LOC can be affected by life experiences (Dyal 1984). People develop and modify these beliefs as they interact with their environment.

There is also evidence of a relationship between LOC and self-efficacy (e.g. Chambliss and Murray 1979). Bandura (1997: 20) too acknowledges that the *interaction* of efficacy beliefs and LOC beliefs will have a significant influence on human behaviour: 'It is when people have the efficacy to perform well [i.e. a high self-efficacy] that belief that outcomes are dependent on their actions [i.e. internal LOC] will create a sense of causative power.' Gist elaborates on the nature of the connection between the two constructs:

> It is likely that persons with an internal locus of control may need fewer enactive mastery experiences to improve efficacy perceptions and performance. They also may respond more readily to modeling [i.e. observational learning], because they tend to believe that they, like the models, generally are in control of their environments. ... In contrast, persons with an external locus of control may be inclined to view enactive mastery experiences as luck. They also may reject modeling because of a tendency to attribute the model's success to skills the observers doubt they have.
>
> (Gist 1987: 480)

In addition, empirical research indicates that entrepreneurial self-efficacy is related positively to internal LOC but negatively to 'chance' control (Chen *et al.* 1998; Scherer *et al.* 1982).

### Self-efficacy and entrepreneurial alertness

From a market-process perspective, it is significant that the recognition of opportunities is likely to be driven by people's situational perceptions of self-efficacy – their perceptions of a situation and their ability to control processes and outcomes in it:

> People's beliefs about their efficacy influence how they construe situations and the types of anticipatory scenarios and visualized futures they construct. Those who have a high sense of efficacy view situations as presenting realizable opportunities. They visualize success scenarios that provide positive guides for performance. Those who judge themselves as inefficacious construe uncertain situations as risky and are inclined to visualize failure scenarios.
>
> (Bandura 1997: 116)

Persons with a strong sense of personal efficacy are quick to take advantage of opportunities. They are also adept at discovering how to bypass institutional constraints. Even in situations that offer few opportunities and serious barriers to their progress, they are creative and alert enough to find ways of exercising some degree of control over events. Conversely, people with a weak sense of self-efficacy are less likely to seize opportunities and are easily deterred by institutional obstacles.

Krueger and Dickson (1993) provide empirical support for the effect of self-efficacy on opportunity recognition. They found that perceptions of self-efficacy reported by 153 upper-class business majors were significantly associated with subsequent perceptions of situational opportunity and threat for two different types of decision-making exercises. Decision-makers whose perceived efficacy is raised through positive performance feedback tend to perceive opportunities worth seeking, whereas those whose sense of efficacy is reduced tend to focus on the threats to be avoided. 'No matter how attractive the positive consequences, individuals are less likely to act in a situation if they perceive that they lack the competence to execute critical behaviors' (Krueger and Dickson 1993: 1236). People who see themselves as inefficacious are at best able to effect only limited change even in environments that offer many opportunities.

There is other indirect evidence that perceptions of self-efficacy influence alertness to opportunities. In a longitudinal field study of East German workers during the transition process ($n$ = 463 to 543), Speier and Frese (1997) found that generalised self-efficacy both partly 'mediated' and 'moderated' the effect of organisational conditions on changes in individuals' levels of personal initiative in the workplace.[8] Personal initiative, of course, is not identical to alertness or spontaneous discovery, but, as defined by Speier and Frese, it does involve identifying opportunities to improve the work process by going beyond the formal duties of the job. It involves carrying out activities that are not directly related to doing stipulated tasks; it may even entail changing these tasks. In economic terms, personal initiative involves the discovery and exploitation of new ends–means frameworks. '[P]ersonal initiative implies that one acts in new and ambiguous situations' (p. 173). It is 'self-starting and proactive' (p. 171).

Given that self-efficacy directly affects opportunity recognition, it follows that perceptions of self-efficacy might play a critical role in the supply of potential entrepreneurs and in the intention to become an entrepreneur. Krueger and Brazeal (1994: 94–95, 102) emphasise the primacy of perceived self-efficacy in their conceptual model of entrepreneurial potential. Entrepreneurial potential is akin to the propensity to be alert in that it pertains to pre-existing cognitive readiness to identify and accept hitherto unknown, personally attractive opportunities. The potential for entrepreneurship is 'causally and temporally prior' to entrepreneurial intentions: a potential entrepreneur need not have a conscious, well-informed intention of pursuing a particular opportunity (p. 91). Some unexpected event is required to precipitate the intention and decision to start a venture.

Conceptual work also emphasises the role of self-efficacy as a determinant of a person's planned intention towards becoming an entrepreneur (Boyd and Vozikis 1994; Scherer *et al.* 1989). 'Perceived self-efficacy is a major determinant of intention' (Bandura 1997: 43). Indeed, Boyd and Vozikis (1994) suggest that individual self-efficacy influences the entrepreneurial process of creating new ventures. They argue that personal efficacy beliefs are a useful concept for explaining the evaluative and decision-making processes that people go through in forming their entrepreneurial intentions and in deciding to embark upon entrepreneurial ventures. More specifically, they hypothesise that self-efficacy determines both the strength of entrepreneurial intentions and the likelihood that those intentions will result in entrepreneurial actions. They did not, however, test their hypotheses empirically.

Empirical research does, however, support the hypothesised role of self-efficacy in the development of entrepreneurial intentions. Chen *et al.* (1998) undertook two studies – one of 140 university students and one of 175 small-business owners and executives. They found that entrepreneurial self-efficacy differentiated entrepreneurship students from management and organisational psychology students and that entrepreneurial self-efficacy is positively related to the intention to start one's own business. (Krueger (1994) also found that perceived entrepreneurial efficacy is higher in business majors who intend to start new ventures.) Another result was that executives who had set up their current businesses ('entrepreneurs') had stronger self-efficacy than did executives who did not found their current companies ('managers'). Chen *et al.* also found that entrepreneurial self-efficacy predicts the decision to become an entrepreneur better than does LOC.

## The causal link between personal agency beliefs and entrepreneurial alertness

We are now in a position to pull together the various threads that have been spun in this chapter. The basic point is that the nature of people's personal agency beliefs (i.e. their LOC and self-efficacy beliefs) is a major factor *determining* their level of entrepreneurial alertness: the more strongly individuals believe that economic outcomes depend largely upon their own actions in a particular domain (rather than on outside factors, such as luck and powerful others), *and* the more strongly they believe that they can perform those critical actions successfully, the more heightened will be their alertness and the higher the level of spontaneous learning that they will exhibit.

### The conceptual model

An advantage of the two psychological constructs, Rotter's notion of LOC and Bandura's concept of self-efficacy, is that they can be linked analytically to Kirzner's economic concept of entrepreneurial alertness. As discussed earlier, empirical psychological studies have shown that entrepreneurs have a high sense of internal control and personal efficacy. However, this correlation does not constitute an explanation of why or how they become entrepreneurs. It is the impact of LOC beliefs and efficacy expectations on alertness which explains entrepreneurship. Internal and self-efficacious people are more alert to profit opportunities, with the result that they are the ones who become entrepreneurs.

The chain of causality is depicted in Figure 3.1.[9] According to the model, generic institutional and specific situational conditions influence the development of people's beliefs about their ability to exercise control over economic events in their lives (i.e. their LOC and efficacy expectations). Subjectively believed LOC and perceived self-efficacy operate as causal factors in cognitive functioning and have a direct effect on alertness to economic opportunities. More precisely, the interaction of strong internal LOC with situationally specific perceptions of high self-efficacy is hypothesised to lead to a heightened level of alertness. Alertness is the mediating variable between people's beliefs in their causal capabilities, on the one hand, and spontaneous learning, on the other. Alertness thus has a direct effect on the entrepreneurial process of spontaneous discovery of profit opportunities:

> The specific entrepreneurial action is a reflection of incidental learning, which depends on a general level of attentiveness. This general level of attentiveness enables the individual to notice opportunities while not suspecting beforehand their specific existence.
>
> (Gilad 1982b: 149)

As a state of mind associated with cognitive readiness, alertness is a necessary condition for spontaneous learning because it 'allows the unsuspecting learner to extract or gain the knowledge about the opportunity from his environment, without having a prior intention to learn' (Gilad 1982b: 140). Because entrepreneurs have no prior intention to perceive specific information, they must maintain a state of constant attentiveness in order to make incidental discoveries of opportunities for profitable action.

Internal LOC and high self-efficacy are each necessary conditions and together they are sufficient for acute and sustained alertness (in the sense of an increased *propensity* to discover previously overlooked opportunities). Believing that one is capable of successfully carrying out entrepreneurial functions, tasks and plans (entrepreneurial self-efficacy) and believing that one's own actions determine desired economic outcomes (internal LOC) intensify alertness to profit opportunities and foster engagement in entrepreneurial activities. In contrast, when people have a very low sense of personal efficacy and a highly external LOC, they feel powerless to improve their situations and they become apathetic and fatalistic. If events are perceived as being dependent completely on external circumstances or chance, there would seem to be little reason for attending to them. As a result, people's alertness diminishes and they become blind to whatever

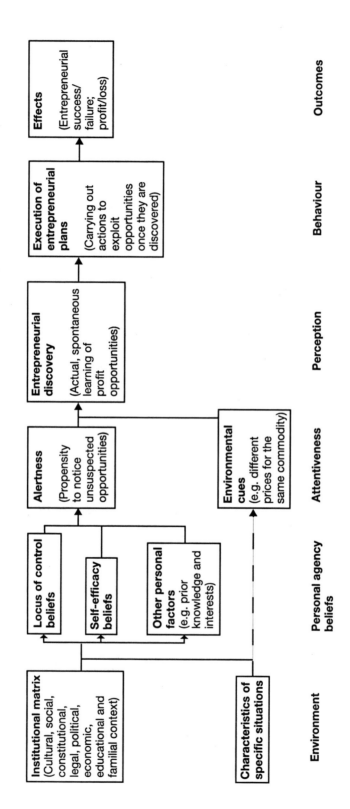

Environment     Personal agency     Attentiveness     Perception     Behaviour     Outcomes
              beliefs

Note: This is a simplified model not including possible feedback loops

*Figure 3.1* The causal link between personal agency beliefs, alertness and entrepreneurial discovery

opportunities might exist for effecting change. In the intermediate case where people have an internal LOC orientation but a low sense of personal efficacy (i.e. when they see events as contingent upon human action but see themselves as incapable of performing the relevant actions satisfactorily), they are also likely to view the world with a sense of futility and to exhibit little alertness to opportunity.

It should be noted that this is a simplified model, emphasising unidirectional causation among environmental conditions, cognition and behaviour. It does not focus upon possible feedback loops. The reality, of course, is that we are both products and producers of our environment. How we act can change our environments as well as our beliefs about ourselves and our capabilities; the environment and our perceptions of self can also change our behaviour. Chapter 8 investigates the issue of reciprocal causation in some detail.

### The determinants of LOC and efficacy beliefs

It is also worthwhile identifying possible determinants of personal agency beliefs (i.e. LOC and efficacy beliefs), which in turn affect alertness and entrepreneurial discovery. The following list is by no means exhaustive. It is merely suggestive of the range of cultural, social, legal, political, economic, familial and educational circumstances that may have an impact upon people's expectations of their personal control and self-efficacy.

Personal agency beliefs are likely to depend upon the type of culture in which people are raised. Different cultural values and norms can cultivate different patterns of perceived efficacy. For example, people in different cultures can turn to different sources of information in order to form their self-efficacy beliefs. In addition, cross-cultural research examines how different LOC orientations might emerge in different cultures. McGinnies *et al.* (1974) compared LOC scores across five cultures (Australia, Japan, New Zealand, Sweden and the USA). The most internal LOC scores were reported for Australia, New Zealand and the USA, three nations with the most similar cultural conditions in terms of language, customs and values. Sweden and Japan produced the most external LOC scores. Similarly, in a cross-cultural study of LOC and innovativeness in nine countries, Mueller and Thomas (2000) found that university students in individualist cultures were more likely to have an internal LOC orientation than were students in group-oriented cultures.

The standard interpretation of these results is that less individualistic or more group-oriented cultures place less value on an autonomous definition of the self, so that an external LOC is to be expected. However, greater care must be taken in interpreting the results of these cross-cultural LOC studies because their methodology is subject to individualistic bias (cf. Furby 1979). As discussed in Chapter 6, the concept of internal LOC needs to be modified and expanded for people in group-oriented cultures because the sources of internal control are not restricted to a narrow conception of the self. There is also an indirect or vicarious source of internal LOC which one, as a communalist, can tap into whenever one attributes desired outcomes to the behaviour of significant others in one's intimate in-group ('extensions of oneself').

Personal agency beliefs also depend upon the general constitutional and institutional framework. The type of political and economic system (especially the degree of decentralisation in economic decision-making and the system of property rights) determines the 'objective' distribution of power over outcomes in the environment. This in turn affects people's experiences of action–outcome sequences and their perceptions of whether outcomes are a function largely of their own behaviour or of external circumstances. These issues are considered in subsequent chapters.

For example, it has been argued that the process of exchange in market economies generates 'self-attribution' or internal LOC beliefs among market participants (Lane 1991). Market exchange is a type of contingent reward that fosters the belief that one is in control of events in one's life: 'Self-attribution is learned from experiences of acting and seeing the world respond, contingent responses. A transaction ... requires mutually contingent responses; therefore *an economy based on {market} transactions teaches self-attribution*' (Lane 1991: 11; emphasis added). Market participants learn that monetary rewards and the denial of these rewards depend upon their prior attempts to act on their environment. No external agency is required to penalise a person who engages in misguided market transactions or misses profitable opportunities for trading. 'Unfavorable exchanges exact their own punishments. ... In many ways, this absence of an external authority and punishing agent is the secret of market success and of the failures of command economies' (p. 162). Consistent with the prediction that entrepreneurs in (former) centrally planned economies have weaker feelings of personal control than those in market-oriented economies, Kaufmann *et al.* (1996) found that Russian entrepreneurs immediately prior to the official breakup of the Soviet Union had scored significantly lower on Levenson's scale of internal control than did US entrepreneurs. Russian entrepreneurs also attributed significantly greater control over events in their lives to 'powerful others' and chance than did their US counterparts.

Over time, one can also expect personal agency beliefs to be affected by the salient features of economic policy, such as the stability and neutrality of fiscal and monetary policy, the nature and magnitude of taxes on business and individuals, and the character of regulatory constraints upon the behaviour of firms and individuals.

In addition, the evidence suggests that intrafamilial processes affect personal agency beliefs during the developmental phase in a person's life. The results of numerous studies into the relationship between parenting practices and children's LOC beliefs present a consistent message: parents who provide stimulation, who are consistently responsive and sensitive to infants' cues, who are emotionally supportive, who encourage independence and who grant autonomy are more likely to have children with an internal control orientation. (In his studies of need for achievement, McClelland (1961) identified similar child-rearing practices as conducive to entrepreneurship.) Conversely, parents who are unresponsive, authoritarian, punitive, overly protective and rejecting tend to produce belief in external control in their children (Flammer 1995; Schneewind 1995). As mentioned previously, the presence of role models – especially entrepreneurial parents – is also important, especially as internal LOC expectancy and high self-efficacy might be transmitted from parents to their offspring (Scherer *et al.* 1989).

An individual's socio-economic background is also likely to affect personal agency beliefs. For one thing, social class has a major impact upon parents' values and their beliefs in their ability to influence their children's development, which in turn determine their parenting practices and children's subsequent LOC beliefs. Lower socio-economic status is likely to be associated with external LOC because people with a poorer socio-economic background perceive the opportunity structure open to them to be narrower and because they are more likely to value conformity to external authority (Jessor *et al.* 1968; Kohn 1969; Kohn and Schooler 1983).

The characteristics of the educational system also play an important role in the development of personal agency beliefs.[10] Oettingen *et al.* (1994) undertook an empirical study of the impact on self-efficacy of the school systems in East and West Berlin before reunification. In line with the Socialist Unity Party's political doctrine, East Berlin educational practices emphasised extensive social comparisons of students' accomplishments in front of the 'class-collective' as well as highly standardised, group-oriented teaching strategies. A key educational goal was to enable students to make self-appraisals of their competence that corresponded with teachers' evaluations of their capabilities. In contrast, the West Berlin system involved more private performance feedback, teaching strategies were more differentiated and the educational philosophy stressed imparting factual knowledge to students rather than reinforcing an official party doctrine or value system.

From their samples of children in grades 2 to 6, Oettingen *et al.* (1994) found that East Berlin children ($n$ = 313) before unification had a significantly lower sense of academic self-efficacy than West Berlin children ($n$ = 516) shortly after unification. East Berlin children judged themselves to have less ability at school, to be less able to exert effort, to attract less luck and to obtain less teacher assistance. The lower perceived efficacy of East Berlin children appeared in the third grade (i.e. at 9 years of age) and was discernible in subsequent school years covered by the study.

This completes the investigation of the psychological determinants of entrepreneurial alertness. It is now appropriate to examine further the antecedent conditions that have an impact upon personal agency beliefs and alertness. Chapters 4 and 5 investigate the institutional framework that is most likely to be conducive to the development of internal LOC beliefs, high self-efficacy and a heightened level of alertness. Chapter 6 considers the impact of culture on people's sense of agency and alertness.

# 4 Institutions I

## Rule of law, property and contract

A free society is fertile and creative in the sense that its freedom generates alertness
to possibilities that may be of use to society; a restriction on the freedom of a society
numbs such alertness and blinds society to possibilities of social improvement.

(Kirzner 1979: 239)

## Institutions and alertness

The purpose of the following two chapters is to examine the institutional
conditions conducive to entrepreneurship. They address the question: what
does the theory of entrepreneurship imply will foster the creation, discovery
and exploitation of entrepreneurial opportunities? In dealing with this issue,
I draw upon the analysis in the previous chapter on the psychological determinants of entrepreneurial alertness. This chapter considers the comparative
effectiveness of alternative institutions for evoking a strong sense of personal
agency and stimulating entrepreneurial discovery. The starting point is to
consider how different conceptions of the entrepreneurial function, its locus
and character will affect such comparative analyses.

The chapter then moves on to examine the ideal of freedom as the pre-
eminent constitutional principle for encouraging entrepreneurship. It
considers how the principle of freedom is embodied in the rule of law, rights
to property and the concept of contract. It puts forward conjectures on what
features of constitutional, legal and regulatory rules would generate strong
beliefs in personal competence and internal control and would therefore best
promote entrepreneurship.

The next chapter investigates other institutions that are conducive to
entrepreneurship. It examines the role of money and the impact of political
and legal decentralisation on the human propensity to be alert to opportunity. Chapter 5 also considers the specific character of the freedom of
entrepreneurial choice and how it is embedded in concrete economic liberties conducive to entrepreneurship. In addition, it reviews empirical studies
on the relationship between economic freedom and national economic
performance.

## What are institutions?

Institutions supply the structures within which people interact with each other. 'They establish the cooperative and competitive relationships which constitute a society and more specifically an economic order' (North 1981: 201). Institutions are humanly generated constraints on people's behaviour, and they thereby exclude exogenously given constraints imposed by natural phenomena. Of course, although institutions are the result of human action, they are not necessarily the product of human design. That is, these constraints on people's activities need not be deliberately established by some human agency. They can evolve spontaneously (Menger 1996; North 1990). No one need ever have consciously intended to bring these institutions about. Furthermore, institutions can be formal in that they are written down and codified, or they can be informal in the sense that we adhere to them without knowing it and without ever formulating them explicitly.

According to North (1981), the institutional framework comprises three classes of institutional rules: constitutional rules, operating rules and normative behavioural codes. Constitutional rules determine the general character of the political order. They represent the 'superstructure' that regulates the ongoing process of making ordinary laws (i.e. operating rules). Operating rules – for example, various statute laws and regulations, specific common law decisions – specify terms of exchange within the framework of the constitutional rules. Normative behavioural rules are codes of moral behaviour that legitimate the constitutional and operating rules.

This and the next chapter focus upon constitutional rules and, to a lesser degree, operating rules. The emphasis on constitutional rules in the following discussion is not meant to imply that the term 'institutions' should only be applied to constitutional rules. Indeed, Chapter 6 considers shared behavioural norms, which are also institutional rules, as they relate to alternative cultural conceptions of the self.

Constitutional rules are the fundamental and general principles that define the underlying structure of people's rights, including property rights. They specify, allocate and limit the different powers of the state. They also define the general attributes which ordinary (i.e. sub-constitutional) laws and rules must possess in order to be implemented and enforced by government (Hayek 1979: 122). Thus, the general principles of the constitution control the content of lower-order constraints or operating rules generated by the legislature, the judiciary, the executive and the administrative bureaucracy. 'The idea of a constitution, therefore, involves not only the idea of a hierarchy of authority or power but also that of a hierarchy of rules or laws' (Hayek 1960: 178). A constitution might also include rules for modifying constitutional rules.

As stated at the outset, the aim of this chapter is to investigate 'the institutional conditions conducive to entrepreneurship'. The choice of this phrase rather than the term 'institutional *prerequisites*' is quite deliberate, the reason being that it is very difficult to identify the necessary and sufficient conditions for entrepreneurship. Certainly, some environments are more supportive than others to the flourishing of entrepreneurial initiative. But it seems that entrepreneurship can emerge in the most hostile of climates. 'Markets are like weeds, they spring up all over and are impossible to stamp out completely. Wherever there is a gap, alert economic actors will attempt to grasp the opportunity available for personal gain' (Boettke 1993: 65).

This chapter assumes that the relationship between economic institutions and outcomes (including the degree of entrepreneurship) best fits a 'multiple-peaked' vision of economic phenomena rather than a 'single-peaked' view of the world, according to which there is only one distinct set of institutional conditions that is optimally suited to a well-functioning market economy. '[T]he institutional basis for a market economy is not uniquely determined. Formally, there is no single mapping between the market and the set of non-market institutions required to sustain it' (Rodrik 2000: 13). Two societies with similar institutions might produce quite different levels of entrepreneurial activity in any given time period. Alternatively, two capitalist economies with very different institutional arrangements can generate similar degrees of entrepreneurship.

Indeed, entrepreneurship is not restricted to economies formally organised on the decentralised model of classical capitalism. In his discussion of the comparative study of long-period change, Easterbrook (1965: 69–77) claims that a profit-oriented, market-economy entrepreneur is only one particular type of entrepreneurship which is identified with a specific (and, in his opinion, historically unusual) set of institutional and ideological conditions. Schumpeter (1947: 150) too, who considered entrepreneurship exclusively within a capitalist framework, conceded that the entrepreneurial function itself 'is not absent from other forms of society; but capitalist entrepreneurship is a sufficiently distinct phenomenon to be singled out'. In the former Soviet Union, for example, entrepreneurs (in the guise of special intermediaries called *tolkachi*) sprung up within the interstices of the official planned economy, buying and selling commodities on behalf of state enterprises and thereby coordinating production and exchange activity within the overall plan itself (Grossman 1981; Hewett 1988).

In addition, we must even take care to define more precisely what we mean by conditions conducive to entrepreneurship. In particular, we must distinguish between demand-side and supply-side conditions.[1] The former relate to the structure of economic circumstances and incentives in the market environment that gives rise to entrepreneurial opportunities (e.g. market ignorance and resulting price discrepancies). In contrast, supply-side conditions relate to the factors which promote or constrain the generation and application of entrepreneurial alertness. Elsewhere a co-author and I have argued that economists should pay more attention to the supply of entrepreneurship (Hamilton and Harper 1994), and accordingly I focus upon supply-side conditions in this chapter.

These two sets of conditions, though interrelated, are not the same. For instance, it is conceivable that in a stationary market environment in which there is no change (i.e. no exogenous disturbances, no disappointment of people's plans over time), there are no entrepreneurial opportunities, even though the individuals in that society are potentially entrepreneurial and would be alert to opportunities if only they existed. On the other hand, it is possible that people's plans to buy and sell could be massively discordant – so that there is an abundance of entrepreneurial opportunities – but these opportunities go unnoticed because people do not have the wit to recognise that they exist, with the result that there is no entrepreneurial activity. Both of these scenarios lead to no entrepreneurship, but the reasons for this inactivity are quite different.

## *The implications of the function, character and unit of alertness*

A further difficulty that arises in connection with examining institutional conditions for entrepreneurship is that certain institutional arrangements may favour one type of entrepreneurship over another. For example, one set of institutional conditions may foster arbitrage but discourage long-term innovation. In such situations, it may be difficult to say whether, on balance, that particular institutional framework is or is not conducive to entrepreneurship. It should be noted that this position differs from Kirzner's (1985: 68–69). Kirzner says that what is conducive for low-level entrepreneurship will also be conducive for high-level entrepreneurship, what fosters short-run arbitrage will also promote long-run innovation. The hypothesis is that numerous incremental acts of entrepreneurship – entrepreneurial discoveries of local and mundane bits of unorganised knowledge – constitute a foundation for the emergence of path-breaking Schumpeterian entrepreneurship.

Similarly, it is important to emphasise the key characteristics of entrepreneurial alertness if we are to try to understand the impact of different institutional frameworks on it. The reader will recall from Chapter 2 that entrepreneurship is *not* a factor of production, not even a special kind of productive factor. Entrepreneurial alertness is non-deployable and tacit, it is costless, people who have it cannot be identified *ex ante*, and it cannot be treated in terms of demand and supply curves.

The non-deployable and tacit nature of entrepreneurial alertness, in particular, has profound consequences for institutional analysis. First and foremost is the fact that the potential stock of entrepreneurial alertness in a society cannot be usefully treated as some 'available' quantity of a resource that is to be allocated and used by an economic system. Rather entrepreneurial alertness is *embedded* in the decisions of individuals so that their actions simply reflect their entrepreneurial hunches (Kirzner 1983b: 64–66). Entrepreneurial alertness 'somehow emerges into view at the precise moment when decisions have to be made' (p. 66).

This property of entrepreneurship in turn implies that the potential stock of entrepreneurial alertness in a society cannot be measured objectively. Thus, it is not possible to derive quantitative relationships between measures of a society's stock of entrepreneurial alertness and institutional variables (such as its degree of economic freedom), although it is possible to enquire analytically into how the institutional framework may affect the alertness in which decisions are implanted.

Another characteristic of entrepreneurship that has a major impact upon institutional analysis is that alertness is costless in the sense that no resource inputs are involved in making entrepreneurial discoveries. As mentioned in Chapter 2, alertness does not involve opportunity costs because entrepreneurial discoveries are made spontaneously in the sense that they are acquired entirely without being planned. Entrepreneurs discover profit opportunities, hitherto overlooked, without a deliberate search for information.

One implication of this feature of entrepreneurship is that operating rules (e.g. public policies, such as subsidies or R&D tax write-offs) which aim to reduce the so-called costs of entrepreneurship or search costs do not necessarily increase the supply of pure entrepreneurship because the latter is costless. The costs of entrepreneurship itself cannot be reduced by public policy or any other means.

In addition, it should be noted that price discrepancies and the resultant opportunities for entrepreneurship cannot be wholly explained in terms of high positive transaction and information costs. For even in a market with zero transaction costs, mutually beneficial exchanges between buyers and sellers might still fail to take place (and hence scope for entrepreneurial alertness may still arise). To have access (even access at zero cost) to information about trading opportunities is by no means sufficient to ensure that these opportunities will ever be discovered and exploited. (Free) *access* to information does not correspond to instantaneous *perception* and *awareness* of the usefulness of that information (Kirzner 1973: 227). The implication is that if one institutional framework has lower transaction costs than another, it may not necessarily generate more entrepreneurial activity. If the members of a society were so blinkered that they failed to exhibit one iota of alertness, there would be no discovery of even the most blatant profit opportunities, even under ideal conditions of zero transaction costs.

How the entrepreneurial function is conceived can also influence how we assess an institution's comparative effectiveness in evoking entrepreneurship. For example, if entrepreneurship is considered to be an element inherent in *all* decision-making (including that by consumers, producers, labourers, etc.), then an institutional framework should be assessed for its relative capacity to foster all types of economic agents to exercise their entrepreneurial faculties. However, if we identify entrepreneurship with the aptitudes of only a small fraction of the population (i.e. 'pure' entrepreneurs), then we must assess the degree to which an institutional framework generates individuals who are representative of the entrepreneurial type and the extent to which it excites their alertness. Different operating rules (e.g. immigration policies) will affect the size of the pool of potential entrepreneurs available to a society.

Having explored the major implications of the characteristics of alertness for institutional analysis, we can now move on to consider how institutional conditions affect people's agency beliefs and the degree of their alertness.

## Rule-of-law constitutions

The institutional framework affects the entrepreneurial alertness in which decisions are embedded and determines the incentives for discovering and exploiting profit opportunities. This section focuses upon those higher-level institutional factors that are conducive to producing people with heightened entrepreneurial alertness. According to the argument developed here, the institutional environment that is most likely to produce entrepreneurs is one that calls for and encourages strong agency beliefs. As discussed in Chapter 3, personal agency beliefs reflect a person's sense of causal potency. They comprise a set of beliefs about the contingency of events on actions (i.e. locus of control beliefs) and about one's personal competence to undertake the relevant actions (i.e. self-efficacy beliefs). It was argued that alertness is an increasing function of the strength of agency beliefs. That is, people with a strong sense of internal control and personal efficacy tend to be more alert to opportunities. This chapter extends this analysis by considering the effects of the institutional frame-work on people's agency beliefs and thereby their entrepreneurial alertness and behaviour. The implication is that personal agency beliefs and entrepreneurship are endogenous; they can be influenced by political, economic and social variables.

As mentioned earlier, the constitutional framework comprises general principles and ideals that people in the community have committed them-selves to and that they respect. These principles determine the underlying rules, which specify the political, legal and economic systems of a society and therefore the basic rights of its members.

Although these general principles are contained in the constitutional framework, this does not mean that they are necessarily articulated in any constitutional documents. Indeed, these principles are often only vaguely perceived. '[C]onstitutions are based on, or presuppose, an underlying agree-ment on more fundamental principles – principles which may never have been explicitly expressed, yet which make possible and precede the consent and the written fundamental laws' (Hayek 1960: 181). For example, a social consensus about the dimensions of the private sphere of the individual might underpin a rule-of-law constitution that frames entrepreneurial and market activities.

Following Kirzner (1992: 51–54), this work regards freedom as the most important political, legal and economic ideal and constitutional principle that is conducive to entrepreneurship. Indeed, freedom can be considered to be the source of and necessary condition for all other entrepreneurial values, and it is to this general principle that the discussion now turns.

## The principle of freedom

This chapter argues that entrepreneurship is most likely to flourish under constitutional arrangements that promote a maximum realisation of the principle of freedom. The central hypothesis is that an environment of freedom, and especially economic freedom, is more likely than other environments to generate strong agency beliefs and acute entrepreneurial alertness. A condition of economic liberty gives all participants the possibility of acting according to their own economic plans and decisions, so that they may direct their energies towards goals that they themselves have chosen rather than towards necessities imposed by powerful others. In an environment of economic freedom, people are more likely to be able to use their skills and knowledge as successfully as possible in the pursuit of their economic ends. Indeed, entrepreneurship in the modern market economy could not exist without a constitutional framework that grants individuals and groups of individuals a large amount of economic freedom. (The next chapter examines the nature of freedom of *entrepreneurial* choice in more detail.)

On the other hand, entrepreneurship is likely to be stifled in conditions where many people are irrevocably subject to the arbitrary will and aggressions of others. People are much less likely to develop a strong sense of agency and hence heightened alertness to economic opportunities if they are constantly coerced into acting or not acting in specific ways by somebody else who has the power to manipulate their environment.

The term freedom has not yet been defined. We must take heed of Leoni's warning that 'we cannot use the word freedom and be rightly understood without first defining clearly the meaning we attach to that word' (1972: 42). This work adopts his definition of freedom as absence of constraint exercised by other people, including the authorities, over the private life and business of each person (p. 78). The terms freedom and liberty will be used interchangeably.

Of course, freedom does not imply the total absence of constraint. There are cases in which at least some people may have to be constrained in order to preserve freedom and to protect individuals from coercion by others, such as murderers or robbers. This also suggests that any analysis of freedom must take into account people's subjective perceptions of the degree of freedom that they enjoy. 'There is no such thing as "freedom" independent of the people who speak of it' (Leoni 1972: 42). At least to the extent that their own interpretation of freedom and of constraint differs from that prevalent within the society to which they belong, some individuals must experience some constraint over their behaviour, even within a 'free' society.

Although freedom is a negative concept – because it describes the absence of something, namely coercion by other people – freedom becomes positive through what people make of it. Freedom can become a shared part of economic, political and ethical life, an ideal that continually brings people together and that provides infinite opportunities for them to cooperate and to adapt themselves to one another, thereby unifying a society (de Tocqueville 1990b: 103–104). Entrepreneurs in particular may make their most valuable contribution to society by exercising freedoms that are seldom used by others. Freedom does not guarantee people any particular opportunity or capacity to get what they want but it allows people to decide for themselves how best to make use of their particular circumstances for their own purposes.

Freedom is a sociological concept that refers to the social relations between one person and other people. It is also, and possibly chiefly, a legal construct because it implies a skein of legal consequences. The law is the most important institution for attempting to protect individual freedom. 'The law is an order of human freedom' (Karl Binding, as quoted in Hayek 1973: 158). Liberty exists according to the law of a society and is defined by it. There can be no liberty without law. 'The law, in the most general sense of the word, is the science of liberty' (Beudant 1891: 5).

Unless specifically indicated otherwise, the emphasis in this work is upon *economic* freedom. The key elements of economic freedom include freedom of entrepreneurial choice, freedom to enter and compete in markets, adherence to the rule of law, the protection of property rights, freedom of exchange and freedom of contract. Economic freedom is to be distinguished from political freedom which encompasses such ingredients as the freedom of opposition parties to organise and compete and the participation of citizens in the electoral process.

### The rule of law

The previous discussion claimed that entrepreneurship in the market is promoted by a constitutional framework that maximises everyone's freedom from coercion, especially in the economic sphere. Here it will be argued that such a framework is most likely to operate according to the rule of law. Indeed, the rule of law is an essential element of constitutional government. 'Fully articulated, the rule of law amounts to a sophisticated doctrine of constitutionalism' (Allan 1998: 369). This section defines what is meant by the rule of law, and it seeks to explain how it affects entrepreneurship.

The rule of law is the legal embodiment of freedom and the basic conception of the law of liberty (Hayek 1944: 61; 1960: 148). The concept is open to various interpretations. The first, most common understanding of the term distinguishes the rule or reign of law from rule by arbitrary forms of government. It emphasises the rule of impersonal law as opposed to powerful persons. According to the rule of law, political power can only be wielded within legal constraints so that government is placed under the law.

It limits the functions of government to those that can be carried out by means of general rules.

The second distinct, but related, interpretation regards the rule of law as a 'meta-legal' principle which serves to guide law-makers. In this sense, it is not strictly speaking a rule of the law but a rule *about* the law. It is an imperative about the general attributes that good laws should possess:

> The rule of law is therefore not a rule of the law, but a rule concerning what the law ought to be, a meta-legal doctrine or a political ideal. It will be effective only in so far as the legislator feels bound by it. In a democracy this means that it will not prevail unless it forms part of the moral tradition of the community, a common ideal shared and unquestioningly accepted by the majority.
>
> (Hayek 1960: 206)

Thus, the rule of law requires that all laws conform to specific principles though it does not specify what the *content* of legal rules ought to be. According to Hayek, these principles include the certainty, the generality and the equality of the law.[2] Taken together, these requirements amount to the ideal of the *universality* of the law.

The rule of law is the prerequisite for the concrete rights of the individual, including those economic freedoms that are most important for entrepreneurship. 'The rule of law can be compared to a tree which, from the invisible strong roots of freedom, lets the fruits of liberty branch out and grow and shine in splendor' (Dietze 1976: 117). In the absence of the rule of law, public authorities are prone to issue a flood of arbitrary and inconsistent decrees that can dampen people's sense of agency and therefore their alertness to opportunities:

> All too frequently, the unsystematic proliferation of rules breeds sullen conformity and dissimulation of an individual's true thoughts and motives, a condition that is the opposite of the open competition of ideas and critical assessment of new ideas and experiments; therefore, it is not conducive to effective coordination and innovation, and hence to prosperity and freedom.
>
> (Kasper and Streit 1998: 138)

It is worth emphasising that a legal system cannot sustain the rule of law if there are no shared beliefs about justice. In a democracy, the enforceability of rule-of-law constitutions requires that laws be consistent with cultural values and ethical norms that are widely held by members of the community. The legitimacy of government is based on an expectation that it will enforce widely shared beliefs about what is just. (For a general discussion of the values, norms and attitudes necessary for or conducive to the rule of law, see Voigt 1993: 505–506.)

More specifically, as Weingast (1995; 1997) argues, the enforceability of constitutions based on the rule of law depends upon the existence of a social consensus about the appropriate limits of state action. In this context, a social consensus does not mean that everyone shares identical values. Rather, there must be a consensus among citizens about which potential actions by the state represent a violation of constitutional constraints as well as a consensus about what they will do to defend the constitution whenever the state tries to transgress its legitimate boundaries. Only then are the constitutional limits on political officials *self-enforcing* in the sense that those in power have the incentive to comply with the restrictions on their behaviour (Hardin 1989; Ordeshook 1992). Only then is the people's threat of retaliation in the event of a fundamental transgression credible. 'The ultimate sanction on a government is the withdrawal of support by a sufficient portion of its citizens so that the government cannot survive' (Weingast 1995: 26).[3] (The discussion of political decentralisation in Chapter 5 deals with the issue of self-enforcing limits in further detail.)

Because it is difficult for citizens to coordinate their views on the legitimate role of the state, the emergence of a consensus is by no means automatic or inevitable. Failure to resolve this coordination problem hinders the enforcement of a rule-of-law constitution. In the absence of a consensus and organised opposition, the state will be able to get away with infringing the rights of all or some citizens, sometimes playing off one group against another. If governments continually succeed in violating constitutional constraints with impunity, citizens are most likely to come to perceive the constitution as a 'book of hopes' with no connection to the real world, as a 'set of *desiderata* largely irrelevant for actual government behavior' (Voigt 1998: 206). Such has been the experience of many societies in Latin America.

In addition, the rule of law requires a civil society in which citizens are, by and large, law abiding and in which informal enforcement mechanisms (such as social ostracism) supplement coercive sanctions administered by the courts. The importance of this becomes all too clear when one considers the limits to the government's ability to enforce the law through compulsion. Kasper and Streit (1998: 139) quote one estimate, admittedly highly speculative, that at any given moment government can enforce by coercion at most 3 to 7 per cent of all formal legal norms.

Let us now return to a more detailed examination of the nature of the rule of law and flesh out its implications for the supply of entrepreneurial alertness. Each of the three attributes of good laws – certainty, generality and equality – will be considered below.

### The certainty of the law

It is desirable to explain what certainty of the law actually means. Leoni (1972: 95) defines certainty of the law as 'the possibility open to individuals of making long-run plans on the basis of a series of rules spontaneously adopted by people in common and eventually ascertained by judges through centuries and generations'. Certainty of the law means that the law is not subjected to sudden and unpredictable changes. Its incidence is predictable. This conception of legal certainty does not mean, and may even be incompatible with, the notion of a series of precisely worded written rules laid down by legislatures. Indeed, many rules implicit in the body of the law may never be articulated explicitly.

The certainty of the law is probably the most important principle for entrepreneurship and other economic activities. 'There is probably no single factor which has contributed more to the prosperity of the West than the relative certainty of the law which has prevailed here' (Hayek 1960: 208). The conventional wisdom is that the legal framework must be sufficiently certain to enable entrepreneurs to make their plans. Entrepreneurs must be able to find out, with reasonable confidence, whether specific actions are either demanded or proscribed by the law. They must be able to foresee with a fair degree of certainty whether their planned conduct is within or outside the law. When the decisions of courts are consistent and predictable, many commercial disputes do not result in litigation because the outcome is already clear once the relevant facts of the case are identified.

It should be noted that the certainty of the law does not mean the absence of change, but it does mean that entrepreneurs can make their plans on the basis of present legal rules without finding that the rules have been overturned overnight by legislative U-turns. In short, entrepreneurs can expect that today's legal rules will be tomorrow's rules. A consequence of such certainty of the law is that an inefficient but stable legal *rule* does not necessarily imply inefficient economic *behaviour*, provided that entrepreneurs and other participants can bargain around the rule. Consider a legal system in which judges decide cases according to precedent (i.e. by applying rulings from similar cases in the past). As Rizzo (1985) explains, this type of legal order can promote the entrepreneurial processes that generate coordination of economic action because it enforces a stable framework of legal rules against which private economic actors can bargain, assuming low transaction costs of exchange.[4] The market prices of goods and services can be in constant flux, but provided that the institutions governing market exchanges are relatively stable, entrepreneurs will by and large be able to adapt to new circumstances and bring about greater consistency in market transactions in different parts of the market. 'The seas may be choppy, but so long as the buoys are anchored firmly navigation can proceed safely' (Wagner 1998: 316). Incessant and unpredictable changes in laws render entrepreneurs unable to use legal rules to orient themselves in making their plans. As discussed later, retrospective (*ex post facto*) laws in particular flagrantly contravene the principle of legal certainty.

In order to exploit perceived profit opportunities, innovators in particular must often plan many years into the future. Innovative entrepreneurs need to foresee that the result of actions decided upon today will be free from legal interference by the authorities tomorrow. The greater the certainty of the law, the more confident they can be of the legal effects of their innovative behaviour, and the more likely they are to discover and to exploit opportunities which involve coordinating transactions entered into at different times.

However, the relationship between the certainty of the law and entrepreneurship is not quite so clear cut. For instance, single-period arbitragers can benefit from accelerated and unpredictable law-making processes which give rise to temporary profit opportunities. This is particularly the case with those entrepreneurs who specialise in the more or less instantaneous discovery and exploitation of tax loopholes created by legislative changes. Speculators too may benefit. Speculative entrepreneurs may seek to profit from legal uncertainty – the uncertainty that current statutes may be replaced at any stage by subsequent laws – especially if they believe themselves to have superior hunches about potential legal developments.

There is thus an element of apparent indeterminacy in the effects of legal certainty upon entrepreneurship. Although this difficulty is still to be resolved satisfactorily, some preliminary conjectures can be put forward now in the interests of furthering the debate.

In the first instance, it seems that expedient changes in legal rules affect what were earlier referred to as 'demand-side' institutional conditions. They relate to the structure of economic circumstances and incentives in the market environment. More formally, these legal changes constitute exogenous disturbances in Kirzner's model of the economic system. They disrupt people's previously coordinated plans and generate fresh opportunities for pure gain. As such, they create scope for entrepreneurial activity.

However, the mere existence of these opportunities is not in itself sufficient to generate entrepreneurial activity – especially if we take into account the possibility that no one may become aware of these opportunities. Some profit opportunities arising from changes in legal rules may never be discovered.

In addition, the entrepreneurial discovery process that is set in motion by successive ad hoc regulatory and legislative changes may be 'wholly superfluous', in the sense that they create entirely new profit opportunities that would not have existed in the absence of these changes (Kirzner 1985: 145). At the same time, these changes also reduce or wipe out opportunities for social improvement that might otherwise have been present in a market governed by general legal rules.

Another point is that the changes in the law that give rise to arbitrage tend not to be holistic changes. They usually involve minor tinkering within a legal *superstructure*, which, to use Lachmann's (1971) terminology, is an external institution which constitutes the outer framework of society. The broad characteristics of this 'external' legal order tend to remain relatively stable over time.

Indeed, the emergence of entrepreneurial *alertness* depends upon certainty of the legal superstructure (i.e. constitutional order). Even when they identify tax loopholes, arbitragers rely upon the fact that legal norms will continue to allow them to exploit the opportunities they discover and to retain the profits they capture. They do not expect their profits to be arbitrarily confiscated by the state. 'Some institutions must be flexible enough to adjust to change, while others, by contrast, must be sufficiently resistant to change to make the outcome of intertemporal [market] transactions predictable' (Lachmann 1979: 77).

## The generality and equality of the law

The second and third principles of good laws implied by the ideal of the rule of law are the generality and the equality of the law. These two principles require that all legal rules apply equally to everybody, including those who are entrusted with political power, and that rules are of such general nature that they can be applied without arbitrary discretion. General and equal laws abstract from the specific circumstances of time and place, and they apply, in a non-discriminatory manner, whenever certain abstractly defined conditions are met (Hayek 1955: 35). This is clearly an ideal. In this sense, good laws are like universal scientific hypotheses: they are general rules rather than specific schemes relating to the state of the world at particular times and places. Indeed, generality is the most significant feature of the abstract character of law.

The generality and equality of the law are important for entrepreneurship especially given that it is not possible to preselect entrepreneurial individuals. General abstract rules are applicable to an unforeseeable range of entrepreneurs and innovative cases. These rules do not make any references to particular persons. Similarly, a fundamental characteristic of entrepreneurship in modern market economies is that entrepreneurs are not known in advance. They are generally those who are alert to possible opportunities. As a result, many unknown entrepreneurs may take part in attempts to solve any particular market problem.

Because it is not possible to identify entrepreneurs *ex ante* (at least for any particular market opportunities prior to their discovery), it is essential that the institutional framework provide each person with the maximum freedom of enterprise compatible with equal freedom for all other people. The equality of the law is aimed at equally improving the chances of as yet unknown entrepreneurs.

General and equal laws provide the most effective protection against encroachment of the state on individual liberty. The ideal of the rule of law requires that the state act under the same law and therefore be limited in the same manner as any private person. It thereby restricts the coercive activities of government:

> It is not to be denied that even general, abstract rules, equally applicable to all, may possibly constitute severe restrictions on liberty. But

when we reflect on it, we see how very unlikely this is. The chief safeguard is that the rules must apply to those who lay them down and
those who apply them — that is, to the government as well as the
governed — and that nobody has the power to grant exceptions. If all
that is prohibited and enjoined is prohibited and enjoined for all
without exception … and if even authority has no special powers except
that of enforcing the law, little that anybody may reasonably wish to do
is likely to be prohibited.

(Hayek 1960: 154–155)

The generality of the law reinforces its certainty. General laws are more
predictable than specific, ad hoc commands issued by a public authority. By
specifying beforehand the circumstances in which action must satisfy certain
conditions and providing the framework within which entrepreneurs can
form their plans, general rules make the legal consequences of
entrepreneurial action more predictable.

The requirement of general and equal laws for all persons is conducive to
freedom, a strong sense of personal agency — particularly internal LOC
beliefs — and hence entrepreneurship. Under the rule of law, entrepreneurs
know that their sphere of personal agency (i.e. the area of legally guaranteed
freedom) includes all actions not explicitly prohibited by general legal rules.
Because general laws specify beforehand the conditions and the manner in
which people can expect to be coerced, entrepreneurs can determine with
reasonable confidence the boundaries of the law within which they can exercise their own will and causal powers. They also know that these boundaries
apply equally to everybody. In this way, general laws allow entrepreneurs to
make the best use of their own unique competences and localised knowledge
in their seizing of profit opportunities.

In a society governed by the rule of law, entrepreneurs know that their
actions do not depend on gaining the permission of any government
authority (provided they keep within the legal delimitation of their private
sphere of agency). In addition, entrepreneurs know they will not be subject
to sudden administrative orders directing them personally to undertake
specific actions. It is true that general rules might eliminate some options
otherwise open to entrepreneurs. But the point is that they do not constrain
the choice sets of entrepreneurs to such an extent that their preferred course
of action will and must be that which most benefits some external authority
(Hayek 1960: 133, 153). Entrepreneurs do still have genuine choices to
make. The contracts they conclude are entered into voluntarily, as acts of
entrepreneurial autonomy.

General, abstract laws are long-term rules and are only ever *forward
looking* in their effect. General rules guide entrepreneurial action; they are
data that entrepreneurs can use as a basis for their planning activities. In
contrast, retroactive legislation cannot affect entrepreneurial action, since
entrepreneurs have already taken and implemented their decisions prior to

the promulgation of such laws. Retrospective legal rules add to entrepreneurial uncertainty since they undermine the standing of laws that are prospective in their effect; the likelihood of retrospective legislation, by definition, places existing and subsequent forward-looking legal rules under the threat of retrospective changes (Fuller 1964: 38–39).

The retrospective enforcement of changes in the law significantly inhibits entrepreneurial freedom and autonomy, and it diminishes entrepreneurs' sense of personal agency. In the first instance, their LOC beliefs become less internal because the outcome of market transactions is seen to be vulnerable to the whims of those in power. In particular, entrepreneurs come to perceive that the legal consequences of their transactions are less contingent upon their knowledge of existing law and their understanding of just conduct. In addition, their sense of self-efficacy is likely to fade because entrepreneurs feel they never know the legal rules that they are expected to observe. They are unable to plan their actions by relying upon the application of pre-existing law. The dampening of personal agency caused by the abuse of retrospective legislation thereby inhibits alertness to market opportunities.

The requirement of general and equal laws also implies the absence of privilege and arbitrary discrimination. General legal rules do not single out particular entrepreneurs or groups of entrepreneurs.[5] Nor do they benefit or harm identifiable business people in a predictable manner. (The principle of legal generality thus forbids so-called 'acts or bills of attainder', which is legislation that prescribes punishment for named or easily identifiable persons, whose conduct might have infuriated those in power.) Under a rule-of-law constitution, entrepreneurs are free to trade and compete as legal equals. Every entrepreneur and economic actor has the same legal status, namely, the status of a person under the law. No entrepreneur is held to be above the law.

Thorough adherence to the rule of law would deprive legislators, governments and administrative agencies of the authority and power to discriminate among economic actors by conferring economic privileges. 'It is the state itself which is to be enjoined to override the rules of the prevailing [constitutional, competitive market] order in favour of one group and at the expense of other citizens' (Böhm 1989: 64). Whenever authorities grant special privileges to one group of entrepreneurs, they are also of course simultaneously discriminating against other entrepreneurs and market participants. The rule of law and the principles of legal generality and equality also extend to the administration of justice, so that judges too are barred from making arbitrary and discriminatory decisions. Judges are bound to decide disputes strictly in accordance with an existing body of established law.

In contrast, modern law is teeming with ad hoc, discriminatory legal commands (or operating rules) that violate the principles of generality and equality, thereby constraining personal agency and stifling entrepreneurship.

Tariffs, tax write-offs, subsidies, price supports, restrictions of entry into professions or businesses, and legislative backing for forming statutory monopolies or cartels – each of these interferences by the state benefits one group of entrepreneurs at the expense of others and is inconsistent with the rule of law. The rampant privilege seeking and privilege granting that characterises the 'rent-seeking' society undermines the legal order of the market economy. It represents a 'refeudalisation of society' (Böhm 1980: 258, quoted in Vanberg 1998: 177).

Codified law is particularly hostile towards entrepreneurship when it is used merely as a means of subjecting path-breaking innovators to the arbitrary will of regulators who have been captured by existing industry players. In such situations, the legislative process may be motivated not by the desire to benefit consumers but by the politically expedient wish to benefit what Baumol (1993) calls 'runners up' – unsuccessful entrepreneurs whose enterprises are being systematically displaced by their more successful counterparts who perceive market conditions more accurately. Lobbying for governmental protection of one sort or another has the appeal that incumbents in the industry are able to insulate themselves from the pressure of competitive entry and yet escape any charge of wrongdoing by elevating misconduct to the legislative and political plane. The opportunity to invoke spurious 'national interest' and 'social justice' arguments makes this strategy even more attractive to them.

In a system replete with economic privileges and discriminatory restrictions on economic activities, 'rent extraction' might also be rife (McChesney 1987; 1991). This occurs when politicians extract wealth from particular individuals or groups by credibly threatening to impose onerous constraints on them. A notable feature of this type of rent seeking is that, when it is successful, there is no obvious trace of government intervention in the form of legislation or regulation, no clear evidence of arbitrary coercion being exercised to appropriate other people's property.

The maintenance of the rule of law requires various substantive institutions and procedural safeguards that can protect economic and political freedom from arbitrary impositions by government. One of the most fundamental institutions is a constitutional *separation of powers* between the different organs of the state – namely, a division of powers and functions between legislature, executive and judiciary. In addition, the rule of law stipulates that the law must be enforced, and violations adjudicated, by an *independent judiciary* that adheres to pre-existing rules of due process (i.e. the principles of *procedural fairness*). The separation of powers implies a *prohibition against acts (or 'bills') of attainder*, which are legislative adjudications of the guilt of particular persons, because they involve an intrusion by the legislature into the judicial sphere. Other procedural rules often used to support the rule of law include judicial review, the prohibition against *ex post facto* laws, trial by jury, the privilege of the writ of habeas corpus, the principle of 'no expropriation without just compensation' and the principle of proportionality (see Allan (1998) for a brief review). The maintenance of the rule of law also requires a political structure, such as 'market-preserving federalism', that produces self-enforcing limits on the actions of political actors (see Chapter 5).

The next sections discuss the twin pillars of the institutions of private property and contract and examine their impact on personal agency beliefs and entrepreneurial alertness. These two sets of institutions are derived from the rule of law and are an essential part of the legal bedrock that is required to support entrepreneurial processes in a market economy. 'Without these institutional prerequisites – primarily, private property rights and freedom and enforceability of contract – the market cannot operate' (Kirzner 2000: 83).

## The institution of private property

A high-level entrepreneurial environment requires more than just an anonymous price system comprising faceless traders. The communication of information on markets and the governance of entrepreneurial transactions also require a diverse set of supporting institutions:

> [P]rices and markets function as part of a social system, not in isolation. A social system generates many kinds of signals and rules besides prices. ... Nonprice constraints are as much a part of a decentralized economy as are the prices they help to generate. These constraints are *reference frameworks* and *orientation points*, in terms of which actors form expectations. Prices are formed on markets composed of contracts, rules, and customs, which are part of the constraints and basis for observed behaviour. ... [Nonprice] constraints are often necessary accompaniments to markets. For example, *it is strictly impossible to imagine a 'price system' devoid of contracts and property rights.*
>
> (O'Driscoll and Rizzo 1996: 106; emphasis added)

Although prior ownership of property is not a prerequisite to entrepreneurial alertness, entrepreneurs would not be able to formulate or carry out their plans unless they were reasonably sure that the people with whom they trade have exclusive control over the relevant resources. In order to reallocate resources in the pursuit of profit, entrepreneurs must often purchase exclusive rights to assets in one period with the intention of selling them for a higher price in a subsequent period. Before the act of purchase, the entrepreneur will need to establish who owns those assets. Having purchased those assets, the entrepreneur will want to be certain of his or her exclusive control over them until the date of their sale. And when selling those assets, the entrepreneur will need to be confident of the claim of the buyer to the resources that are being offered in exchange for those assets. Thus, to be in a position to carry out their plans of action, entrepreneurs must rely upon a secure system of property rights.

### Principles embodied in the concept of private property

The institution of private property is an essential condition for safeguarding individuals against coercion and protecting liberty. 'While property in some form is possible without liberty, the contrary is inconceivable' (Pipes 1999: xiii). As the term implies, private property rights are held in a private capacity by individuals, a group of people or a firm. They are to be distinguished from public rights, which are exercised by those who control the state or one of its political organs. As discussed later, the distinction between these two types of rights and the relative prevalence of these rights have important implications for the nature of the economic system and the scope and character of entrepreneurship.

The institution of private property embodies two main principles. The first is that people have an assured private sphere of things which they can control and which we call their property ('the right to control and benefit from resources'). One's private sphere consists of those things in one's environment with which others cannot interfere. The second principle is that these things can be transferred from the sphere of one person to that of another only by mutual consent ('the right to dispose of resources') (Hayek 1955: 31–32). Although they guarantee a certain area of freedom, these principles do not constitute absolute property rights. Under very exceptional, narrowly defined circumstances, such as war or imminent peril to life, the state and private individuals may be permitted to infringe the property rights of others in exchange for some form of just compensation (see Epstein 1995: 113–116).

The institution of private property (and the principles it embodies) has an important psychological dimension that enhances our feelings of self-efficacy, internal control and personal agency, and it thereby promotes entrepreneurial alertness. Private property rules offer people the possibility of self-determination or autonomy. 'For it is by using one's own property according to one's own values and goals, without the necessity for consultation with one's neighbour, or any collective authority, that one can most nearly approximate the status of an autonomous agent' (Gray 1989: 142). Ownership of property causes objects that we possess to be become part of our protected private sphere. By controlling, exploiting and transferring property, we can express our subjective sense of agency in the external material world of physical and intangible assets and can carry out, with varying degrees of success, the tasks necessary to sustain ourselves. When our right to own and control property is curtailed or taken away from us, we experience a dilution of our sense of personal agency.

The psychological aspect of the institution of private property (especially as it relates to consumer goods) is evident in early stages of child development, in both individualist and group-oriented cultures (Gesell and Ilg 1949; Spiro 1975). Empirical studies of children have found that psychological attachment to property (i.e. feelings of ownership) is closely associated with the development of personal identity and a perception of the contingency of events upon one's own behaviour: 'The first notions of possession revolve around what *I* control and what responds to *my* actions' (Furby 1980: 35). (For a brief literature review, see Pipes 1999: 71–76.) In addition, Furby's studies found that, across different ages and cultural groups, a sense of personal competence and efficacy was fundamental to one's understanding of, and motivation for, possession and property.

The second principle embodied in private property rules (referred to above) implies that people have the freedom to transfer the things they own to others. It thus presupposes that property is *alienable*. The alienability of property means that people are able to separate themselves from the things that they produce, so that they do not have to consume their own output. Thus, they are willing to sever the connection between the production of a good and the consumption of its services in order to obtain gains from trade. What people produce with their own labour is objectified and depersonalised, so that they are willing to make it available for use by others and to claim title to goods that they did not produce themselves (Casson 1990: 138–139).[6] The alienability of property is essential for fostering markets and for facilitating the entrepreneurial processes to coordinate market transactions.

### Economic versus legal structure of property rights

The conception of property rights most relevant to entrepreneurship is economic rather than legal. The economic notion is broader than the legal conception of property rights as defined in the laws of various societies. In essence, an economic property right gives an entrepreneur the effective decision-making authority or actual power to choose the uses of an economic good, to draw the fruits from its use and to transfer the good to other people. This right is of crucial importance if entrepreneurs are to be free to exploit opportunities for reallocating specific capital goods from low-valued uses to new, hitherto unimagined, higher-valued uses. The economic conception of rights is the one most akin to the notion of internal LOC, competence and personal agency. Because economic property rights give an entrepreneur the freedom to capture profit from trading an asset and to contract over the terms with other participants, they strengthen the entrepreneur's perceptions of the contingency of potential economic rewards upon their actions, thereby increasing their internal LOC and alertness.

Economic rights may be, but are not necessarily, supported by registered legal title or formal laws enforced by the state. These rights constitute *de facto* ownership of assets and may or may not correspond to legal definitions of property (i.e. *de jure* ownership). 'While property in the legal sense of the word has something to do, and particularly historically had to do, with the property in the economic sense of the word, the legal structure of property does not reflect necessarily its economic counterpart' (Bajt 1968: 1). Indeed, economic rights can be maintained by means of physical force and the threat of social sanctions, such as ostracism. In contrast, legal property rights are defined as what the legal authority or system formally recognises and enforces as a person's property. In the legal sense, private property rights 'designate the legal institution in which the main economic rights in a resource are bundled in the hands of a single title holder' (Mackaay 1997: 4). For many types of transactions, legal rights can reduce the costs of contracting, especially with strangers, because they facilitate third-party enforcement primarily effected through the courts.

Although legal rights are neither necessary nor sufficient for the existence of economic rights, the delineation of legal rights can in general enhance economic rights, people's perceptions of personal agency and hence entrepreneurial processes. '[M]arkets without clearly defined rules tend to be limited and constrained as vehicles for economic development' (Boettke 2001: 242). This is vividly illustrated by de Soto. Although people in Third World and former communist nations may have large holdings of assets, the rights to which are governed by social conventions, they lack well-defined, universally recognised and readily alienable property rights. They also lack a formal process for legally registering their property: 'They have houses but not titles; crops but not deeds; businesses but not statutes of incorporation' (de Soto 2000: 7). According to de Soto, more than half the city-dwellers of Peru and the Philippines live in housing to which there is no clear legal title and in which rights of occupancy are supported only by informal custom (p. 33). In de Soto's view, the absence of formal legal property rights means that people cannot use their houses as collateral for loans in order to raise finance for their new entrepreneurial ventures. In the underground economy, people by and large can borrow only from those they know.[7]

Without well-developed legal property rights, entrepreneurs often encounter prohibitively high costs in contracting with strangers. Such a high level of transaction costs eliminates opportunities for mutually beneficial exchange of assets, and it therefore limits the extent of the market and the ability to realise many of the largest gains from specialisation and trade. 'A legal failure that prevents enterprising people from negotiating with strangers defeats the division of labor and fastens would-be entrepreneurs to smaller circles of specialization and low productivity' (de Soto 2000: 71). In the absence of precise and uniform legal rights to property, the investment required to exploit long-term profit opportunities is restricted, and entrepreneurship cannot develop much beyond 'kiosk capitalism'. If nations do not have the institutions that make private property rights in capital goods secure over the long run, they lose most of the gains from longer-term, capital-intensive, 'roundabout' processes of production. ('Round-aboutness' refers to a deepening in the capital structure.)

## *Economic decentralisation and private versus public (state) property rights*

The scope for entrepreneurship and its character also depend upon the relative importance of different types of property rights in an economic system. As mentioned earlier, the private–public continuum is one of the most important dimensions over which property rights can vary. Capitalist economies depend upon private property rights, whereas socialist and communist systems stress public property rights.

Only within a decentralised system of private property are productive resources voluntarily exchanged in real markets against money, thereby enabling entrepreneurs and other market participants to attach meaningful prices to them. 'The existence of markets for productive assets is the most important feature of a market exchange system based on private property, capitalism' (Eggertsson 1990: 37). Market prices for productive resources reflect the interplay of the subjective valuations of all the individuals participating in buying and selling. The existence, in different parts of the market, of multiple money prices for the same bundle of private ownership rights over an asset represents a simple arbitrage opportunity. Indeed, entrepreneurial profit presupposes the institution of private property and associated market prices. The institutions of private property and money are essential for guiding entrepreneurs in their judgements of the potential profitability of alternative ventures (i.e. the process of monetary 'economic calculation').

In contrast, a socialist system of economic organisation is based on constitutionally established public or state ownership of the means of production, which implies the absence (or constitutional abolition) of private property rights, markets and market prices for productive resources. In its pure form, the state is the exclusive owner of all productive assets and the allocation of these assets is orchestrated by the one central planning authority only. It is only the imagination and alertness of a single mind – namely, that of the central planner – that shapes the pattern of decisions made within the single attempted plan. However, without markets for productive resources, the socialist-planning agency cannot allocate resources rationally. Because it lacks indices of the relative importance of those resources (i.e. market prices for factors of production), it is unable to reallocate scarce resources to higher-valued uses as economic conditions change. 'Every step that leads away from private ownership of the means of production and the use of money is a step away from rational economic activity' (Mises 1981: 102). In the absence of market price signals for capital goods, the central authority has no basis for reckoning the results of its planned actions. The agency has no basis for determining the full implications of one set of decisions for other decisions in its overall plan (Kirzner 2000: 146). Consequently, even if the central agency's objective were to satisfy as much as possible the wants of consumers in the socialised economy, its plan would necessarily fail.

The legal structure of property rights under socialism offers no scope for the decentralised entrepreneurial acts of discovery, motivated by the lure of pure profit, that involve trading bundles of ownership entitlements. Agents in the socialised economy are legally precluded from holding and trading property and from keeping the entrepreneurial gains from such activity:

> Government officials whose status, by definition, precludes their being able personally to profit from their commercial discoveries, cannot be depended upon to achieve through planning, or through bureaucratically setting nonmarket 'prices' to stimulate effective market activities, those discoveries the generation of which constitutes the real contribution of free markets.
>
> (Kirzner 2000: 70)

To the extent that decentralised state agents in a nominally socialist regime do engage in monetary exchanges or do exercise *de facto* (i.e. economic) private control rights over public property, then the regime is not truly socialist. For instance, in the former Soviet Union, private property rights in the economic sense were never abolished but were implicitly allocated to specific individuals, such as incumbent managers of factories. The situation is well described by Boettke:

> The Soviet system not only relied on the decentralized decisions of thousands of economic actors to coordinate plans that were supposed to be pre-reconciled by the organs of central administration, but it also remained at heart a commodity production economy. ... In other words, the Soviet economy was not a centrally planned economy radically different from any other economic system witnessed in history. It was over-regulated, abused and distorted, but it was, nevertheless, a market economy.
>
> (Boettke 1993: 69)

That different forms of property rights and entitlements will always coexist in real-world economies must also be appreciated.[8] Even in the modern market economies of Western Europe and North America, individual, private property is not the only system of rights at hand. '[M]ost of the important and difficult economic decisions taken by citizens of advanced industrial societies involve attempts to cooperate in the management of resources in which they hold some form of *common* property rights' (Seabright 1998: 594; emphasis added). In particular, *local* common property rights are by no means extraordinary. (Local common property rights in a resource are characterised, among other things, by *partial* excludability and *incomplete* contracts – the members of the group can control access to the scarce resource by excluding outsiders but they cannot exclude other members from consuming the resource, and entitlements of each are not precisely defined.) The joint-stock company, for example, is a type of common property in whose ownership separate, tradeable shares (i.e. private property rights) have been created and then sold to private, individual owners (Seabright 1998: 594).

## The moral dimension of private property rights

The discussion so far has left open the question of what exactly people are *morally* entitled to claim as their property. What is considered fair or just title to the control of a resource will often be reflected in the system of legal rules. Property rights do not evolve in a moral vacuum. The definition and enforcement of property rights requires a socially recognised notion of ownership and shared ethical principles. 'The core of the institution of ownership is a matter of unquestioned and largely unconscious social and economic practices that must be rooted in non-legal developments' (Rapaczynski 1996: 88). According to John Stuart Mill, the institution of private property is founded on the notion that producers have a moral right to what they themselves have produced. Typically, in the literature this is taken to mean that people have a just title to what is produced by the resources they themselves own, including their own labour.

Kirzner rejects this identification of production solely with what derives from the ownership of factors of production. He consequently rejects the 'factor ownership' theory of property to which it gives rise (including Locke's labour theory) and its ethical implications. The reason is that this conception of production and its associated theory of property exclude the exercise of pure entrepreneurship in production (which involves no resource ownership) and the entitlement of entrepreneurs to what they have discovered. To rectify the situation, Kirzner advances an entrepreneurial view of 'what people have produced':

> In this view, a producer is entitled to what he has produced not because he has contributed anything to its physical fabrication, but because *he perceived and grasped the opportunity* for its fabrication by utilizing the resources available in the market. This is clearly an example of finding and keeping.
>
> (Kirzner 1979: 196; original emphasis)

> The finders-keepers rule asserts that an unowned object becomes the justly-owned private property of the first person who, discovering its availability and its potential value, takes possession of it.
>
> (Kirzner 1989: 98)

In sum, entrepreneurs have a right to own what they have discovered with their own alertness. A widely shared moral conviction that recognises the justice of this 'finders-keepers' rule as well as the injustice of confiscating what someone else has discovered reinforces a strong sense of personal agency in entrepreneurial endeavours. The discussion below on the freedom of contract examines the finders-keepers principle more closely.

### Are property rights an institutional prerequisite for the emergence and existence of markets?

There are two opposing views about the underlying conditions that precede the emergence of the entrepreneurially driven market economy. The first approach, to which Kirzner subscribes, holds that the requisite ethical norms and social institutions (e.g. property and contract rights) must *pre-exist* in a society before markets and market entrepreneurship can emerge. The rival view is that the institutional conditions conducive to market entrepreneurship can be generated spontaneously as a by-product of the market process itself.

According to Kirzner, property rights are largely rooted in an extra-market ethical framework, so that there is an overriding moral basis for the assignment and evolution of property rights. Like Platteau (1994a; 1994b), Kirzner argues that a generalised morality, emphasising honesty and fair dealing, is a precondition to the creation and expansion of the market order: '[Market] forces can only be relied upon *provided a widely shared ethic already exists* which firmly recognizes the "rightness" of the property rights system and the corresponding "wrongness" of theft and fraud' (Kirzner 2000: 85; emphasis added). These ethical principles consist of explicit or implicit rules of conduct that inform people's evaluation and expectations of others' actions (p. 84). Consequently, the formation and delineation of property rights are not exclusively or principally driven by utilitarian calculations which weigh costs and benefits, though they might be partly shaped by economic conditions. 'No understanding of the market can afford to ignore the fundamental insight that its institutional foundations are to be sought directly, not in economic considerations but in ethical ones' (p. 84).

Furthermore, Kirzner argues that the institution of private property and its moral underpinnings have evolved over time in a manner quite different from the spontaneously benevolent, coordinative processes of competitive markets. He sees a clear demarcation between the sub-constitutional issue of how market processes operate within a given institutional–legal framework ('the outer limits of the market') and the constitutional issue of how the rules of the game that facilitate competitive market processes themselves come into being. The market economy cannot spontaneously generate the ethical system or the institution of private property rights that must exist in the society *before* a market economy can successfully emerge. Indeed, 'we cannot rely upon *any* spontaneous social forces to foster those institutions' (Kirzner 2000: 83; original emphasis).

The competing perspective is that the formation of market-supporting institutions, such as the property rights system, is a spontaneous process that is subject to evolutionary *economic* forces. Adherents of this view include Hume (1969), Hayek (1979; 1988) and Demsetz (1967). Through repeated experiences of market transactions in an incipient market economy, individuals come to adopt consciously or unconsciously moral beliefs, property rules and other customary practices that sustain social order in modern societies. Thus, markets arise coextensively with the legal–institutional framework in a society:

> Property rights, like most other goods, are produced in response to market demand. Although the state may satisfy a portion of this demand, market responses often come first and provide more effective solutions. Indeed, the legal responses are often only effective against a background of self-enforcing market mechanisms.
>
> (Rapaczynski 1996: 102)

In contrast to Kirzner who depicts entrepreneurs as accepting the status quo structure of property rights, Anderson and Hill (1988) describe how profit-motivated entrepreneurs respond to new situations with significant contractual innovations that recombine existing property rights and establish new ones. Entrepreneurs often create new forms of property rights when they seek to introduce innovations for which there are as yet no known rights or effective 'fences'. (A fence is defined as a technique for securing exclusive control over an asset. It includes physical barriers, such as encryption devices, but also institutional arrangements, such as rules of an industry association.) According to this view, entrepreneurs are always on the lookout for new means of making *de facto* rights more valuable, and they play a central role in extending the property rights system to new objects.

> Given that they control their [novel] product at the outset, they can design new fences, using whatever devices and techniques are available to them as part of the existing property rights order and making contractual arrangements. The fences must secure them sufficient control to bring the product to market and make a profit from it.
>
> (Mackaay 1997: 17)

It is important to note that the economic assets to which property rights refer are not *unidimensional* (Barzel 1997). These assets typically have multiple attributes, and there are often separate rights to different attributes of any given asset. Consequently, the experimental rights or fences that entrepreneurs might introduce in the pursuit of profit opportunities do not necessarily cover novel products as such but may be aimed at securing control over new attributes of *existing* assets that have only just been discovered.[9] According to the condition of presumptive control, the owners of existing assets are presumed to hold any future, but as yet unknown, rights to newly discovered attributes of those assets when those rights come into being (Demsetz 1998: 146). Thus, the development of property rights systems is a dynamic and open-ended process.

## Freedom of contract

The freedom of contract is an essential component of economic liberty and is pivotal to entrepreneurial processes in a modern market economy. Contractual freedom means that entrepreneurs and other market participants are free to pursue their own interests through making binding promises, however prudent or imprudent, in the course of economic transactions. It gives entrepreneurs and other market participants the freedom to place themselves under a legal, and perhaps moral, obligation regarding their future conduct (thereby voluntarily reducing the possibilities open to them in the short run) for the purpose of expanding their range of choices in the market later on. It goes without saying that the freedom of contract guarantees neither entrepreneurial success nor any preconceived outcome.

### *Freedom of contract and entrepreneurs' personal agency beliefs*

Like the institution of private property, the freedom of contract evokes feelings of internal LOC and reinforces people's propensity to be alert to opportunity. The concept of contract is one of the most important means that the law offers people to control their own destiny: 'The whole network of rights created by contracts is as important a part of our own protected sphere, as much the basis of our plans, as any property of our own' (Hayek 1960: 141). By voluntarily adhering to the rules of contract law, a person can broaden the scope of their protected domain. 'Inasmuch as he validly contracts, his claims on others become, as it were, an extended "property right" (just as their claims on him become part of their extended property rights)' (Rizzo 1985: 869).

If defining and specifying property rights is the central economic function of the law of property, then providing for the *transferability* of those rights to higher-valued uses is the main economic function of the law of contracts. In order to be able to advance their plans, entrepreneurs must be able to enter binding commitments with the holders of property rights over resources that have the potential for improved coordination. That other people's property can be hired or sold to other market participants in the achievement of entrepreneurs' aims is largely due to the *enforceability* of contracts.

By enforcing long-term promises, the judicial system enables entrepreneurs and other market participants to make credible commitments to cooperate with each other. In other words, contract law provides the legal scaffolding that helps contracting parties to invest in the physical and human capital that is specific to particular entrepreneurial transactions and relationships. Such investments have the potential to enhance the gains from trade since the cost of supply from highly specialised capital (e.g. customised plant and equipment) is presumably lower than that from fungible (i.e. multipurpose) capital items. But because specialised capital goods cannot, in the event of a breakdown of exchange relations between the entrepreneur and the other party, be redeployed to alternative uses or users without a significant loss of productive value (perhaps because there is no lease or resale market), the party making such investments is tightly locked into the transaction and is exposed to the threat of *ex post* hold-up by the other contractual partner (Williamson 1979; 1985). In the absence of legal safeguards upon which they can rely, parties who anticipate such opportunistic behaviour may be unwilling to sink resources into relationship-specific investments. 'Many substantive contract doctrines, ranging from the traditional common law's pre-existing duty rule to the modern duty of good faith, are designed to provide precisely this protection' (Katz 1998: 427).

## Freedom of contract and the rule of law

The freedom of contract is derived from the rule of law.[10]

> Freedom of contract ... means that the validity and enforcibility [*sic*] of a contract must depend *only* on those general, equal, and known rules by which all other legal rights are determined, and not on the approval of its particular content by an agency of the government.
>
> (Hayek 1960: 230; emphasis added)

Adherence to the rule of law means that the substantive content of entrepreneurial contracts (including the agreed terms of trade) is not subject to supervision by the courts or any other public authority. The role of the courts is to enforce binding agreements; it is not to police the adequacy of consideration being exchanged to support a contract. Freedom of contract requires that the courts respect, in the absence of coercion, the contracting parties' subjective valuations of what is given or pledged in exchange for a promise. It is for participants themselves, and not the courts, to decide whether their contracts are profitable or unprofitable, wise or foolhardy, fair or unfair.

The ideal of the rule of law also implies that the general principles of contract law must be sufficiently universal and abstract to govern both discrete (i.e. one-off) and relational contracts. In a complex market economy, entrepreneurship consists of more than numerous one-shot, arbitrage transactions effected by discrete or spot contracts. Indeed, entrepreneurs often enter into relational contracts which entail not only an exchange arrived at by way of a bargain, but also an ongoing relationship between the trading partners that is supported by the contract. Innovative entrepreneurs, especially, use these contracts to govern the ongoing conduct of what Eisenberg calls '*thick relationships*' – 'relationships characterized by an involvement which is both personally intensive and broad in scope' (1998: 447). These contracts – which include business partnerships and employment contracts – are unavoidably incomplete, and they omit variables and contingencies that are relevant to the subsequent evolution of entrepreneurs' relationships with other participants. As a result, entrepreneurs and their contract partners might come to require general legal principles that enable them to cope with specific unforeseen events in reasonably predictable ways. The obligation to perform contracts in good faith is just such a principle, and it is as applicable to discrete contracts as to relational contracts. In any case, since most contracts have both discrete and relational aspects, the existence of both general-purpose contract law and special relational contract law can create uncertainty among market participants as to which set of legal rules will apply for any particular contract (Eisenberg 1998).

The rule of law also implies that there are serious risks in empowering courts to modify the terms of contracts because of changed circumstances. In New Zealand, for instance, the Employment Court's interpretation of the Employment Contracts Act 1991 (since repealed) led to the development of a body of case law which limited contractual freedom with respect to terms relating to redundancy and dismissal (New Zealand Business Roundtable and New Zealand Employers Federation 1992). The Court's decisions imposed obligations on employers, which were contrary to the express intentions of both parties at the time of entering the employment contract.

Similarly, if courts were given the power to adjust price terms of contracts in the event of changed market conditions, then they could, in the interests of evening out the burden, impose a price that reduces the loss otherwise borne by one party at the expense of the profit of the other.[11] This follows from the zero-sum quality of price adjustment within bilateral contracts. This judicial interference in economic affairs would frustrate the ability of entrepreneurs to predict, on the basis of general rules, the legal consequences of entering into contracts. This legal indeterminacy might reduce entrepreneurs' sense of control over events, diminish their sense of agency and may therefore reduce their alertness to market opportunities. If legally mandated adjustment of the contract price (a rare instance of which occurred in *Alcoa v. Essex Group, Inc.*, 499 F Supp. 53 (Pa 1980)) were the norm rather than the exception, the courts would curtail the freedom of entrepreneurs and their contractual partners to choose the price adjustment rule that is most appropriate for them (Goldberg 1998: 293).

### Entrepreneurship, contractual mistakes and non-disclosure

Preserving incentives for speedy entrepreneurial discovery requires general, equal and certain rules of contract that allow entrepreneurs to take advantage of market ignorance. In considering this principle, it is useful to consider cases involving unilateral mistake and non-disclosure, which arise when one party, say the purchaser, simply remains silent and lets the unsuspecting seller contract on the basis of a mistaken belief concerning relevant material facts. For example, suppose that a team of entrepreneurs has a strong hunch that a block of land might contain valuable subsurface mineral deposits and suppose further that the entrepreneurs know that the current owner is completely unaware of its mineral-bearing potential at the time of contract formation. (Assume, for the sake of argument, no duress, fraud, misrepresentation or breach of fiduciary duty on the part of the entrepreneurs or cognitive incapacity on the part of the seller.) The entrepreneurs contract for the purchase of the land at a low price that reflects only its existing agricultural uses and, upon finding their earlier hunch to be correct, they subsequently sell the property at a much steeper price signalling its higher-valued use as a mineral reserve. (For relevant common law cases, see Kronman 1978: 19.)

At the normative level of philosophical and ethical evaluation, permitting the entrepreneurs to capture the arbitrage profit arising from the other contracting party's genuine error does not deprive that party of the freedom necessary to make his or her promises entirely voluntary and binding – at least not if the relevant concept of voluntary consent is grounded in Kirzner's theory of distributive justice. As mentioned earlier, Kirzner's finders-keepers ethic insists that entrepreneurs have full title to the 'discovered gain' that they unearth as a result of superior alertness. The gap between the prices that entrepreneurs pay and receive for resources represents pure arbitrage profit and is a gain that is spontaneously discovered solely by them without deliberate search:

> The additional value now seen by all to have resided in the resource was in fact found by the innovative entrepreneur. *If we follow a finders-keepers rule we can no longer countenance any simple revocation of the resource sale.* Simply to revoke the sale will be to assign to the seller a gain which someone else, not he, discovered. Precisely because the seller had no inkling of the 'true' higher value residing in his unit of resource he must recognize that the gain to be derived from the discovery of the higher value, justly belongs to another under a finders-keepers rule.
> (Kirzner 1989: 108; emphasis added)

At the level of positive economics, a rule requiring disclosure of the other party's error during contract formation would eliminate the profit of the entrepreneurial team. If the entrepreneurs were to disclose the known mistake, the current owner would then seek a higher price reflecting the surprisingly favourable new knowledge about the attributes of the resource. Alternatively, if the entrepreneurs failed to disclose the mistake, they would not be able to enforce their contract rights. Their non-disclosure would give the mistaken party grounds for avoiding any contractual obligations to the entrepreneurs. By defaulting on the transaction, the current owner would be able to appropriate the entrepreneurs' information. Thus, a disclosure rule would undermine the incentive for entrepreneurial discovery of socially valuable knowledge. There would be little, if any, incentive for entrepreneurs to discover higher-valued uses for productive resources, and the entrepreneurial process of economic coordination would become very sluggish.

> Ignorance, by checking the response of some, may be a necessary condi-tion for any response by others. ... A general profit opportunity, which is both known to everyone, and equally capable of being exploited by everyone, is, in an important sense, a profit opportunity for no one in particular.
>
> (Richardson 1960: 57)

This account contrasts markedly with Kronman's (1978) analysis of advan-tage taking in the context of contractual mistake and non-disclosure. Kronman distinguishes between two kinds of information, 'information which is the result of deliberate search and information which has been casually [i.e. accidentally] acquired' (p. 2). The main economic difference between the two is that the former entails costs that are only incurred in the hope of acquiring the information in question, whereas no costs are expressly incurred for the sole purpose of acquiring the latter type of infor-mation. He argues that, on economic efficiency grounds, a party to a contract should be legally entitled to withhold information that he or she knows the other party lacks (and to profit from the other's party error) *provided* this special information results from *deliberate and costly search*. Kronman argues that a legal rule permitting non-disclosure of deliberately acquired information (which is essentially a property right in such informa-tion) is required to provide an incentive to invest in the production of such knowledge at a socially desirable level. By implication, a party should be required to disclose casually acquired information because so doing would not affect how much of this sort of information he or she will produce in the future. In effect, Kronman's analysis falls into the same trap as equilib-rium economics: it fails to consider a third type of knowledge – namely, entrepreneurial knowledge, which results from neither deliberate search nor pure luck. As it stands, Kronman's rule would most likely impose a duty to disclose upon alert entrepreneurs because their superior 'knowledge' results, not from deliberate search, but from costless, spontaneous discovery of hitherto unnoticed opportunities. His rule would deny entrepreneurs a private advantage which they might otherwise obtain from their hunches, and it would therefore undermine incentives to be alert to opportunities in the future.

*Contract enforcement*

It should be noted that the freedom of contract in the legal sense does not just comprise the freedom of individuals to use available types of contracts for their own purposes. It also refers to the types of contracts that the legal authority will enforce. For example, in modern Western societies, the state does not try to enforce all classes of contract, such as contracts for criminal purposes, gambling contracts, price-fixing agreements and liability insurance policies against fines. In the case of contracts to sell voting rights and human organs, the state intervenes to such an extent that it prohibits the market exchange of these entitlements under all circumstances, even between a willing seller and a willing buyer. In the terminology of Calabresi and Melamed (1972), *rules of inalienability* protect the entitlement, even against the owner's temptation to sell it. By barring contracts to trade these legal entitlements, inalienability rules may be thought of as attenuating the grant of the entitlement itself.

The focus so far has been on the role of the judiciary in enforcing contracts, but there are other mechanisms besides the courts for governing contractual relations. State-supplied or judge-made contract laws often serve as a comprehensive set of default rules around which entrepreneurs and their trading partners can contract. The public legal system for enforcing contracts is far from perfect, and judicial enforcement of contracts (i.e. 'court ordering') is costly. Contracts can be enforced unilaterally, bilaterally or trilaterally. (However, these mechanisms generally still presuppose that the state will uphold the freedom of contract and set the legal baseline of entitlements in the event of possible judicial enforcement.) *Unilateral or internal governance* of contracts occurs when two contracting parties belong to the same hierarchical firm (e.g. a business start-up) established by the entrepreneur and are both subject to the authority of the latter when contractual difficulties emerge. Unilateral governance also includes the use of the household, extended family network or clan to govern economic transactions in the absence of *de jure* property rights. When both sides of a transaction to supply an input are contained within a single organisational entity, the entrepreneur can exercise greater control over whatever quantity adjustments are needed as economic conditions change.

Entrepreneurs and other participants may also depend upon *bilateral governance* structures. They may resolve their contractual disputes directly themselves through 'private ordering' and might only turn to judicial enforcement of their contracts as a last resort. Entrepreneurs' reliance upon self-enforcement mechanisms to ensure fulfilment of bilateral contracts rather than external enforcement organisations, such as the courts and police, preserves their autonomy and it may enhance their feelings of internal control over how unanticipated events will be handled. The freedom to engage in private ordering may thus strengthen entrepreneurs' sense of agency and their alertness to opportunity.

Indeed, many, if not most, contractual disputes that could be litigated under current law are resolved by private means, such as 'tit-for-tat' strategies, the threat of terminating the business relationship altogether, or self-help. The reason why private ordering is so common is that in 'many instances the participants can devise more satisfactory solutions to their disputes than can professionals constrained to apply general rules on the basis of limited knowledge of the dispute' (Galanter 1981: 4).

In addition, entrepreneurial contracts are also facilitated by the development of private *trilateral governance* structures to which traders have the right of recourse in the event of contractual disputes, thereby reducing transaction costs. A good example is the range of third-party arbitration tribunals that exists for resolving disputes under private commercial law. In the USA alone, merchant entrepreneurs and managers in more than fifty industries, including diamonds and cotton, have opted out of the public legal system and, through their trade associations, they have collectively developed systems of private commercial law (Bernstein 1992; 2001). These systems each comprise a network of contract default rules that are specific to the particular industry. Merchant arbitration tribunals operated by trade associations interpret and enforce these rules as codified by industry trade rules. The private commercial law systems still operate within the ambit of the public legal system in that the awards of merchant tribunals are legally enforceable by the courts. (To this extent at least, entrepreneurs operate within a state-provided superstructure of the law of contracts within which there is a plurality of *decentralised* private systems of contract laws.) However, a party rarely needs to seek judicial enforcement of a tribunal's decision because formal and social sanctions are so effective. The next chapter examines more closely decentralised processes for the production and enforcement of legal rules and their consequences for entrepreneurship.

This concludes the discussion of the institution of private property and freedom of contract. The next chapter takes a different tack. It focuses upon the phenomenon of money and the political decentralisation of economic regulatory authority, and it examines the impact of these institutional factors upon the development of personal agency beliefs and entrepreneurial alertness. It also considers the substantive economic liberties, conducive to entrepreneurship, that are provided by an institutional framework based on the rule of law, the institution of private property and freedom of contract.

# 5 Institutions II

Money, political and
legal decentralisation
and economic freedom

This chapter continues the analysis of the institutional conditions for entrepreneurship. In the previous chapter, I considered the fundamental principles and rules that must be embedded in a constitutional order if it is to produce agents who are causally efficacious and alert in the economic sphere. I paid particular attention to the bedrock institutions of private property and freedom of contract. As yet, I have remained silent about the role of money or of the political order in competitive market processes.

The conventional wisdom is that the phenomenon of money presupposes the institution of private property, and like the institution of private property, money expands the extent of the market and facilitates the division of labour. Money prices are viewed as an aid to entrepreneurial decision-making ('a powerful cognitive simplifier') that, in conjunction with other kinds of knowledge, helps entrepreneurs zero in on the latent economic potential of productive resources. By signalling profit opportunities, disequilibrium money prices are a sophisticated device that spurs entrepreneurs to correct these prices and to discover new knowledge.

In contrast to previous scholarship, this chapter pays attention to how the emergence of money affects entrepreneurial alertness. It extends Kirzner's ideas on entrepreneurship by relating psychological determinants of alertness to 'monetary calculation', a particular form of cognitive operation. In particular, it focuses upon how the phenomenon of money influences people's personal agency beliefs and the complexity of the entrepreneurial knowledge problem. Among other things, money reinforces entrepreneurs' perceived self-efficacy because it gives them the means to engage in the economic calculation necessary to select, initiate and monitor capital projects and production processes.

After considering money and its surrounding institutions, the focus shifts to examining how the decentralisation of political and legal decision-making helps secure the foundations for market entrepreneurship. (Economic decentralisation has already been examined in the discussion of alternative property rights systems in Chapter 4.) It is hypothesised that political and legal systems based on decentralised control appear more likely than centralised structures to produce economic agents who have a strong sense of personal agency and are alert to profit opportunities. The more decentralised are political and legal systems, the clearer are the signals of internal locus of control, since people's economic success is visibly dependent more on their own actions and less on the activities of 'powerful others', such as the state.

Having analysed the role of the political and legal order, the chapter moves on to reconsider the principle of freedom more closely. In particular, the discussion fleshes out the implications of Kirzner's notion of alertness for how we conceive entrepreneurial freedom. It also examines how the law institutionalises or embeds the principle of freedom in a framework of concrete economic liberties that are essential for entrepreneurial discovery. The last section of the chapter then surveys the empirical literature on the relationship between economic freedom and economic growth. It presents impressive empirical results that show the positive contribution that economic freedom can make to a nation's economic performance.

## The phenomenon of money

Money is one of the key institutions contributing to human freedom and the development of civil society. It is one of the great social phenomena that rationalise economic life:

> It [the use of money] gives society the technical machinery of exchange, the opportunity to combine personal freedom with orderly cooperation on a grand scale, and the basis of that system of accountancy which Sombart appropriately calls 'economic rationalism'.
>
> (Mitchell 1937: 170–171)

It plays a significant role in the cultivation of entrepreneurial alertness and the ability to make judgemental decisions about the coordination of economic resources. In the absence of money, a complex economic order based on specialisation and the division of labour could not emerge. The scope for entrepreneurship would be limited to an extremely rudimentary form of production and exchange.

As discussed in Chapter 2, the scope for entrepreneurship is provided by the existence of more than one price for the 'same' good in the 'same' market. The price differential (in the form of interlocal or intertemporal price discrepancies) represents an opportunity for pure arbitrage profit arising from market participants overlooking current economic facts. The analysis of market entrepreneurship proceeded on the unstated assumption that all prices are *money* prices and that all market transactions involve exchanging goods or services for *money*. Specifying prices in cardinal numerical values presupposes that there is a specialised and universally accepted medium of exchange used in trading goods and services in which prices for market transactions can be expressed.

The analysis of market entrepreneurship has also assumed implicitly that money is 'neutral': that is, that the working of the market and the direction of market activity are exactly as they would be in the absence of money.

It should be noted that these assumptions were made for heuristic purposes only. In the real world, the introduction of a money supply into a market system affects both demand-side and supply-side conditions conducive to entrepreneurship. Because it induces changes in the degree of division of labour and specialisation in production and exchange, the division of knowledge among market participants, the extent and number of markets and goods, the duration of the period of production (degree of 'roundaboutness'), and the transaction costs of exchange, money changes the structure of economic circumstances and the totality of exchange ratios between commodities that give rise to entrepreneurial opportunities. To state it simply: the emergence of money increases the range of goods and services available on the market and the potential set of disequilibrium prices open for correction. It thereby increases the scope for entrepreneurial opportunities.[1]

The focus of this section, however, is upon how money impinges on supply-side factors that affect the generation of entrepreneurial alertness. As argued in Chapter 3, the supply of entrepreneurial alertness is a function of people's sense of agency, which in turn comprises their beliefs about their own efficacy (competency) and locus of control (contingency). This section argues that the introduction of money and a system of money prices potentially strengthens the sense of personal agency and the degree of alertness of (as yet unknown) entrepreneurs. The existence of money promotes personal agency by enhancing entrepreneurs' perceptions of self-efficacy and particularly their beliefs about their own capacity to secure the relevant knowledge, to plan rationally and to coordinate resources successfully in the pursuit of profit opportunities. In addition, a generally accepted medium of exchange bolsters entrepreneurs' perceptions of the contingency of desired economic outcomes (profit, success) upon entrepreneurial actions. It raises their expectation that economic rewards are controlled by behaviour rather than external forces. In other words, it reinforces an internal locus of control.

### Money and entrepreneurs' self-efficacy beliefs

How does money affect entrepreneurs' sense of self-efficacy? This section argues that the existence of money and money prices enhances perceived self-efficacy by improving the epistemic basis of entrepreneurial action, by reducing the complexity of entrepreneurial transactions and by facilitating cognitive operations such as economic calculation and the rational planning of entrepreneurial activities. Although it comes later in history than barter, the use of money simplifies economic problems. Money changes how people think and act because it can reduce the cost of cognition and can serve as a substitute for cognition (Gifford 1999). Money is part of the institutional

framework that facilitates the mental division of labour and extends specialisation in cognition.

One mechanism by which money affects entrepreneurs' agency beliefs is
through its impact on their perceptions of their problem situation.
Entrepreneurs' estimates of their self-efficacy and degree of agency may
include a cognitive appraisal of the situational context in which
entrepreneurship occurs, including the nature of the goals to be achieved
and the requirements of the transactions to be carried out. Transactional
attributes include the degree of complexity and interdependence of activities, the frequency and number of sequential and coordinative steps
necessary, and the quantity and quality of resources and knowledge required
to complete the transaction successfully. The adequacy of the resources and
knowledge that the entrepreneur has access to in a domain of activity is
another contextual factor.

Money prices reinforce a sense of efficacy and agency because they
improve the epistemic and informational basis of entrepreneurial action.
Money prices reduce the amount of detail that entrepreneurs need to know
in order to make the right decisions. They make it possible for entrepreneurs
to make plans as if they had much more knowledge than they actually do.
They increase the ability of entrepreneurs to 'know' their environment, even
if that knowledge contains a heavy tacit component.

Money prices supply the knowledge base upon which entrepreneurs'
cognitive processes can operate, and they condense a tremendous amount of
contextual and historical knowledge relating to each good into a single
cardinal number (Horwitz 1998: 442). In the absence of money prices,
entrepreneurs would have to obtain and aggregate masses of *additional* data
on resource availabilities, production technologies and consumer preferences
as the basis for their activities. 'The most significant fact about this system
[the price system] is the economy of knowledge with which it operates, or
*how little the individual participants need to know in order to be able to take the
right action*' (Hayek 1948: 86; emphasis added). In exploiting the particular
price differences and profit opportunities they themselves have discovered,
entrepreneurs decide tentatively to treat many observed prices as unprob-
lematic and reasonably reliable. In so doing, entrepreneurs make their plans
against a background of money prices, some of which they single out and
test but many of which they accept unquestioningly for the time being. 'The
economy of knowledge with which the [price] system works is due ... to a
division of entrepreneurial labor caused by the fact that each individual
"disagrees" only with a few prices while "accepting" all others' (Thomsen
1992: 60). This buffer serves to protect entrepreneurs from cognitive overload, a condition that would threaten their capabilities and self-efficacy
(Lavoie 1985b: 83–84).

Money prices signal, more or less faithfully, underlying economic fundamentals. 'The state of the market at any instant is the price structure, i.e. the
totality of the exchange ratios as established by the interaction of those eager

to buy and those eager to sell' (Mises 1966: 258). Money prices serve as objective proxies of the subjective valuations of individuals on both sides of the market. They are 'knowledge surrogates' that to varying degrees reduce or summarise a host of supply and preference data (Thomsen 1992: 41). Movements in money prices are interpreted as reflecting changes in relative scarcity and/or relative urgency of wants (in the absence of monetary mismanagement). Many entrepreneurs and other economic actors do not need to know the source of the change in relative scarcity of some particular commodity – be it an increase in demand and/or a decrease in supply – in order to respond to it. A market system economises on information by making the response of most agents independent of cause (Loasby 1982a: 124).

Although the price system economises on information, it must be recognised that entrepreneurs cannot treat money prices as perfect substitutes for relevant knowledge of market data. Money prices are not 'sufficient statistics' that fully convey everything that entrepreneurs need to know. As Garrison points out: 'Hayek called our attention to the *marvel* of the market economy functioning as it does on the basis of such little knowledge; he did not insist on a *miracle* in which the economy functions in the total absence of knowledge' (1982: 133; emphasis added). Prices are not the only pieces of information that potential entrepreneurs need to know in order to take the right action. Potential entrepreneurs must still be alert to a mass of *real* variables that affect money prices and the profitability of business opportunities (though, even in this connection, money prices may help entrepreneurs direct their attention to the most significant real variables). For example, most, if not all, entrepreneurs will be very keen to know why the market price of some key input into their venture has risen. They will want to know the cause of the price increase, whether the good has become scarcer because of a loss in one of its sources of supply or because new uses have been discovered for it.

But the point is still that, because of the complexity of the technical connections between capital goods and other factors in roundabout processes of production, entrepreneurs would not be able to make good use of their stocks of qualitative knowledge of market data without a system of money prices that serves as the basis for their computations of profit and loss:

> [W]ithout the ability to calculate [with meaningful numerical data or money prices], producers, *no matter how much qualitative knowledge of the economic data* they discovered or were endowed with, would never be able to use such knowledge in pursuit of their purposes.
>
> (Salerno 1993: 120)

Furthermore, even though disequilibrium money prices are imperfect and insufficient conveyors of information, they still perform an important epistemic function. They provide information to entrepreneurs that would otherwise be absent. Disequilibrium money prices signal the existence of a faulty pattern of resource use and they provide entrepreneurs with an incentive to eliminate this discoordination. '[D]isequilibrium prices provide through profits a *feedback mechanism* for their own correction that makes them a more sophisticated informational device than they may seem when concentrating only on their equilibrium role' (Thomsen 1992: 3; emphasis added). The advantage of this feedback mechanism is that entrepreneurs do not have to identify instances of imperfect coordination between market transactions per se; they simply have to identify price discrepancies for the same good.

The existence of money and money prices enhances the self-efficacy of entrepreneurs because it enables them to engage in 'economic calculation', which is an advanced cognitive operation. Money enhances the capacity of the entrepreneurial mind to deal with problems of a higher order. '[T]he very possibility of purposive action within the framework of social division of labor depends on the faculty of the human intellect to conceive cardinal numbers and manipulate them in arithmetic operations' (Salerno 1990b: 27).

Money strengthens the ability of entrepreneurs to make *rational* judgemental decisions about reallocating scarce productive resources in light of the higher-valued uses that they have discovered. '[M]onetary economic calculation is the intellectual basis of the market economy' (Mises 1966: 259). In an economy based on a complex division of labour, economic calculation is pivotal to the ability of entrepreneurs to make rational economic decisions and systematic production plans under uncertainty. 'Every single step of entrepreneurial activities is subject to scrutiny by monetary calculation' (Mises 1966: 229).

So what exactly is economic calculation? Economic calculation is an individual's numerical computation, in terms of money prices, of the consequences of his or her actions in the market (Mises 1966: 201–213). It includes the *ex ante* computation of the expected outcomes of planned actions (e.g. the expected costs and expected revenues of a project) and the retrospective computation of the results of past transactions (i.e. entrepreneurial success and failure, profit and loss).

Money is necessary for economic calculation because computation requires a common denominator (a common unit of calculation), to which exchange ratios can be reduced. 'The whole structure of the calculations of the entrepreneur and the consumer rests on the process of valuing commodities in money. Money has thus become an aid that the human mind is no longer able to dispense with in making economic calculations' (Mises 1971: 48–49).

The numbers that entrepreneurs employ in economic calculation are money prices – that is, the numerical ratios of exchange between money and other economic goods and services. '[P]rices are not measured in money; they consist in money' (Mises 1966: 217). Money prices are the mental tools of rational entrepreneurial planning and economic calculation.

The bounded rationality of entrepreneurs means that, in the absence of money prices, it would be impossible for them to monitor directly all the changes in market conditions and to determine the corresponding alterations in exchange ratios between numerous pairs of goods and services. If there were $n$ commodities in a direct barter economy, and each commodity could be exchanged with each of the other $n - 1$ commodities, then an entrepreneur participating regularly in the market would have to monitor $\frac{1}{2}n(n - 1)$ separate exchange ratios. If, however, one of the commodities were to become a generally accepted medium of exchange and a unit of account, then the exchange matrix would be reduced dramatically to $n - 1$ exchange ratios (Brunner and Meltzer 1971: 787). By establishing money prices for every good and service, money enables market participants to compare prices easily: 'Instead of a myriad of isolated markets for each good and every other good, each good exchanges for money, and the exchange ratios between every good and every other good can easily be estimated by observing their money prices' (Rothbard 1993: 203).

Psychological research on numerical cognition supports the suggestion that money reduces the cost of obtaining, comparing and remembering exchange ratios. By supplying a common unit of calculation (i.e. a common denominator), money reduces the *problem difficulty* effect (Ashcraft 1992; Dehaene 1992). Without money, individuals would have to engage in more complex cognitive processes. The absence of a common denominator reduces the efficiency of direct memory retrieval as the predominant strategy for performing simple arithmetic in price comparisons. It also greatly increases the need to use relatively slow calculation procedures, and it affects more than just the encoding of numerical stimuli. The reaction time to perceive and quantify price differences, and the scope for error, will all be greater under barter than for comparable transactions involving exchange ratios expressed in a common unit of account.

Money prices are set by unconditional market exchanges of goods and services against money. It follows that entrepreneurs can only engage in economic calculation within an institutional framework that supports private ownership of the means of production and the exchange of goods and services against money. 'Economic calculation cannot comprehend things which are not sold and bought against money' (Mises 1966: 214).

If fallible entrepreneurs are to have the competency (efficacy) to distinguish, from among the myriad technologically feasible projects, those ventures which are profitable from those that are not, they must have recourse to calculative 'aids' of the 'human mind', such as that provided by money, in assessing the possible consequences of planned actions. Monetary calculation provides 'a guide amid the bewildering throng of economic possibilities' (Mises 1981: 101). Moreover, economic calculation does not require perfect-knowledge surrogates. In spite of the 'imperfect configuration of disequilibrium relative prices' that occurs in a world of out-of-equilibrium trading, economic calculation can still aid entrepreneurs in separating out the profitable investment projects from those that are not (Lavoie 1985a: 57).

Before embarking upon a full-scale operation, entrepreneurs are able to assess alternative methods of production by means of monetary calculations, to evaluate them symbolically and to reject or tentatively accept them on the grounds of their predicted consequences. 'Through the medium of symbols people can solve problems without having to enact all the various alternative solutions' (Bandura 1977b: 13). The cognitive capacity for economic calculation is thus embedded in symbolic ability. For example, a business plan with projections of money income and money outlay is an objective symbolic depiction of the entrepreneur's ideas. Because economic calculation enables entrepreneurs to sift their way early on through possible projects whose implementation would consume a great deal of time and effort, it quickens the pace of their learning.

Economic calculation is not only required at the *ex ante* stage of forming an entrepreneurial plan, however. It also facilitates implementation of plans and their evaluation *ex post*. '[I]n a world of partial ignorance, there is much more to effective decision-making than the selection of the correct alternative from the choice set' (Loasby 1976: 88). Because entrepreneurial decisions are made in conditions that are liable to lead to error, economic calculation is also required in assessing the success of the decisions that they have made.

Once entrepreneurs have chosen a project, they may engage in monetary calculation and profit and loss accounting so as to gauge the progress of their ventures. Feedback that conveys successful accomplishment and competence strengthens entrepreneurs' perceptions of their self-efficacy. But even negative feedback may facilitate entrepreneurial learning and the development of entrepreneurial capabilities and perceived self-efficacy. Feedback in the form of a discrepancy between actual performance and the planned decision is an important source of information in the formulation of entrepreneurs' efficacy perceptions (cf. Bandura and Cervone 1986). The frequency and immediacy of these signals help entrepreneurs to discover their errors earlier than they would otherwise in the course of carrying out their plans. In the absence of money prices, entrepreneurs would not be able to avoid errors that they can now avoid because of the condensed and detailed (albeit imperfect) information made available to them by price signals.

A whole host of abstract pecuniary concepts and practices has evolved from the use of money and economic calculation. These products of the human mind are essential tools of entrepreneurial thought and action and support what Mitchell (1937: 160) calls the 'whole countinghouse attitude toward economic activities'. For example, entrepreneurs rely upon the system of double-entry bookkeeping and the process of capital budgeting. These methods enable entrepreneurs to establish business hierarchies in which they delegate subordinate entrepreneurial tasks to their managers, thereby enabling themselves to focus on the big picture. The system of business accounting, in conjunction with market-based transfer prices for factor inputs, enables entrepreneurs to calculate the profit or loss imputed to different divisions of the enterprise and to determine their contribution to overall performance. Lewin (1998) adds the twist that business hierarchies are also *necessary* for the smooth functioning of market processes because they facilitate economic calculation by supplying a cognitive backdrop and set of procedures for the attribution of input costs.

A less obvious point is that economic calculation *always* pertains to the future. The introduction of money and monetary calculation supports 'futurity', which Lane defines as 'longer-term purposiveness, a teleological orientation that necessarily points to the future' (1991: 87). Entrepreneurs engage in economic calculation to handle changes in market conditions and to anticipate the future. They use past money prices as a starting point for forming their expectations of the future structure of market prices for particular goods and services (what Mises calls entrepreneurial 'appraisement') (Mises 1966: 331–332).[2] Entrepreneurs only take past money prices into account in economic calculation to the extent that it assists them in adjusting their actions to their current expectations of the future. But because future prices cannot be deduced from past prices, economic calculation does not supply entrepreneurs with certain knowledge of the future constellation of the market or definitive knowledge of a profit opportunity. '[I]t does not deprive action of its speculative character' (Mises 1966: 214). Even retrospective assessments of past action may rely upon speculative anticipations of future prices (e.g. the prices that will be paid on the market for assets acquired in previous transactions).

### Money and entrepreneurs' locus of control beliefs

The discussion so far has focused upon the impact of money upon entrepreneurs' perceptions of self-efficacy as a determinant of alertness. The introduction of money might also have a tendency to strengthen entrepreneurs' beliefs that economic outcomes are contingent upon action rather than external forces beyond their control. That is, it might reinforce a sense of internal locus of control – the other component of personal agency beliefs that enhances alertness.

A system of direct exchange or barter is one in which all market transactions involve 'the exchange of one useful good for another, each for purposes of direct use by the party to the exchange' (Rothbard 1993: 160). There is no universally used medium of exchange; money does not exist. Goods and services are directly traded on the market against other goods and services. Each party acquires a good either for the direct satisfaction of his or her wants or for the services it renders directly to the production of other goods.

Barter is a very cumbersome and high-transaction-cost system in which every entrepreneurial transaction requires a 'double coincidence' of wants. At the very least, the entrepreneur must find two individuals, each of whom possesses a different good, and each of whom simultaneously values the good of the other more highly than his or her own. (In addition, a precondition for the existence of a profit opportunity is market ignorance: the parties are unaware of the existence of the other and do not know of the goods that the other party has and is willing to trade.)

In more complex cases of arbitrage involving the coordination of multiple direct exchanges between the entrepreneur and several other parties (i.e. multilateral clearing), the entrepreneur might anticipate a high cost in adapting his or her plans to slight changes in expected market conditions. Under barter, the success of the entrepreneur's plan is very vulnerable to surprises or exogenous shocks, such as the unexpected loss of one source of supply and the failure to complete a planned barter transaction. The cost of adjusting the plan in response to an exogenous change represents an obstacle to action that must be overcome if the entrepreneur is to continue pursuing the profit opportunity. (Of course, the cost may eliminate the profit opportunity entirely from the entrepreneur's subjective viewpoint, in which case he or she pulls the plug on the venture.) For example, if an entrepreneur employs a labourer to pick kiwifruit on the entrepreneur's orchard in exchange for a share of the orchard's kiwifruit output, and the labourer for whatever reason unexpectedly withdraws his or her services, the entrepreneur incurs the additional search cost of finding another labourer who not only wants to pick fruit but who also wants to acquire kiwifruit in exchange for services rendered.

The fragility of entrepreneurial plans involving barter transactions applies to the production and sale of even the simplest commodities. Within a barter system, the problem is substantially exacerbated in the case of indivisible goods, such as a house or boat. (The defining characteristic of an indivisible good is that it loses all, or almost all, its value when split into smaller pieces. Individual pieces have no value to other market participants.) The upshot is that under full barter entrepreneurs consider the success and profitability of even relatively simple transactions to be extremely sensitive to those external forces that can generate significant costs of adaptation. This sensitivity to external shocks dampens their perceived level of internal control, which in turn dims their alertness.

In contrast, in a fully monetised economy, the entrepreneur knows, as a result of the tacit agreement among market participants, that others will accept only one particular commodity – namely, the one that serves universally as money – as payment for the other goods and services they supply. Money represents a linking pin in all market transactions. 'Money ... is one half of all exchanges, i.e., it is the joint linking all transactions' (Boettke 1993: 116). Economic goods and services are traded in exchange for money, and money exchanges for economic goods and services. 'Every single market ... includes the money commodity as one of the two elements' (Rothbard 1993: 201). Money thereby lubricates the wheels of exchange by reducing the costs of market transactions.

In particular, the interpolation of money into market transactions removes the problems arising from a lack of coincidence of wants and the indivisibility of commodities. For example, if the entrepreneur needs to employ a new labourer for the orchard, all the entrepreneur has to do is find a labourer who is willing to supply the relevant services, and then the entrepreneur pays the agreed amount of money. It does not matter that the labourer does not want kiwifruit in exchange for services rendered. The unexpected loss of a source of supply or a prized customer has less serious consequences for the profitability of the entrepreneur's plan because the entrepreneur incurs a lower cost in searching for a replacement.

The introduction of money therefore increases the robustness and flexibility of entrepreneurial plans over a range of environments. From a different perspective, it can be said that money increases the decomposability of entrepreneurial plans. Decomposability means that a complex plan comprises subsets of transactions that are to some extent independently stable. For instance, the existence of money enables entrepreneurs to extend specialisation to every facet of the production process and to divide production into various stages, each of which might comprise relatively autonomous sequences of transactions (e.g. the production of assemblies and subassemblies in manufacturing vehicles). Unexpected disruption in one subset of planned exchanges does not completely undermine the carrying out of the entrepreneur's overall plan. 'Decomposability is of significance primarily in conditions of change – either random or systematic. ... Decomposability matters above all because it facilitates adaptation [to a change in the environment]' (Loasby 1976: 33).

The effect is that entrepreneurs perceive the profitability of their ventures to be more contingent upon action and less contingent upon unforeseeable, external changes. They see the successful execution of their plans as less subject to the vicissitudes of the market. The entrepreneur has a deeper sense of internal locus of control and of agency and is thus more alert to opportunities.

The implications of the introduction of money for economic stability have of course been considered in the wider economic literature. In contrast to Keynes (1936: viii, 293–4) who argued that a monetary economy is more subject to destabilisation than a barter system, Marshall (1920: 335, 793) noted that the use of money often stabilises markets and leads to decomposability in people's plans to buy and sell.[3]

## Discretionary monetary policy and entrepreneurs' perceptions of agency

It should be noted that the origin of the phenomenon of money is independent of the power of the state. 'Money is not an invention of the state. It is not the product of a legislative act. Even the sanction of political authority is not necessary for its existence' (Menger 1994: 262).[4] A detailed analysis of the process by which money emerges is outside the scope of this chapter.[5]

But it suffices to emphasise that not only can money emerge spontaneously out of a barter economy through the interaction of market participants, but also money can *only* evolve organically through private market exchanges and cannot be consciously created by the state through central planning (Menger 1892; 1994). It is 'epistemologically impossible for the State to create a common medium of exchange outside the context of exchange practice' (Boettke 2001: 255). The state by itself does not have the power to transform a commodity into a generally accepted medium of exchange.[6] Although the legal order of a society can have an effect on the money character of commodities, it is only the common commercial practice of all the individuals who participate in the market that can create money. (This also implies that the institutions of property and contract must exist before money can emerge.) Furthermore, as a result of changes in economic conditions, business customs and the marketability of various assets, a commodity that once served as money may eventually be displaced over time by another more liquid commodity. 'Advanced transactions technologies, liquid spot and futures markets, and the development of financial intermediaries all contribute to the replacement of one set of exchange media by another' (Cowen and Kroszner 1994: 596–597).

Although, as a Big Player, the state or its central bank does not have the power to create a medium of exchange, it does have the power to change the value of the monetary unit and to discoordinate market processes. A Big Player is defined as 'anyone who habitually exercises *discretionary power* to influence the market while himself remaining wholly or largely immune from the discipline of profit and loss' (Koppl and Yeager 1996: 368; emphasis added). It is clear that as a Big Player, a central bank is an archetype of a 'powerful other' in Rotter's (1966) psychological sense of the term. When a central bank pursues inflationary monetary policies or intervenes to influence short-term interest rates or to defend an exchange rate, its actions distort the structure of relative prices and reduce the information content of market signals – money prices less accurately reflect underlying market fundamentals (Butos and Koppl 1999: 269).

A change in the epistemic quality of money prices brought about by discretionary monetary policies inhibits entrepreneurial alertness to market opportunities through its stifling effects on entrepreneurial self-efficacy and locus of control beliefs. Big-Player intervention in the monetary sphere reduces entrepreneurs' sense of self-efficacy because it reduces their ability to obtain useful information about market developments. 'Big Players weaken the epistemic foundations of entrepreneurial action' (Butos and Koppl 1999: 272). Discretionary policy reduces the capacity of entrepreneurs to know their environment. Entrepreneurs become less confident in the reliability of their expectations, and they feel less able to respond to changes in the data of the market.

In addition, the discretionary actions of a central bank diminish the internality of entrepreneurs' locus of control beliefs because they weaken the perceived contingency of events upon what entrepreneurs discover and do in the market.[7] Economic outcomes (profit and loss) become more dependent upon external forces, that is the actions of key central bank officials and politicians. 'Entrepreneurial success now becomes more closely tied to discovering or anticipating the behavior of the Big Player' (Butos and Koppl 1999: 270). As mentioned earlier, money is the linking pin in market transactions, the other side of all market exchanges in a monetary economy. This implies that if state intervention alters the value of the monetary unit, it also changes the pattern of exchanges in the market, the constellation of relative prices, the structure of profit opportunities and therefore the allocation of real productive resources among competing uses. When a Big Player enters the game, observed market events and the pattern of relative prices are no longer as tightly linked to shifts in the data of the market, such as changes in consumer preferences, technology and resource endowments, because they depend more and more upon political factors. '[D]iscretionary policy attenuates the link between action and the economic environment by making the underlying reality [of the market] less important. ... In short, Big Players introduce free parameters into the environment that may change in unpredictable and arbitrary ways' (Butos and Koppl 1999: 270). As a result of the declining contingency of entrepreneurial outcomes upon their actions, entrepreneurs shift their attention away from market opportunities towards political developments and the capricious actions of the monetary authority.

As long as there is a central bank and government monopoly of money, political tinkering with the money supply is likely to continue (Wagner 1989a). The state monopoly over money gives decision-makers who control or influence government an additional means for pursuing their political interests. The incumbent political party can try to buy votes through monetary manipulations that change the structure of relative prices and the distribution of income for the benefit of those whose political support is desired. Greater economic instability is thus the inevitable by-product of the rational pursuit of political gain (electoral success) in a democracy in which the state has a monetary monopoly. Cartelisation of the banking industry is also a possibility:

> Instead of being the agency for the provision of a public good, a central bank seems more reasonably seen as an agent for cartelizing a banking system that otherwise would be competitive. The member banks gain from the formation of this cartel, as the members of any cartel gain from the cartel's formation. It is the government that makes this cartel possible, and which enforces the cartel, so it too would share in the gains from the monopolization of money and credit.
>
> (Wagner 1980: 14)

One approach to constraining discretionary monetary interventions is to denationalise money and to introduce competition into the monetary sphere.

In addition to providing a sounder banking system and more effective administration of the money supply, a free banking system of competitive note issue is likely to enhance the alertness of entrepreneurs both within and outside the banking sector.[8] Under free banking, entrepreneurs in the market for monetary services are free from interference by monetary authorities, such as a central bank or a government deposit insurance agency. They have the freedom to issue bank notes bearing their brand name, set interest rates and introduce new types of loans and deposits, subject only to the general laws of contract. Entrepreneurs recognise that there is no official lender of last resort that will provide them with emergency loans if they make poor business decisions. Eliminating the central bank and privatising the money supply credibly signals to all potential entrepreneurs that the government is committed to a limited role in economic affairs. It takes away the ability of the government to finance its expenditures through inflation, and it thereby assures entrepreneurs that government officials will not manipulate the value of the monetary unit and distort the structure of relative prices. All in all, free banking is likely to strengthen entrepreneurs' sense of personal agency and to heighten their alertness to profit opportunities.

## Political decentralisation

By itself, the rule of law, even in Hayek's thoroughgoing version, does not secure a system of personal liberty and vigorous entrepreneurship. The rule of law, and the formal requirements it imposes (certainty, generality and equality), does not guarantee an effective bulwark against the discretionary power of government. It is a mistake to present the rule of law as a *sufficient* condition for individual freedom and the unimpeded operation of spontaneous market forces, when it is possibly only a *necessary* condition (Hamowy 1971: 375). The same could be said of well-defined property rights and freedom of contract.

The fundamental problem is one of *credible political commitment* to maintaining markets and protecting economic liberties. If entrepreneurs are going to discover lucrative business opportunities and engage in the innovation that creates wealth, a political infrastructure is needed that credibly restricts the power of the state to expropriate entrepreneurial profits and other people's property.

### Federalism

A sound political foundation for market processes requires political decentralisation of the authority to determine economic policy, which so far has been best achieved by a federal constitutional order. A federal system of government is one of the institutional configurations most conducive to economic freedom and development (de Tocqueville 1990a: 172). It is a way of minimising the potential for political coercion by injecting the principles of the market into the political structure (Buchanan 1995; 1995/96). The processes of entry, exit and intergovernmental competition that are essential features of federalist structures serve as a constitutional limitation on governmental power. By protecting the autonomy of private decision-makers, federalism strengthens people's beliefs in their ability to exert power over what happens in their lives, and it raises their general level of attentiveness to market opportunities. 'In a federation economic policy will have to take the form of providing a rational permanent framework within which *individual initiative will have the largest possible scope* and will be made to work as beneficently as possible' (Hayek 1948: 268; emphasis added).

So what exactly is federalism, and what form of federalism is most conducive to a strong sense of agency and heightened entrepreneurial alertness? If the overall objective is to maximise people's entrepreneurial propensity to discover opportunities in the dynamic world in which they live, then it is relatively straightforward to define the ideal of competitive federalism:

> A central government authority should be constitutionally restricted to the enforcement of *openness of the whole nexus of economic interaction*. Within this scope, the central authority must be strong, but it should not be allowed to extend beyond the limits constitutionally defined. Other political-collective activities should be carried out, if at all, by separate state-provincial units that exist side-by-side, as competitors of sorts, in the inclusive polity.
>
> (Buchanan 1995/96: 265; emphasis added)

Riker's (1994) definition of federalism captures the main elements common to most conceptions of this polycentric political order. He defines federalism as a political system that comprises a *hierarchy of governments*, each of which has its own clearly specified *sphere of authority*, and that institutionalises the autonomy of each government by means of *self-enforcing limitations* on political discretion.

Though necessary, these conditions are not sufficient for activating acute levels of entrepreneurial alertness and promoting wealth creation. Not all forms of federal organisation generate thriving market processes and vibrant economic development. A case in point is the *de jure* federal system in Argentina, once the world's fourth-richest country in the 1930s. Thus, extra criteria are needed for pinpointing the subset of federal systems that effectively supports competitive markets. To this end, I draw upon Weingast's (1995) concept of '*market-preserving* federalism'.

It is predicted that market-preserving federalism is the political structure that is most conducive to internal locus of control beliefs, strong self-efficacy and heightened alertness on the part of economic actors. To qualify as market preserving, according to Weingast (1995), a particular federal system must satisfy three additional requirements beyond those identified by Riker. First, the *primary authority for regulating economic activity* must reside with lower-level governments in order to curtail the national government's control over economic policy-making. Second, there must be a *unified (i.e. common) market*, unhampered by internal trade restrictions and other kinds of regional protectionism, in order to ensure free movement of goods, labour and capital among individual states or provinces. Third, the lower-level governments must be subject to *a hard budget constraint* in order to maintain fiscal discipline.

The institution of market-preserving federalism accounts for some of the most spectacular economic miracles in the economic history of the West. During the last three or four centuries, the wealthiest nations in the world have been either *de jure* or *de facto* federalist systems (Weingast 1995: 3). For instance, the economic miracle in the first half of the seventeenth century was the new Dutch Republic. In addition to sound rights to property, free trade and tolerance of religious differences that led to an influx of well-connected immigrant merchants and moneymen, the Dutch Republic was distinguished from other countries by its polycentrism: '[T]he Dutch state drew power from federalism when absolutist centralization was the norm' (Schama 1988: 223).

The Dutch were not the only people to enjoy the beneficial economic effects of market-preserving federalism. Weingast (1995) explains how this system contributed critically to the Industrial Revolution in England in the eighteenth century, the economic take-off of the USA from the ratification of the Federal Constitution in 1789 through until the Great Depression, and the success of economic reform in southern China since the late 1970s. (For an analysis of the *demise* of competitive federalism in the USA, see Higgs 1987.) Eighteenth-century England is a good example of a nation that qualifies as a *de facto* federal state, even though it was formally a unitary polity. In practice it exhibited all the characteristics of market-preserving federalism (Weingast 1995: 6). Most significantly, the national government was constrained in its power to impose regulations on the domestic economy, while local governments were an autonomous source of political authority constrained by competition among each other.

## *Impact of federalism on entrepreneurs' agency beliefs and alertness*

So how does market-preserving federalism affect entrepreneurial alertness and the cognitive factors that switch it on? More specifically, what impact does this political structure have on people's causal beliefs about the contingency of economic outcomes upon action? What effect does it have on people's perceptions of their ability to successfully carry out entrepreneurial functions and tasks?

In general, federalism affects the 'objective' distribution of power over outcomes in the economic environment. In particular, it limits arbitrary interference by 'powerful others' in the economic affairs of private decision-makers because it separates economic policy-making responsibilities that might otherwise be bundled together in a single, all-powerful centralised government. Federalism sets an effective limit on the powers of government by dividing and balancing these powers among several rival political units, so that no one unit can transcend the delineated scope of its authority without being reined in by the others:

> The reason why a division of powers between different authorities always reduces the power that anybody can exercise is not always under-stood. It is not merely that the separate authorities will, through mutual jealousy, prevent one another from exceeding their authority. More important is the fact that certain kinds of coercion require the joint and co-ordinated use of different powers or the employment of several means, and, if these means are in separate hands, nobody can exercise those kinds of coercion. ... *Federal government is thus in a very definite sense limited government.*
>
> (Hayek 1960: 184–185; emphasis added)

Federalism is a self-enforcing set of institutions governing political decision-making that simultaneously restricts the power of the government and strengthens the economic freedom of private individuals and groups. '[U]nitary states are at a disadvantage relative to federal ones in establishing and maintaining credibility about keeping their governments in check' (Brenner 1994: 240). A political system of federalism is self-enforcing in that it makes it in the self-interest of political officials to limit their inter-ference in market processes. By credibly constraining future decisions of policy-makers, a federalist system supplies the basis for the rule of law and the political foundations of economic freedom.

The three additional characteristics of market-preserving federalism referred to above – namely, a subnational locus of economic regulatory authority, a unified market region and a hard budget constraint – signifi-cantly reinforce market participants' feelings of personal control and efficacy, and they stimulate alertness to market opportunities. According to the first requirement, the federal government's scope of economic control and regulation must be much narrower than that of the several states or provinces. Indeed, domestic economic policy-making by the states is meant to be the rule and that of the national government the exception. Thus, federalism protects entrepreneurs and other economic actors from big, centralised government. The limitation on the national government's ability to regulate the domestic economy makes the government much less responsive to lobbying by established interest groups that are being displaced by the innovations of more alert entrepreneurs. It thereby limits the ability of lacklustre 'runners up' to use the political process to under-mine the success of their competitors. This dimension of federalism means that both actual and potential entrepreneurs will come to expect that economic outcomes will be free of arbitrary interference, at least in the form of ad hoc national economic controls and legislation, imposed by an external central authority. Their experiences of action–outcome sequences will then become more predictable and controllable. Thus, the first additional characteristic of market-preserving federalism endows entrepreneurs with a greater sense of internal locus of control and heightens their alertness to profit opportunities.

As mentioned, the second characteristic of market-preserving federalism is a unified market together with a prohibition on trade restrictions among lower-level governments. The absence of regulatory barriers to the movement of goods, people and capital among individual states enables new entrepreneurs to set up (or to relocate) their new enterprises in regions outside established commercial centres so as to evade onerous local regulations of economic life. In the language of Hirschman (1970), entrepreneurs within a federal structure are free to exercise the 'exit' option provided by mobility whenever they judge that the quality of the local regulatory framework has deteriorated relative to that in other localities. Entrepreneurs will migrate to the state in which the bundle of regulatory laws and the supply of public goods are most consistent with their aims. They will vote with their feet.[9] If exit is to bring about improvement in the coordination of resources within a federal structure, however, there needs to be a mix of alert and inattentive market participants. If all participants were highly alert and instantaneously withdrew from one state to go to another in the event of a slight relative deterioration in the quality of the former state's institutional framework, the under-performing state would lack the necessary resources to implement improvements.

As well as the freedom to start up their ventures in new areas and to transfer their business activities across states, entrepreneurs obtain from market-preserving federalism the freedom to engage in interstate trade of goods and services. They are therefore free to exploit any interregional arbitrage opportunities that they discover in the entire unified market region. Their contractual freedom includes the freedom to transfer property rights in consumer and capital goods across state boundaries. Market-preserving federalism thus expands the extent of the market and gives entrepreneurs opportunities to capitalise on gains from further specialisation.

The prohibition on barriers to interstate commerce has important consequences for the effectiveness of ad hoc state-level industrial policies designed to favour one group of entrepreneurs at the expense of others. To be effective, industry assistance measures (such as the establishment of statutory marketing boards) that aim to limit supply and raise prices require the joint use of two or more coercive powers. But if a state lacks the power to prevent the movement of people and capital across its borders, regardless of its power to control other conditions, the state will not be able to successfully pursue coercive industrial policy: 'If goods, men, and money can move freely over the interstate frontiers, it becomes clearly impossible to affect the prices of the different products through action by the individual state' (Hayek 1948: 258).

Thus, although state governments have more scope than the federal government to regulate economic activity, their power to make economic policy is still severely limited by political competition among each other.[10] The mobility of people and capital within a common market serves as a check on the activities of state governments.

By pre-committing the federal government to respect the autonomy of lower-level governments, federalism does, however, encourage states to engage in economic experimentation. The prohibition on internal trade restrictions and the decentralisation of political decision-making set in motion a competitive discovery process among state governments that involves experimenting with different social arrangements and learning through trial and error the best method of providing public goods (Vihanto 1992; Streit 1996; Vanberg and Kerber 1994). Entrepreneurs have an important role to play in local experimentation in providing the service activities of government, such as participating in competitive bidding processes to contract out local government services. Decentralising the supply of local public goods might even allow entrepreneurs to establish private profit-seeking clubs to compete for members, each of whom pays a user charge to consume the club good (Buchanan 1965). A climate of economic experimentation, aimed at adapting institutions of governance to local conditions, fosters a sense of personal efficacy, internal locus of control and alertness of individuals.

The third additional requirement of market-preserving federalism is a hard budget constraint imposed on lower-level governments. This arrangement makes political officials accountable for their fiscal decisions. As a consequence, people see that even public decision-makers have to take responsibility for their own decisions. It affects the sequences of actions and rewards that people observe in the world around them. A hard budget constraint signals that the federal government will not bail out state governments with a cash injection if they cannot repay their debts. (For an analysis of the economic and political institutions necessary to control local defaults and central bailouts, see Inman 2001.) It makes market participants realise that they will not receive special privileges or subsidies from the federal government. People see that economic successes and failures are contingent upon action and not upon the arbitrary interference of 'powerful others', such as the federal government. Good-quality fiscal management raises people's confidence that the federal government will not overawe other decision-makers, whether public or private. Thus, a hard budget constraint imposed on subnational governments indirectly reinforces people's internal locus of control beliefs. It evokes a stronger sense of human agency and heightened alertness to commercial opportunities.

Furthermore, the fiscal discipline of market-preserving federalism might reduce the future tax burden on entrepreneurs and other market participants from what it would otherwise be in the absence of that constraint. The hard budget constraint is thus consistent with limiting the use of the government's monopoly to tax. From the point of view of entrepreneurs, the effect is that some hitherto marginally unprofitable arbitrage transactions might become profitable once the lower tax rate is taken into account.

A final point is that market-preserving federalism is bound to result in gaps in legislative control in some areas. These interstices in the statutory framework present entrepreneurs with additional degrees of freedom for hunting out opportunities and exercising their initiative. These gaps arise because states often cannot reach an adequate consensus on whether and how certain economic powers should be used, so that these powers end up not being exercised at all by either the federal government or the individual states. 'Indeed, this readiness to have no legislation at all on some subjects rather than state legislation will be the *acid test* of whether we are intellectually mature for the achievement of suprastate organization' (Hayek 1948: 266; emphasis added).

## Legal decentralisation

> In fact, centralized law, like socialism, is not even plausible for a technologically advanced society. The forces that reversed the trend towards socialism and destroyed central planning are also undermining legal centrism. ... [A]s economies become more complex, efficiency demands more decentralized lawmaking, not less.
>
> (Cooter 1994: 216)

This section considers different sources of law and alternative institutions of law-making and examines their consequences for human agency and entrepreneurial alertness. It first compares the ideal type of the system of common law (i.e. judge-made law) with that of law-making processes centred on legislation. It then examines customary law as a decentralised process for producing and enforcing legal rules.

### *The organic common law process versus centralised law-making*

A relatively decentralised law-making process, such as the common law tradition, which evolves spontaneously and gradually by judicial decisions, is more conducive to the development of a robust sense of personal agency and heightened entrepreneurial alertness than is a centralised legal system codified by the authorities and based on legislation. A decentralised process treats the law as something to be discovered rather than enacted. It is 'both incremental and purposeless. ... The process of [legal] change is as close to a continuous development as one is likely to see in human affairs' (Rizzo 1985: 872).

The impact of a common law system on personal agency beliefs (and therefore alertness) is shaped by the fact that it corresponds more closely to the ideal of the rule of law. The common law provides a system of abstract and general rules that does not impose a specific hierarchy of ends or values on society and, in this sense, it is 'policy neutral' (Rizzo 1985: 865). It enhances the prospect of a spontaneous market order in which entrepreneurs and other economic actors can effectively pursue their various purposes on the basis of their own knowledge. In other words, the abstract order of the common law promotes economic coordination, and it increases the coincidence of individual expectations and plans (Hayek 1973: 102–106). Because it offers a greater chance of many economic expectations being correct, the common law process is more likely to make the success of people's planning activities contingent upon their own actions. That is, this legal order is more likely than a centralised law-making process to generate internal LOC beliefs and alertness.

Under a common law system, entrepreneurs are better able to make and fulfil their long-run plans because the overall character of the legal order tends to be highly predictable. The long-run certainty of the common law means that entrepreneurs can enter into commercial relationships with other market participants and enjoy reasonable assurance of the governing rules of law. The power to affect the overall properties of the common law system is widely dispersed among a multitude of judges located at different times and places so that no single judge can do much to alter its overall character. One set of judges can be substituted for another without affecting the general properties of the spontaneous order of the common law. In this sense, common law judges are interchangeable personalities who lack individuality (Leoni 1972: 94). An internal LOC is encouraged as entrepreneurs can expect that the overall pattern of the common law and the legal foundations of their decision-making will not be undermined by 'powerful others'.[11]

In addition to the dispersal of power in the legal order, a key institutional source of the certainty and stability of the common law is the rule of precedent, which in the mid-nineteenth century developed into the formal doctrine of *stare decisis* ('stand by what has been decided previously'). This doctrine refers to the obligation that requires a judge to follow prior applicable precedent even when the judge, in considering the case anew, might have good reasons for reaching a different decision. In practice, the judge may be obliged to adhere to prior decisions of the same court (horizontal *stare decisis*) and/or to prior decisions of a superior court within the same jurisdiction (vertical *stare decisis*).

The doctrine of *stare decisis* contributes to an internal LOC because entrepreneurs perceive greater contingency between the legal effects of their actions in the future and legal decisions in the past. It also enhances their sense of self-efficacy because it improves their capacity to predict reasonably accurately how cases that might affect them would be determined in the courts.

The common law *doctrine of standing* is another institutional rule that strengthens the legal foundation for entrepreneurial discovery and that reinforces entrepreneurs' beliefs in strong personal agency. This traditional judicial doctrine determines who has the right to bring an action in court. In the common law, only the original parties to a contract had the right to go to court in order to enforce the contract or to sue for damages in the event of contractual non-completion. The class of potential plaintiffs granted standing was closed and highly restricted. Third parties – those who were not original parties to the contract – were denied standing to sue even when they might have gained directly from the completion of that contract (Holderness 1985).

A restrictive standing doctrine, such as those in the common law, increases entrepreneurs' sense of control over events. It enhances their capacity to adjust their individual plans in the event of unexpected economic changes. If an entrepreneur discovers a change in economic conditions that makes it no longer profitable for him or her to execute a contract that he or she has already entered into, all the entrepreneur has to do is to settle the amount of damages for the breach and negotiate new terms (such as a later date of delivery for a new product) with the person who paid his or her consideration. Restrictive standing means that the entrepreneur does not have to go about identifying and negotiating with numerous third parties who were not original parties to the contract but would benefit from the performance of the contract as written. A restricted standing doctrine thereby reduces the transaction costs that entrepreneurs incur in revising their plans in the light of new knowledge, and it increases their flexibility in coping with change.

Restrictive standing also facilitates market processes and economic coordination by increasing the transferability of property rights. It enables entrepreneurs to reallocate resources from their current uses to the higher-valued uses that they discover. In addition, a restrictive standing doctrine secures economic freedom by reducing the threat of third-party interference in the right to exercise ownership in private property.

In contrast, modern statutes, such as the Clean Air Act in the USA, have significantly expanded standing from its narrow common law basis. They thereby limit the alienability of property (including pollution rights) and entrepreneurial freedom (Jensen *et al.* 1986).

More generally, within a legal system based on legislation, people are often less free and more vulnerable to the will of others – especially legislators, politicians, their advisers, lobbyists and bureaucrats. Individuals who occupy powerful official positions can seek to produce legislation that reflects their own personal aims or the preferences of sectional interests upon whose political support they rely. Consequently, this type of legal system provides entrepreneurs with less certainty than a common law tradition, as there is a greater chance of abrupt and unpredictable changes in the legal rules governing their behaviour:

The legal system centered on legislation, while involving the possibility that other people (the legislators) may interfere with our actions every day, also involves the possibility that they may change their way of interfering every day. As a result, people are prevented not only from freely deciding what to do, but from foreseeing the legal effects of their daily behavior.

(Leoni 1972: 8)

The problem is that the people and institutions that have the power to produce legislation also have the power to repeal it. '[L]egislation cannot guarantee its own permanence' (Sugden 1998: 489). The problem is magnified because a new legislative rule applies to the entire state or nation, not just a localised site where a court case is decided. In addition, because no single legislative group is able to conceive of all contingencies, precisely formulated statutes are likely to need revising as unanticipated developments unfold. Even though political institutions might create rights structures and practices, such as logrolling, that slow the rate of legislative change, statute law can still be expected to provide economic decision-makers with less stability than the common law. As a result, they are likely to perceive a weaker degree of contingency between actions and events so that their alertness is likely to be dampened.

Another important difference between these two processes of law-making is that flows of knowledge in centralised legal systems are much less dense and rich in detail than those in decentralised legal orders, and the flow is mainly in one direction from the top to the bottom:

In these respects a legal system centered on legislation resembles in its turn ... a centralized economy in which all the relevant decisions are made by a handful of directors, whose knowledge of the whole situation is fatally limited and whose respect, if any, for the people's wishes is subject to that limitation.

(Leoni 1972: 22)

In contrast, like a decentralised market system, the spontaneous common law process taps into a diffuse body of detailed knowledge of the circumstances of time and place that is unavailable to any single human mind or group of legislators. In the course of hearing cases, courts come to examine real-world practical problems in concrete terms. By depending on litigants' efforts in a case, the common law process draws upon richly contextual information otherwise only accessible to the parties. In addition, courts enjoy a significant informational advantage over a centralised group of legislators in observing the revealed preferences of parties under current legal rules (Parisi 2000: 3–4). For example, courts might observe that many contracting parties are opting out of a set of default rules currently provided by the legal system and are instead choosing alternative provisions that they perceive to be a lower-cost means of governing their relationship.

A general hypothesis advanced in this section has been that, other things being equal, people are likely to enjoy greater freedom in a common law system than in a legal system centred on legislation.[12] Indeed, the empirical evidence on the source of law and the extent of liberty corroborates the claim that the extent of liberty under common law is greater than that under codified legal systems (Scully 1992). Furthermore, and more anecdotally, seven of the ten most economically free nations in the world in 1999 (ranked by Gwartney and Lawson's (2001) Economic Freedom of the World index) are based on common law systems. The legal systems of Hong Kong, Singapore, New Zealand, the UK, the USA, Australia and Ireland are all based on English common law. (Rounding out the top ten, Switzerland, Luxembourg and the Netherlands are all based on civil law systems.)

### Common law under threat

Unfortunately, the traditional emphasis in the common law on abstract and general rules is being eroded by the expansion of administrative law and common law doctrines that favour a balancing of economic or social interests. The balancing method of legal reasoning mutes the signals of internal control that economic agents perceive, and it dulls their alertness to profit opportunities. The stimulus to this disturbing trend appears to be the emergence of the administrative and regulatory state, and the proliferation of legislation and bureaucratic discretion that comes with it. (The following explanation draws from Ackerman 1984: 9–18.) In many countries, there is now a multiplicity of different, if not conflicting, areas of laws that encroach upon almost every conceivable domain of human action. 'Specific-goal-oriented legislation, passed in an *ad hoc* piecemeal fashion, destroyed the idea of law as a seamless web' (Rizzo 1985: 882).

In addition, numerous administrative agencies, created by statute, have been granted far-reaching discretionary powers to make ad hoc decisions that affect the business and personal lives of individuals: '[T]his area of discretionary power touches upon the average person to a much greater extent than that area governed by rigid rules' (Hamowy 1971: 366). The discretion enjoyed by these agencies typically takes the form of balancing particular costs and benefits in the pursuit of specific policy goals. Moreover, in a further departure from the rule of law, these agencies are in practice subject to only limited judicial scrutiny.

The upshot is that, in response to growing pressure for consistency across the legal system, the rule-oriented approach in the common law is being displaced by cost–benefit (i.e. balancing) methods of legal reasoning that were prominent in the development of legislation. As a consequence, entrepreneurs' property and freedom are increasingly subject to the threat of interference by judicial decisions and the exercise of wide discretionary powers by officials. This has the effect of diminishing their sense of causal efficacy and their perceptual sensitivity to economic opportunities.

## Customary law

Customary rules are another source of law. A customary legal system is a spontaneous and highly decentralised process of law-making that has consequences for human agency and entrepreneurial alertness that are in some respects similar to those of the common law.

Customs are norms that emerge spontaneously outside the state's machinery for producing law. They are more than just behavioural regularities; they are internalised obligations or 'felt norms' that direct behaviour of members of a group (Cooter 1993: 426). A behavioural pattern that many people do not regard as socially necessary (e.g. shaking hands upon making someone's acquaintance) does not constitute a binding custom. In addition, in order to become a customary legal rule, a behavioural practice must receive widespread recognition and acceptance from members of the relevant social group (Pospisil 1971: 63–64). Reciprocities and the recognition of mutual benefits from cooperation play an important role in the formation of customs.

There are many historical examples of customary legal systems but the most impressive is medieval commercial law or the Law Merchant (*lex mercatoria*). This law was a dynamic system of evolving legal rules that was customarily produced, privately adjudicated and privately enforced. The medieval Law Merchant illustrates how the role reversibility of merchants (who are buyers one day, sellers the next) induced them to adopt mutually desirable rules that benefited them all. Customary medieval commercial law was subsequently absorbed into the common law. Its modern-day counterpart is the 'new' Law Merchant, which includes private international commercial law and the customary rules of international trade relating to negotiation, mediation and arbitration. The new Law Merchant also includes domestic private commercial law systems, such as that in the diamond and the cotton industries in the USA, which are enforced by trade associations through the use of private reputation-based sanctions (Bernstein 1992; 2001).

Customary law percolates up from the everyday practices of business communities. Customs are created by the independent choices and ongoing interactions of members of a social group. They evolve from the *spontaneous and voluntary* behaviour of individuals in society. Because the formation of customary law requires a very high level of participation and agreement among individuals affected by the rules of conduct, it serves to strengthen people's sense of personal causation and alertness: 'Individuals are bound by a customary rule only to the extent that they concurred – actively or through voluntary acquiescence – in the formation of the emerging practice' (Parisi 2001: 22–23). In the decentralised process of making customary law, individuals are free to assess for themselves the desirability of accepting alternative behavioural practices. They can express their preferences by adopting or not adopting behaviours that accord with various rules of conduct before these practices ripen into customary obligations.

Unlike other sources of law, the process for forming customary law does not require the participation of third-party decision-makers, such as judges and legislators, who are backed by the coercive powers of the state. 'In a customary law setting, the group of lawmakers coincides with the subjects of the law' (Parisi 2000: 2). Because the formation of customary law is not under the control of any single individual or group, customary legal rules cannot be designed to satisfy the ends of policy-makers or any coercive authority. Compared with statute-making, the process of custom formation is much less vulnerable to the arbitrary pressure of special-interest groups. The very high level of participation among individuals in the formation of enforceable customs reduces the scope for powerful incumbent interests to impose constraints on unwilling minorities and innovators. Consequently, customary legal rules are likely to emphasise individual freedom and private property and to conform to the requirements of the rule of law. 'Because the source of recognition of customary law is reciprocity, private property rights and the rights of individuals are likely to constitute the most important primary rules of conduct in such legal systems' (Benson 1990: 13).

Customary law requires much less force to maintain social order. It is not imposed or enforced from above by some coercive central authority or powerful minority. The threat of boycott or total expulsion from the relevant business community (and the potential reputational loss and forgone gains from repeated-dealing arrangements) is usually sufficient to obtain a member's compliance with customary dispute-resolution processes and rulings.

In order to address potential collective action and other problems in the enforcement of customary law, proposals have recommended combining the decentralised process of making customary law with centralised law enforcement by the state (e.g. Cooter 1994; 1996; de Soto 1989; 2000). Accordingly, the role of the state is to provide authoritative codifications of customs and to give them the full backing of its coercive power. These proposals, however, underestimate the knowledge problems that law-makers encounter in discerning the customs of specialised business communities and in evaluating the efficiency of incentive structures that produce social norms. They also ignore the dynamics of interventionism: once customary property rules are codified in public law, there is a risk that politicians and law-makers will seek to alter those rights and to transfer them to special interests.

In light of the problems with centralised law enforcement, some free-market advocates have proposed a fully privatised model of decentralised, customary law. In such a model, there is no government involvement in the production and enforcement of law. The enforcement of legal custom depends on the private initiative of aggrieved individuals who have a direct personal stake in a dispute. The strong signal that people must take personal responsibility for their affairs encourages highly internal LOC beliefs. Benson (1990) visualises private cooperative arrangements emerging to internalise the deterrent benefits of private enforcement of customary laws. The kinds of arrangements he has in mind include informal voluntary associations, private surety organisations and firms specialising in enforcement services. In addition, Friedman (1979) suggests that free-rider problems in enforcement will not emerge if the rights of aggrieved parties to seek restitution can be sold to specialised firms that are willing to pursue alleged offenders and collect fines.

In conclusion, the decentralised, bottom-up process involved in the formation of customary law is conducive to strong feelings of personal agency and more intense alertness. In this system, entrepreneurs and other business people have the capacity to regulate their own activities through their own customary practices and to form their own mechanisms to adjudicate disputes. The obligation to comply with customary law arises voluntarily from a mutual recognition by individuals that they perceive net benefits from participating in the legal system. Furthermore, entrepreneurs in a customary legal system are free from interference by legal authorities. The emphasis in these systems upon individual freedom, private property rights and voluntary cooperation through reciprocal arrangements reinforces an internal LOC and sustained alertness to opportunities.

## Freedom of entrepreneurial choice and concrete liberties

In the previous chapter, I examined the principle of freedom embodied in the rule of law. In this section, I investigate the unique character of the freedom of entrepreneurial choice and how it contrasts with the notion of freedom implicit in mainstream economics.

The standard conception of choice in economic theory identifies individual freedom with the power to achieve *given* goals. In mainstream economics, the ends between which the agent can select and the criteria of selection are given, as are the means to achieve each end. Freedom of choice in such circumstances is empty (Shackle 1969: 273). Individuals are denied the freedom to choose ends and means: they are not free to decide what to do or how to do it. Their freedom is limited to economising in the allocation of given means to achieve a set of given ends.

Moreover, in the world of mainstream economic models, the optimal course of action is determined uniquely by objective situational characteristics, such as costs, prices, consumer preferences and technology (Latsis 1972). The solution is implicit in the definition of the maximisation problem. 'Any other decision would have been unthinkable' (Kirzner 1982c: 142). This notion of freedom turns out to involve no choice at all: 'One has, in this conception of choice, in effect already chosen *before* the moment of decision' (Kirzner 1979: 227).

Such a restrictive view of freedom is totally inadequate as a basis for entrepreneurship and for explaining the role of freedom in the workings of the market economy. Apart from confusing freedom with power, this view of freedom *precludes* entrepreneurship in the sense of alertness to opportunities and the discovery and creation of *new* ends–means frameworks.

The freedom of entrepreneurial choice is a 'meta-freedom' in the sense that it applies to all the other freedoms, which relate to some or other aspect of choice. Kirzner has been the first to elaborate in detail this important perspective on freedom, though it clearly derives from the Misesian conception of human action. This broader perspective grants entrepreneurs far more than just the freedom to implement the optimum solution implied in some automatically known or given problem situation:

> Freedom of choice can now be seen to encompass the *liberty to make up one's own mind as to the ranking of ends to be pursued and the means judged available for the purpose.* Once a given ends–means framework has been adopted, freedom can only mean the freedom to achieve what one has already announced that one wishes to achieve. It is this narrow view of freedom that many economists seem to have adopted. But, with the acting man seen as approaching choice without having firmly adopted any one framework of ends and means, freedom of choice is at once seen as freedom to announce (i.e., to choose) what it is one wishes to achieve.
> …
>
> [T]he wider view of freedom recognizes that, when people refer to the freedom to choose, they have in mind liberty to select among a wide range of moral and value frameworks, of ethical systems, of tastes; to make their own guesses concerning present realities and future uncertainties; to determine for themselves what opportunities they are in fact confronted with.
>
> (Kirzner 1979: 226–227)

The entrepreneurial view of liberty emphasises how freedom of choice may evoke the discovery of opportunities that would be unthinkable to those to whom this freedom is denied. It stresses the open-endedness of an unimpeded market process. It also serves to warn us that the biggest perils arising from limiting freedom of entrepreneurial choice are likely to be hidden. As a general rule, individuals and groups cannot know what welfare losses have been suffered as a result of reducing entrepreneurial freedom, since no one can know what they (or the market) might have discovered in the absence of the constraint. Kirzner (1985) applies this important insight to examining the costs of regulating economic activity.

The law 'transmutes' the general principle of freedom into concrete liberties or rights. 'By means of this transmutation, the law economizes intangible freedom into tangible properties' (Dietze 1976: 115). In any particular society, the principle of freedom may or may not be applied to many kinds of human activity. Its application to property rights and contractual activity has already been discussed in the previous chapter. Table 5.1 lists some other freedoms, which are conjectured to be highly important to entrepreneurship. (Note that the inspiration for this table was Machlup (1969: 137) upon which its structure is heavily based.) These economic freedoms serve to secure a reliable sphere of unimpeded entrepreneurial action.

This list is not intended to be exhaustive. Indeed, by the very nature of liberty, it *cannot* be exhaustive. The definition of liberty and our knowledge of it are open ended. Over time, entrepreneurs and other market participants may discover and exercise liberties that have not yet been dreamed of:

> It also follows that the importance of our being free to do a particular thing has nothing to do with the question of whether we or the majority are ever likely to make use of that particular possibility. To grant no more freedom than all can exercise would be to misconceive its function completely. The freedom that will be used by only one man in a million may be more important to society and more beneficial to the majority than any freedom that we will all use.
>
> It might even be said that the less likely the opportunity to make use of freedom to do a particular thing, the more precious it will be for society as a whole. The less likely the opportunity, the more serious will it be to miss it when it arises, for the experience that it offers will be nearly unique. ... It is because we do not know how individuals will use their freedom that it is important.
>
> (Hayek 1960: 31)

Indeed, it might be that innovators come to create wealth by exercising freedoms that have hitherto been rarely exercised by other members of society. For example, an entrepreneur might be the first to see and seize the opportunity to trade with 'outsiders' from another culture. By using the freedom to have commercial dealings with strangers, the entrepreneur successfully adapts to new trading conditions and prospers relative to those who limit their opportunities to trading with 'insiders'. From an evolutionary perspective, the entrepreneur's behaviour and its imitation by less adventurous participants tend to have a positive impact upon the long-run adaptational prospects of human society (see Rizzo 1992b).

Many of the freedoms listed in Table 5.1 are conducive to the development of personal competence, internal LOC, personal agency and entrepreneurial alertness. It should also be noted that these freedoms are often connected. For example, the freedoms of choice of occupation and of consumption are so comprehensive in their scope that they *presuppose* or *include* several of the other freedoms in the list. In addition, although some of the freedoms may be independent of each other, others are *complementary* or *competing* in the sense that

*Table 5.1* A catalogue of economic freedoms important to entrepreneurship

| Freedom of | would mean that economic actors, including entrepreneurs, are free to: |
|---|---|
| Entrepreneurial choice | make their own discoveries, to discover and exploit perceived profit opportunities through arbitrage, speculation and innovation, 'to identify for themselves what the opportunities are which they may endeavor to grasp' (Kirzner 1992: 53) |
| | attempt to coordinate any transactions in any market in any place in any time period |
| | attempt to coordinate any kind of resources for any kind of venture in any industry or market |
| Achievement of rewards | 'seize benefit for themselves from the opportunities they have discovered' (Kirzner 1992: 54), to make profits, to appropriate the rewards of arbitrage, speculation and innovation |
| Trade | import or export any kind, quantity and quality of goods and services |
| | discover and exploit domestic and international price differentials for the 'same' commodities |
| | adjust prices, quantities and qualities bid or offered in response to new market conditions |
| Markets | buy or sell any quantity and quality at any mutually agreed price |
| Contract | pursue their interests through voluntarily making binding promises, however prudent or imprudent, with any other individual, group or organisation |
| Competition, entry and exit | enter (or exit from) any market or industry and compete as best they can, provided that they do not interfere with the freedom of others |
| | displace existing organisations and industries that fail to adapt to their environment |
| Choice of production | adjust the bundle of inputs and methods of production in order to exploit profit opportunities arising from imperfect coordination between factor and product markets |
| | choose a suitable location when starting a venture |
| Choice of marketing | promote, advertise and distribute anything in any way |
| Choice of occupation | enter the occupation of their choice, to become an entrepreneur, trader or a business person rather than to work in some other kind of occupation, and not to work at all |
| Movement | travel according to their own choice (within and across national boundaries), to make their residence anywhere they choose and to hire employees from other countries |
| Ownership | own and acquire property |

*Table 5.1 continued*

| Freedom of | would mean that economic actors, including entrepreneurs, are free to: |
|---|---|
| Choice of ownership form | choose the ownership form (limited liability company etc.) most appropriate to the individual circumstances of their ventures |
| Coalition and association | network with other entrepreneurs and economic actors and combine with anybody for any purpose not interfering with the freedom of others |
| Privacy and secrecy | develop and communicate their novel ideas without the oversight of any unwelcome party |
| | keep their entrepreneurial hunches and knowledge secret |
| Expression and speech | speak privately and publicly, to express their novel ideas in any tangible form (such as a business plan or prototype) and to print and publish on any subject whatsoever |
| Non-conformance | be different in behaviour, habits and business practices |
| Experimentation | try something new, to commission R&D in any field (including marketing research), to test their ideas, to make mistakes and fail, and to bear the consequences of their own errors |
| Search | investigate and acquire information on any subject by any method, except with use of violence, theft or fraud |
| Choice of consumption | purchase any goods or services that they choose to satisfy their current wants |
| Revision | change their plans and decisions made in the course of exercising any of the freedoms in this list (e.g. to revise their choices of occupation or of marketing) |

*Source*: Table is significantly adapted and expanded from Machlup (1969: 137)

more of one may allow either more or less of another. Thus, a greater degree of liberty in one sphere of human activity may make it either easier or harder to achieve freedom in another sphere (Machlup 1969: 128, 138).

## Empirical studies on economic freedom and economic performance

A key argument of this work is that economic freedom is conducive to entrepreneurship and competitive market processes. But what empirical evidence, if any, is there that economic freedom spurs entrepreneurial alertness? Unfortunately, there are as yet no empirical studies that directly investigate the impact of economic freedom on people's cognitions and entrepreneurial alertness. However, if we accept that entrepreneurship is the main driver of economic growth and development, then we might be able to gain insights indirectly from empirical research on the relationship between economic freedom and economic performance.

### Potential pitfalls

Unfortunately, empirical analysis in this area is bedevilled by problems that frustrate attempts to test hypotheses about the interplay between economic freedom and growth. The first significant problem has been the absence of a precise operational definition of economic freedom and a lack of a clear specification of the crucial components of economic liberty. This makes it difficult to classify particular countries according to the degree of government intervention in the economy. Economic freedom is a subtle and elusive concept. It represents a highly complex, multi-dimensional aspect of a country's institutions.

The second set of problems is concerned with how to measure economic freedom and in particular how to quantify and weigh the components of economic liberty. Because economic freedom is not one dimensional, no single statistic can fully reflect its many features. Thus, economic freedom cannot be captured merely by measuring the size of the state in a nation – typically measured as total government expenditures as a percentage of GDP. Instead, it is necessary to compare alternative forms of government involvement in the economy, and to assess how they change the economic incentives that individuals face and how they might violate economic freedom.[13]

Moreover, the level of economic freedom in nations can at best only be ranked in ordinal terms; it is not amenable to cardinal (absolute) measurement in terms of some unit or other. In other words, it might be possible to order countries by their degree of economic freedom but it is not possible to say by how much freedom differs between one nation and the next nation in the ranking.

There is also a lack of readily available data on the relevant components of economic freedom for a broad cross-section of countries and over a sufficiently long time span. Many dimensions of economic freedom are inherently difficult to quantify objectively across a large number of countries. For example, regulatory interventions are often complex, and their application is often subtle and idiosyncratic to a country, which makes it extremely difficult to quantify the effects of regulation objectively. Because data on many attributes of economic freedom are not available, it is often necessary to use various proxies for these attributes. 'These proxies may mirror the underlying element of liberty with some distortion' (Hanke and Walters 1997: 122).

The next problem is how to combine various components of economic freedom into a single summary measure for each nation. The problem is how to weight the components in order to construct aggregate indices of economic freedom. Different weighting techniques might yield different relative rankings of countries by their degree of economic freedom (Caudill *et al.* 2000; Scully and Slottje 1991). Similarly, the robustness of the statistical relationship between economic freedom and the growth rate of real per capita GDP depends crucially upon how freedom is measured (De Haan and Sierman 1998).

Another problem arises in connection with the protracted and variable time lags involved. How long will it take for the changes in public policy that impinge on economic freedom to affect the growth rate of output? 'The advantages that freedom brings are shown only by the lapse of time, and it is always easy to mistake the cause in which they originate' (de Tocqueville 1990b: 96). The time lag occurs because credibility in public policy is not immediate but must be secured over time, and the time period required depends upon historical factors and current political conditions (such as previous political instability and the strength of political opposition to policy initiatives already implemented). These time lags will weaken the empirical relationship between growth and changes in economic freedom in the short run. Thus, we need data for relatively long periods of time in order to test for a potential relationship between economic growth and economic freedom (both level and change).

## *Empirical findings*

Having explored the potential pitfalls in this area, we can now consider the various studies that have been conducted into the relationship between economic freedom and economic growth.

In the early studies, democracy was used as a proxy for individual freedom. Statistical evidence that democracy is conducive to economic growth is inconclusive at best. In their survey of political regimes and economic growth, Przeworski and Limongi (1993: 64) concluded that 'the simple answer to the question with which we began is that we do not know whether democracy fosters or hinders economic growth'. Their hunch is that 'political institutions do matter for growth, but thinking in terms of regimes does not seem to capture the relevant differences' (p. 51).[14] Barro (1996) analysed the interplay of political institutions and economic outcomes in a panel of about 100 countries from 1960 to 1990. After adjusting for various factors, including the initial level of GDP, he found that democracy has, overall, a weakly negative impact on economic growth. However, there was some suggestion that more democracy has a weak positive effect on growth for countries that start with low levels of political freedom.

Gastil and Wright were the first to try to develop direct systematic measures of *economic* freedom across countries (Wright 1982; Gastil 1984; Gastil and Wright 1988). Their overall measure of economic liberty is an aggregation of four separate sub-indices of economic freedom: the right to private property, the freedom of association, the freedom of internal and external travel, and the freedom of information. Building on Gastil and Wright's earlier work, Scully and Slottje (1991) developed broader measures of economic freedom that include fifteen attributes of economic liberty. They found a statistically significant and positive correlation between the level of economic liberty in a nation for the year 1980 and the average growth rate of real per capita GDP (RGDP) for the period 1950–1985. They reported that their results show that:

> [C]ountries that rank low with respect to their relative degree of economic freedom also have relatively low levels of economic growth and overall RGDP as a consumption share. The consistency of the results across all the rank indexes suggests *compelling evidence for a basic hypothesis that economic freedom is essential for economic development.*
>
> (Scully and Slottje 1991: 137–138; emphasis added)

Subsequent empirical investigations seek to develop much more comprehensive measures of economic freedom. The three major studies are conducted by the Economic Freedom Network (Gwartney and Lawson 2001), Freedom House (Messick and Kimura 1996) and the Heritage Foundation (O'Driscoll *et al.* 2001). The content and explanatory power of the economic freedom indices developed in these three studies have already been the subject of an extensive critical survey and need not be examined in detail here (see Hanke and Walters 1997).

For several reasons, the Economic Freedom Network's index (hereafter, the EFW index) is probably the best measure for grappling with issues concerning the institutional conditions for economic prosperity. It is the only economic freedom index that covers a substantial time period (1970–1999), which means that it is the only index that can be used to investigate the effect of changes in economic freedom on changes in levels of national income over the long run. In addition, the EFW index is based on transparent procedures that can be replicated by other researchers. The regular EFW index tries to avoid subjective assessments of variables and is derived almost exclusively from regularly published international data sources. It relies primarily on objective quantifiable variables that are used to develop finely calibrated ratings for each component for a large number of countries. Furthermore, the latest version of the EFW index employs an objective method for determining the weights that are used in constructing summary ratings of economic freedom – namely, principal component analysis (Gwartney and Lawson 2001: 7). This technique combines various attributes of economic liberty into a single summary measure that best reflects the original data. Moreover, in contrast to Freedom House's emphasis on democratic institutions and civil liberties as an essential dimension of economic freedom, the EFW index is a measure of economic freedom that deliberately excludes elements of political freedom.

In Gwartney and Lawson (2001), the regular EFW index comprises twenty-one components that are grouped into seven major categories: size of government, the structure of the economy and use of markets, monetary policy and price stability, freedom to use alternative currencies, legal structure and property rights, freedom to trade with foreigners, and freedom of exchange in capital and financial markets. 'Reliance on markets, sound money, legal protection of property rights, free trade, and market allocation of capital are important elements of economic freedom captured by the index' (Gwartney and Lawson 2001: 5).

Employing the EFW index, Gwartney and Lawson track changes in economic freedom of 123 countries during the last thirty years (1970–1999), where data are available. Higher ratings are given to countries with institutions and policies more consistent with economic freedom. In 1999, Hong Kong received the highest rating of 9.4 (out of 10), followed by Singapore (9.3), New Zealand (8.9), the UK (8.8) and the USA (8.7). In the sample, the five least-free economies are Myanmar (1.9), Algeria (2.6), the Democratic Republic of Congo (3.0), Guinea-Bissau (3.3) and Sierra Leone (3.5).

In their analysis of economic freedom and growth, Gwartney and Lawson first grouped all the countries into quintiles according to their 1999 EFW index. The EFW index for quintile groups was then related to national income (the level of per capita GDP, measured in 1998 purchasing power parity US dollars) and the rate of economic growth in the 1990s. While not rigorous, the results of this simple tabulation are consistent with those of Scully and Slottje (1991): more economic freedom is strongly correlated with higher levels of income and higher rates of economic growth. The top quintile of the most economically free nations has an average per capita real GDP of $19,846 and an average growth rate of per capita real GDP of 2.27 per cent over the period. Nations with lower levels of economic freedom tend to have lower incomes and rates of economic growth. The bottom, least-free quintile of countries had an average per capita real GDP of $2,210 and an average growth rate of minus 1.45 per cent.

The analyses of economic freedom and growth by Scully and Slottje (1991) and Gwartney and Lawson (2001) suffer from the same shortcoming: they both rely upon snapshots of the *level* of economic freedom in one year only. Such measures do not tell us anything about how long economic freedom in a nation has been at that level or whether it has been increasing or decreasing over time.

For a more rigorous econometric examination of the contribution of changes in economic freedom over time to the process of economic growth, we must turn to the study by Gwartney *et al.* (1999). They examined the determinants of the average annual growth rate in per capita real GDP during the period 1980–1995. Their sample comprised eighty-two countries and is fairly representative of the world's economies, except that a lack of data required them to omit the former Eastern bloc and other centrally planned economies, such as Cuba. Economic freedom was measured by an early, more restricted version of the EFW index.[15] Because they expected that changes in economic freedom would exert a lagged effect on growth, their models included as independent variables both the *level* of the EFW index in 1975 and the *change* in the index over the four subsequent five-year intervals.

The results of the study are striking and provide further evidence that an institutional framework that supports economic freedom is a key determinant of economic growth. The first finding is that there is a *strongly positive and robust correlation between changes in economic freedom (as measured by the EFW index) and economic growth*, and that this relationship holds even after taking into account the impact of other variables, such as investment in physical and human capital. 'Our analysis indicates that differences in economic freedom along with differences in investment in physical capital explain about 40 per cent of the variation in cross-country growth rates during the last two decades' (Gwartney *et al.* 1999: 652).

Of course finding a statistically significant correlation between economic freedom and growth is not proof that economic freedom causes growth. The correlation could arise because countries that grow faster tend to become freer. Though this alternative hypothesis seems reasonable, Gwartney *et al.* found no empirical support for this idea. Thus, the second important result of their study is that causation proceeds in one direction only: increases in economic freedom in a nation generate a faster rate of economic growth, but higher growth does not cause an increase in economic freedom in future years.

Another notable result of their regression analysis relates to the relative explanatory power of economic and political freedom. They found that economic freedom is a substantially more powerful determinant of economic growth than is political freedom (defined as the degree to which citizens are able to organise, participate and compete in the political process). More specifically, the components of the EFW index are much more strongly correlated with economic growth than are the components of political freedom, as measured by combining Freedom House's ratings of political and civil liberties for 1995–1996 (Karatnycky 1996). Political freedom explains little of the variation in growth rates across countries.

> This indicates that adoption of policies consistent with economic freedom – greater reliance on markets, freedom of exchange, openness of the economy, and monetary stability – is more important as a source of economic growth than the nature of the political regime.
>
> (Gwartney *et al.* 1999: 658)

In conclusion, the overall picture that emerges from empirical research is that greater economic freedom is a major determinant of higher rates of economic growth. The main ingredients of economic freedom are 'personal choice, protection of private property, and freedom of exchange' (Gwartney and Lawson 2001: 4). Societies which bind themselves to the principles of the rule of law, security of property rights, market coordination of resources, free trade and sound money grow faster than societies in which economic freedom is curtailed. Because many of the components of economic freedom are the result of public policy and explicit political decisions, it follows that the choice of institutional framework has immense consequences for economic prosperity and the wealth of nations. These empirical studies shed light on the positive effect on economic growth and development of institutions and policies that promote economic freedom. If we assume that entrepreneurial discovery is the basic microeconomic mechanism that generates growth within a particular institutional framework (Steele 1998: 52), these results thereby provide indirect evidence of the positive effect of market-oriented institutions on people's alertness to economic opportunities.

## Conclusion

The last two chapters have examined how the institutional framework moulds and determines people's agency beliefs and the degree of their entrepreneurial alertness. Economic freedom is considered to be the most important institutional principle for promoting entrepreneurship. The central hypothesis is that the more freedom people enjoy, the more likely they are to hold strong beliefs in their self-efficacy and to have an internal LOC, and the more acute will be their alertness to profit opportunities.

It has been argued that the extent of freedom individuals enjoy depends, among other things, on the constitutional rules that operate within a society. A maximum of freedom is most likely to be provided in a society based on the rule of law, a spontaneous and decentralised legal order that corresponds to this rule, laws that transmute economic freedom into tangible liberties, a system of private property rights and contracts, a depoliticised monetary system that facilitates economic calculation and political decentralisation of economic regulatory authority (so-called market-preserving federalism). It follows that entrepreneurship will prosper most in a society embodying these institutions. It is most likely to flourish within a framework that maximises everyone's freedom from coercion, compatible with equal freedom for all people.

Speculations in these chapters have been limited to the issue regarding the dependence of entrepreneurship and market processes on individual liberty. The analysis has not, as Kirzner (1992: 53–54) rightly points out, investigated the dependence of a liberal social order on entrepreneurial alertness to opportunities for enhancing market coordination.

Furthermore, the institutional analysis in this and the previous chapter is expressed in terms that are most applicable to industrial and post-industrial societies of the West and to relatively individualist cultural settings. Chapter 8 will address the question of whether the institutions identified as supportive of entrepreneurship are generally applicable across different cultural contexts. It argues that much of what is contained in these pages is directly relevant and capable of being adapted to the modern industrial societies of East and Southeast Asia and other group-oriented cultures.

# 6   Culture and alertness

> Entrepreneurship necessarily takes place within culture, it is utterly shaped by culture, and it fundamentally consists in interpreting and influencing culture. Consequently, the social scientist can understand it only if he is willing to immerse himself in the cultural context in which the entrepreneurial process occurs.
>
> (Lavoie 1991: 36)

## The entrepreneurial power of individualism, and cultural convergence

Investigations of culture and entrepreneurship commonly assume or argue that individualism and economic development (itself an entrepreneurially driven process) are intrinsically and ineluctably related to one another. This idea can be decomposed into two additional theses that may or may not be made explicit in any particular study:

1   Individualism is more conducive to (or, more strongly, is a necessary condition for) entrepreneurship and economic development in a modern economy. Consequently, individualist cultures and nations are more entrepreneurial than group-oriented ones.
2   As societies modernise and industrialise, the cultural values of their members tend to converge towards individualism. The process of modernisation dissolves group-oriented communities and cultures, and it promotes individualist values.

The first thesis, hereafter referred to as the *cornerstone hypothesis*, presents individualism as an *antecedent* to entrepreneurship and economic development. In contrast, the second thesis, the *convergence hypothesis*, presents individualism as a *consequence* of economic and other social processes through which societies develop and modernise.

### The cornerstone hypothesis

The distinctive individualism of Western culture can be argued to have provided a climate that was very congenial to the emergence of modern entrepreneurship and industrial capitalism. That individualism is a crucial element in modernisation[1] has, of course, been a conventional theme ever since Weber's seminal work. Weber (1930) argued that the Protestant emphasis on the enhancement of individuals and the rational pursuit of economic gain was a main source of rapid Western economic development. In particular, the Calvinist notion of demonstrating one's faith through the performance of good works in worldly activity spurred individuals to choose business as an occupation, thereby releasing and channelling their entrepreneurial energies and increasing entrepreneurial supply. According to at least one interpretation, Weber argued that the Protestant ethic[2] provided a necessary though not sufficient condition for the emergence of modern capitalism (Berger 1991b: 19). Hayek (1979: 161–163) too seems to argue that modernisation requires Westernisation and that the market economy requires a cultural substratum comprising individualist rules of conduct.

In addition, the belief that individualist cultures are more entrepreneurial than group-oriented ones is a 'cornerstone of entrepreneurship theory and research' in the organisational sciences (Tiessen 1997: 368). For example, Shane (1993) tested the hypothesis that individualist societies are more innovative than group-oriented societies. Having controlled for national differences in industrial structure and per capita income, he found that national rates of innovation (as measured by per capita numbers of trademarks granted in the US market and world markets) were significantly associated with Hofstede's (1980) index of individualism in 1975 but not in 1980. He concludes that 'the positive relationship between innovation and individualism suggests that the possession of the beliefs that individualism represents – autonomy, independence and freedom – make some countries more innovative than others' (p. 70).

In his review of firm-level studies, Tiessen reports that international research into the founders of business start-ups also shows a strong association between individualism and entrepreneurship (p. 372).[3] In general, entrepreneurs in this line of enquiry are narrowly defined as individuals who start a stand-alone business. For instance, in their cross-cultural study of value differences between entrepreneurs and non-entrepreneurs in eight (mostly Western) countries, McGrath *et al.* (1992a) reported that 'in a number of quite different societies, entrepreneurship is associated with high individualism' (p. 133). They found support for the thesis that entrepreneurs (business founders) generally hold individualist values when compared with non-entrepreneurs, so that 'entrepreneurs favor independent action and separation from groups and clans', no matter what the cultural orientation of the broader society (p. 131).

Similar results were reported by Holt (1997: 495) and McGrath and MacMillan (1992). In fact, Holt suggests that if the similarity between the value systems of mainland Chinese entrepreneurs and of US entrepreneurs reflects changes occurring in China's transition, then 'it is possible that convergence is beginning to occur, although on a parsimonious scale'

(p. 500). This brings us to the second hypothesis for consideration, the convergence hypothesis.

## The convergence hypothesis

The convergence hypothesis relates to the dynamics of cultural change. It assumes that, with sufficient diffusion of technology and the appropriate introduction of other resources, all societies will go through a similar growth process and will come to share characteristics (including cultural values and patterns of social relatedness) that are typical of modern societies in Western Europe and North America. 'Modernization, then, in the essentialist view of evolution, was seen as a convergent process wherein all societies as they developed were assumed to become more alike' (Greenfield and Strickon 1981: 494–495). All societies are expected to have a common destination, regardless of the uniqueness of their cultural origins.

Hayek (1979; 1988) too explained the emergence of individualism within an evolutionary framework. Although Hayek (1976: 27) accepts that many societies exist which subscribe to very different systems of rules, he suggests that the general and abstract rules of conduct in individualist society tend to prevail over the practices of the 'tribal' or 'small-group' society, which he sees as encompassing aggressiveness towards strangers, within-group solidarity and striving towards common concrete goals. According to Hayek, the latter values evolved very early on in humanity's cultural history. Individualist norms and precepts have displaced many small-group values and have spread throughout Western civilisation because the groups that adopted individualist values prospered more than other groups and grew:

> Some economists, most notably Hayek, have seen the importance of the cultural correlates of a market economy as an important element in its functioning, with Hayek even arguing for a form of cultural evolution that has in an unplanned and unintended way led to a move from a Stone Age culture, with its sense of community and shared purpose, to a modern culture where there is respect for abstract rules, such as the rule of law, and 'a detachment from communal cooperative ends'.
>
> (Lal 1998: 5)

## Past critique of received view

The convergence hypothesis has been subject to strong criticism.[4] Critics argue that processes of economic development and modernisation in different countries are unique, diverse and open-ended. Socio-cultural change is not assumed to be directional or convergent. The position is well summarised by Abraham:

> [T]he theory of convergence, or what Lauer calls the fallacy of unidirec-
> tionality, which postulates that the end product of modernization in
> developing countries is the Western type 'modern' industrialized
> society, not only rests on false premises but also draws dangerously erro-
> neous conclusions. ... The experience of Japan, which modernized itself
> while maintaining and utilizing premodern traditional institutions ...
> not only questions the notion of the antithesis between tradition and
> modernity ... but also rejects the unilinear assumption underlying
> various models of modernization.
>
> (Abraham 1980: 249–250)

Thus, the belief that the relationship between individualism and
entrepreneurial capitalism (or, more generally, modernity) is universal has
been challenged in recent decades by the development path of Japan, as
Abraham observes, as well as the track records of several other East Asian
nations, namely, the 'four little tigers': Taiwan, South Korea, Hong Kong
and Singapore. During the second half of the twentieth century, these
economies achieved spectacular economic success in world markets and
became a major force in international trade, industrial and textile production, banking and technological development. Making a success of
entrepreneurial capitalism in the modern global economy does not, it seems,
require economies to converge towards a specific set of cultural values.
Capitalism permits differences in cultural traits and patterns of behaviour to
endure.

Indeed, the blossoming of an entrepreneurial drive in these East Asian
societies is sometimes explained as having occurred because of, rather than
in spite of, some aspect of their group-oriented cultures, whether it be the
key tenets of Confucianism, East Asian Buddhism or Chinese folk religion.
Studies refer to the 'entrepreneurial power' of Confucian values and practices
(Harrison 1992: 85), 'entrepreneurial familism' (Wong 1985) and the
future-oriented, economically dynamic mindset of 'Confucian work
dynamism' (Chinese Culture Connection 1987).

Moreover, the industrialisation of these societies has not led to a convergence towards individualism across all domains. 'The "Five Tigers" were
adopting and modifying the technological knowledge of the West, but were
not forgetting their traditional [cultural] psychologies. Change was encouraged and promoted, but the cultural psyche was not sacrificed' (Marsella and
Choi 1993: 204). The focus in these societies is still upon the family, clan,
work group, firm, school or other in-group. They still prize a group orientation rather than individuality. In Japan, for instance, people have in general
retained a non-individualist, interdependent conception of self as their
economy and society have undergone dramatic transformation (Yamaguchi
1994): 'Thus the Japanese have been able to adjust to the needs of *modernization without westernizing their selves*' (Lal 1998: 150; emphasis added).
Similarly, a survey study of two generations of South Koreans has shown

that, in spite of changes towards individualism in some domains, the great majority of Korean adults, whether young or old, endorse group-oriented values, such as the acceptance of relational obligations and in-group favouritism (e.g. preferential treatment of school alumni) (Cha 1994). They remained 'largely collectivist rather than individualist in absolute terms' (p. 173). Ho and Chiu (1994) report a similar overall result for Hong Kong university students.

More generally, Peter Berger makes a similar observation about the constancy of group-oriented values in East Asia:

> [I]t can plausibly be argued that East Asia, even in its most modernized sectors, continues to adhere to values of *collective solidarity* and discipline that strike the Western observer as very different indeed from his accustomed values and patterns of conduct. ... Could it be that East Asia has successfully generated a *non-individualistic* version of capitalist modernity? If so, the linkage between modernity, capitalism and individualism has not been inevitable or intrinsic; rather it would have to be reinterpreted as the outcome of contingent historical circumstances.
>
> (Berger 1988: 6; emphasis added)

Although the crises of the Asian economies in the late 1990s highlighted severe weaknesses in their legal and financial systems and the nature of business–government relations, these events still do not undermine the fact that processes of entrepreneurship and economic development in industrial societies can assume cultural forms quite different from that in the West.

> Asia will continue to modernize and, in doing so, will produce forms and practices that are distinctive. ... Cultural differences will endure, and in most cases *there is little point in trying to say which cultures are superior and which ones inferior*.
>
> (Pye 2000: 255; emphasis added)

The convergence thesis is also brought into question by empirical entrepreneurship research in the organisational sciences. McGrath *et al.* (1992b) undertook a cross-cultural study comparing the values of entrepreneurs (defined as new business founders) from the People's Republic of China, Taiwan and the USA. They found that the two groups of Chinese entrepreneurs continue to share a group-oriented perspective for six of the eight discriminating items related to individualism–collectivism. In none of the items related to individualism did the Taiwanese entrepreneurs score significantly closer to the US sample than to the mainland Chinese sample of entrepreneurs.

> Our interpretation is therefore that along the individualism/collectivism dimension of culture, collectivist values are generally highly enduring –

50 years of exposure to very different ideologies [i.e. political, economic and social interventions] has done little to break down the traditional collectivist Chinese culture that is each group's heritage.

(p. 452)

## The approach in this chapter

The theory developed here is a preliminary step towards an account of why and how different cultures might promote a high degree of alertness and why significant cultural diversity can be expected to persist even among advanced capitalist societies. More specifically, and in contrast to the corner-stone and convergence hypotheses, the approach in this chapter explains why we can expect a subset of group-oriented cultures to be highly entrepreneurial and why we do not expect all market-based economies to converge on a single dominant pattern of individualist values. '[T]here is no inexorable convergence of countries towards greater individualism in values with the march of time and progress' (Smith and Bond 1993: 216). The approach acknowledges the possibility of 'multiple adaptive peaks' in evolu-tionary processes (Gould and Lewontin 1994: 84) – that is, it recognises that cultures can develop along different evolutionary paths to that of Western civilisation and still survive and prosper. In the language of Freeman (2000), the approach emphasises 'diversified' rather than 'single-peaked' capitalism. The underlying premise is that divergent cultures that we observe in the world today would not have survived to this point if they were absolutely lacking in entrepreneurship and adaptability to changes in economic condi-tions.[5] 'Casual empiricism reveals a wide degree of cultural variety consistent with the survival of a group in the modern world' (Vaughn 1984: 126).

The observation that economic development and modernisation may assume significantly different cultural forms raises the question: could it be that a society's path towards economic prosperity depends at least in part on entrepreneurs discovering and exploiting those aspects of its culture(s) that constitute its *comparative cultural advantages* (given the institutional and situ-ational context)? Following Lavoie and Chamlee-Wright (2000: 64–67), this chapter takes the view that each society has cultural characteristics particular to its own circumstances that might influence how entrepreneurship is manifested and how markets are coordinated and that might therefore promote different patterns of economic development.[6] Each society can prosper economically by taking advantage of its own cultural traditions and heritage. Just as two countries with a comparative advantage in two different products can trade those products to their mutual benefit, so too can each country benefit from focusing on those entrepreneurial activities in which its culture gives it relative strengths (Berger 1988: 11). 'Comparative advantage is a *story of diversity*; of gains that come from differing from one's neighbor, not from aping him' (Freeman 2000: 5; emphasis added).

Accordingly, the approach adopted here suggests that we need to reject the notion that individualism or communalism (i.e. group orientation, collectivism) per se is either categorically pro- or anti-entrepreneurship. That is, we need to acknowledge that the cornerstone hypothesis can lead us badly astray. Individualist and group-oriented cultures neither inherently promote nor inhibit processes of entrepreneurial discovery. The distinctive individualism generated in the West is neither a necessary nor a sufficient condition for the emergence of entrepreneurial alertness. More generally, there is no universal, contextually independent scale by which one can assess and rank the dominant culture of an entire nation in terms of its 'entrepreneurial content' or 'growth-friendliness', as do Casson (1990) and Harrison (1992): 'It is unscientific to try to draw up a universal list of positive and negative cultural values for economic development. What may be positive in some circumstances can be quite counterproductive under other conditions' (Pye 2000: 255). Lavoie and Chamlee-Wright (2000: 62) refer pejoratively to such exercises in scoring national cultures according to their entrepreneurial content as 'checklist ethnography'.

This chapter focuses upon just one, though crucial, aspect of the complex phenomenon of culture – namely, *different construals of selfhood* – and how they affect the supply of entrepreneurial alertness. The analysis distinguishes between two notions, the *independent* and *interdependent* self, and it examines the key differences between them. The independent self represents how people in an individualist cultural group typically define themselves. The interdependent self is the corresponding conception for group-oriented cultures. This distinction is considered to be one of the most important and deeply rooted sources of cultural variation. Cultural self-conceptions are culturally evolved rules that are of a very general and basic nature. The specifics of any particular culture's comparative advantages will depend, at least partially, upon the conception of self that is most prevalent in that culture.

## The impact of cultural self-conceptions on psychological determinants of alertness

An important mechanism by which cultural self-conceptions influence entrepreneurial alertness is through their effects on people's cognitive processes. More specifically, how personhood is construed in a particular culture affects the *structure*, *content* and possibly the *intensity* of people's agency beliefs. Chapter 3 argued that personal agency beliefs are cognitive factors that can switch on and direct alertness. It explained how these beliefs are an amalgam of perceptions of *locus of control* (LOC) and *self-efficacy*. That is, one's subjective perceptions of personal agency ('What is *my* causal power over events?') combine two sets of expectations: (i) LOC beliefs about whether actions influence outcomes ('Are target events contingent upon doing $x$?'); and (ii) self-efficacy beliefs about whether one can produce the relevant actions ('Can I do *x*?'). The main proposition of Chapter 3 was that the degree of alertness of people is an increasing function of the strength of their agency beliefs.

This chapter investigates how the effects on alertness of alternative cultural self-construals are *mediated* by people's perceptions of agency. As mediator variables, personal agency beliefs represent a causal, generative mechanism through which culture influences entrepreneurship. Thus, culture causes personal agency beliefs, which in turn cause alertness.

The chapter considers in detail how different cultural notions of person-hood might affect various aspects of people's agency beliefs, the main cognitive drivers of entrepreneurial alertness. Indeed, how we conceive our selves might affect how we conceive of the very notions of 'agency', 'control' and 'efficacy' in the first place. For instance, what does 'personal agency' mean to people within different cultures? Cultural differences in self-conceptions might lead individuals in one group or society to think of agency as primarily about changing the environment to fit the self's needs, while people in another group or society might view agency as mainly about changing themselves to fit their environment.

In addition, the chapter examines how independent and interdependent self-conceptions affect the meaning and sources of internal control within a culture. Do people perceive internal control as stemming solely and directly from the inner self, or do they perceive internal control as extending to indi-rect sources, such as other in-group members who are extensions of themselves and over whom they have some control? Do self-conceptions affect the culturally dominant perception of the *degree* of contingency between actions and intended outcomes (i.e. people's LOC expectations)?

Another issue is how differences in cultural self-conceptions affect the meaning of efficacy within cultures. Does efficacy inhere in individuals and/or social groups? How does variation in cultural notions of personhood affect people's perceptions of their competency to produce relevant actions? Are there cultural differences in situational influences on efficacy beliefs, and thereby on alertness?

### *The impact of cultural self-conceptions upon the unit and character of alertness*

As explained later, the two notions of selfhood also influence how entrepreneurship is manifested and the nature of the opportunities that entrepreneurs discover. They determine in part the different channels through which entrepreneurship is likely to proceed in different societies. In particular, they determine the most prevalent *unit* or *locus* of alertness within a cultural group: 'The typical entrepreneur will reflect the specific cultural context out of which he or she emerges' (Lavoie and Chamlee-Wright 2000: 70). The notion of selfhood dominant in a culture determines the definition, structure, boundaries and character of the entity that does the perceiving and discovering of profit opportunities in that culture. In an individualist culture, the most common unit of alertness is the *independent, autonomous person*. In contrast, the primary centres of alertness in a group-oriented culture are *interdependent members of an in-group*. These two units of alertness are different units of analysis: they are different entities, they behave according to different rules, and their 'mental models' differ.

Cultural construals of the self give *form and direction* to people's alertness and entrepreneurial potential:

> Entrepreneurship is not only a matter of opening one's eyes, of switching on one's attentiveness; it requires *directing* one's gaze. ... And this raises the question of what gives a *predirectedness* to the entrepreneur's vision, of why he is apt to read some things and not others. I submit that the answer to this question is culture.
>
> (Lavoie 1991: 46; emphasis added)

Cultural differences in the degree of people's autonomy and social embeddedness affect the *character* of alertness to opportunities. In individualist cultural groups, independent selves are alert to opportunities that are relevant to *direct, personal gain*. Their alertness is *solely self-referential*. In addition, alertness is commonly manifested in *individual entrepreneurship*. Independent selves have a tendency to be more alert to entrepreneurial opportunities for litigation, opportunities for the application of new commitment devices that reduce principal–agent problems, and opportunities requiring a nexus of formal, legal arrangements or contracts.

In communalist cultural groups, the alertness of interdependent selves is multi-layered and multi-dimensional. Their alertness has both *role-referential* and *group-referential* aspects. Interdependent selves each exhibit alertness to opportunities relevant to the successful fulfilment of their own roles in the group ('micro-alertness'). They may also exhibit alertness to profitable opportunities for collective action by the in-group as a whole ('macro-alertness'). The alertness of interdependent selves is manifested in *collective or corporate entrepreneurship*. Group-oriented entrepreneurs are likely to be more alert to opportunities for leveraging resources through informal networks and to be more vigilant of opportunities requiring consensus decision-making and teamwork. They are likely to be more alert to opportunities for non-legal conflict resolution.

Table 6.3 (pp. 157–160) summarises the impact of different self-conceptions on various aspects of entrepreneurship, such as the primary locus of alertness, the scope for entrepreneurship, the nature of opportunities discovered, the dominant situational influences on alertness and entrepreneurial discovery, the entrepreneur's prior local knowledge, innovative activity, modes of conflict resolution, the speed of entrepreneurial decision-making, and entrepreneurial contracting and its enforcement.

*Caveats*

The focus of this chapter is upon independent selves (i.e. individualists) and interdependent selves (i.e. communalists) and the cultural groups within a society that exemplify these categories of personhood. Where possible, we must try to avoid relying – as do some versions of the cornerstone and convergence hypotheses – upon a grossly aggregated, homogeneous notion of national culture that is employed in crude comparisons that, for example, describe the USA as 'individualist' and Japan as 'communalist' or 'collectivist'. One estimate is that there are around 10,000 cultures in the world, compared with 192 independent countries (Triandis 1995: 3–4). Thus, many nations comprise many cultures and subcultures. Nations are 'systems of interacting cultures' rather than unified cultures (Lavoie and Chamlee-Wright 2000: 59). On occasion, however, this chapter unavoidably resorts to the nation-state as the unit of analysis, especially when reporting on the findings of others.

At the outset it is important to note that within societies and nations there might be significant cultural variation. In addition, there are people who hold interdependent values residing in individualist cultures, and people who hold independent beliefs living in group-oriented cultures, though the proportions of each in both cultures vary. Moreover, any particular person, whether in an individualist or a group-oriented culture, is likely to be a mix of independent and interdependent aspects. 'Self-conceptions embody both personal and collective facets, although their relative emphasis will vary depending on the type of culture in which people are raised' (Bandura 1997: 32).[7] For instance, Indian culture and the Indian sense of self display a juxtaposition of individualist and communalist orientations. In considering the Indian culture and psyche, Sinha and Tripathi (1994: 134) write that 'individualism and collectivism often coexist in individuals' behavior, and ... the cultural system reflects both these elements as well'. In particular, they found that group-oriented values are prominent in family contexts (namely, extended family and kinship ties) but that Hindu religion and ethics emphasise realisation of the self through individual-based discipline, self-control and meditation (pp. 130–132). Similarly, Ho and Chiu (1994) found that the form of communalism in Hong Kong contains strands of individualism in its endorsement of self-reliance (but not self-interest narrowly defined).

Another caveat is that the approach adopted in this chapter does not stress reciprocal causation. It construes culture as an antecedent condition that has an impact upon the cognitive processes of human agency and alertness. Consequently, the analysis does not take account of important feedback mechanisms by which personal agency beliefs, entrepreneurial behaviour and economic development can affect culture. For example, it does not explain how cultural change can be brought about by the successful imitation of 'maverick' entrepreneurs who profitably breach well-established moral codes (such as prohibitions against trading with members of a foreign culture) when those moral rules no longer help people to adapt to economic changes. Reciprocal causation is discussed more fully in Chapter 8.

A final note of caution relates to terminology. *The terms 'group orientation', 'communalism' and 'collectivism' are used interchangeably.* In many respects it would be preferable to refrain from using the term 'collectivism', with its connotations of dictatorial political systems and central economic planning, but the term is now so well established in the cross-cultural literature (especially in analyses of the 'individualism–collectivism dimension') that to avoid using it proves difficult. *In any case, 'collectivism' in this context does not refer to 'forced', state-imposed collectivism.* It does not mean a planned economic system in which a centralised hierarchical body attempts to determine crucial economic processes and in which the state owns all the means of production and distribution.

Similarly, group orientation or collectivism should not be conflated with a high degree of hierarchy in human relations. Although collectivism is empirically correlated with power distance, collectivism as a construct does not necessarily involve hierarchical organisation, with its emphasis upon vertical (e.g. top–down) relationships and authority, an acceptance of asymmetry in social status and of the privileges of high rank. For instance, there are variants of communalism, such as Israeli kibbutzim, that are 'horizontal' in that they emphasise oneness with in-group members, discomfort with 'standing out', similarity of status, and unease with dominating other members of the in-group (Triandis 1995: 44–46).

Furthermore, individualist cultures are not necessarily horizontal in all domains. *Within* the class of individualist groups, some groups may exhibit *relatively* vertical relations in some situations, such as commerce, when compared with the typical individualist culture. However, it should be noted that even 'vertical' individualist cultures might be relatively horizontal when compared with most (but not necessarily all) group-oriented cultures.

## Variation in cultural conceptions of the self

### Defining culture

In line with recent thinking in cultural anthropology and psychology, I place little emphasis on 'material' culture and its external manifestations, such as inherited artefacts. Instead, I focus upon 'subjective' or 'mental' culture – the 'software of the mind', to use Hofstede's (1991) evocative phrase. Cultural and social phenomena are largely mental phenomena: 'without the contact of mind with mind, they would not exist' (Davis 1948: 6).

For the purpose of studying the cultural context of entrepreneurship, I choose to adopt a contemporary social science definition of culture as 'a *complex system of shared symbols* that expresses and that regulates codes of conduct that sustain particular forms of human sociality' (McGavin 1993: 96; emphasis added). I maintain that the essential core of culture consists in the underlying values, moral principles, beliefs, norms, roles and cognitive styles that are shared to some degree by members of a human social group.

The fundamental value priorities prevalent in a society are at the very heart of culture and have a major impact upon entrepreneurship. Values (in the form of both moral prohibitions and ideals) pervade an individual's overall conception of self: 'Cultural traditions ... regulate ... the human psyche, resulting in ethnic divergences in mind, self and emotion' (Shweder 1990: 1). How one conceives oneself and one's relationship to others is intimately tied to the values and ethics of one's own cultural group.

Culture is a 'packaged variable' (Whiting 1976). It must be unbundled if we are to use it as an explanatory construct in our analyses of entrepreneurship and in our critical appraisal of the cornerstone and convergence hypotheses. The approach here unbundles and operationalises the concept of culture by focusing on higher-order dimensions of values that are appropriate for comparing cultures.

In particular, this chapter takes individualism–collectivism (I/C) to be the most critical high-order dimension for understanding differences in entrepreneurship across diverse cultures around the world. (To this extent, at least, the approach is in accord with the cornerstone and convergence hypotheses.) Individualist values emphasise giving priority to personal goals, independence, personal achievement and competition. Collectivist (i.e. group-oriented) values stress giving priority to group interests, interdependence, group achievement and cooperation with other in-group members (Triandis 1995).

The I/C dimension has so far proven to be the most coherent, integrated and empirically testable dimension of cultural variation in values (Kim *et al.* 1994b: 2). However, the I/C continuum is a very broad dimension that can be defined more precisely in terms of more specific types of values. Most significantly for present purposes, the central feature of the I/C dimension pertains to the issue of the independence (autonomy) vs. interdependence (embeddedness) of the person vis-à-vis the group. Thus, at a fundamental level, individualist and group-oriented cultural values reflect how people in a particular cultural setting define themselves and how they experience their personhood:

> [A major theme of the I/C dimension] concerns thinking about or *construing the self as an independent entity* motivated by personal standards *or as an interdependent part of social groups* motivated by social expectations.
>
> (Smith and Schwartz 1997: 88; emphasis added)

In essence, the I/C dimension reflects people's views on whether they see themselves as independent, bounded, autonomous individuals, or as interdependent persons who are inseparable from their social relationships. In psychological lingo, these two views are referred to as the *independent* and *interdependent* conceptions of the self, and these constructs are taken to be the most significant source of cultural differences.

## *The self as a cultural artefact*

The conception of self is a crucial element of a cultural group's 'subjective culture' (to the extent that it is shared by members of that group) (Triandis 1972). It reflects the shared understanding of what it means to be human. The self-concept is not just influenced by culture; it is deeply culturally constructed. Self-conceptions are highly symbolic constructions that are artefacts of the cultural system of symbolic meaning. Developments in cultural psychology suggest that our construal of self is a social construction generated by our active participation in the practices and shared meanings (including values and norms) of particular cultural contexts. It is influenced and constrained by the patterns of social interaction with parents, peers, teachers, and so forth, that are characteristic of a particular culture. There is no such thing as a *human* nature independent of culture (Geertz 1973: 49). Without culture, there is no person or self, there is only a biological entity. Hayek (1979: 157) made a similar point in his analysis of the concurrent evolution of mind and culture: without mind, no civilisation; but equally significantly, no mind without civilisation.

Self-conceptions are an integral part of personality. They affect how we construe the qualities and attributes of being a person. They underpin our social identity and influence how we act and handle different situations in the social and economic sphere.

How personhood is conceived in a particular culture is clearly related to the most prevalent unit of decision-making (or agency) in that society. Is it the autonomous individual or an interdependent self embedded in a close social group? 'One cannot … simply assume [autonomous] individuals are always and everywhere agents, because one's ideological predilections encourage one to think this must be the case' (Davis 2001: 121). Similarly, as discussed later, the cultural construal of self also has a bearing on the nature of the entity that does the discovering and exploiting of profit opportunities. Is it an independent entrepreneur acting autonomously or interdependent members of an entrepreneurial team?

Cultural groups differ in their conceptions of selfhood and have divergent views of the relationship between 'the self' and 'others'. By emphasising individual autonomy or interpersonal connectedness, a culture both expresses and regulates how people in a society construe themselves and it can thereby potentially affect cognitive functioning, including alertness to opportunity.

## The independent self

As mentioned already, empirical research in cross-cultural psychology and anthropology draws the distinction between two cultural conceptions of self-hood: the *independent* and *interdependent* self. Table 6.1 summarises the key differences between these two ways of thinking about the self that are found in different cultural groups.

*Table 6.1* Key differences between cultural conceptions of the independent and interdependent self

| Feature | Independent conception of self | Interdependent conception of self |
|---|---|---|
| Definition of the self | The person is an autonomous entity, existing independently of society | The person is an inseparable part of a larger social whole |
| | A person's identity is not rooted in, or bounded by, social context or group membership | The characteristics of one's clan or social group are an integral part of one's personal identity |
| | Weak dependency of each individual on any specific group | Strong dependency of each person on his or her in-group |
| | Clear, strong boundaries between the self and others | Fluid, augmented boundaries – relationships with close in-group members included in boundaries of the self |
| | Knowledge of inner self is more detailed than knowledge about other people (Greenwald and Pratkanis 1984) | Knowledge of inner self is less elaborated than knowledge of other in-group members and the self's relationship to them (Markus and Kitayama 1991) |
| Perceptual and cognitive focus of the self | Perceptions focus on individuals; relationships and groups are in the background | Perceptions focus on relationships and groups; individuals are in the background (Triandis 1994a: 167) |
| | Egocentricism | Socio-centricism or in-group egoism (rather than altruism) |
| | The individual is the unit of analysis in both the evaluation of ends and the selection of means | Ends are evaluated and means chosen on the basis of their consequences for the in-group and the fulfilment of one's social role |
| | Personal goals have priority and often conflict with group goals | In-group goals have priority or overlap personal goals |
| | Cognitions are context independent | Cognitions are context dependent (Triandis 1994b: 47) |
| | Cognitions focus upon inner, private thoughts, feelings, attitudes, personal needs and abilities | Cognitions focus upon the self in relation to specific others, social roles, relationships, statuses, norms, obligations, duties and the needs of the in-group |

*Table 6.1 continued*

| Feature | Independent conception of self | Interdependent conception of self |
|---|---|---|
| | Explanations of individual behaviour focus upon the actor's general dispositions, traits and inner attributes (Miller 1984) | Explanations of individual behaviour focus upon the actor's social role and interpersonal relationships |
| Stability and consistency of the self | Personality and individual behaviour are supposed to be stable over time and across different situations | Personality and individual behaviour are supposed to vary over time and across different situations |
| Cultural values | Autonomy; freedom of individual thought, feeling and action; mastery over nature; assertiveness; ambition; creativity; stimulating activity; self-reliance; separation from family and community; individual achievement; and material success (Bellah *et al.* 1996; Schwartz 1994) | Dynamic orientation towards the future, perseverance in obtaining long-term goals, group achievement, harmony in interpersonal relations, respect for tradition, modesty, reciprocity of favours, and unity with nature (Chinese Culture Connection 1987; Hofstede 1991; Schwartz 1994) |
| Rights conception | Individuals are endowed with independent legal, moral and religious rights | Rights are more likely to adhere to various social entities or positions |
| | Rights are ascribed to individuals, apart from and prior to their entering into social relationships | Rights are subordinate elements of more basic norms governing social relationships and are ascribed to social roles and relationships rather than individuals |
| | Rights are primarily rights *against* others in the society and the threats they present | Rights are primarily rights held because of one's *connection with* others in associational webs of the society |
| Culturally mandated tasks of the self | Be unique, express oneself, promote one's own goals, develop one's potential | Belong, restrain oneself, occupy and fulfil one's proper role within the in-group, promote in-group's goals (Markus and Kitayama 1991) |
| Exemplary cultures | Anglo-American, Anglo-Celtic, Australian, English, Dutch, New Zealand European, Swedish, French | Japanese, Han Chinese, Korean, Taiwanese, Thai, Balinese, Malay, Samoan, Maori (New Zealand), Greek, Turkish, Berber (Morocco), Yoruban (Nigeria), Akan (Ghana), Kikuyu (Kenya) |

The first conception of the self sees the individual as a 'self-contained, individuated, separated, independent self defined by clear boundaries from others' (Kagitçibasi 1997: 19). The person is a 'bounded, coherent, stable, autonomous, free entity' (Markus and Kitayama 1998: 68). The independent view typically means that the self is conterminous with the body: 'a sense of self with a sharp boundary that stops at one's skin and clearly demarks self from nonself' (Spence 1985: 1288). As independent selves, we believe that we are each separate from each other and from the group.

Geertz provides an eloquent, and now classic, description of this way of thinking about the self:

> [The person is] a bounded, unique, more or less integrated motivational and cognitive universe, a dynamic center of awareness, emotion, judgment, and action organized into a distinctive whole and set contrastively both against other such wholes and against a social and natural background.
>
> (Geertz 1975: 48)

The cultural model of the person as an independent entity sees the self as a distinct configuration of qualities and characteristics that is integrated into a single, coherent package. 'Others are typically cast as part of the situational context that should not have much influence on person factors' (Markus and Kitayama 1998: 65). People are considered to be egocentric: the focus is upon oneself and on finding out and expressing one's unique attributes. In these cultures, the presumption is that we are knowable through our actions and that our behaviour is largely determined by our unique configuration of internal attributes rather than the exigencies of the external situation.

In an extensive series of empirical studies on values across cultures, Schwartz (1992; 1994) has identified higher-order dimensions that summarise the structure of values at the individual level and the cultural level. He surveyed up to forty-one cultural groups in thirty-eight nations. On the basis of his research, we can expect such values as openness to change (self-direction, stimulation and hedonism), self-enhancement (achievement and power), intellectual and affective autonomy, and active mastery of the environment to be important in societies where an individualist, independent conception of the self is dominant. Additional independent values identified by other researchers include freedom of choice, self-determination, personal control, uniqueness, pleasure, competition, fair exchange, individuation, self-fulfilment, assertiveness and privacy.

It must be made clear that a self that is independent, autonomous and distinctive is still socially constructed. '[E]ach distinct, individualized, independent person is *collectively constructed* through his or her engagement in a cultural world that is organized by and made up of practices and meanings based on the model of the person as independent' (Markus and Kitayama 1998: 74–75; emphasis added). From a cultural psychological perspective, independent selves are neither socially isolated nor self-contained; their very character is determined by their lifelong participation in society. (See too Hayek 1948: 6.) Even though an individualist culture emphasises being unique and realising one's individual potential, it legitimises only a restricted range of ways to be a unique and self-actualised person. There is pervasive social pressure to conform to cultural definitions of being a unique (rather than a peculiar) individual.

Anglo-American, English, Dutch and other Western and North European cultures exemplify this conception of the independent, separated self.

## The interdependent self

The notion of the person as an autonomous entity that can be separated from others and the surrounding social environment is a conception that is 'a rather peculiar idea within the context of the world's cultures' (Geertz 1975: 48). Indeed, people in most cultures around the globe subscribe to the *interdependent* construal of personhood.

As Table 6.1 shows, the interdependent model of the person stresses 'a relational, interdependent self with fluid boundaries' (Kagitçibasi 1997: 19). The person is cast as an entity that is *embedded* in society and culture. The major difference between this and the independent model is the emphasis given to 'the other' in people's self-conceptions. The interdependent self includes relationships with other actors within the boundaries of the self because a person's relationships to others in specific situations are central to his or her identity. 'What is a person? Answer: A connected, fluid, flexible, committed being who is bound to others' (Markus and Kitayama 1998: 69). The focus of individual experience is upon the self *in relation to* others: it is the other that is fixed as the reference point for defining the self (Price-Williams 1985: 1007).

The interdependent conception of the self is well captured by the traditional African concept of *Ubuntu* (humanness), which is expressed in the Zulu maxim usually translated as 'a person is only a person through other people' (Ramose 1999). *Ubuntu* is both a world-view and a philosophy of life that expresses mutuality and that shapes human action. It describes personhood as both a state of 'being-with-others' and a dynamic process of reaching one's full potential as a human being through one's ongoing interaction with others. Viewed through the lens of *Ubuntu*, a person is not a solitary and self-sufficient entity but is defined in terms of their relationships to others:

> [I]ndividuals only exist *in* their relationships with others, and as these relationships change, so do the characters of the individuals ... *Ubuntu* unites the self and the world in a peculiar web of reciprocal relations in which subject and object become indistinguishable.
>
> (Louw 2002: 5)

Interdependent selves are in some sense mere fragments, only becoming fully whole when they fulfil their proper roles within their social groups. People constitute and reveal themselves through social roles and relationships, and, as MacIntyre explains, many cultures, such as the Japanese, have some difficulty in separating a private idea of self from its social aspects:

[T]he individual without and apart from his or her social role is not yet complete, is a set of potentialities waiting to be achieved.

(MacIntyre 1990: 493)

There is no inner self definable apart from the defined relationships of the social world.

(p. 494)

For, take the Japanese self, in its self-understanding, away from social roles, and what you have is a self that is not yet or no longer.

(p. 495)

The interdependent construction of the self includes aspects of the larger social unit, such as roles and statuses, within the boundaries of the self. This characteristic leads to differences in learning: whereas Anglo-Americans in the USA learn to 'stand out', in order to highlight their individuality, people in Japan learn to 'stand in', so as to become so identified with the group that they subordinate their individuality (Barnlund 1975).

The boundaries of the interdependent self are fluid. (Just as the business firm is a hierarchical order with malleable boundaries, so too is this type of self-system, it seems.) The distinction between fluid and fixed boundaries is highlighted by comparing one of the Japanese concepts of the self (*jibun*) with that of the West:

The Western concept of 'self' refers essentially to the uniqueness of the individual, or the substance of the person, which has maintained its sameness and continuity over time and across situations, although it is recognized as a product of interaction with other humans. Whereas [*sic*], the Japanese concept of *jibun* refers to one's sharing which is something located beyond a boundary of 'self' in the Western sense. The amount of one's sharing varies depending upon dynamics of a situation. *Jibun* does not have a definite consistent boundary.

(Kimura 1973: 154)[8]

In these cultures, behaviour is determined by people being responsive to others in particular social contexts. We are knowable through our actions within particular social relationships. Because the detailed characteristics of social situations differ and people are sensitised to these differences, the behaviour of the interdependent self will vary significantly across situations and over time – unlike the independent self that seeks to be relatively consistent from one situation to another. This variability in behaviour is regarded as desirable (Markus and Kitayama 1998: 63).

The interdependent view of the self leads to a conception of rights that differs from that in the West, where individual rights are of prime impor-tance. For example, in Japan, 'rights ... are characteristically understood as secondary aspects of more fundamental norms and relationships, belonging therefore in practice not to individuals *qua* individuals, but to the roles and relationships through which individuals realize and constitute themselves' (MacIntyre 1990: 496).

On the basis of Schwartz's empirical research referred to earlier, we can expect cultures stressing an interdependent view of the self to favour such values as conservatism (security, conformity and tradition), self-transcendence (benevolence and universalism), hierarchy and harmony. Obedience, duty, personalised relationships, succour, nurturance, compliance and persistence are other values that have also been cited as likely to prevail in such cultures.

However, as Kagitçibasi (1997: 16) has noted, it is not clear why collectivism (group orientation) as a cultural dimension must necessarily be conflated with conservative values, such as tradition and conformity, that emphasise maintaining the status quo and rigidly adhering to in-group norms (nor is it obvious why individualism must necessarily be related to openness to change). Although they are related, collectivism and the dimension of cultural 'tightness' can also remain distinct for analytical purposes. 'It is theoretically possible for a group to be collectivist (give priority to in-group goals) yet allow considerable deviation from group norms before imposing sanctions' (Triandis 1989: 511).

The interdependent model of the self is prevalent in many of the world's cultures. It characterises Han Chinese, Japanese, Korean and Thai cultures. It is also common in many cultural groups in South America, especially among indigenous people, such as the Quechua, as well as in Africa, such as the Kikuyu in Kenya and the Yoruba in Nigeria (Beattie 1980; Markus and Kitayama 1998; Marsella *et al.* 1985).

## Effects of different cultural self-conceptions upon agency beliefs

The cornerstone hypothesis makes no claims about the causal psychological mechanism by which culture affects entrepreneurship. This section remedies this deficit by considering how culture affects the cognitive drivers of alertness (namely, agency beliefs and subcomponents of agency).

The concepts of agency, internal LOC and efficacy can have different meanings in different cultures. There is considerable cross-cultural variation in the understanding of these terms. Where does the culture typically locate agency in the world? Are agents primarily single individuals (i.e. independent selves) or are they primarily members of intimate social groups (i.e. interdependent selves)? Given the culturally specific definitions of 'self', 'agency', 'internal LOC' and 'efficacy', what is the structure of relations between perceived locus of control and perceived efficacy in the determination of agency beliefs? What is the culturally dominant perception of the contingency of intended events upon human action? Are there differences between cultures in the magnitude, generality and duration

with which agents are seen to exercise their causal powers? Table 6.2 high-
lights some of the main differences across cultures in the locus and scope of
agency.

### Effect on conceptions of agency

As discussed in Chapter 3, personal agency beliefs are a person's expectations of their capacity to cause events that are desired or intended. These
beliefs are a joint function of beliefs about LOC (i.e. action–outcome
contingency) and of beliefs about self-efficacy (i.e. personal competence).
LOC refers to one's belief about the degree to which target events are
contingent upon human action. Efficacy refers to one's judgement about
the degree to which one can produce the actions on which target events are
contingent.

   We know little about cultural variations in personal agency beliefs. But it
is likely that there are differences in the conceptions, strength and domains
of agency beliefs in different cultures. The model of agency beliefs in
Chapter 3 reflects an independent or individualist conception of the self that
is generally characteristic of Western cultures. The independent self is an
autonomous self that does not feel significantly subject to group influences.
Consequently, in the individualist model in Chapter 3 that explains the
psychological determinants of alertness, there are no group-level variables
depicting the person's perceptions of the competence and agency of the
groups to which they might belong. All variables pertain to *self-referential*
variables of one kind or another (i.e. personal internal LOC, personal efficacy,
personal agency).[9]

### Personal and group agency

More refined distinctions of agency may be required to reflect the diversity
of meanings of agency across cultures, especially in group-oriented societies.
The first distinction is between the *personal* and *group* agency beliefs of the
*interdependent self*. The personal (or role-relevant) agency beliefs of the interdependent self comprise judgements about his or her causal power to
successfully fulfil his or her role in the group (e.g. by way of analogy, to be a
good goalie in a soccer team).

   The personal agency of the interpersonal self is directed towards trying to
complete the self through the performance of social roles. 'The collective [i.e.
interdependent] self seeks to gain favorable evaluation from a reference group
by fulfilling a particular role and helping to achieve the goals of the group'
(Yamaguchi 1994: 178). Interdependent selves regard outward role demands
to be the 'really important center of the self' (Smith 1985: 28). MacIntyre
explains that in the case of Japan, people differ in the extent to which they
succeed in completing themselves through performing their roles:

*Table 6.2* Cross-cultural variation in the locus and scope of agency

| Feature | Independent conception of self | Interdependent conception of self |
|---|---|---|
| **1 Agency beliefs** | | |
| (a) Personal agency beliefs | One's judgements about one's own causal power to generate target events | One's judgements about one's causal power to successfully fulfil one's role in the group |
| | A combination of *personal* LOC beliefs (2a) and *personal* efficacy beliefs (3a) | A combination of *personal* LOC beliefs (2a) and *personal* efficacy beliefs (3a) (as defined in this column) |
| (b) Group agency beliefs | Not applicable | One's judgements about the causal power of one's in-group to achieve its overall goals |
| | | A combination of *group* LOC beliefs (2b) and *group* efficacy beliefs (3b) |
| **2 LOC beliefs (i.e. contingency expectations)** | | |
| (a) Personal LOC beliefs | One's judgements about the extent to which target events are contingent upon certain actions | One's judgements about the extent to which successful fulfilment of one's role within the group (the target event) is contingent upon certain actions, both *directly* and *indirectly* |
| (b) Group LOC beliefs | Not applicable | One's judgments about the degree to which achievement of the group's goals is contingent upon certain collective actions |
| **3 Efficacy beliefs (i.e. competence expectations)** | | |
| (a) Personal efficacy beliefs | One's judgements about one's own capacity to produce desired actions | One's judgements about one's own capacity to produce the actions upon which successful fulfilment of one's role within the group is contingent |
| (b) Group efficacy beliefs | Not applicable | One's judgments about the capacity of one's in-group to produce the collective actions upon which achievement of the in-group's goals is contingent |

It is not, of course, that every Japanese individual relates to the social world in the same way and to the same degree. The Japanese individual may be more or less successful in completing him- or herself by assuming those social roles in which he or she gives particularized life to socially and conventionally ordered institutional arrangement; but to the degree to which someone *fails* to realize him- or herself in the medium of social forms, and thereby produces discrepancies between inner feelings and thoughts on the one hand and manifest performances on the other, 'between *omote* and *ura*,' between '*tatemae* and *honne*,' such an individual will approach a condition of crisis of identity.

(MacIntyre 1990: 494–495; emphasis added)

The personal agency beliefs of an interdependent self are a function of *self-referential* (or *role-referential*) expectations of contingency and competence: namely, his or her *personal* internal LOC beliefs and *personal* efficacy beliefs. These beliefs are defined in Table 6.2 and the discussion below.

In contrast, the *group agency beliefs of the interdependent self* comprise his or her judgement about the in-group's causal power to achieve its overall objectives (i.e. to score goals, to win the soccer game). They entail an evaluation of his or her group's capacity collectively to produce intended effects, which includes an assessment of the coordinative dynamics and synergy between group members. People who have a strong sense of group agency will mobilise their efforts and resources to overcome external impediments to their innovative ventures. People who regard their group as collectively powerless will not persevere in their efforts to initiate and adapt to change. The group agency beliefs of an interdependent self are a function of *group-referential* judgements of contingency and competence, namely, his or her group LOC beliefs and group efficacy beliefs.

Distinguishing between personal and group agency is not just for taxonomic convenience. It also has causal implications. As discussed later, this distinction as well as the distinctions between personal and group LOC and between personal and group efficacy (defined below) help explain what determines different aspects of the alertness of interdependent selves. In particular, the degree of *micro*-alertness they each exhibit – that is, the extent to which they are alert to role-relevant opportunities – is an increasing function of the strength of their *personal* agency beliefs. In contrast, the degree of *macro*-alertness that they each exhibit – that is, the extent to which they are alert to opportunities for profitable collective action by the group – is an increasing function of the intensity of their *group* agency beliefs.

*Primary and secondary agency*

There are also other distinctions between types of agency that are important from a cross-cultural perspective. Rothbaum *et al.* (1982) supply a detailed two-process model which distinguishes between two aspects of agency.[10] According to their model, a sense of agency can entail either (i) a capacity to *change the environment* (outside events, other people, circumstances) so as to make it conform to one's goals and wishes, or (ii) a capacity to *change the self* so as to bring about a better fit between self and the environment. The former notion refers to *primary* agency; the latter, to *secondary* agency.

Primary agency was the focus of Chapter 3. Secondary agency might involve controlling one's facial gestures, spoken words and manifest behaviour to ensure that they are socially appropriate to specific relationships with specific people in specific situations. It might also involve regulating 'that which is concealed, what belongs to the heart, the sphere of unspoken thoughts and feelings' (MacIntyre 1990: 493) so that they are brought into accord with socially appropriate expressions and actions.

Both the primary and secondary types of agency are consistent with the broad conception of agency described in Chapter 3 – namely, the power to cause an event consistent with intention. In the case of primary agency, the intended event comprises a change in the objective or external world. With secondary agency, the intended event comprises a change in the self, an internal change, which influences the psychological impact of external reality. It might include changing one's perspective on a situation or relinquishing unattainable goals.

These two aspects of agency are directly relevant to the individualist–collectivist dimension and related cultural conceptions of the self. Cross-cultural research suggests that primary agency beliefs are given relative emphasis in individualist cultures, whereas secondary agency beliefs are relatively emphasised in group-oriented cultures (Weisz *et al.* 1984). Conceiving of agency as a person's capacity to change objective conditions to meet the self's needs and desires is highly congruent with individualist cultural values. The close connection between an independent conception of the self and primary agency is identified by Markus and Kitayama:

> The sense of individuality that accompanies this [independent] construal of the self includes a sense of oneself as an *agent*, as a *producer of one's actions*. One is conscious of being in *control over the surrounding situation*, and of the need to express one's own thoughts, feelings, and actions to others. ... Such acts of *standing out* are often intrinsically rewarding. ... Furthermore, the acts of standing out, themselves, form an important basis of self-esteem.
>
> (Markus and Kitayama 1991: 246; emphasis added)

Similarly, Markus and Kitayama posit a close relationship between the interdependent self and secondary agency:

> An interdependent view of the self does not result in a merging of self and other, nor does it imply that one must always be in the company of

others to function effectively, or that people do not have a sense of them-selves as agents who are the origins of their own actions. On the contrary, *it takes a high degree of self-control and agency to effectively adjust oneself to various interpersonal contingencies. Agentic exercise of control, however, is directed primarily to the inside* and to those inner attributes, such as desires, personal goals, and private emotions, that can disturb the harmonious equilibrium of interpersonal transaction.

(Markus and Kitayama 1991: 228; emphasis added)

Primary agency is neither universally applicable nor universally reinforced by socialisation patterns. Indeed, secondary agency might have significant adaptive advantages in some situations and cultures. It might be highly functional for people pursuing in-group goals, and it might thus reinforce the development of group efficacy in group-oriented cultures. Consequently, through their expectations and child-rearing patterns, parents in different cultures can emphasise different notions of agency in their attempts to assist their children's integration into society.

In a cross-cultural empirical study, Trommsdorff (1989) (as reported in Schneewind 1995: 137) identified systematic differences in agency beliefs in Germany and Japan, representing an individualist and a group-oriented culture, respectively. He found that German children held more primary agency beliefs whereas Japanese children scored higher on secondary agency. These differences were reflected in differences in parent–child relations and approaches to child rearing. German parents emphasised their children's independence and learning by sanctions. They anticipated parent–child conflicts. In contrast, Japanese parents expected their children to be more compliant and interdependent, to learn through imitation and to remain closely and harmoniously aligned with their parents.

Similarly, Weisz *et al.* (1984) argue that primary agency is more highly valued and more sought after in the US cultural context. In contrast, secondary agency is more pivotal in everyday life in Japanese culture than in the USA. Their exploratory study illustrates this cross-cultural difference by comparing US and Japanese views and practices in child rearing, socialisa-tion, religion, philosophy, work and psychotherapy. 'In each area, behavior patterns in Japan appear to reflect a pursuit of secondary control more than do patterns in the United States' (p. 957).

Distinguishing cultures dichotomously on the basis of whether they invoke primary agency or secondary agency is open to question. People of all cultures may exhibit both kinds of agency simultaneously. Even with an enormous confidence in their ability to change the world to fit their goals (primary agency), successful, independent entrepreneurs need a strong sense of secondary agency. They need to be able to bring into play powerful self-regulating psychological processes that sustain their motivation and positive outlook in response to major environmental impediments that block them in their endeavours.

## Effects on LOC beliefs

Just as there is cultural differentiation in how people construe personal agency, so too there is cultural differentiation in meanings of LOC and beliefs about the sources of internal control.[11] An independent conception of self underlies the characterisation of LOC in most psychological research (Furby 1979; Stam 1987). This individualistic bias is significant since LOC might work quite differently in cultures that emphasise the interdependent self (see Table 6.2).

## Personal and group LOC beliefs

The LOC beliefs of the independent self were examined in Chapter 3 and need not be considered in detail here. It suffices to say that LOC beliefs of the independent self are always personal and purely self-referential. They pertain to the strength of the contingency of target events upon individual behaviour rather than collective action.

In the case of the interdependent self, the nature of LOC beliefs is more complex because a person's perceptions of the relevant in-group clearly matter. As discussed above, the interdependent self is an inseparable part of an intimate in-group. His or her relationships to close in-group members are included in the boundaries of the self.

Consequently, a distinguishing feature of interdependent selves is that they each have two sets of LOC beliefs: *group-relevant* LOC beliefs and *personal (or role-relevant)* LOC beliefs. A LOC belief is an expectation of the degree of contingency of a class of target events upon a class of actions. In the case of *personal* LOC beliefs, the relevant target event is meeting the requirements and obligations of one's social role; the relevant class of actions is one's own behaviour. In the case of *group* LOC beliefs, the relevant target event is achieving the group's objectives; the relevant class of actions is the collective behaviour of the group.

Thus, *personal* LOC beliefs entail judgements about the degree to which successful fulfilment of one's role within the group is contingent upon certain actions, both directly and indirectly. Thus, it would be a mistake to assume that an interdependent self does not have any interest in self-relevant factors (Markus and Kitayama 1991: 228).

In contrast, *group* LOC beliefs entail a person's judgements about the degree to which achievement of the group's overall goals is contingent upon the collective actions of the group as a whole rather than external forces.

The soccer analogy referred to earlier can help clarify the distinction between personal and group LOC beliefs of the interdependent self. In the case of one of the team players, let us say the goalie, *personal* LOC beliefs comprise his or her expectations about the extent to which fending off goals by the attacking team and 'keeping a clean score sheet' (the goalie's social role and target event) depends upon the goalie's own shot-stopping actions (e.g. catching and kicking the ball, doing diving saves) rather than on outfield players' actions or external forces. The goalie's *group* LOC beliefs comprise his or her expectations about the extent to which the team's scoring goals and winning games (the team's objective and target event) is contingent upon the collective efforts of team-mates (rather than upon external forces, such as luck or biased judgements of a corrupt referee).

### Direct and indirect sources of internal LOC

In order to reduce the individualistic bias in previous research on LOC, Chia *et al.* (1998) suggest another modification (in fact a broadening) of the concept of *internal* LOC for group-oriented cultures. Recall from Chapter 3 that Rotter's social learning theory explains how internal LOC is considered to exist *within* the self. 'Internality was equated with *a sense of control originating from the self*, and externality was equated with a sense of control other than the self' (Chia *et al.* 1998: 565; emphasis added).

In contrast, Chia *et al.* argue that for people in group-oriented cultures, such as China, there are sources of internal control that are not limited to the self, narrowly construed. In particular, there are both *direct* and *indirect* sources of internal control.[12] The direct source corresponds to that identified by Rotter – namely, the inner self. The indirect source of internal control arises from other members of one's intimate social group whom one sees as extensions of oneself. Thus, people with an interdependent self-conception can still perceive internal LOC *through* significant others if they believe that target events (such as role fulfilment) are directly contingent on the actions of other close in-group members over whom they themselves exert some influence. As Chia *et al.* (1998: 570) put it: 'When any extended self in this special relationship group has control, I can feel that I too have control.' In earlier research, this indirect source has been considered a source of external control for people in individualist cultures.

Chia *et al.* subjected their hypotheses to empirical testing. They undertook a study of the LOC beliefs of 86 US college students and 180 college students from Taiwan. Their empirical work corroborates the hypothesis that there can be direct and indirect sources of internal control for people from group-oriented cultures. Indeed, they found that a sense of internal control can come (in order of priority) from the self, the family, 'others' and even the government. The data were also consistent with the hypothesis that for people from individualist societies, there is only one single (namely, direct) source of internal control, namely, the self. The US students in their sample also had a stronger sense of (overall) internal control than the Taiwanese students.

Indirect internal control also finds its parallel in Weisz *et al.*'s (1984) analysis of the emphasis in Japan (relative to the USA) on *vicarious* control. They examine how people can associate with powerful others in order to bolster their own sense of control and to tap into the capacity of others to influence events. They suggest that child rearing in Japan seems to promote this vicarious control:

> When a Japanese youngster's parent, sibling, or peer group member exerts control at work, at school, or elsewhere, that youngster has been prepared by elaborate child-rearing patterns to experience that control *vicariously*. Certainly this is true of some American children, but the cross-cultural literature … strongly indicates that this *capacity for vicarious control* runs deeper and broader in Japan.
>
> (Weisz *et al.* 1984: 959; emphasis added)

In the Japanese workplace, procedures and practices, such as *nemawashi* and *ringi-seido*, that encourage wide participation and consensus in business decision-making also promote vicarious control. The former refers to the process of group consultation to forge a consensus, whereas the latter refers to the drafting and circulation of written proposals in order to obtain approval from the managers and the divisions that will be affected by the proposed decision.

### Effects on self-efficacy beliefs

Although they involve self-referential cognitive processes, efficacy beliefs are not bound solely to individualism (Bandura 1995a: 34; 1997: 33). Judgements about whether the self is efficacious or not will presumably depend on the cultural conception of the self that is being invoked (i.e. independent vs. interdependent). Self-efficacy is in part culturally constructed, and the construction of self-efficacy may vary as a function of culture. See Table 6.2.

In order to understand the impact of culture (especially alternative self-construals) upon efficacy beliefs, it is useful to distinguish between *personal* efficacy and *group* efficacy in much the same way as was done between personal and group LOC beliefs. Perceived personal efficacy refers to one's beliefs about one's own ability to produce the actions upon which success in prospective situations (more specifically, success in fulfilling one's role in the group) is contingent. Group efficacy relates to people's beliefs about their capacity to solve, through collective endeavour, the problems they face as a group as a whole. More specifically, it involves judgements about the group's capacity to produce the particular collective actions upon which achievement of the group's overall goals is contingent. Group efficacy is especially relevant for the interdependent conception of the self with its emphasis upon commitment to a few, small, stable in-groups.

Within any group, of course, there can be variability in members' beliefs about the efficacy of their in-group. In particular, people with different statuses or roles within the same group may differ markedly in how they perceive their group's efficacy.[13] With high interdependence, a person's group efficacy belief is not just the aggregation of that person's perceptions of individual members' capabilities; rather it is the perception of an *emergent property* of interactive group processes (Bandura 1997: 478). Group efficacy beliefs are likely to depend, among other things, on people's appraisals of the depth, variety and balance of competences in the group. Consequently, in evaluating the calibre of talent available to an entrepreneurial venture, people will assess the functional balance of the team (including the mix of managerial, marketing and financial expertise) and the extent of prior joint experience of team members (i.e. the degree to which they have previously worked together).

Although personal and group efficacy are analytically distinct concepts, a person's estimates of them are likely to be related to some extent. Our judgements of our personal efficacy are not unconnected to the social groups in which we participate. This is especially the case for interdependent selves. In appraising their personal efficacies in group contexts, they inevitably consider group processes that promote or undermine their individual capabilities. Their sense of personal efficacy is likely to be weaker if they find themselves in a group of no-hopers rather than star performers. In addition, both types of efficacy beliefs depend on similar sources of information, they serve similar functions, and they operate through similar cognitive and social processes.

Different cultural values and norms cultivate different meanings of perceived efficacy in different contexts. For example, Western notions of what it means to be a capable person do not necessarily correspond to indigenous notions of efficacy in non-Western cultures. For example, in their empirical study, Berry and Bennett (1992) found that Cree conceptions of cognitive competence differed substantially from Western notions of general intelligence in that they emphasise taking time, being careful and self-sufficient rather than being fast and analytic. Multi-dimensional scaling techniques revealed that the Cree term for 'lives like a white person' was opposite the core cluster of terms for the Cree conception of competence.

In addition, culture affects the development and pattern of efficacy beliefs: '[C]ultural values and practices affect how efficacy beliefs are developed, the purposes to which they are put and the way in which they are best exercised in particular cultural milieus' (Bandura 1997: 32). We must remember, however, that there is significant variation within cultures, and Bandura is at pains to note that this variation will affect the emergence of efficacy beliefs in different contexts: 'Because there is variability within cultures, understanding how cultural background affects efficacy beliefs and functioning requires analysis of individual orientations as well as the prevailing cultural orientation' (p. 471).

The way people in a cultural group construe the self will guide how they sample, process and assess information from the social environment. In particular, cultural differences in self-concepts and values might affect the various information sources that people use to form their personal and group efficacy beliefs:[14]

[F]orming beliefs of personal efficacy is a complex process of self-appraisal which entails selecting, weighting, and integrating information from multiple sources. It is in this appraisal process that culture may play its influential role. Culture may affect not only the type of information provided by the various sources, but also which information is *selected* and how it is *weighted* and *integrated* in people's self-efficacy judgments.

(Oettingen 1995: 151; emphasis added)

Employing Hofstede's typology on the dimensions of cultural diversity, Oettingen suggests that efficacy beliefs depend upon whether cultural values are rooted in individualism or collectivism (group orientation), whether they support an equal or unequal distribution of power, the extent to which they avoid uncertainty by enforcing strict codes of conduct, and the degree to which sex roles are differentiated. Cultural variations on these dimensions generate different social and institutional practices in families and schools, which in turn influence the *prevalence, form* and *valuation* of different sources of efficacy information.

Independent and interdependent selves differ in the relative emphases they give to personal and group-level forms of efficacy, and they sample information from their social environment in different ways. Independent selves emphasise personal efficacy. They are more alert to, and more often search for, efficacy information that is self-relevant rather than group rele-vant, and they process self-relevant information more quickly. In addition, they mainly base their personal efficacy beliefs on information about their own performance experiences and achievements. For instance, in families in which children are encouraged to act independently, children are likely to access information about their own performance, actions and capabilities when they face new challenges. *Direct mastery experiences* are thus the most significant source of self-efficacy information for independent selves.

Furthermore, since their cognitions typically focus on private thoughts and feelings, individualists may also be more likely to judge their own coping ability and self-efficacy on the basis of how positively or negatively aroused (e.g. enthusiastic, anxious) they feel when confronted with particular situations (Oettingen 1995: 153). Hence, in general, *private emotional states* are a more accessible and more salient source of self-efficacy information for independent rather than interdependent selves.

Interdependent selves largely base their judgements of personal efficacy on assessments from members of their in-group. They tend to evaluate their personal capabilities in terms of others' evaluations. In addition, they infer their own competence by observing the successes and failures of other in-group members and comparing those attainments with their own. That is, *vicarious experiences* provided by role models are likely to be a more influential source of self-efficacy information for interdependent selves than for individ-ualists. Thus, the way in which a society is structured along age, gender, ethnic and socio-economic dimensions is highly pertinent because it largely determines the types of role models to which its members are exposed, and the type of competences, attitudes and attainments that those members will observe, imitate and compare with their own.

Earley (1994) showed that the cultural dimension of individualism–collectivism is relevant in explaining how training influences self-efficacy. Earley compared the impact of individual- vs. group-focused training on self-efficacy in two intercultural studies conducted in countries that differed in terms of their degrees of individualism–collectivism. He studied managers in Hong Kong, the People's Republic of China and the USA. His results show that the cultural orientation of employees influences their use of training information. As hypothesised, group-focused job training was found to have a stronger effect on collectivists' personal efficacy beliefs and performance than did individual-focused training. In contrast, individualists were found to respond best to individual-focused job training (p. 112).

In a subsequent study, Earley and his colleagues (1999) undertook a laboratory experiment to determine how people from different cultures use different types of performance feedback in the formation of their self-efficacy beliefs. Their study involved managers from an individualist culture (the USA) and two group-oriented cultures (the People's Republic of China and the Czech Republic). Based on Triandis's (1989) work on how people sample information about different aspects of the self, they put forward the following hypothesis about self-efficacy judgements:

> *Hypothesis 1*: Individualists who were provided with both individual- and group-referenced feedback on a performance task would base their self-efficacy and self-evaluations of performance on individual-referenced feedback. Collectivists who were provided with both individual and group feedback on a performance task would use feedback concerning their group's performance.
>
> (Earley *et al.* 1999: 597)

A surprising and key result was that they found that individual-referenced feedback played a consistent role for *both* individualists and collectivists, whereas group feedback seemed to be crucial only for the formation of collectivists' self-efficacy judgements (p. 611). Collectivists' self-efficacy judgements were strong if they received either high individual or high group performance feedback, but they were strongest if they received both. Thus, interdependent selves do *not* rely solely upon group-relevant information in determining their sense of self-efficacy. They also prefer to have feedback on their own personal capabilities too.

> [A] collectivist's sense of self is based on both personal and group-based information. ... Not only does a collectivist benefit from knowing that

his or her work group has been successful, but he or she needs to know about personal success as well.

(p. 614)

## Effects of different self-conceptions upon alertness

The distinction between the independent and interdependent construals of the self is important in explaining variations in psychological processes across cultures. This section takes up this theme by investigating the major effects of alternative cultural self-conceptions upon the unit of alertness and other aspects of entrepreneurship. See Table 6.3.

*Table 6.3* Effects of alternative self-conceptions upon entrepreneurship

| Feature | Independent conception of self (in individualist culture) | Interdependent conception of self (in group-oriented culture) |
|---|---|---|
| Primary locus of alertness | Independent, autonomous person | Interdependent members of an in-group |
| Alertness is most attuned to opportunities that are relevant to … | direct, personal gain | (i) successful fulfilment of one's social role in the group (i.e. *micro-alertness*) |
| | | (ii) collective action by the in-group and successful achievement of the overall goals of the group (i.e. *micro-alertness*) |
| Alertness typically manifests itself in … | individual entrepreneurship | clan, team-based or corporate entrepreneurship that draws upon the pooled talents of interdependent members in the group (e.g. the Chinese family business, Japanese 'quality circles') |
| Innovation often entails…. | *generating variety* through new combinations of resources (Tiessen 1997) | *leveraging resources* internally or building close external relations with other firms (thereby pursuing opportunities without regard to the resources already controlled) (Tiessen 1997) |
| | taking discrete steps that involve independent action | taking connected steps that involve groups and businesses working together |
| | violating established practices without consensual decision-making | 'consensual rule-breaking' (McGrath *et al.* 1992b; Shane 1994) |
| | a partitioned sequence of activities | a non-linear, parallel process |
| | compartmentalised organisation of functions (e.g. shop-floor manufacturing staff are not involved in sales and marketing) | highly integrated organisation (e.g. interdivisional transfers of researchers and engineers) (Harper 1994a) |

*(continued over)*

*Table 6.3 continued*

| Feature | Independent conception of self (in individualist culture) | Interdependent conception of self (in group-oriented culture) |
|---|---|---|
| Innovation often entails.... | 'renegade' championing strategies and corporate venturing approaches that free innovation efforts and venturing groups in a firm from the formal corporate structure, organisational norms and rules (Shane and Venkataraman 1996) | firm-wide corporate venturing strategies that are linked to the company's collective goals and norms and that rely upon cross-functional support (Shane *et al.* 1994; 1995) |
| Scope for entrepreneurship | Opportunities rarely limited by people's expectations of the boundaries of their society (in the absence of government intervention) | Opportunities possibly limited by partitioning of the social structure and by norms about trading with strangers (at least in some group-oriented cultures that are vertical and 'tight' in their social organisation) (Greif 1994) |
| Prior localised knowledge of entrepreneur includes ... | richly elaborated knowledge of self and of the abstract and generic attributes of other (classes of) autonomous market participants | richly elaborated knowledge of relationships with other in-group members, position of in-group relative to out-groups, requirements of specific social contexts, and concrete and contextually embedded attributes and roles of other market participants |
| | deep knowledge of objective conditions required to meet the self's needs and desires | deep knowledge of perspectives, expectations, goals and desires of significant others in the in-group that impinge upon successful fulfilment of one's role |
| Situational influences on people's alertness | Most alert when working independently on tasks that can be solved by one person (i.e. 'disjunctive' tasks) | Most alert when working in their in-group on tasks that require a team effort (i.e. 'conjunctive' tasks) |
| | Most alert when they have individual goals, individual responsibility and individual-based rewards (because then their sense of agency is strongest) | Most alert when they have group-focused goals, shared responsibility and group-based rewards (Earley and Gibson 1998) |
| | Alertness does not depend significantly upon the cultural similarity of the group members that the entrepreneur leads or interacts with | Alertness is dampened when working in a group of strangers and in culturally heterogeneous teams (Earley 1993) |

*Table 6.3 continued*

| Feature | Independent conception of self (in individualist culture) | Interdependent conception of self (in group-oriented culture) |
|---|---|---|
| Situational influences on people's alertness | Social pressure to develop one's uniqueness and potential (according to cultural definitions of being a unique, self-actualised person) encourages creativity and innovation but channels them *within* socially accepted bounds | In the case of those group-oriented cultures that are 'tight' in their social organisation, the need to consider the reactions of in-group members in every situation may inhibit entrepreneurial initiative, creativity and innovation (Liu 1986) |
| | Alertness is more generalised and diversified but less attuned to any one particular social situation (partly because individuals belong to many non-intimate groups, they frequently shift from one group to another and their prior knowledge is more generalised) | Alertness is more finely attuned to specific social situations (because people belong to fewer and more stable groups, their social interactions are less diverse and their prior knowledge is much more contextual) |
| Information structures relevant to entrepreneur(s) | Low investment in the sharing and coordination of information | High investment in the sharing and coordination of information |
| | Less intimate communication between entrepreneurs and other actors | High level of in-group communication and extensive informal, low-cost transmission of latest available commercial information ('thick information exchange') (Gudykunst *et al.* 1987; 1992) |
| | Frequent opportunistic withholding of information | Much less frequent opportunistic withholding of information vis-à-vis other in-group members (Aoki 1986) |
| Conflict resolution and alertness | More alert to opportunities to litigate via the courts to obtain or secure a competitive advantage at the expense of rivals | More alert to opportunities for non-legal conflict resolution and for middle-ground solutions to opposed opinions when dealing with in-group members (Leung 1997) |
| | More alert to new 'commitment technologies' and contractual innovations that reduce principal–agent problems | More alert to the changing requirements of informal institutions that build trust and that reduce the payoff to socially uncooperative strategies (Fukuyama 1995) |
| Entrepreneurial decision-making | Individual based | Generally team based, more participatory and consensual |
| | Potentially rapid decision-making – especially for short-lived arbitrage opportunities | Relatively slow decision-making |

*(continued over)*

*Table 6.3 continued*

| Feature | Independent conception of self (in individualist culture) | Interdependent conception of self (in group-oriented culture) |
|---|---|---|
| Entrepreneurial contracting and its enforcement | Explicit and/or shorter-term contracts | Implicit, ongoing, highly personal, relationships supported by extensive networks |
| | Entrepreneurs readily enter into contracts with people from different groups and cultural backgrounds | Entrepreneurs prefer to interact with members from their specific ethnic, religious or familial group and they may forgo contracting with particular out-groups even when they perceive profitable opportunities (ignoring agency costs) (Greif 1994) |
| | High functional division of labour between individuals (in the sense of 'who is to do what') but less structural differentiation among individuals (in the sense of 'who is in charge') (Kashima and Callan 1994) | Lower functional division of labour between individuals but greater structural differentiation among individuals |
| | Employees are more likely to pursue personal or localised interests within their specific functional unit (thereby increasing contractual problems for the entrepreneur) | Employees more likely to apply skills and knowledge in the overall interests of the firm |
| | Hierarchical and vertical control in firms | Horizontal communication and coordination among production units |
| | Higher degree of formal vertical integration of production | Extensive networks of long-term subcontractual relationships (e.g. Japanese *keiretsu*) (Aoki 1990) |
| | Contract enforcement is achieved mainly through self-enforcing bilateral agreements, formal control mechanisms and specialised third-party organisations, such as the court system | Contract enforcement is achieved through informal economic and social mechanisms, such as social intimacy, close personal relationships and customs |

## Cultural variation in the unit or locus of alertness

The cornerstone and convergence hypotheses do not recognise cultural foundations of the self as a significant source of cultural variation. Nor are they expressed in terms of the actions and interactions of human actors. As a result, these hypotheses tell us very little about whether or how the entities that discover profit opportunities might vary in different cultural contexts.

In contrast, the approach in this book argues that different cultural conceptions of personhood lead to variation in the *unit or locus of alertness* across cultures. It is necessary to ask: what is the entity that does the perceiving and discovering of entrepreneurial opportunities in individualist and group-oriented cultures? The unit of agency and of alertness is endogenous to culture. In individualist cultures, the predominant unit of alertness is the independent self. But the independent person is not to be confused with the isolated, culture-free decision-maker that is epitomised in 'Robinson Crusoe' analyses of individual entrepreneurship (e.g. Kirzner 1979: 158–162). The independent self is not 'atomistic' in the sense that the existence and actions of the self are independent of any relationship that the self has to other entities. As mentioned before, individualism is a cultural system of independent values characterised by high levels of social commitment. Real-world independent entrepreneurs are imbued with cultural values locating their individualism and sense of self in a legitimated wider social order.

In group-oriented societies, on the other hand, it is interdependent members of a group who are the primary centre of entrepreneurial alertness. It is *not* the group. Interdependent selves are the sole possessors of cognitive and perceptual faculties. Groups have no consciousness; a group cannot be the first to spot an opportunity. Though interdependent selves share the same physical boundaries as independent selves, they are different units of analysis.

The interdependent selves belonging to the group must relate and fit together in a functionally adaptive way if each self is to be highly alert to opportunities relevant to the fulfilment of his or her social role in the group and/or to be alert to opportunities for the successful achievement of the overall goals of the group as a whole:

> In endeavors involving high system interdependence, members must work well together to achieve group results. Such endeavors require close *coordination of roles* and strategies, effective communication, cooperative goals, and *mutual adjustment to one another's performances*.
>
> (Bandura 1997: 480; emphasis added)

In examining collective action by groups, it is useful to consider again the analogy of a successful soccer team, whose players must coordinate their specific roles with one another, share a common aim of trying to score goals and win the game, and continually be alert to the actions of other players, so that they can adjust their own actions.

The 'overall order of actions' in a group, whether a soccer team or a Chinese family business, is 'more than the totality of regularities observable in the actions of the individuals and cannot be wholly reduced to them' (Hayek 1967: 70). A social group is more than a mere aggregate of interdependent selves: 'The social group is *more* than the mere sum total of its members, and it is also *more* than the mere sum total of the merely personal relationships existing at any moment between any of its members' (Popper

1961: 17). The group is a particular relationship of interdependent selves. The interaction among interdependent selves, the interaction of each with the outside world, and the interaction of the group as a whole with the external selection environment, all affect and account for the operation and evolution of the group.

The distinction between independent and interdependent selves has a major effect on the nature of the opportunities to which people are alert and the character of their alertness. See Figures 6.1, 6.2 and 6.3. In contrast to the independent self, for instance, an interdependent self potentially exhibits two types of alertness: *micro*-alertness and *macro*-alertness. Micro-alertness is defined as one's propensity to notice opportunities, events and conditions that are specifically relevant to the successful fulfilment of one's role in the group (and that relate to the commitments and obligations that the role confers). Macro-alertness, on the other hand, is defined as one's propensity to notice opportunities, events and conditions relevant to the achievement of the overall goals of the group as a whole, including the propensity to discover profitable opportunities for collective action by the group. It should be noted that micro- and macro-alertness are two aspects of the alertness of an interdependent self. Macro-alertness is *not* the alertness of a group.

Given the centrality of roles as a constituent of the interdependent self, micro-alertness entails being alert to changes in the perspectives, expectations and goals of significant others in the group that have an impact on the effective operation of one's role. Alertness to these changes helps one adapt oneself to others' needs and demands and to create and maintain a connection to them. Micro-alertness is directed to the immediate requirements of each specific situation and to the key people who make up that situation. It manifests itself in finding new ways of becoming part of various interpersonal

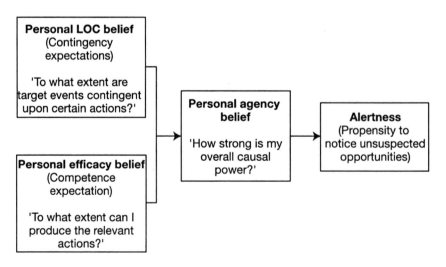

*Figure 6.1* Determinants of alertness of an independent self

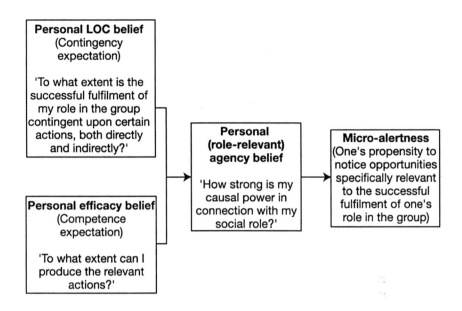

*Figure 6.2* Determinants of micro-alertness of an interdependent self

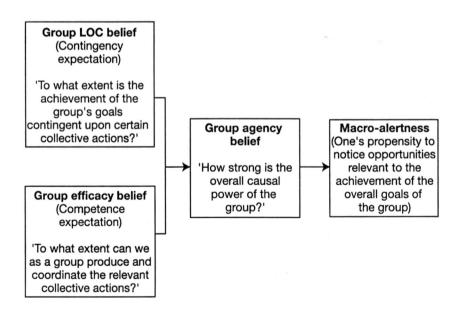

*Figure 6.3* Determinants of macro-alertness of an interdependent self

relationships within the group and of enhancing one's goodness of fit with significant others – for instance, by discovering opportunities to create and fulfil obligations and to promote the goals of other in-group members (e.g. one's supervisor or boss). Micro-alertness also entails being vigilant about the process and sequence by which collective decisions will be taken that might have an effect on one's role in the group and one's relationship to others.

Macro-alertness relates to noticing opportunities for profitable collective action on the part of the group. It is relevant to the achievement of the goals of the in-group as a whole. It might involve discovering opportunities to compete against rival out-groups. It might involve ideas about new products and new markets that an entrepreneurial team might explore. Macro-alertness might also manifest itself in forming new alliances with other entrepreneurial teams. It includes vigilance towards external signs of danger and potentially threatening events to which the team must adapt.

The degree of micro-alertness of an interdependent self is likely to be an increasing function of the strength of his or her personal agency beliefs, which in turn is a function of his or her beliefs of personal internal LOC and personal efficacy. In contrast, macro-alertness depends on the interdependent self's perceptions of the group's agency, which in turn is a function of his or her beliefs of group internal LOC and group efficacy.

Micro- and macro-alertness are probably loosely coupled. For instance, an interdependent self's perception of personal agency (a determinant of micro-alertness) is influenced by his or her perception of group agency (a determinant of macro-alertness). The interdependent self's sense of personal efficacy is after all likely to be influenced by group context and group processes. At least some minimal degree of micro-alertness is necessary (but not sufficient) for non-trivial degrees of macro-alertness: how could one possess a high degree of alertness to relatively distant opportunities for collective action by the group but fail to exhibit one iota of alertness to more proximate opportunities ('right under one's nose', so to speak) that are related to the successful realisation of one's own social role? Thus, some degree of mutual interdependence and positive correlation between these two types of alertness seems plausible.

## Revisiting the cornerstone and convergence hypotheses

As discussed earlier, the cornerstone hypothesis maintains that individualist cultures are inherently more conducive to entrepreneurship than are group-oriented cultures. This hypothesis is often stated in terms that rely upon the notion of 'national culture'. For example, it is predicted that individualist nations, such as the USA, are likely to be more supportive of entrepreneurship than are group-oriented nations, such as the People's Republic of China. More robust formulations of this hypothesis eschew such overly aggregated concepts as 'national culture' and take subnational cultural groups as the relevant unit of analysis.

This chapter makes a case for rejecting the cornerstone hypothesis and its underlying assumption that individualism or communalism is intrinsically pro- or anti-entrepreneurial. In particular, it claims that individualism is neither a necessary nor a sufficient condition for the discovery of profit opportunities. Indeed, the propensity to be alert exists in all individuals and groups of people, whether individualist or group-oriented. Interdependent selves are not necessarily less alert or entrepreneurial than their independent counterparts. Before jumping to the conclusion that a vibrant entrepreneurial economy requires a Western brand of individualist culture, it is recommended that we first take a look at those developing countries in which group-oriented values are prevalent and then see what happens when they adopt political institutions and property laws that can bolster people's perceptions of agency and that can channel their alertness in the economic sphere.

Furthermore, this chapter asserts that the cognitive factors that switch on people's alertness are similar across cultures. In particular, people's perceptions of agency – their beliefs in the causal power of the relevant loci of decision-making and alertness – are the main psychological mediators through which culture influences entrepreneurship in all societies. (However, it is acknowledged that the structure and content of agency beliefs do differ between individualist and group-oriented societies. The approach explains how the propensity to be alert works its way through different channels in different cultural contexts.) Although it specifies when certain effects will hold, the cornerstone hypothesis says nothing about *how* and *why* culture affects entrepreneurial *alertness*, the essence of entrepreneurship. It makes no claims about the causal or generative role of cognitive processes (especially agency beliefs) in cultural phenomena.

One problem with the cornerstone hypothesis is that it assumes that there is a one-dimensional, culturally neutral scale for measuring and comparing degrees of entrepreneurship across different cultural groups. However, alertness is a complex perceptual faculty and there is as yet no scale for measuring it that has cross-cultural validity. Opportunities and market events may be perceived differently depending on whether one is looking through individualist or group-oriented lenses (in a manner akin to Ichheiser's '*Kulturbrille*' (cultural glasses)). Different units of entrepreneurship (i.e. independent versus interdependent selves) exhibit different *types* of alertness that lead to differences in the *nature* of the opportunities that entrepreneurs discover. As explained earlier, interdependent selves have a greater propensity to recognise particular types of entrepreneurial opportunities than do independent selves, and vice versa.

Because they are alert to different types of opportunities, it is very difficult to compare the degrees of alertness of independent and interdependent selves in general and absolute terms. For any given opportunity, one type of self may be more or less predisposed to its discovery than is the other. In other words, entrepreneurial alertness is not a contextually independent phenomenon. It is a psychological propensity that is laden with cultural values. Although they are not recognised by the cornerstone hypothesis, situational influences can have a significant effect on how entrepreneurial people are. That is, the alertness of independent and interdependent selves is heightened in different types of situational contexts (see Table 6.3). For example, the independent self is most alert when working alone on tasks that can be performed by one person (so-called 'disjunctive' tasks) and when operating in organisational contexts that provide individual-based rewards. In contrast, interdependent selves are most alert when working as a team with members of their in-group on tasks that require a team effort (i.e. so-called 'conjunctive tasks') and when they face group-based rewards. An increase in the intensity of out-group competition may also further enhance their alertness.

Although there are conceptual and measurement difficulties in comparing people's degrees of alertness across cultures, some tentative claims will be put forward. In particular, in contrast to the cornerstone hypothesis, the approach in this chapter predicts that some group-oriented cultures can generate a high degree of entrepreneurial alertness among their members (at least relative to other group-oriented cultures). In addition, the approach identifies the distinguishing characteristics of those group-oriented cultures in which people are likely to be intensely alert and entrepreneurial.

It is argued that the members of group-oriented cultures that are highly entrepreneurial will typically possess a strong sense of *personal* agency in fulfilling their role within the group as well as a strong belief in their group's *collective* agency. They each perceive events that are relevant to both self and group to be contingent on actions, and they perceive both self and group to have the capacity to produce the relevant actions. That is, they typically exhibit a strong sense of contingency (i.e. internal LOC) and competence (i.e. efficacy) at both the personal and group level. They feel able to affect the external conditions that impact upon their roles when necessary (primary agency), and they are confident in their ability to adapt how they perform their social roles when circumstances change (secondary agency). They also consider themselves capable of regulating their inner thoughts when under stressful conditions. They are also confident in their in-group's capacity to coordinate its activities and adapt to new environmental pressures. They consider their group's internal dynamics to be highly functional to the achievement of collective goals.

Because the degree of people's alertness is directly related to the perceived strength of their agency, we can expect interdependent selves in such group-oriented cultures to be highly alert to entrepreneurial opportunities that specifically enhance their fulfilment of their role (an expression of micro-alertness). They are also expected to be alert to rewarding opportunities for collective action by the group (i.e. to exhibit a high degree of macro-alertness).

Thus, the cornerstone hypothesis is conceptually unsound. The cornerstone hypothesis is a bold proposition that disintegrates upon closer scrutiny. A group-oriented culture that emphasises relatedness between people is not inherently incompatible with robust entrepreneurship. On the contrary, a subset of group-oriented cultures may generate heightened alertness to opportunity on the part of its members, as demonstrated by real-world examples of spectacular entrepreneurial performance in some East Asian nations.

The second hypothesis examined in connection with the relationship between culture and entrepreneurship is the convergence hypothesis. This hypothesis predicts that as societies develop, they will all become more alike. In particular, they will come to share individualist cultural values. Like the cornerstone hypothesis, the convergence hypothesis is often expressed at an aggregate level. Group-oriented nations are predicted to become more individualist as they modernise and become more affluent.

The cornerstone and convergence hypotheses are right to focus upon the continuum of individualism–collectivism because it is the most significant and coherent dimension of cultural variation in values. However, they fail to emphasise that this dimension is very broad and encompasses many separate elements. Moreover, they fail to focus upon the most fundamental aspect of the individualism–collectivism dimension: cultural self-construals.

Culture is a complex symbolic system of shared meanings. Shared understandings of personhood are artefacts of this cultural system. This chapter argues that culture is a major influence on whether people define themselves as independent entities or as interdependent parts of a larger social whole. Different self-conceptions are a key phenomenon in explaining psychological processes that vary across cultures.

The analysis suggests that cultural conceptions of the self are often relatively stable from generation to generation. These self-construals underpin the ingrained identity of a people. Adaptation in cultural conceptions of the self is very slow, especially in relatively homogeneous cultures where a dominant cultural framework is identifiable and tangible. The persistence of group-oriented values and the culture of the relational self in highly developed nations, such as Japan, is a case in point (Iwawaki 1986). Taking a broad historical perspective, MacIntyre observes that:

> It is this capacity for adaptive change which suggests that even those radical transformations which Japan has undergone between the sixteenth century and the present are compatible with *a certain constancy in the understanding of the self*. ... If this is so, then, in certain important respects, *convergence*, increasing resemblance between Japanese and Americans, *is unlikely to occur*.
>
> (MacIntyre: 1990: 496; emphasis added)

There is no compelling evidence that collectivist cultures that have prospered economically are becoming overwhelmingly individualist in many different behavioural and cognitive domains (see the various studies in Kim *et al.* 1994a). The conception of the interdependent self is not giving way to that of the independent self. Kagitçibasi suggests that psychological aspects of group-oriented cultures, such as close-knit human bonds, may be expected to endure if they do not conflict with the demands of urban life in modern economies and other social structural changes:

> For example, belonging to more than one homogeneous group may be necessitated by urban living and working conditions. *However, how one relates to other in-group members and how closely one is interconnected with them may remain the same.* Thus, for example, work organizations are prevalent in all urban contexts in the world, but whereas such organizations are typically 'secondary' groups in Western societies, they assume 'primary' group qualities in Japan.
>
> (Kagitçibasi 1994: 61; emphasis added)

Furthermore, she suggests that some aspects of individualism in the West are on the wane as people seek out more human relatedness in post-industrial societies.

In contrast to the convergence hypothesis and its rigid demarcation between individualist and group-oriented cultures, there is some evidence that individualist and group-oriented cultural elements may *coexist* in the process of economic and social development. For example, it is incorrect to portray Chinese culture globally as collectivist because it affirms both group-oriented values (e.g. a cooperative orientation) and some individualist values (e.g. self-reliance, individual responsibility) (Ho and Chiu 1994). Mishra (1994) also found a coexistence of individualist and group-oriented values among fathers and sons in eastern Uttar Pradesh in India (see too Sinha and Tripathi 1994). Indeed, Kagitçibasi (1990; 1996) has proposed a coexistence model of selfhood that combines independent and interdependent elements. She claims that intensification of urbanisation in group-oriented cultures weakens *material* intergenerational interdependencies in the family but does not diminish *emotional* interdependencies. Because strong emotional interdependencies persist, she argues, an interdependent conception of the self is still the net outcome (i.e. the predominant notion of personhood).

Individualism and collectivism should not be characterised as *opposing* configurations of cultural values as is implied by the cornerstone and convergence hypotheses. They are not *opposite* ends of a *single* continuum (Ho and Chiu 1994: 155). We must avoid the trap of 'misplaced polarities' (Gusfield 1967). Independent and interdependent selves are not complete antitheses of one another. An interdependent conception of the self does not imply a total melding of inner self and other. It does not imply that the interdependent self is only ever entrepreneurial when performing team-based tasks. Nor does it imply a fatalistic view that people are always pawns of external forces. Indeed, interdependent selves can see themselves as causally efficacious agents who are the catalysts of events in their lives.

Consequently, interdependent selves do not rely solely upon group-referential data and group-based expectations when planning and acting in the world. As we have seen, they also use self-referential data to form self-referential judgements of their own personal efficacy, personal LOC and personal agency in connection with their social roles. Thus, self-referenced data perform a similar role for both independent and interdependent selves in the formation of their personal agency beliefs. In addition, as mentioned above, the alertness of interdependent selves has self-referential aspects as well as group-referential aspects.

Thus, in contrast to the convergence hypothesis, significant cultural variety can be expected to persist even among post-industrial capitalist societies as they continue to develop. It is most unlikely that all market-based economies will converge on a unified cultural pattern of individualist values. 'Diversified capitalism' with multiple adaptive peaks is more likely than 'single-peaked capitalism' (cf. Freeman 2000).

## Conclusion

Economic analyses often treat institutions with the same neglect as they do the law of gravity: 'These factors are implicitly assumed to exist but appear neither as independent nor as dependent variables in the models. Such economy in model making can be eminently reasonable' (Eggertsson 1990: xi). The same could be said of how culture and social rules are treated in most economic discourse. Ignoring the role of culture in market processes might be an admissible, heuristic strategy for developing a line of pure economic analysis. However, we need to explore the significance of the cultural dimension for entrepreneurship if we wish to gain a more complete picture of what influences the human propensity to be alert to economic opportunities, and if we want to determine whether this propensity exists in all individuals and groups of people and whether it will be manifested similarly irrespective of cultural milieu, whether a society has the cultural conditions in place that will help market-preserving institutions to emerge and 'stick', or whether and how a greater understanding of the cultures of various groups in a nation might assist in the development of public policy for entrepreneurship.

This chapter examines the cultural aspects of entrepreneurship and economic development. It provides a preliminary account of why and how culture influences entrepreneurship. It examines how differences in cultural conceptions of selfhood shape alertness. It explains how this important aspect of culture might lend 'predirectedness' to entrepreneurial alertness as well as influence the psychological determinants of the basic propensity to be alert. The approach delves into the highest level of social analysis – the 'social embeddedness' level (Williamson 2000: 596). This level consists of shared mental models, conceptions of personhood, values, norms and customs. The approach thereby integrates a sophisticated account of entrepreneurship (supplied by Austrian economics) with a deep appreciation of the nature of culture as a symbolic phenomenon (supplied by some schools of cultural anthropology and cross-cultural psychology).

In contrast to the cornerstone hypothesis, this chapter predicts that a subset of group-oriented cultures might generate a high degree of entrepreneurial alertness among their members. People in this subset possess a particular constellation of agency beliefs that promotes alertness to economic opportunities. A culture of relatedness and interdependence is thus not inconsistent with vigorous entrepreneurship. This chapter also argues against the 'convergence hypothesis' – the belief that all cultures will tend towards a single dominant cultural pattern, such as individualism, as they industrialise.

# 7 The market-process approach to public policy

> [T]he theory of entrepreneurial discovery has implications which go beyond the simple satisfaction of scientific curiosity. The explanation which it provides drastically alters the way in which significant features of the market economy and of contemporary economic reality are understood or appreciated. The differences in understanding should, in turn, entail important modifications ... in the formulation of practical economic policies to permit the economy to reap its greatest potential in efficiency and in prosperity.
>
> (Kirzner 1997b: 53)

## Policy goals and assumptions

This chapter spells out some general principles that can be used as a basis for developing public policy in general and policy towards entrepreneurship in particular. These principles are derived from the theory of entrepreneurial discovery and the framework developed in previous chapters. As well as providing a starting point for developing public policy, these principles can be used to evaluate current and prospective public policies. Among other things, these rules emphasise taking into account the (often unintended) effects of policy on entrepreneurship and market processes.

Taken as a whole, this general policy approach constitutes what will be referred to as the 'market-process' policy programme (MPP). The specification of the MPP arises out of a desire to provide in a succinct and systematic way the key implications of 'Austrian' market-process theory for public policy. (For the purposes of this chapter, the term 'Austrian' is read to mean the broad subjectivist and market-process school of economic thought.) After defining a public policy programme in more detail, the chapter outlines the specific hard-core assumptions and rules of the MPP. It then examines the relationship of the applied policy analysis of the MPP to the school of theoretical Austrian economics. The next step distinguishes the MPP from two other public policy frameworks based on the 'market-failure' paradigm and the 'perfect-markets' approach, respectively.

It should be noted that this chapter does not aim to come up with detailed and specific policy recommendations for encouraging entrepreneurship. The objective is to provide insights and to suggest guidelines and directions for further policy analysis. For any particular real-world policy problem, the policy recommended will depend upon the specific empirical characteristics of that situation and some assessment of the expected range of possible effects of alternative policies. Detailed policy recommendations are not possible without information about the particular situation.

However, we can begin to use the principles described in this chapter to provide examples of concrete policy options. Indeed, Table 7.2 and the surrounding discussion offer selected 'stylised' policy prescriptions based on the entrepreneurial-discovery perspective to provide a flavour of the sort of policy recommendations that an Austrian market-process scholar might make in order to encourage entrepreneurship and enhance economic coordination. It also compares these prescriptions with those derived from competing policy approaches.

### On the relevance of Austrian market-process theory for public policy

As a by-product of this chapter, I also hope to indicate that applied market-process theory is capable of being operationalised in a policy setting. To this extent, this chapter challenges the criticisms of Austrian economics put forward by Stiglitz (1994) in *Whither Socialism?*.[1] The Austrian theory of entrepreneurial discovery can assist policy decision-makers in solving practical and important policy problems. 'The strength of the [Austrian] school can best be gleaned in the application of its theoretical principles to understand real world problems' (Boettke 1995b: 40).

This raises the question: for which sets of policy problems is Austrian market-process theory likely to have a comparative advantage relative to other approaches? Austrian economics can contribute greatly to enhancing our understanding of the big picture – to explaining how markets and entire economic systems operate within different institutional contexts (Yeager 1997a: 154). It has a comparative advantage in examining fundamental questions concerning the evolution and design of institutional frameworks and their implications for the coordination of economic activities and decisions. Its focus is the constitutional and basic institutional structure of society. To use Vanberg's distinction (2001), the market-process approach favours general regulatory rules that *frame* market processes rather than specific regulatory commands that *intervene* in market processes. Its emphasis is on how, if at all, the functioning of markets might be improved indirectly by modifying the superstructural rules of the game of the market economy rather than upon how desired economic outcomes might be brought about directly by altering particular actions by market participants (e.g. price, quality and quantity decisions). Similarly, in terms of Williamson's taxonomy of four levels of social analysis, Austrian economics has significant value for the second level of analysis, whose aim is to 'get the formal rules of the game right':

The second level is referred to as the institutional environment. The structures observed here are partly the product of evolutionary processes, but design opportunities are also posed. ...

Constrained by the shadow of the past, the design instruments at Level 2 include the executive, legislative, judicial, and bureaucratic functions of government as well as the distribution of powers across different levels of government (federalism). The definition and enforcement of property rights and of contract laws are important features.

(Williamson 2000: 598)

In dealing with the institutional environment, Austrian economics addresses the big policy problems. And given that these problems are most prevalent in societies undergoing significant economic change, the theory of entrepreneurial discovery is especially applicable to examining policy issues related to the transition from a socialist economy (such as East European economies) and those economies facing or going through a process of liberalisation (e.g. the UK in the 1980s, New Zealand in the 1980s and early 1990s). Austrian economics can provide a richer and more sophisticated story of processes of economic adjustment (including economic growth and development) than mainstream economics.

In addition to examining general constitutional principles, Austrian economics has significant implications for the content of substantive public policies (what North calls 'operating rules'), such as competition policy, monetary policy, fiscal policy, tax policy, the treatment of externalities, policy towards state-owned enterprises and so on. It provides guidance on how the coercive powers of the state are to be implemented and advice on the conduct of government in its allocation of scarce means to particular ends, as in the provision of collective goods.

Austrian economics can equip policy-makers with an understanding of aspects of real-world market behaviour that other schools of economics have either ignored or struggled to account for. The theory of entrepreneurial discovery is necessary to help us explain *how* the market economy works. At this time, only Austrian economics can shed light on the implications of dynamic economic processes, uncertainty and the subjective character of knowledge and expectations for the operation of a decentralised market economy and the design of public policies. Only Austrian economics can give a true picture of the nature and role of competition in markets, the entrepreneurial function and the institutional conditions for entrepreneurship. 'Yet one may search in vain for any non-Austrian exposition of the market process. ... If the market process envisaged is not that developed by Austrians, what is it?' (Littlechild 1986: 92).

More importantly, Austrian economists can play an essential role in tracing out the full range of consequences of government intervention for coordination and entrepreneurial discovery processes both in the original market that is the target of that intervention and in adjacent markets. (See the discussion of the heuristics of the MPP later in this chapter.) '[I]nterventionism both increases the level of discoordination within the system (throwing you farther from your destination) and makes it more difficult to eliminate this discoordination (by damaging your compass)' (Ikeda 1997: 122). Austrian economists can determine whether an intervention or set of interventions is giving rise to negative unintended consequences that even the supporters of the policy find undesirable. In particular, they can examine the discoordination that results from the entrepreneurial actions that frustrate the achievement of policy-makers' ends (pp. 91–151).

Furthermore, Austrian economics helps policy-makers to avoid the 'pretence of knowledge' that Hayek warned us against. It reminds policy-makers of the implications of their bounded rationality for acquiring and processing information necessary for centralised economic decision-making. It urges caution in the use of formal 'models' of markets and the economy as a basis for judging economic performance and for establishing the mix and design of policies. The Austrian theory of entrepreneurial discovery makes policy decision-makers recognise their inability specifically to predict and effectively to control people's reactions to intervention in the market:

> To act on the belief that we possess the knowledge and the power which enable us to shape the processes of society entirely to our liking, knowledge which in fact we do *not* possess, is likely to make us do much harm. ...
>
> If man is not to do more harm than good in his efforts to improve the social order, he will have to learn that in this, as in all other fields where essential complexity of an organized kind prevails, he cannot acquire the full knowledge which would make mastery of the events possible. He will therefore have to use what knowledge he can achieve, not to shape the results as the craftsman shapes his handiwork, but rather to cultivate a growth by providing the appropriate environment, in the manner in which the gardener does this for his plants.
>
> (Hayek 1978: 34)

Although it does not reject possible piecemeal reforms, Austrian economics does serve as an analytical check on the hubris of holistic social engineers. It explains how important institutions, such as money, the common law, and even markets themselves, can evolve spontaneously without deliberate planning or design. It reminds us that undesirable conditions and genuine inefficiencies that might emerge in unregulated markets might well be corrected spontaneously by the future course of market processes without the need for deliberate government intervention. The Austrian approach prescribes more than a modicum of modesty in attempts to reconstruct and replace these spontaneous institutions on the basis of definite blueprints. It 'counsels a certain humility against temptations to overthrow spontaneously evolved institutions and practices merely because their rationales have not been fully understood and articulated' (Yeager 1997a: 154).

## *What is the goal of public policy?*

Before I embark upon describing the Austrian market-process approach to public policy, it is important to say a word or two about the nature of public policy goals in general and the policy goal emphasised in this chapter and elsewhere. Clearly, it is not possible to have coherent policy without objectives. The selection of ends depends on value judgements and is beyond the scope of economic analysis (though economic analysis can clarify the implications of the different ends we may select (Robbins 1932: 152)). Hence, the choice of policy goals depends on policy decision-makers' own value judgements or their estimates of the value scales of those people they seek to serve. The choice of means (policies) to achieve given ends, however, can be value neutral.[2] In this case, policy analysis does not reflect personal valuations but rather the analyst's conjectures about the degree of success with which particular policies achieve particular purposes – namely, the purposes of those people who are wanting or proposing the particular policies. Economic analysis can help policy-makers decide on the means to be applied for the attainment of the ends they have chosen: 'science never tells a man how he should act; it merely shows how a man must act if he wants to attain definite ends' (Mises 1966: 10).

The policy goal has been described loosely so far as enhancing entrepreneurship and market processes. This is not entirely straightforward, however. Does 'enhancing entrepreneurship' mean that we seek to increase entrepreneurial *alertness* (= a propensity) or entrepreneurial *activity* (= action)? Does it mean that we aim to promote all entrepreneurship, or just successful entrepreneurship? If it means successful entrepreneurship, from whose perspective is 'success' to be judged: the acting entrepreneur, the observing economist or policy-maker, or someone else? Does 'enhancing entrepreneurship' mean that we wish to increase the number of successful entrepreneurial ventures (with no regard to the magnitude of their effects) or does it mean that we are concerned with the magnitude of their effects (but not with their number), or are we interested in both?

The aim here is merely to alert the reader to the difficulties of defining this policy goal precisely. A rigorous and careful analysis of these issues would require a lengthy exposition and is beyond the scope of this chapter. In addition, the results of such an analysis may well still be quite inconclusive. These difficulties are to some extent inherent in the concept of entrepreneurship itself. Because entrepreneurship is not a factor of production, we cannot talk about increasing the stock of entrepreneurship available to a society. There is no yardstick available for quantifying the supply or degree of entrepreneurship in a society (i.e. it is not amenable to measurement on a cardinal scale). Ordinal measurement (the ranking of social systems by their degree of entrepreneurship) is also problematic.

However, in spite of all these difficulties, it seems reasonable to assume that policy decision-makers (and consumers) would prefer a single case of entrepreneurship which successfully brings about significant coordination of market plans where there had been (or could have been) massive discoordination and severe disappointment of plans (e.g. substantial shortages leading to unsatisfied consumer demand) to several entrepreneurial activities which, taken together, only lead to a slight improvement in market coordination. (The greater degree of coordination achieved in the former case would also be reflected in greater profits being captured by that entrepreneur.) It is the significance of entrepreneurial activities for economic coordination rather than their number per se which is of primary interest.

Consequently, for present purposes, *I will define the policy goal as to enhance successful entrepreneurial alertness that gives rise to significant improvement in economic coordination.* Thus, in this context, the goal of enhancing entrepreneurship is an intermediate goal for achieving the ultimate goal of improved coordination of economic activities. These goals are consistent with a modern Austrian approach to normative welfare economics. This modern approach emphasises the norm of economic coordination as a welfare criterion, not only in the *stationary* sense of a coordinated pattern of economic affairs, but especially in the *dynamic* sense of an economy's potential to promote entrepreneurial discovery processes which detect and correct (though never fully eliminate) previous error and discoordination and which thereby generate a *tendency* towards coordination in the stationary sense (Kirzner 1992: 190–192).

The implication of the entrepreneurial discovery approach is that we should judge the economic performance of a social system not just by the degree of efficiency it achieves in the allocation of resources but, more importantly, by 'the speed and accuracy with which the system is able to identify and overcome the waste and discoordination of disequilibrium situations' (Kirzner 1997a: 76). The socialist calculation debate (and the argument against the possibility of comprehensive central economic planning) suggests that the coordination criterion might be useful for the comparative evaluation of economic systems. At a lower level of analysis, it has also been suggested that the norm of economic coordination (in the dynamic, process sense) can be used as an objective criterion for judging the economic goodness or badness of individual economic policies within a given institutional structure (Kirzner 2000: 132–148). Although the serviceability of this criterion has not yet been conclusively demonstrated for practical policy purposes, we can put forward some conjectures on the impact of a particular policy on the incentives for entrepreneurial discovery and the pace with which sheer ignorance is being reduced. That is, we can tentatively associate specific public policies with greater or lesser likelihood of producing economic coordination.

Using the coordination norm as an index of 'economic goodness' corresponds to Hayek's idea that the goal of policy in a free society is to maximise the fulfilment of people's largely unknown purposes within an abstract social order rather than to achieve a particular, preselected optimal result that satisfies a given set of concrete, known ends.

> A policy making use of the spontaneously ordering forces ... must aim at increasing, for any person picked out at random, the prospects that the overall effect of all changes required by that order will be to increase his chances of attaining his ends.
>
> (Hayek 1976: 114)

A final comment on policy goals is that the discussion in this chapter is concerned largely with increasing entrepreneurship *in isolation of other objectives*. The objective of enhancing successful entrepreneurial alertness (and of increasing economic coordination) is taken as given. This chapter does not investigate the advantages and disadvantages of this goal but it does assume implicitly (i.e. invoke the value judgement) that increasing the degree of entrepreneurship and social coordination is worthwhile. That is, a greater degree of coordinatedness in economic activity is assumed to be good (as asserted by some independently established moral philosophy). 'When we identify coordination as being the criterion for economic "goodness", we are asserting that, from the perspective of those whom economists aspire to serve, the function of an economic system is to coordinate the activities of its participants' (Kirzner 2000: 137). The relationship between increasing the level of entrepreneurship in a society and other objectives of public policy is a high priority for future research since economic well-being is only one component of human welfare.

## Treating political institutions as given

This chapter largely abstracts from public-choice considerations – that is, it does not apply economic theory to analyse 'non-market' decision-making or political behaviour. The approach treats existing political institutions as exogenous. That is, it assumes that the rules of the game of politics ('the political constitution') are given. In particular, it assumes a democratically structured constitutional state, organised on either unitary or federal lines.

However, this does not mean that the policy analysis developed in accordance with the MPP is solely at the sub-constitutional level. Indeed, it can be conducted at both the constitutional and sub-constitutional levels. To the extent that policy analysis involves comparing the properties of the spontaneous market order with those of alternative arrangements (e.g. deliberate organisation, central planning), policy analysis is being conducted at the constitutional level. 'Opting for the market system is a matter of *constitutional choice*' (Vanberg 2001: 140; original emphasis), however implicit that choice might be. Thus, examining the different patterns of entrepreneurial actions and discovery processes that emerge under different kinds of rules of the game (i.e. alternative 'economic constitutions') is a constitutional issue. So too is analysis of how to set up and maintain the rules of the game that make markets function well (as do Chapters 4 and 5). To the extent that policy analysis developed in line with the MPP examines the effects of policy options on competitive market processes within a particular framework of property rights and other constitutionally determined rules, analysis is being conducted at the sub-constitutional level.

Although political institutions evolve through internal forces, there is as yet no well-developed Austrian theory of political economy which provides a full account of these endogenous changes or which explains human action in the political sphere. Indeed, Littlechild (1986: 89) has commented that the lack of progress in investigating regulatory discovery and adjustment processes in a political context limits the usefulness and applicability of Austrian insights into current policy problems.[3]

Accordingly, the MPP does not focus on the political processes by which public policies emerge or the procedures that allow people in the polity to engage in organised collective action. It does not examine decision-makers in political markets or the results of political entrepreneurship. It studies coordination in economic markets but not in political markets, and there are important differences in these two types of process.

> The political process, just like the market process, should not be expected to generate optimal allocations. Both are imperfect. Unlike the market process, however, democratic politics does not engender the incentives and information for its own error detection and correction.
>
> (Boettke 1995a: 24)

The aim of this chapter is to apply to public policy what is unique in Austrian economics. The lack of an explicit treatment of public-choice issues should not be read as a disregard for this line of research. Indeed, the public-choice perspectives of the Virginia and Chicago schools have much to offer, and they complement the MPP (Ikeda 1997: 149–152). In particular, Buchanan (1986), Tullock (1987), Vanberg (1994) and Wagner (1989b) are modern scholars within the public-choice tradition who have applied Austrian-style insights on economics, law and politics in the development of modern political economy. The lack of emphasis upon public-choice considerations merely reflects the current state of Austrian political economy and the fact that public-choice perspectives have not yet been adequately integrated with an Austrian approach to the analysis of government intervention.

Although this work does not deal explicitly with the analytical issues raised by public-choice scholars, the analysis in previous chapters is consistent with much of the literature on public choice and rent seeking. Indeed, many of the rules of the MPP only make sense if the conclusions of public-choice theory are correct. For example, the examination of the rule of law is presented with an awareness of the logic of concentrated benefits and dispersed costs (Chapter 4). General, equal and certain rules eliminate opportunities for special-interest groups to capture bureaucrats and legislators and to manipulate the political process for their own benefit at the expense of the general citizenry. These constitutional rules make it harder to seek wealth through redistribution via the political mechanism. Furthermore, and in line with public-choice proposals, the analysis in Chapter 5 emphasises the importance of federalism as a constitutional constraint on democratic government and the discretionary power of the legislature and other public decision-makers. Both public choice and Austrian political economy recognise the need for effective constitutional rules that safeguard private property rights.

## The MPP

### *What is a public policy programme?*

As the name implies, a public policy programme (or, simply, 'policy programme') is a set of ideas and rules that policy advisers and decision-makers can use for thinking about, and for developing, public policy. It is a prospectus for developing a general public policy framework. The notion of a public policy programme must not be confused with concrete policy initiatives that are often referred to as government programmes (e.g. housing and urban development programmes). As used here, the term 'policy programme' is a conceptual apparatus for policy analysis and development.

The idea of a policy programme adapts the concept of a scientific research programme which was developed by Lakatos (1970; 1978) in the philosophy of science. Broadly speaking, a scientific research programme is a distinctive framework of scientific enquiry that contains a descriptive and a normative hard core. The descriptive hard core comprises propositions about the nature of the world, which are treated as irrefutable by scientists working within the programme. The normative hard core includes a positive heuristic which is a set of methodological decision rules for solving problems and a set of instructions for developing the research programme. A research programme is also shielded by a protective belt of auxiliary hypotheses and propositions that are subject to scientific testing and experimentation.

Similarly, a policy programme is a conceptual framework characterised by two essential components: a set of descriptive *hard-core propositions* upon which policy analysis is based and a set of rules or *heuristics* for doing policy analysis (the normative hard core). A policy programme represents a particular perspective on the world. It makes explicit the foundations of our thinking, including the economic foundations of our policy analysis. The hard core and heuristics determine the nature of policy analysis that an adviser gives.

The growth of our knowledge requires a set of conventions, which imposes a structure for enquiry (Popper 1959; 1963). Accordingly, a policy programme constitutes a coordinative framework for policy analysis and development. It assists learning by organising the policy-maker's problem solving and decisions. It coordinates the policy analyst's choice and interpretation of policy problems, and it guides the analyst's selection and application of economic theories and models to the solution of those problems. A policy programme performs a useful heuristic role in guiding the policy decision-maker's search for information and explanations.

The policy programme provides general instructions on how institutions and policies should be developed in order to meet policy-makers' objectives. It guides them in adapting to changes in the environment, and it gives directions on how to respond to feedback about the apparent success or failure of policy. It should be noted that it is not so much the effect of one particular hard-core proposition or rule taken in isolation that is important in developing policy analysis but rather the effect of the policy programme as a whole.

Having a hard core is useful because it means that policy analysts do not have to keep returning to square one each time they encounter difficulties or empirical anomalies. This is particularly important when policy advisers have to provide analysis at short notice and under stressful conditions of great urgency. In practice, much policy analysis rests on the ability to apply rapidly a tentatively accepted framework to policy problems in order to develop policy recipes for the attainment of prescribed goals. Thus, the hard core and heuristics economise on the bounded rationality of policy decision-makers. In a complex and uncertain world, such rules are an economical way of filtering and analysing information.

Specifying the policy programme underlying our policy analysis also helps us build the foundations for fresh strategic thinking. It enables us to meet a former Secretary of the New Zealand Treasury's suggestion that we should be 'aware of our biases, think about how we think, and avoid being rigid or defensive' (Scott 1992). Specifying the policy programme makes us aware of the domain of application and the limits of our approach to policy decision-making. It enables us to monitor and review how we approach policy problems, and it helps us to keep our thinking processes sharp.

The following sections attempt to specify the policy programme based on the Austrian theory of entrepreneurship and competitive market processes. The MPP summarises the conventional wisdom that Austrian economists have about public policy. It reflects the entrepreneurial-discovery perspective on the role of the state in the catallaxy. It provides a coherent approach for consistently applying the methods and results of Austrian economic analysis to policy problems. Specifying the fundamental claims of the Austrian school in the form of a policy programme also serves a useful function in avoiding misunderstandings about the nature of Austrian economics, which is sometimes mistaken for an ideological advocacy of free-market policies.

The MPP involves the *practical* application of well-corroborated intellectual developments in *theoretical* Austrian economics, especially market-process theory. Thus, we must differentiate the MPP from the school (or scientific research programme) of theoretical Austrian economics. The MPP treats the results of that research programme largely as given. I have more to say on the relationship between the MPP and the Austrian scientific research programme later in the chapter.

This chapter attempts to define the MPP in a way that will be acceptable to almost all Austrian market-process theorists and policy analysts. It seeks to identify the set of hard-core propositions and rules relevant for policy purposes that is considered beyond question by the great majority of Austrian economists. As a consequence, the description of the hard core and heuristics of the MPP is a conjecture of what the consensus is among Austrian economists (*qua* economic scientists) about the hard core rather than a proposal of what should constitute the hard core of the MPP. In other words, it is a positive rather than a normative statement of the MPP.

Because it is meant to represent the widely held views of Austrian economists, the following statement of the MPP is *inherently individualist* in its orientation, which is the norm amongst Austrian economists. It takes the individual decision-maker, not interdependent members of a group, to be the sole locus of alertness and the unit of analysis in policy development (see *H8* and *R6* below). At least at this stage, it does not draw upon the cultural approach to entrepreneurship developed in Chapter 6.

Furthermore, the following description of the MPP should not be taken as definitive. It is an initial attempt at specifying this programme. *By its nature, a policy programme will always be incompletely specified.* For one thing, there will always be some hidden assumptions and tacit rules which economists use in their policy analysis which neither they nor others are aware of yet. The assumptions they hold may be neither stated explicitly nor subject to scrutiny in their day-to-day work. In addition, like other policy programmes, the MPP is not static. The hardening of a programme's hard core is a process that takes place in time. Moreover, the set of heuristics has to be developed piecemeal as the programme itself unfolds. The programme and its specification may need updating as changes occur in both background knowledge (including intellectual developments in Austrian market-process theory and experience of public policies) and the external environment in which policy decision-makers operate. 'Austrian economics is still in the process of self-creation' (Rizzo 1996: xvii).

It must also be remembered that not everything that Austrian economists say and write about is necessarily Austrian economics (e.g. they may sometimes dabble in political philosophy as *obiter dicta* to their economic analyses). The description of the hard core attempts to distil what is essentially Austrian policy analysis rather than to catalogue exhaustively everything that can be found (often incidentally) in the works of Austrian economists. This point is important. For instance, it bears on the question of what the future of the MPP is likely to be.

## *The hard core of the MPP*

The MPP is organised around several key groupings of hard-core propositions that applied Austrian economists and policy analysts believe firmly and decide not to question for now. (See the box below.) The hard core includes central assumptions and hypotheses about the nature of the policy environment and the basic tenets of Austrian policy analysis.

---

### The hard core of the MPP

#### *H1 Spontaneous ordering processes*

There is a tendency in markets towards coordination of individual economic activities.

> To assert that there is such a tendency is to make no claim about the frequency with which [actual] coordination comes about. ... The presumption that action is coordinating does not have direct empirical applicability. Nevertheless, it can still be a useful tool in identifying important features of actual markets.
>
> (Rizzo 1982: 59)

In other words, there is a tendency for the whole of the economic order based on private property and voluntary exchange to run itself. It is not in the power of policy-makers (or of anyone else for that matter) to acquire the full knowledge that would enable them deliberately to control or replicate this social order.

#### *H2 Dynamic competition*

The competitive market is a dynamic process of entrepreneurial discovery rather than a state of equilibrium in which there is no need and no opportunity to compete. The competitive market process tends to discover what goods and services consumers want, how much they are willing to pay and how goods and services can be produced at lower cost. Changes over time in prices, production, the range of products, plans, knowledge and expectations are more important than prices and output at any point in time. There exist entrepreneurs who adjust prices and modify other elements of the marketing mix (quantities, qualities and product characteristics). Competitive

---

entrepreneurial-discovery processes are the engine of economic development. In other words, economic development is the overall, unintended result of a myriad of individual profit-motivated discoveries of previously overlooked opportunities for trading and innovation.

## H3 Market dominance and profit

Neither the number of firms operating in a market nor the magnitude of profits seized is, in itself, a cause for concern. Market dominance may result when there are wide differences in industry participants' alertness to profitable opportunities. Profit arises from successful entrepreneurial activity. It is the reward for discovering and correcting errors in other people's buying and selling decisions. It is not the result of monopoly power. Monopoly rents tend to be transient in the context of competitive market processes, and they are likely to develop and persist in the context of arrangements that inhibit such processes.

## H4 Structural uncertainty

Policy decision-makers and economic agents act in an open-ended world of structural uncertainty, complexity and real time.[4] Their knowledge is highly imperfect, incomplete, fragmented, contextual and often tacit. There is real indeterminism in the world of public policy and economic affairs. As a result, policies often have unintended and undesirable consequences. 'Even moderate amounts of intervention produce results that are unsatisfactory from the point of view of the benevolent interventionist' (Rizzo 1992a: 251). Through the operation of an entire complex system, the effects of policy decisions may be very different from, and even opposite to, intentions. 'The competitive-entrepreneurial process, being a process of discovery of the as yet unknown, can hardly be predicted in any but the broadest terms' (Kirzner 1985: 145). Thus, economists cannot provide reliable numerical forecasts of particular events but they can strive to supply qualitative predictions and explanations of the possible effects of alternative policy proposals.

## H5 Superior plan-coordinating properties of markets

Government is presumed to be more prone to failure than the market since the incentives to correct errors in public policy are weaker than those to correct poor decisions in the market, and the information requirements for central planning (vis-à-vis decentralised decision-making in markets) are logically and practically impossible to fulfil. 'The profit and loss system has greater coordinating properties than any other feasible system of allocating resources' (Rizzo 1992a: 251). In general, alleged cases of 'market failure' tend not to result from inherent deficiencies of the market as a type of economic organisation but from shortcomings in the framework of laws and institutions within which the market operates (see Kirzner 2000: 86). 'Externalities exist because the facilities to make relevant transactions do not exist' (Littlechild 1986: 64).

### H6   *The spontaneous origin of money, and monetary disequilibria*

Money is the spontaneous outgrowth of market activity rather than the product of state action or a social contract (Menger 1892; 1994). Money is

> not merely one good among many (e.g. the numeraire in a general equilibrium system), but a good whose (near) perfect liquidity gives it an influence over economic activity qualitatively different from any other good. It is the medium through which almost all exchanges take place.
>
> (Horwitz 2000: 3)

The emergence of money makes possible a complex division of labour, and it enables entrepreneurs to make profit and loss calculations. Excess demands or supplies of money affect all markets and weaken the capacity of markets to perform their coordinative function. The way that money supply increases enter the market affects how and when particular banks, customers and sectors receive additions to their money balances. It thereby affects the pattern of market exchanges and distorts the array of relative prices and the intertemporal structure of capital. In a fully market-driven monetary regime or 'free banking' system, the quantity of money would be an unintended result of a market-discovery process involving individual customers and private profit-seeking banks that produce competing brands of currency (redeemable in some base money) (Selgin and White 1994).

### H7   *Extra-market institutional framework*

The market process relies upon the presence of extra-market (including governmental) institutions that support processes of discovery, production and exchange, such as the emergence of private property rights, arbitration in disputes about the interpretation of such rights and freedom and enforceability of private contract (Kirzner 2000: 77–87). These extra-market institutions include widely shared ethical principles that require us to respect the truth and other people's property. The best way to improve the performance of markets is to improve the framework of rules and institutions that underpin them rather than to try to reconfigure final market outcomes. An institutional framework that maximises individual economic freedom (consistent with equal freedom for all) is most conducive to entrepreneurship and economic development.

## H8 Methodological individualism and subjectivism

Economic phenomena arise from the actions or inactions of individuals. Individuals engage in purposeful behaviour: they try to reach ends and goals they have chosen; and they act in order to remove or alleviate some uneasiness or dissatisfaction with the state of their affairs (Mises 1966: 11–17). Only individual economic agents have aims, beliefs and preferences, and only individuals can make decisions. Individuals inevitably differ in their purposes, judgements, preferences, knowledge, perceptions, expectations and degree of alertness. Different people know different things about resource availabilities, technology and consumers' wants. Consequently, knowledge is localised and dispersed.

## H9 Subjective costs and benefits

The costs and benefits that determine choice are unique to the economic actor and are inherently subjective. The true character of the cost of adopting a course of action is that it reflects the chooser's own evaluation of the utility of the best alternative opportunity that must be forgone as a result of choosing (Buchanan 1973; Rizzo 1994). It follows that 'social cost' and 'net social benefit' (e.g. from a change in government policy) cannot be objectively measured. Ultimately, public policy must depend on the value judgements of the policy-makers or of their own estimates of the value scales of those they wish to serve.

## H10 Non-neutrality of government intervention

No government intervention (in the sense of a specific act aimed at a particular result) is ever neutral (Rothbard 1981). All regulatory commands, taxes, and activist monetary and fiscal policies have real effects on economic activity. They distort the formation of relative prices and hamper processes of entrepreneurial discovery and economic coordination. Developing and implementing supposedly 'efficient' regulatory commands (e.g. externalities taxes) and 'optimal' monetary and fiscal policies entail knowledge problems akin to that of central economic planning. Government interventions in market processes not only change the relative desirability of *already perceived* alternative courses of action. They also distort or weaken the incentive to discover *as yet unnoticed* opportunities or courses of action (Kirzner 1985: 93–111). A policy of limited government intervention into the market process generates unintended consequences that increase the likelihood of further intervention.

### H11 *Path dependence*

History matters and so do the timing and sequencing of changes in institutions and public policies. The process by which institutions and policies develop is significant because it constrains future choices of both economic actors and policy-makers.

> Historical events can have an effect in the short run, on how a market or economy evolves, and this short run effect can, in certain circumstances, be maintained, or amplified in such a way that it changes the long run evolution of that market or economy.
>
> (Cowan 1995: 3)

Economic processes in real time, such as learning in the market, innovation and economic development, are irreversible and path dependent. These processes always run asymmetrically because they entail novelty.[5]

Though they can be of various levels of complexity, generality and abstraction, the hard-core propositions tend to be high-level postulates and hypotheses upon which policy decision-makers build their analyses, advice and choices. These fundamental presumptions correspond to Schumpeter's (1954) pre-analytic vision and to what Converse (1964) calls 'central idea-elements' in a person's political 'belief system'. They are the propositions from which the policy decision-makers derive all others in elaborating their policy approaches. In a sense, these assumptions determine and entail all the lower-level predictions and prescriptions that policy analysts and advisers make about the world.

## *The heuristics of the MPP*

A policy programme also contains a set of rules or heuristics that we use to guide policy analysis and development. This set of rules is just as 'hard' as the hard core. These rules are the hard core's normative component. They can be stated in both positive terms ('Do *x*') and negative terms ('Don't do *y*'). Positively expressed, these rules specify which analytical methods we are to apply to policy problems. They guide how we identify, interpret and deal with possible policy problems and how we develop tentative solutions. Negatively stated, these rules indicate which kinds of policy analysis and methods are to be avoided. They specify what we must not do. In other words, the rules of a policy programme may prescribe or proscribe particular techniques of thinking.

The next box specifies the heuristics of the MPP. Many of these sets of rules correspond to a relevant hard-core assumption, so that there is a high degree of complementarity between the various components of the MPP. The pieces of the programme fit together into a coherent pattern. (Note that some categories of heuristics have been combined because of substantial synergies between them, such as exists between rules about dynamic competition and market dominance. Hence, the labelling of these rules does not correspond perfectly with that of the hard-core assumptions.)

---

## The heuristics of the MPP

### R1 *Spontaneous ordering processes*

- Seek to explain complex social phenomena in terms of spontaneous ordering processes.
- Take account of potential spontaneous ordering processes (especially entrepreneurial-discovery processes), and their strength and speed, in analysing perceived problems with market outcomes and investigate the reaction of spontaneous market forces to government intervention.
- Assess rules of the game and institutional arrangements according to the principles of certainty, generality and equality. Determine the extent to which rules will be stable and predictable, the degree to which they can be applied without arbitrary discretion and the extent to which they apply equally to everybody, including those who govern.
- Examine the pattern of outcomes arising from market processes rather than particular results, and acknowledge that the particular results that emerge from the choices of market participants must remain indeterminate.
- Pay particular attention to the factors that can frustrate the attainment of coordination of economic activities in real-world markets.

In particular, identify the effects of legal rules and policies on the scope for voluntary mutually beneficial exchange.

- When economic activities appear discoordinated and the policy goal is greater coordination, search for the source of the 'relevant communication breakdown among economic agents' (Rizzo 1982: 64).
- If in given circumstances government intervention is deemed necessary to support the supply of particular collective goods, then do so in a manner that as much as possible avoids impairing the spontaneous forces of markets for other goods and services (Hayek 1979: 46).
- Determine how to conduct fiscal affairs so as to give greatest scope to market forces in the private sector.

### R2 *Dynamic competition, market dominance and profit*

- Treat the market as an open-ended, dynamic competitive process. Do not base policy analysis upon 'single-exit' economic models, that is, closed models that yield a determinate equilibrium.
- In tracing out the direct and indirect effects of public policies, pay particular attention to the impact on entrepreneurship and new market entry. Focus upon the effects on: the incentive for entrepreneurs to discover arbitrage, speculative and innovative opportunities; the incentive for, and ability of, entrepreneurs to exploit the opportunities that they have discovered; the pattern of entrepreneurial activity; and the degree of people's entrepreneurial alertness, including its psychological determinants. Identify institutional barriers to entrepreneurship, examine the effects of policies on competitive selection pressures, and consider the effects of policies on entrepreneurial choices with respect to inputs, outputs, production, prices, quantities and qualities.
- Identify sources of monopoly power and monopoly rents. Focus on discovering which arrangements or government-imposed barriers may be inhibiting competitive market processes from reducing or eliminating these rents.
- Do not base policy analysis on a priori views about what the market structure or the size distribution of firms should be.
- Recognise that starting up a new firm is neither necessary nor sufficient for an act of entrepreneurship.

### R3 *Structural uncertainty*

- Recognise the severe knowledge problems inherent in centralised decision-making and the bounded rationality of policy-makers (especially government planners) in a complex and uncertain world. Avoid any 'pretence of knowledge'.

- Recognise that, in complex economic structures, policies may have effects that are not only different from, but also the opposite to, those intended. Attempt to identify the range of such possible policy effects.
- Recognise that as policy analysts and decision-makers, we can only learn from our mistakes. Proceed, step by step, carefully comparing the results expected with the results achieved. Always keep on the lookout for the unintended undesirable consequences of any policy initiative (Popper 1961).
- Favour qualitative predictions of likely consequences of policy options rather than spuriously precise numerical forecasts.
- Use econometrics as one tool to explain complex historical phenomena but do not interpret econometrically derived relations as universally applicable, time-invariant relations (Rizzo 1978: 53).

## R4 Comparative institutional approach

- Take account of the institutional rules of the game in which economic processes are embedded.
- Seek to improve the functioning of markets indirectly by improving the rules of the game that frame market processes rather than directly by ad hoc interventions in the market order (Vanberg 2001: 40–41).
- Search for the source of alleged 'market failures', arising from 'externalities', in potential loopholes in the institutional (especially property rights) framework within which markets operate. Do not attribute such undesired market outcomes to the failure of the market to coordinate plans with respect to that framework (Mises 1966: 654–661; Kirzner 2000: 86).
- Recognise that the error-correcting mechanism of regulatory processes is likely to be weaker than that of the market.
- Avoid using the standard of Pareto efficiency because it presumes omniscience on the part of the observing economist (Hayek 1948: 104–105).
- When the policy goal is greater economic coordination, judge the performance of an economy or economic system not only by the efficiency with which it allocates given and known resources at a point in time (taking as given production technologies and consumer tastes) but also, and more importantly, by the speed with which it discovers and responds to new opportunities over time. Evaluate institutional arrangements in terms of their potential to inspire entrepreneurial discovery of genuine error (i.e. previously overlooked opportunities) (Kirzner 1992: 191).

### R5  Money and monetary disequilibria

- Treat seriously money and its surrounding institutions by emphasising money's role as a generally accepted medium of exchange that lacks a price and a unique market of its own (Yeager 1997b: 228).
- Recognise that money plays a crucial role in competitive discovery processes and price formation in real-world markets.
- Recognise that 'any analysis of excesses or deficiencies in the money supply must involve the institutions that are responsible for supplying money' (Horwitz 2000: 4).
- Recognise that changes in the nominal supply of money (with money demand unchanged) frustrate the coordination function of markets because they systematically distort the formation of relative prices and entrepreneurial plans and because they have real (i.e. non-neutral) and unsustainable effects on the intertemporal structure of heterogeneous capital.[6]
- Identify the relative-price effects and allocative (or 'first-round') distortions of a monetary disturbance (e.g. a money supply increase required to maintain price-level stability in a growing economy) (Garrison 2001: 5).
- Recognise that a recession (following inflationary credit expansion) is the recovery stage of the business cycle, in which entrepreneurial errors and wasteful uses of capital are revealed and corrected (Rothbard 1963: 20–21).

### R6  Individualism and subjectivism

- Develop policy analysis in a way that is consistent with the principles of methodological individualism. That is, make the individual decision-maker the unit of analysis in policy analysis. Explain economic phenomena and policy problems in terms of the valuations, perceptions, expectations, choices and behaviour of individual economic agents (e.g. individual consumers, producers, investors, entrepreneurs, etc.). Base policy analysis on economic theories that are consistent with methodological individualism.
- Consider the impacts of public policies on individual decision-makers' goals, incentives, degree of entrepreneurial alertness, expectations, knowledge (including knowledge of constraints and opportunities available), learning behaviour, the revision of their plans and the compatibility of their actions with those of other people. Pay particular attention to the expectational element of policy analysis and consider whether the policy or policy change can be credible and effective in light of its effects on people's expectations and their learning from experience.

- Determine whether individuals will acquire the knowledge necessary to modify their conduct in line with policy-makers' intentions. Identify what type of information people need to make decisions and investigate how they can be expected to acquire that information, once the policy is implemented.
- Determine whether the individuals involved have the incentive to change their behaviour in line with policy-makers' intentions. Investigate whether it will be in the self-interest of individuals to act in the way desired by policy-makers, once the policy is implemented (i.e. determine whether the policy is incentive compatible).

## R7 Subjective costs and benefits

- Emphasise the subjectivity of costs and benefits in policy analysis. Recognise that 'cost must be borne exclusively by the person who makes decisions' and that 'cost cannot be measured by someone other than the chooser because there is no way that subjective mental experience can be directly observed' (Buchanan 1973: 15).
- Refuse to recognise 'meaning in statements concerning the "welfare of society" that cannot, in principle, be unambiguously translated into statements concerning the individuals in society (in a manner which does not do violence to their individuality)' (Kirzner 1992: 181).
- Do not accept analyses or statements that depict the 'economic well-being of society as expressible in terms (such as physical output) that are unrelated to the valuations and choices made by individuals' (Kirzner 1992: 181). Do not depend upon aggregate notions of welfare, such as gross domestic product.
- Reject standard neoclassical welfare analysis of public policy and do not rely on social cost–benefit analyses of policies (Cordato 1992).
- Do not attempt to provide a basis for policy decisions by trying to measure the relative utilities or satisfactions of different persons.

## R8 Non-neutrality of government intervention

- Identify both the direct effects of the initial government intervention as well as the indirect effects that result from subsequent interventions likely to be required to address negative unintended consequences of the former government action.
- Identify the likely relative-price effects (i.e. the standard or Type-I incentive effects) of a regulatory command or tax and examine how it encourages or discourages decision-makers from selecting particular actions out of a set of already perceived alternative courses of action.

- Consider the potentially significant negative effects (i.e. the discovery or Type-II incentive effects) of a regulatory command or tax upon barriers to entrepreneurial entry and the incentive of entrepreneurs to discover as yet unnoticed opportunities or courses of action that might otherwise have been discovered but now will not be.
- Consider how a government intervention enhances the potential of opportunities to be discovered and exploited that would not have existed in the absence of the intervention and that are superfluous to the process of market coordination (another discovery effect of intervention).
- Consider the effects of government intervention on entrepreneurial adjustment in both the original market that was the target of the intervention and adjacent markets.
- Identify the likely consequences of a government intervention for heterogeneous elements of the intertemporal capital structure.

### R9 Path dependence

- In explaining economic phenomena and analysing policy issues, consider the genesis of those phenomena and issues. That is, examine the historical process that gives rise to their emergence.
- Emphasise obtaining empirical and historical information about the relevant features of the policy problem.
- Recognise path dependence in the analysis, design and implementation of policies.
- Identify potential bottlenecks arising from particular timing and sequences of policy options.

The rules of the MPP tend to be general in nature, recommending how to do policy analysis rather than elaborating specific policy prescriptions. They are general rules whose application to any particular policy problem will require detailed empirical information about the specific circumstances of time and place.

Of particular interest are the rules that relate to the non-neutrality of government intervention (*H10, R8*). The heuristics of the MPP direct us to trace out in detail the full spectrum of effects of different types of government intervention (in the sense of specific regulatory commands aimed at particular results). In particular, it directs us to identify and explain the largely unintended consequences of public policies for entrepreneurial discovery and market processes. More than any other policy approach, the MPP quite rightly requires us to evaluate the hidden 'dynamic effects' of government intervention, such as the stifling and misdirection of entrepreneurial-discovery processes and the distortion of the intertemporal capital structure. Consequently, unlike other policy approaches that ignore the entrepreneurial discovery process, the MPP is less likely to understate the adverse consequences of regulatory interferences in the market and less likely to understate the potential beneficial effects of economic liberalisation.

In the case of each government intervention, the MPP requires us to consider various types of unintended consequences for entrepreneurial discovery and economic coordination (see Ikeda 1997: 99–137). In particular, we are instructed to assess the:

1  *direct* effects that result from the initial intervention;
2  *indirect* effects that result from subsequent interventions likely to be required to address unintended problems caused by the initial intervention;
3  *internal* consequences that affect coordination in the particular market that is the original target of the intervention;
4  *external* consequences that affect coordination in adjacent markets for complementary and substitute goods and services.

In analysing each of the above effects, we must also examine the *standard (or Type-I) incentive* effects that change the relative desirability of already perceived alternative courses of action. More importantly, for each of the above, we must also examine and emphasise the *discovery (or Type-II incentive)* effects that change the propensity to discover as yet unnoticed opportunities or courses of action. The analysis of discovery effects requires us to investigate how an intervention might generate impediments (such as barriers to new market entry) that inhibit entrepreneurial discovery and the exploitation of opportunities within and between markets. It also requires us to examine how government interference in the market might create 'wholly superfluous' entrepreneurial opportunities (e.g. tax loopholes) that would not have existed in the absence of the intervention(s).

As a general observation, it is worth noting that the MPP rejects 'single-exit' methods of policy analysis (Latsis 1972; 1976b). Austrian policy analysts do not see their job as calculating the optimal policy:

> In Austrian thinking, the task is not primarily one of computing the optimal solution to a well-defined 'problem', but rather one of discovering the 'problem' in the first place (and the possibility of making some improvement), then gathering and utilising the necessary information, and finally implementing an improved solution.
>
> (Littlechild 1986: 65)

It is for this reason that the MPP tends to emphasise considering spontaneous ordering processes in policy analysis *(H1, R1)*.

Finally, it should be noted that these rules are heuristics, not algorithms that entirely and deterministically direct policy analysts' choices. They provide plenty of scope for the creativity of policy decision-makers.

## *The relationship of the MPP to the Austrian school of economics*

In this and the next section, I relate the MPP to the Austrian school of economics, and I compare it with other policy programmes derived from other schools of economic thought. This discussion aims to highlight the distinctive characteristics of the MPP rather than to provide an appraisal of it.

The MPP deals purely with applied economic and policy analysis, and as such it needs to be distinguished from the school, or more formally, the scientific research programme, of theoretical Austrian economics. The Austrian scientific research programme has been specified precisely by Rizzo (1982) and Langlois (1982). In contrast, the specification of the MPP is by its very nature less exact.

The MPP involves the practical utilisation of the provisionally accepted results and methods of the Austrian scientific research programme. For their purposes, policy-makers take the 'well-corroborated'[7] hypotheses and predictions of the Austrian research programme largely as given and adopt these hypotheses as a basis for policy analysis and action. From the point of view of policy decision-makers, the Austrian scientific research programme is relatively autonomous. They treat it as a decomposable system, which is not affected by their experiences of success or failure in public policy. Similarly, theorists in Austrian economics consider that their discipline develops largely independently of the verdict of policy experiments.[8]

There is some overlap between the hard cores and heuristics of the MPP and those of the Austrian scientific research programme. For instance, the spontaneous-ordering postulate *(H1)* is in the hard core of the MPP, and it is also in the hard core of the Austrian economics research programme.[9] However, they need not coincide entirely. Public policy-makers may consider propositions to be in the hard core of the MPP even though they are only part of the auxiliary protective belt of the Austrian economics research programme.[10] (This gives rise to a kind of core/demicore map of the sort described by Remenyi 1979.) *H3* on market dominance and profit, *H7* on the extra-market institutional framework and *H11* on path dependence may fall into this category.

Finally, it must be emphasised that this specification of the MPP is not the only conceivable policy programme derivable from modern Austrian economics. Other variants are clearly possible and the programme can be expected to evolve over time. For instance, a follower of Rothbard's approach is likely to modify or remove the hard-core proposition *H7*, which assumes a role for government in setting rules of the game, and develop an anarcho-capitalist variant of the MPP which denies the need for a publicly provided institutional framework. In addition, Austrian economists who place a high value on positive freedom could conceivably develop a policy programme based on Austrian economics that implies a different role for government.

Thus, it is conceded that there is more to Austrian economics and policy analysis than market-process theory. A greater emphasis upon other important areas within modern Austrian economics, such as business cycle theory, monetary theory and capital theory, might contribute to other distinctly Austrian policy approaches. However, the Austrian market-process theory is sufficiently central to the revival of interest in Austrian ideas that it warrants individualised attention (Kirzner 1997a: 61).

## Comparison of the MPP with other policy programmes

Just as there are several schools of economics, so too there are potentially several public policy programmes. Indeed, the existence of competing policy programmes is potentially more profitable in terms of increasing our knowledge of market-preserving institutions and public policies than is a situation in which a policy programme has achieved monopoly.

This section compares the MPP with two other policy approaches: the 'market-failure' policy programme and the 'perfect-markets' policy programme.[11] These policy programmes represent three readily identifiable perspectives on policy analysis, which, although interrelated, are distinct enough to warrant comparative analysis. This classification scheme is not idiosyncratic or arbitrary. It is familiar to many economists and policy analysts, and they often see themselves as adopting one or other of these approaches.

The taxonomy of policy approaches is more analytical than sociological. It classifies policy programmes by the particular stance they take regarding the workings of the market. It seeks to describe objective interrelations among ideas. Each policy programme provides principles that are sufficiently precise to provide clear guidance on policy.

### *The perfect-markets policy programme*

The first of these programmes, the perfect-markets policy programme, considers that the neoclassical model of perfect competition provides an accurate description of most real-world markets – that is, the conditions of the real world often match the approximations of the model. According to this programme, unregulated markets generate economically efficient outcomes. Consequently, proponents of this programme often claim that there is a very minimal role for government in the economic sphere.

Unlike the MPP, which depicts the market as a dynamic process of discovery in disequilibrium, the perfect-markets policy programme relies upon an equilibrium market-clearing perspective, and it often seeks to analyse economic behaviour and policy problems within a general equilibrium setting. It focuses upon states of equilibrium in which there are no profit opportunities. It assumes that all economic agents are consistent and successful optimisers within the limits of their information. They are limited to economising in the allocation of given and known means to achieve a set of given and known ends. Economic decision-makers are seen to be forward looking and to have rational expectations. They do not make systematic errors in evaluating their environment and they typically have true actuarial knowledge of the past, present and future. They do not face structural uncertainty.

The focus on perfect markets sufficiently captures the dominant perspective of the Chicago school that it seems reasonable to regard this policy programme as in some sense the 'essence' of the overall Chicago approach. However, the perfect-markets policy programme is also neoclassical in a broader sense to the extent that it adheres to the tenets of maximising behaviour, stable preferences through time and market equilibrium, and to the extent that there are perfect-markets theorists who are neoclassical but not Chicago economists. The perfect-markets approach includes policy analysis derived from Friedman's ideas on economic methodology and monetarism, Stigler's theory of search, Becker's theory of human capital and Lucas's and Sargent's elaboration of the new classical macroeconomics.[12]

New classical economics is a paradigmatic exemplar of the perfect-markets programme. Its proponents believe that we can explain short-run macroeconomic fluctuations while maintaining the assumptions of the classical economic model. Indeed, they believe that the Walrasian general equilibrium model is a good approximation of the operation of actual economies. They assume that the economy is efficient, that economic actors are fully rational and process available information efficiently, that they hold rational expectations about the future, that prices are fully flexible and adjust instantaneously to clear all markets even in the short run, and that all resources are fully employed (Hoover 1988). For instance, as a leading new classical explanation of macroeconomic fluctuations, real-business-cycle theory asserts that the labour market and other markets always clear, with wages and prices adjusting swiftly to any exogenous shocks in technologies (see Plosser 1989). Real-business-cycle scholars base their policy recommendations on simple economic models of markets that assume perfect information, rational expectations, perfect competition, zero transaction costs and a complete set of markets. New classical economists typically conclude that systematic monetary and fiscal policy cannot affect real outcomes, so that government policy is ineffective.

### The market-failure policy programme

The market-failure (or imperfect-markets) view is much less sanguine about the extent to which the real world corresponds to the assumptions of the model of perfectly competitive general equilibrium. Market-failure proponents believe that, in general, market economies are not (constrained) Pareto efficient. They often see significant discrepancies between the model and what they observe when they study actual markets. In their eyes, these discrepancies can arise because actual competition in factor and product markets is limited (e.g. small-numbers bargaining problems, monopoly), transaction costs are high, people are unable to appropriate all the benefits of their investment, prices are sticky in the short run, information is imperfect or unevenly dispersed between buyers and sellers, people have short time horizons, markets are incomplete (especially markets which distribute risk), factors of production are immobile or indivisible, or because goods have externalities (spillover effects) associated with them. The approach argues that prices, wages and interest rates will not adjust quickly to market-clearing levels.

In its crudest formulation, this programme holds that the existence of 'market failures', where one or more of the assumptions of the perfectly competitive model are violated, implies that there is *necessarily* some scope for collective or government action of some sort to improve allocative efficiency. Accordingly, central agencies that are not governed by profit and loss criteria can better perform the usual allocative functions of a market in situations where markets fail or are more costly than substitute arrangements (Noll 1977: 170). Government intervention in the market can make everyone better off, and it is often required to stabilise the level of economic activity. More sophisticated proponents in this programme contend that, even if a market failure is identified, problems with government action (i.e. 'bureaucratic failure') mean that government intervention may not improve economic efficiency. However, they would still hold that there are significant market failures that require at least selective intervention by government in the market.

The market-failure approach represents the dominant perspective on policy analysis derived from much of mainstream neoclassical economics (excluding Chicago). The approach also reflects the policy perspective of new Keynesians, such as Mankiw, Gordon and Stiglitz, who, although not necessarily regarding themselves as neoclassical economists, adopt neoclassical tools of analysis (such as constrained optimisation and rational expectations equilibrium) but reach Keynesian policy conclusions about the frequent need for government intervention to stabilise the aggregate level of economic activity. 'Although new Keynesianism tends to focus on disequilibrium or non-market-clearing phenomena, analysis is conducted within the standard neoclassical equilibrium framework' (Keenan 1994: 582).

The basic argument put forward by an important strand of new Keynesianism (in which Stiglitz is a major figure) is that markets fail to function perfectly because participants typically have imperfect and asymmetric information. Even when prices and wages are flexible, these market failures exacerbate the shocks that an economy experiences, increasing both the magnitude and persistence of their effects, and can lead to high levels of unemployment and sharp fluctuations in aggregate output (Greenwald and Stiglitz 1993). Consequently, these new Keynesians advocate structural reform of labour and financial markets. Their policy analysis focuses upon the causes and effects of labour- and capital-market failures arising from incomplete contracts, such as imperfect indexing (as occurs, for example, when debt contracts are denominated in nominal terms). Other variants of new Keynesianism emphasise macroeconomic market failures arising from the stickiness of nominal prices for goods (e.g. the menu cost theory), nominal wage rigidity (e.g. long-term contract theories), imperfect competition and game-theoretic coordination failures.

### Comparing the hard cores and heuristics of the three policy programmes

The major differences between the three policy programmes are identified in Table 7.1. The table compares the hard cores and heuristics of these three policy programmes.

So what are the key distinguishing characteristics of the MPP? One of the most significant distinctions of the MPP approach is that it does not, unlike the other two policy programmes, use the perfect-competition model either as a description of actual markets or as a benchmark for evaluating markets when conducting policy analysis. As the name suggests, this policy perspective focuses upon the processes of market adjustment rather than upon states of market equilibrium. Although it recognises general economic interdependence between different markets (especially factor and product markets), the MPP does not focus upon multi-market equilibria. The market is treated as an open-ended, indeterminate, dynamic competitive process. The MPP is concerned with comparing the outcomes arising from alternative real-world institutional arrangements rather than with comparing the real world with some ideal of perfect competition.

More specifically, the MPP can be distinguished from the other policy programmes in terms of its domain of enquiry and methodology. The domain of enquiry refers to the sets of policy problems and issues with which the programme is primarily concerned. To a greater degree than the other policy programmes, the MPP focuses mostly upon problems arising from *a breakdown in the coordination of economic plans*. Adherents of the market-process approach aim to explain observed market outcomes in terms of spontaneous economic processes and when economic activities appear discoordinated (or when market outcomes are considered undesirable in some other respect) they first seek to identify potential impediments to the proper functioning of these spontaneous processes. Correspondingly, the heuristics of the MPP direct the policy analyst to pay particular attention to factors that can frustrate the spontaneous ordering of individual activities in real-world markets. When economic activities seem

Table 7.1 Comparison of public policy programmes

| | Market-process programme | Perfect-markets programme | Market-failure programme |
|---|---|---|---|
| Hard-core propositions: | | | |
| Spontaneous ordering processes | Yes. Entrepreneurs' pursuit of profits sets in motion a tendency towards coordination of economic activities, though complete coordination may never actually be attained. Market ignorance may prevail for an indefinite period until entrepreneurs discover and correct it | No. Market adjustment is virtually instantaneous, so that markets essentially always clear. Prices fully reflect all available, relevant information at (almost) every instant of time. There are no processes of spontaneous ordering in real time | No. Markets do not solve the coordination problem efficiently. Wages and prices do not adjust rapidly to market-clearing levels. Prices are 'noisy' (they do not aggregate information perfectly). Natural economic forces can magnify economic shocks (Greenwald and Stiglitz 1993) |
| Dynamic competition | Yes. The competitive market is a dynamic process of entrepreneurial discovery. Entrepreneurs set and adjust prices, choose quantities and qualities and introduce new products, all under conditions of competitive rivalry | No. In general, an economy is (approximately) in long-run competitive equilibrium, with all profit opportunities captured and no further adjustments necessary. Most market participants are price-takers (Reder 1982) | Limited. Informational asymmetries and principal–agent problems are inherent in dynamic competition. Imperfect competition enables firms to set prices and wages |
| Maximising behaviour | No. Human action includes entrepreneurial discovery of new ends–means frameworks and not just allocation of known scarce means among known competing ends | Yes. All individuals independently optimise expected utility (or profit) subject to constraints. They engage in purely calculative economising activity | Yes. As for perfect-markets programme (though the objects of choice and the constraints might differ) |
| Anti-monopoly | No. Market dominance and high profits are not in themselves a cause for concern. An industry will be more highly concentrated the greater the difference in participants' alertness to profit opportunities | No. Genuine monopolies are infrequent, short-lived and eliminated by free entry, and they have a limited effect. Firms do not earn supernormal profits in equilibrium | Yes. Monopoly may significantly affect relative prices or quantities and may greatly distort the allocation and utilisation of resources (relative to that in competitive equilibrium) |

(continued over)

Table 7.1 continued

| | Market-process programme | Perfect-markets programme | Market-failure programme |
|---|---|---|---|
| Structural uncertainty | Yes. Neither policy-makers nor economic agents have full knowledge of the structure of the future, not even in a probabilistic sense (i.e. they are radically ignorant and do not possess rational expectations) | No. Economic agents tend to have full and relevant (probabilistic) knowledge of market data. Information bearing on prices and qualities can be acquired at an economically optimal level. People always hold rational expectations | No. Highly informed governments can improve on competitive market outcomes through appropriate mixes of taxes, subsidies and regulations (Stiglitz 1987: 14). Information bearing on prices and qualities can be acquired at an economically optimal level |
| Superior plan-coordinating properties of markets | Yes. The unhampered market coordinates the economic plans of individuals better than any other feasible resource allocation system | No. The market renders consistent all prices and quantities so that all prices clear all markets. The market is more efficient than any other resource allocation system | No. The relative efficiency of a market economy and a centrally planned system depends on the costs of operating each system in any particular case (Grossman and Stiglitz 1976) |
| Spontaneous origin of money | Yes. Money is a spontaneous by-product of the market economy. It is no one's invention | No. Money is a deliberate artefact of government policy | No. As for perfect-markets programme |
| Subjective costs and benefits | Yes. 'The opportunity cost involved in choice cannot be observed and objectified and, more importantly, it cannot be measured in such a way as to allow comparisons over wholly different choice settings' (Buchanan 1973: 15) | No. Costs and benefits can be objectively measured. Observed prices of inputs are good approximations of the opportunity cost of using them (Reder 1982: 15) | No. Costs and benefits can be objectively measured |
| Non-neutrality of monetary and fiscal policy | No. Both monetary policy and fiscal policy can have real effects. No tax is ever neutral | Yes. Monetary policy and fiscal policy have no systematic effects on real variables (Sargent and Wallace 1975) | No. Both monetary policy and fiscal policy can have real effects |
| Path dependence | Yes. History and the sequencing of policies matter. Market processes take place in real time, which is asymmetric and unidirectional | No. History has no tangible effect on competition. 'Time is fully analogized to space' so that time is reversible (O'Driscoll and Rizzo 1996: 53) | No in general (except for new Keynesian theories of hysteresis and theories of technological lock-in) |

|  | Market-process programme | Perfect-markets programme | Market-failure programme |
|---|---|---|---|
| *Heuristics:* | | | |
| When economic activities appear discoordinated, find the source of the relevant failure in communication among participants (e.g. distorted price signals) | Yes | No | No |
| Treat the market as an open-ended, dynamic competitive process and treat arbitrage as a disequilibrium activity in real-time | Yes. Avoid basing policy analysis upon closed 'single-exit' models of competition, which yield a determinate equilibrium | No. Continually push the use of equilibrium ('single-exit') theorising in policy analysis to the limits of its applicability. Analyse observable market phenomena with reference to equilibrium states | No. As for perfect-markets programme. Employ temporary equilibrium modelling techniques. Treat arbitrage as an equilibrium activity |
| Recognise that entrepreneurship is the engine of economic development | Yes | No | No |
| Pay attention to the impact of policy on (the determinants of) people's alertness, the incentives for entrepreneurial discovery and the pattern of entrepreneurial activity | Yes | No | No |
| Develop policy analysis on the assumption that individual economic agents only optimise subject to constraints | No | Yes | Yes |
| Emphasise the subjectivity of costs and benefits in policy analysis, and reject aggregate notions of welfare and social cost–benefit analysis for assessing policies | Yes | No | No |
| Recognise the severe knowledge problems of centralised decision-making and the bounded rationality of government planners | Yes | No | No |
| Apply market-process analysis to the institutional design of the monetary regime | Yes | No | No |

(continued over)

Table 7.1 continued

| | Market-process programme | Perfect-markets programme | Market-failure programme |
|---|---|---|---|
| Recognise that nominal money supply changes (with money demand unchanged) frustrate market coordination because they distort relative price formation and entrepreneurial plans and have real and unsustainable effects on the intertemporal structure of heterogeneous capital | Yes (Mises 1971; Hayek 1935) | No | No |
| Determine how to conduct fiscal affairs so as to give maximum scope to market forces in the private sector | Yes | Yes | No |
| Prescribe, for each 'market failure', the specific government interventions that will lead to a Pareto improvement and identify the parameters (e.g. supply and demand elasticities) that determine the optimal corrective policy | No. Seek to identify the sources of alleged 'market failures' in gaps in the institutional framework, especially the private property rights system, and eliminate any loopholes identified | No. Treat alleged 'market failures' as highly suspect and as being most likely the result of the failure of policy analysis to consider all the relevant variables (Toumanoff 1984: 529) | Yes |
| Emphasise obtaining empirical and historical information about the problem situation and investigate the historical, path-dependent process that gives rise to the policy issue(s) | Yes | No (except for the monetarists' emphasis on historical facts) | No |
| Judge the performance of economic systems and arrangements by how quickly and accurately they discover and reduce the waste and discoordination associated with disequilibrium situations | Yes | No. Assess economic systems and arrangements according to the standard of Pareto efficiency | No. Assess economic systems and arrangements according to the standard of 'constrained' Pareto efficiency (thereby taking into account the absence of complete markets and imperfections of information) (Stiglitz 1987) |

discoordinated, the analyst is instructed to search for the source of the relevant failure in communication among individual economic agents and to find out why information has failed to be transmitted correctly and quickly (Rizzo 1982: 64). In particular, the analyst examines the impacts of public policies on individual decision-makers' knowledge, expectations, learning behaviour and plan revision. For example, the analyst investigates whether government intervention has significantly distorted the array of relative prices.

Another, clearly related, set of policy problems addressed by the market-process approach concerns processes of coordination, that is *entrepreneurial-discovery processes*. More than any other, this programme emphasises the importance of appreciating the entrepreneurial perspective. As discussed earlier, the corresponding rules of the MPP require policy analysts to pay special attention to the impact of public policy on entrepreneurial alertness and entrepreneurial processes of adjustment. In particular, they are instructed to investigate the effects on people's incentives to discover profit opportunities, the incentives for entrepreneurs to exploit what they have discovered, the pattern of entrepreneurial activity and the impact on people's degree of alertness and the psychological determinants of that alertness (i.e. agency beliefs). In addition, the MPP requires the policy analyst to assess the extent to which policies affect entrepreneurs' choices over time regarding inputs, outputs, production, prices, quantities and qualities. To a greater degree than the perfect-markets policy programme, the MPP focuses upon assessing the institutional impediments to entrepreneurship, especially government-imposed barriers to new market entry. Furthermore, the policy analyst is required to be ever vigilant of the unintended and undesirable consequences of any policy initiative, especially in terms of its adverse effects on entrepreneurship and market processes.

The methodology of the MPP is also distinctive. Unlike the perfect-markets and market-failure approaches, the MPP rejects exclusive use of single-exit methods of policy analysis. (Single-exit methods of analysis involve specifying economic problems in such a way that the optimal policy is determined uniquely by objective situational characteristics, such as costs, prices, consumer preferences, technology and so on.) The MPP directs us to avoid developing policy solutions to problems on the assumption that people only optimise subject to constraints. In addition to rejecting single-exit methods and the assumption of maximising behaviour, the MPP rejects the neoclassical assumption of stable preferences. Indeed, people's preference maps ('scales of values') are considered to be in continual flux.[13] It also refrains from treating technology as given, as do some neoclassical policy analyses.[14]

The MPP also supplies a unique toolkit of standards or appraisal criteria for evaluating and choosing between policy analyses. The MPP is unique in at least three respects. First, it requires thoroughgoing *subjectivism*, stressing the subjectivity of costs and benefits in policy analysis, the expectational component of policy issues and the implications of radical uncertainty. Second, it requires an emphasis upon *process*, paying particular attention to the open-ended and indeterminate nature of dynamic competition, the function of entrepreneurial discovery and the impact of policies on market processes. Third, it requires an *empirical and historical focus* in policy appraisal.

More so than the two other policy approaches, the MPP emphasises obtaining empirical and historical information about the relevant features of the problem situation and specific conditions of the environment. It requires policy analysts to take account of path dependence in analysing policy options and their timing and sequencing. In addition, it requires analysts to understand the historical processes giving rise to the emergence of economic phenomena and policy issues and it urges them to construct 'conjectural histories' of how unintended results develop from individual actions. Empirical work also includes detailed historical case studies.

This emphasis upon the empirical aspects of the MPP may seem at odds with the criticisms of commentators, such as Rosen (1997), who regard the Austrian market-process approach as lacking in empirical content and limited in its power to generate new empirical facts. Yeager's (1997a) response to such negative assessments is instructive. Describing himself as a 'mere fellow-traveller' of the Austrian school, he claims that the Austrian approach is empirical in a wider sense of the term in that it embraces qualitative predictions of patterns of economic phenomena rather than quantitative predictions of the timing and magnitude of specific concrete events (e.g. numerical forecasts of macroeconomic aggregates in a particular year). Austrians are interested in understanding how the real world ticks:

> Austrians do take seriously the most pervasive and dependable facts about empirical reality. These include human purpose and other introspectively known realities, scarcity and the necessity of choice, the phenomenon of diminishing marginal returns, and the fragmentation of knowledge. They include other features of the real world that unavoidably restrict atomistic competition to being the exception rather than the rule and that accord entrepreneurs a large role in the working of markets. ... Austrians are guilty less often than the neoclassicals of what P. T. Bauer (1987) aptly diagnosed as the 'disregard of reality'.
>
> (Yeager 1997a: 156)

Although proponents of the market-process view usually assume that there is a role for government in the establishment and maintenance of an institutional framework within which markets operate, they do not presume that specific government intervention is necessarily required to correct market outcomes.

As mentioned earlier, the taxonomy of policy approaches is more analytical than sociological. As a consequence, the classification scheme does not provide an exact one-to-one correspondence with established schools of economic thought. For example, the market-process view encompasses almost all Austrian economists except Rothbard and Salerno. In addition, some Chicago economists (e.g. Demsetz and Brozen) and some members of the mainstream neoclassical school (e.g. Fisher 1983; 1987) have also, whether consciously or not, been market-process theorists of a sort (though Demsetz can also be interpreted as straddling the fence between a perfect-markets and a market-process view of the world).

## *Comparing 'stylised' policy prescriptions of the three policy programmes*

Table 7.2 identifies selected 'stylised' policy prescriptions that indicate the flavour of policy recommendations forthcoming from the MPP and the perfect-markets and market-failure policy programmes. There is some risk in this sort of presentation, however. It must be emphasised that these 'stylised' prescriptions do *not* represent general policy rules of the MPP. Nor do they form part of the heuristics of the MPP. They are tentative implications only.

> Austrian economics is, first and foremost, a way of looking at the world and of framing questions. It is only secondarily a system of conclusions about market economies which, when combined with some very commonly held value judgments, produces a free-market 'advocacy'.
>
> (Rizzo 1992a: 252)

In practice, the specific policy solution that proponents of any policy programme will actually recommend for any particular policy problem will depend upon the application of their respective hard-core assumptions and heuristics to the empirical details of the case and their conjectures about the range of possible effects of alternative policies. Indeed, policy-makers may be able to draw upon empirical work (including econometric research) that provides insights on 'the magnitude of the effect of, $x$, [say, some quantifiable policy variable] on the whole complex phenomenon, $y$, at some specific point in time' (Rizzo 1978: 52). In addition, it should be noted that these policy recommendations are not value neutral and that they are imbued with implicit value judgements about the ends that are worth pursuing.

An interesting observation to emerge from a comparison of Tables 7.1 and 7.2 is that the specifications of the perfect-markets and market-failure policy programmes are very similar to each other and both different to the MPP, and yet the 'stylised' policy prescriptions derived from the perfect-markets programme and the MPP are similar to each other and both different to the market-failure policy prescriptions. How can we account for the fact that when we juxtapose the key components of the MPP and perfect-markets policy programmes we see great divergence but that when

Table 7.2 Comparison of selected 'stylised' policy prescriptions

| 'Stylised' policy prescriptions | Market-process programme | Perfect-markets programme | Market-failure programme |
|---|---|---|---|
| Favour market-oriented policies within a stable, rule-bound institutional framework that maximises individual freedom and the scope for voluntary mutually beneficial exchange | Yes | Yes | No |
| Establish and maintain a minimal regulatory and welfare state, and avoid supplanting private arrangements with centrally determined solutions | Yes (except for Rothbardians who are anarcho-capitalists) | Yes | No. There is a large role for the state in the provision of 'public goods', regulation and redistribution (Stiglitz 1994) |
| If the policy goal is to enhance plan coordination, do not reduce the rewards for successful entrepreneurship (by taxing pure profit) or increase the penalties for entrepreneurial error and failure | Yes | No | No |
| Look initially to spontaneous ordering processes to address perceived problems with market outcomes (e.g. rely upon entrepreneurial-discovery processes to handle alleged externalities) | Yes | No | No |
| In general, if government action is thought necessary to address 'externalities', choose market-based regulation by rules (e.g. the creation of water rights) over specific regulatory commands, taxes or subsidies | Yes (Mises 1966: 654–660; but not Arnold 1995) | Yes | No |
| Remove government controls on inputs, outputs, wages and prices, quantities and qualities | Yes | Yes | No |
| Remove government-imposed barriers to new entry in all industries (including statutory monopolies and occupational licensing laws) | Yes | Yes | No |

| Policy | | | |
|---|---|---|---|
| Abolish patent rights to allow new competition in innovation | Mixed. Yes – Rothbard (1993: 652–660); Mises straddled the fence (1966: 661–662) | No | No |
| Prescribe government intervention (i.e. specific regulatory commands) in order: (a) to control the use of monopoly power; and (b) to prohibit 'anticompetitive' behaviour | No. Do away with antitrust policy, and abandon governmental control of mergers, takeovers and trade practices (Armentano 1990; O'Driscoll and Rizzo 1996: 130–159) | No in general (except for 'natural monopolies' if their services are regarded as essential and their market power is sizeable (Friedman 1982: 29)). Seek an efficiency explanation for why the behaviour in question is not really anticompetitive | Yes |
| Eliminate all tariffs, import quotas and restrictions on exports | Yes | Yes | No |
| Remove all international capital controls (i.e. controls on inward and outward foreign investment, whether direct, portfolio or equity investment) | Yes | Yes | No |
| Remove direct regulation of exchange rates | Mixed. Yes – Mises (1966: 800–803), Rothbard, Salerno; no – White | Yes | No |
| Establish a sound monetary framework (as the role of a central authority) | Mixed. Yes – Mises, early Hayek, Kirzner, no – later Hayek, Rothbard, White, Selgin | Yes (Friedman 1982) | Yes |

(continued over)

Table 7.2 continued

| Stylised policy prescriptions | Market-process programme | Perfect-markets programme | Market-failure programme |
|---|---|---|---|
| Choose stability in the general level of output prices as the principal objective of government's monetary policy | No. Stabilise M (Rothbard 1993: 850). Stabilise MV (Hayek 1935). Hold MV constant and let changes in Q cause inverse changes in P, preferably under a 'free banking' monetary regime (Selgin 1995; 1997) | Yes | Mixed. Yes (menu cost theory); no – focus on raising employment through expansionary monetary policy (e.g. staggered wage contract theory) |
| Avoid using government spending and taxation as countercyclical policy tools that try to correct alleged 'market failures' | Yes | Yes | No |
| Reduce as much as possible the level of government expenditure, and maintain fiscal balance (i.e. a balanced budget) | Yes | Yes | No |
| Broaden the tax base as much as possible, and reduce and flatten tax rates | Yes. Use income not consumption as the tax base. Emphasise reducing tax rates more than flattening them | Yes | No |
| Privatise state-owned enterprises or go for partial privatisation (and divestment of assets, sale of rights, share sales, etc.) where full privatisation is not possible | Yes | Yes in general (except 'natural monopolies' under some circumstances) | No. Advocate state ownership and/or control where economies of scale are so important that monopoly is inevitable |
| Separate funding from provision of state health and educational services, and encourage private sector crowd-in | Yes | Yes | No |
| Tighten eligibility requirements and reduce levels of governmental social transfer payments (e.g. unemployment benefits) | Yes | Yes | No |

we compare their 'stylised' policy prescriptions we see much resemblance? How can these two policy programmes based on vastly different hard-core propositions and heuristics generate such similar economic policy prescriptions?

In a somewhat different context, Paqué provides a clue to the answer to these questions:

> In the Austrian view of the market as a ceaseless process of discovery and information dissemination, there is no single individual and no board of directors who knows how the relative scarcity of goods will look like in the future. Granted this premise, it must be unwise to put the power of resource allocation into the hands of some committee, even if it is a democratically elected one. Hence setting up a stable institutional framework and letting the simultaneous adjustment of all private economic agents proceed on its own is the best way to ensure the most rapid growth of knowledge.
>
> Tight prior equilibrium theorizing along Chicago lines has similar consequences for policy making: If markets can rightly be assumed to work efficiently (including the efficient use of available information), there is simply no rationale for government intervention apart from setting up a stable institutional framework (including an unambiguous definition of property rights).
>
> (Paqué 1985: 431)

Alternatively, it could be argued that, in order to be consistent in their position, Chicago economists ought to be open to the prospect of a high degree of government intervention in markets because the assumptions of perfect competition are frequently violated. Their perfect-markets, equilibrium-clearing perspective would tend to imply that government is needed to bring the unregulated market closer to the conditions of perfect competition. For example, Friedman's prescriptions on competition policy cannot be derived from his economic analysis of monopoly. According to this line of argument, the free-market prescriptions of the Chicago school are not so much the result of their economics as of their political philosophy (classical liberalism). Only Austrian market-process economics is capable of deriving market-oriented policy prescriptions analytically.

## Conclusion

This chapter has put forward an Austrian entrepreneurial-discovery approach to developing public policy. It has sought to identify the key propositions and rules that market-process economists apply to guide their analysis of policy issues.

The market-process policy programme (MPP) is a set of analytical arguments and methods for doing policy analysis and policy development. It is a set of techniques for solving problems and not a set of doctrines. It is not to be confused with dogmatic prescriptions to adopt a policy of wholesale laissez-faire. Austrian economics per se does not provide a scientific imprimatur for unrestrained laissez-faire economic policies. To argue that it does is a 'far too oversimplified – and inaccurate – conclusion' (Kirzner 1997a: 81). Laissez-faire is a rough-and-ready rule of thumb that has 'never provided a criterion by which one could decide what were the proper functions of government' (Hayek 1973: 62). In contrast, the MPP provides consistent and definite principles for guiding policy that can be subject to rational criticism and can be successfully defended. Its principles are grounded upon a clear explanation of how government intervention in competitive market processes is likely to obstruct entrepreneurial adjustments that tend to bring about greater economic coordination. When supplemented by some widely shared value judgments (e.g. that economic coordination is a 'good thing'), this explanation is sufficient to support a tentative presumption – though not a doctrinal insistence – in favour of market-based solutions to a society's economic problems.

Furthermore, the Austrian market-process approach must not be conflated with the policy position of the Chicago school of economics. As has been shown, there is a distinct Austrian perspective to policy analysis, which is markedly different from both the perfect-markets and market-failure policy programmes. Among other things, the MPP is distinguished by its focus upon explaining the workings of market *processes*, the function and requirements of *entrepreneurial decision-making*, and the effects of public policies upon *dynamic competition* and the *coordination* of economic plans.

# 8 Empirical testing and conceptual development

Economic explanations of the great differences in the wealth of nations have typically focused upon differences in resource endowments, including stocks of physical and human capital and technological knowledge. Much less attention has been paid to the role of entrepreneurial processes in the creation of wealth and to the potential capacity of institutions to promote entrepreneurship. This book takes the view that entrepreneurship is the mainspring of economic growth and development. It is crucially important for the market process and affects firms' responsiveness to new market conditions, especially the changing requirements of consumers and the strategies of rivals. As a consequence, processes of entrepreneurial discovery have far-reaching effects on the nature, direction and coordination of economic activities.

This book explores the circumstances that are most favourable to a robust sense of personal agency and a heightened level of entrepreneurial alertness. It examines the institutional, cultural and psychological contexts in which entrepreneurial processes become manifest. It identifies the possible effects, both direct and indirect, of different institutional rules of the game on incentives to be alert. It also examines how cultural values influence how alertness is channelled and manifested. The intention has been to promote a more critical stance so that economists and policy decision-makers will be more sensitive in their analyses to potential consequences for entrepreneurship.

It must be emphasised that the analysis contained in these pages is a weigh-station on the route to a more comprehensive examination of the institutional and cultural foundations of entrepreneurship. The analysis is subject to several limitations. In the first instance, no empirical tests have been conducted to test the predicted relationships among institutions, personal agency beliefs, entrepreneurial alertness and economic performance.

In addition, the institutional conditions identified in Chapters 4 and 5 as being conducive to entrepreneurship are framed in terms that seem more compatible with individualist rather than group-oriented cultures. The analysis so far has not looked at the issue of whether the institutional framework outlined in earlier chapters can apply to group-oriented cultures. Nor has the analysis investigated reciprocal effects and feedback loops that may operate among cultural and institutional factors, people's cognitive properties and entrepreneurial activity. The chain of causality has been implicitly assumed to be linear. Cultural values and institutions have generally been viewed as antecedent conditions that affect people's cognitive processes and entrepreneurial propensities. This is a significant drawback since cultures and institutions both mould, and are moulded by, people's actions.

The present chapter makes some tentative first steps at filling these gaps. First, it sketches out a rudimentary outline of empirical research to test the hypothesised relationship between institutional arrangements and personal agency beliefs.

Second, it looks at the relevance and applicability of the institutional rules of the game, identified in previous chapters as conducive to entrepreneurship, for group-oriented societies. It is argued that a group orientation by no means necessarily entails rejecting the idea of negative freedom, the rule of law, private property rights, freedom of contract and freedom of entrepreneurial choice.

Third, it deals with the issue of reciprocal causation explicitly. It recognises that feedback effects might occur when people's cognitions and entrepreneurial actions interact and combine to affect the cultural norms and institutions of society. It is noted that reciprocal causation does not, of course, imply simultaneous causation. Culture, institutions and people's cognitive properties can affect each other at different speeds.

The last section of this chapter identifies opportunities for future research on policy analysis as it relates to entrepreneurship and market processes.

## Potential empirical tests

One of the more general hypotheses advanced in this book is that institutions and economic policies that inhibit economic freedom dampen people's alertness to profit opportunities through their negative effects on people's personal agency beliefs (i.e. by weakening people's sense of internal locus of control and personal efficacy).

There is as yet no widely accepted scale for measuring the strength of a person's propensity to be alert. Frese *et al.*'s (1997) Personal Initiative Scale, Kirton's (1976) adaption–innovation scale and McCline *et al.*'s (2000) Entrepreneurial Opportunity Recognition scale do not adequately capture the notion of alertness to profit opportunities. If researchers are to be able to measure individual differences in people's degrees of alertness, further work is needed to operationalise the idea of a person's general level of attentiveness or cognitive readiness to recognise and grasp opportunities in particular economic contexts.

Because the tacit character of entrepreneurial alertness frustrates empirical testing of hypotheses given currently available measurement techniques, what follows is limited to a discussion of how one might go about testing subsidiary hypotheses about the effects of government regulation on market participants' sense of personal agency. In particular, it is hypothesised that, relative to entrepreneurs in heavily regulated industries, entrepreneurs in less regulated industries have: (i) a higher degree of internal locus of control; (ii) a greater sense of personal efficacy; and (iii) a greater sense of personal agency.

The preliminary outline of the following potential empirical tests adapts and considerably expands the proposals put forward by Gilad (1982a: 199–209; 1984: 278–279). The first test involves a cross-sectional study of the personal agency beliefs of entrepreneurs in heavily regulated and less regulated industries at a point in time. The second test involves a longitudinal study of the agency beliefs of entrepreneurs in industries that are going through significant deregulation over time.[1]

The first study would involve measuring the mean personal-agency scores of samples of entrepreneurs from highly regulated industries (e.g. public utilities, video gaming, commercial banking) and relatively less regulated industries (e.g. e-commerce) and then testing for significant differences. (On the selection of appropriate samples for research on entrepreneurial characteristics, see Gartner 1989.) A more sophisticated approach to a binary classification of industries as either 'heavily' or 'lightly' regulated would be to construct a more comprehensive measure of the extent of regulatory interference in an industry. A ten-point index variable, for instance, could measure the extent of regulatory intervention in particular industries in particular regions (or states). As such, it would correspond to an industry-specific, subnational version of Gwartney *et al.*'s index of economic freedom considered elsewhere in this book.

In order to control for the effects of culture, the entrepreneurs sampled should be drawn from a relatively homogeneous ethnic group. An individualist cultural setting is preferable for a preliminary study because measuring the agency beliefs of independent selves is less complicated than doing so for interdependent members of a group (Table 6.2). In particular, by limiting itself to individualist subjects, the study only needs to measure *personal* (and not group) locus of control, efficacy and agency beliefs.

In order to measure entrepreneurs' personal agency beliefs, it will first be necessary to develop more sophisticated measurement scales of personal locus of control and personal efficacy that are specifically designed for economic and entrepreneurial settings. Rotter's (1966) original Internal–External scale for measuring locus of control has been the most widely used instrument in previous entrepreneurship research (e.g. Begley and Boyd 1987; Mueller and Thomas 2000). However, this scale has been shown to contain up to nine dimensions (see Ferguson (1993) for the relevant literature), and at least one of the dimensions (e.g. the 'political responsiveness' factor) does not seem to be pertinent to entrepreneurial behaviour (Shaver and Scott 1991). Alternatives to Rotter's scale include

Levenson's (1973) three-factor LOC scale and the economic LOC scale used by Bonnett and Furnham (1991). Any newly developed or modified LOC scale targeted at entrepreneurship must of course be tested for its reliability and validity (see Angleitner and Wiggins 1986).

Similarly, measures of personal efficacy must also be tailored to the specific needs of entrepreneurship research. Entrepreneurship poses special problems because it encompasses a wide range of interrelated tasks, and measuring self-efficacy requires that each task has relatively well-defined performance levels. (On the measurement of self-efficacy, see Bandura (1986) and Gist and Mitchell (1992).) Rather than using an omnibus measure that compromises predictive power, one option is to develop an entrepreneurial self-efficacy construct (ESE) along the lines of Chen *et al.* (1998). Their construct measures how strongly people believe that they are capable of successfully performing key roles and tasks associated with entrepreneurship. With its focus upon specific tasks rather than generic functions or beliefs, the ESE is superior to the scale used by Scherer *et al.* (1989) and the personal efficacy subscale of the Paulhus (1983) Spheres of Control scale. However, the ESE as specified by Chen *et al.* would have to be adapted, because it includes some tasks, such as risk taking, that are specifically excluded from Kirzner's conception of entrepreneurship.

Once component scores of LOC (contingency) and perceived self-efficacy (competence) have been obtained for entrepreneurs in the two samples, the next step is to construct a total measure of personal agency which is a joint function of these two subordinate constructs. There are many possible ways in which people themselves might combine LOC and efficacy expectations in the formation of their own agency beliefs. For instance, people might integrate contingency and competence information in a multiplicative or an additive fashion. If a multiplicative model is used to generate a summary measure of personal agency, then the strength of personal agency belief ($AGN_i$) of person $i$ is the product of their scores for personal internal locus of control ($LOC_i$) and personal efficacy ($EFF_i$). That is, $AGN_i = f(LOC_i \times EFF_i)$. Specifying a multiplicative model is not arbitrary. It captures the idea that *both* a high level of perceived internal LOC and of efficacy is required for a strong sense of agency (and a high degree of alertness). Individuals with a weak sense of internal LOC are restricted to a relatively narrow and mediocre range of personal agency, irrespective of how competent they feel.

The survey instrument for the study would comprise a battery of questions and items derived from the scales for measuring LOC and personal efficacy. For example, items related to entrepreneurial self-efficacy would require respondents to indicate their degree of certainty in performing each entrepreneurial role or task on a five-point Likert scale ranging from 'completely unsure' to 'completely sure'. To minimise the effect of response bias arising from the tendency of some respondents to give more extreme responses than others, the original scores for LOC and personal efficacy could also be converted to binary data. Thus, each entrepreneur's scores for LOC and personal efficacy could also be reduced to either 'high' or 'low' ratings, as could the scores on personal agency.

It is not necessary at this juncture to go into a detailed specification of the statistical tests that need to be conducted. However, it is clear that the hypothesis-testing procedures should include ANCOVA (analysis of covariance) and multivariate logistic regression methods.[2]

An ANCOVA test would remove the extraneous effects of pre-existing individual differences among entrepreneurs in the study. It would provide statistical control of variability in a situation in which experimental control could not be used. Thus, a one-way ANCOVA procedure would be employed to test the significance of the main effect of the degree of industry regulation on entrepreneurs' original (unadjusted) personal agency scores, after controlling for the effects of each entrepreneur's gender, age, education and other covariates (control variables). (Because ANCOVA assumes that the dependent variable is continuous and measured on an interval scale, it would be necessary to use the original LOC and efficacy scores and not binary data.) The hypothesis that entrepreneurs from less regulated industries have higher personal agency scores than entrepreneurs from heavily regulated industries is clearly directional so that a one-tailed statistical test is appropriate. (If, instead of total personal agency scores, component scores for LOC and efficacy were treated as the dependent variables, multiple analysis of covariance (MANCOVA) could be performed.)

If LOC, efficacy and agency scores were converted to binary data (i.e. 'high' or 'low' ratings) in order to minimise response bias, logistic regression would be the most appropriate form of regression analysis because it is used when the dependent variable is dichotomous (and the independent variables are continuous variables, categorical variables or both). It would be preferable to use a ten-point index of the degree of regulation in an industry than a simple binomial classification of heavily and lightly regulated industries. A series of logistic regression analyses could be run to test the subsidiary hypotheses (cited above) about the effect of regulation on entrepreneurs' expectations of LOC, personal efficacy and personal agency (i.e. combined LOC/efficacy beliefs). Control variables for gender, age and education should also be included in all the regression models.

The second investigation would involve a longitudinal study that would compare mean LOC, self-efficacy and personal agency scores of a sample of entrepreneurs in an industry before and after a major episode of economic deregulation. The same set of control variables would be included. The hypothesis-testing procedure would be similar to that described for the first study. A one-way ANCOVA would be performed to test the one-sided hypothesis that entrepreneurs' sense of personal agency strengthens after deregulation (and a consequent increase in economic freedom).

A major difficulty of this type of test would be not knowing how much time it would take for the deregulatory measures to feed into people's revisions of their agency beliefs. Because of the time lags involved, economy-wide and political events (e.g. a foreign exchange crisis) might overwhelm the impact of changes in industry regulation on participants' agency beliefs. One solution would be to conduct regular surveys of people's agency beliefs both before and after deregulation.

## Are market-preserving institutions generally applicable across cultures?

As stated at the outset, the institutional conditions identified in Chapters 4 and 5 as being conducive towards entrepreneurship were examined in terms that seem more compatible with individualist rather than group-oriented cultures. In group-oriented (or communalist) cultures, legal, customary and moral rights are more likely to adhere to various social entities (e.g. the extended family, clan) rather than independent individuals. Because property rights can only be attributed to persons or groups of persons, and contractual agreements can only be entered into among persons or groups, it follows that the conception of what is a person must be sufficiently defined beforehand.[3] If the concept of personhood varies across cultures, it might be the case that the entities, to whom property rights are attributed and among whom contracts are agreed, might also vary in different cultural contexts. In any case, the unit or locus of alertness in a group-centred society is typically the interdependent member of a group rather than an independent individual, so that the relevant institutional rules must unleash the alertness of a different type of entity.

Nevertheless, the group orientation of a culture (and its associated conception of the interdependent self) by no means necessarily entails rejecting the idea of negative freedom, the rule of law, private property rights, freedom of contract, freedom of entrepreneurial choice and other liberal ideals (Wellmer 1991). Similarly, 'the core of liberalism cannot be identified with a particular cultural stance' (Raico 1992: 269). The institutions of the civil society are not pitted against non-coercive group norms and social arrangements. Indeed, the concept of freedom under the law is inherently social and can be defined only with reference to interpersonal relationships. Private property can belong to a kinship group or an association of people, and not just to an individual (Pipes 1999: xv). Legal property rights offer people in any culture the possibility to express their sense of agency in the external world.

> I doubt that property per se directly contradicts any major culture. Vietnamese, Cuban, and Indian migrants have clearly had few problems adapting to U.S. property law. If correctly conceived, property law can reach beyond cultures to increase trust between them and, at the same time, reduce the costs of bringing things and thoughts together.
>
> (de Soto 2000: 226)

In a group-oriented society, it is perfectly possible for people to have a high regard for negative freedom and the basic rights that protect them against coercion by other people, including arbitrary interference in their affairs by agents of the state. In these societies, arbitrary action may be constrained by unwritten rules of interpersonal relationships, such as the general duties pertaining to different social roles (e.g. father, son, ruler, subject). However, members of group-oriented cultures may seek to utilise their freedom in a manner different from that of individualists. For example, they might exercise their freedom of choice by choosing actions on the basis of their consequences, not for themselves as isolated individuals, but for the group(s) with which they are identified and for the social role(s) they perform. All individualists are very likely to value freedom of choice and protection from coercion, but all the people who value freedom are not necessarily individualists. '[N]o matter how communally focussed some cultures may appear to us, one can usually find underneath a fundamental, perhaps even somewhat principled respect for the autonomy of individuals' (Lavoie and Chamlee-Wright 2000: 68).

Both among societies and within any particular cultural group, there is a diversity of property rights structures. Anthropological research shows that within clan-based cultures, especially of indigenous peoples, there is a spectrum of rights that includes not only property of the nuclear family, of the extended family, and common property of all members of the group, but also, with rare exceptions, strictly personal property for each adult (Bailey 1998: 156). Within group-oriented societies, effective (i.e. *de facto*) control rights are often in practice allocated to specific individuals (or the particular social roles they occupy). In addition, even within societies typically regarded as highly individualistic, common property is neither unusual nor rare: the joint-stock company, for instance, is best conceived as a form of common property with privately owned and traded shares (Seabright 1998). Among other things, social factors, such as the size and degree of cohesiveness (i.e. homogeneity) of a particular group, affect the costs of creating, elaborating and readjusting property rights and thus the specific pattern of rights that evolves within that group (Libecap 1989).

Although we should be very wary of using the nation-state as the unit of analysis in cultural analyses, free trade and the institution of private property are as crucial for sustained economic prosperity in modern group-oriented societies as they are in individualist ones. The point is well put by Lavoie and Chamlee-Wright:

> The study of hundreds of years of experience has shown rather conclusively that no matter what the cultural advantages held by a particular society, without the policies of free trade, a reliable legal framework, a stable monetary system, and a functioning system of private property rights, economic success is highly unlikely if not impossible. ... In examining the reasons for success in Hong Kong and Singapore, Pang

Eng Fong (1988) finds that economic growth was the result of free trade, low tax rates, and minimal levels of state intervention.

(Lavoie and Chamlee-Wright 2000: 76–77)

Hong Kong and Singapore are good case studies of how the institutions analysed in this book are applicable to group-oriented societies. Hong Kong and Singapore were ranked thirty-seventh and fortieth, respectively, out of fifty-three countries and regions according to Hofstede's (1983) ratings of national cultures on the individualism–collectivism dimension. These rankings place these two countries well towards the group-oriented end of the spectrum. If we compare their economic performance with that in areas with similar cultural characteristics (e.g. Hong Kong versus mainland China), we see that their greater per capita wealth is largely attributable to superior institutions and economic policies rather than a relative abundance of physical resources or marketable human capital (Olson 1996: 19).

Indeed, according to the series of studies of *Economic Freedom of the World* conducted by Gwartney and his associates, Hong Kong and Singapore provide exemplars of market-preserving institutional arrangements that secure economic freedom. For the entire thirty-year period for which summary ratings of the regular EFW index are available (1970–1999), Hong Kong's institutional structure has ranked first in the world, and by a substantial margin, in terms of its degree of economic freedom (Gwartney and Lawson 2001). (Since becoming a Special Administrative Region of China in July 1997, Hong Kong continues to enjoy a high degree of autonomy, except in foreign and defence affairs, and it has maintained its ranking as the most economically free place in the world.) Since 1990, Singapore has ranked second and was a hair's breadth behind Hong Kong in 1999 in terms of its overall economic freedom. Over the last couple of decades, Hong Kong has received perfect (i.e. 10 out of 10) or near perfect ratings for the degree of freedom it offers to trade in capital and financial markets. In addition, Hong Kong and Singapore have consistently offered the greatest freedom to trade internationally during the last thirty years. It should also be noted that Singapore received perfect ratings in 1995 and 1999 for the extent to which its legal institutions support the principles of the rule of law, and Hong Kong did too in 1995.

## Reciprocal causation

This book offers only a partial solution to the problems of explaining what determines the 'supply' of entrepreneurial alertness and of accounting for how culture, institutions and human psychology affect the intensity and prevalence of the human propensity to be alert. It is an intermediate step along the way to a more complete explanation of the complex nexus of causal relationships among cultural and institutional factors, people's cognitive processes, their alertness, entrepreneurial behaviour and economic development.

The approach identifies and analyses key cultural and institutional elements in terms of their *partial effects* (i.e. *tendencies*) on personal agency beliefs and alertness. Because it is focusing upon tendencies, it does not account for all the possible disturbing causes that affect people's perceptions of contingency and personal competence, their alertness and entrepreneurial behaviour.

Furthermore, the approach assumes that causality operates primarily in one direction: the causal sequence is from the 'cultural and institutional matrix' (social, customary, constitutional, legal, political and economic rules) through personal agency beliefs to entrepreneurial alertness and action. Personal agency beliefs and alertness are depicted as shaped and controlled by cultural and institutional factors. (See, for instance, the descriptive model in Figure 3.1.) In particular, it is argued that the degree to which people are free to choose ends and means in accordance with their own decisions and plans determines how responsible they feel for shaping their own lives and how alert they will be to opportunities for economic gain.

However, the direction of causality among cultural and institutional conditions, personal agency beliefs and entrepreneurship is not necessarily one-way. Under most real-world conditions, there exist important feedback mechanisms and other tendencies whose disturbing effects cannot be readily disentangled from the effects of the particular subgroup of causes tentatively isolated for special study. Indeed, the spontaneous ordering processes and institutions of civil society might depend on dynamic entrepreneurial discovery of opportunities for improving economic coordination. 'Only in the context of free markets is there genuine scope for human liberty in society' (Kirzner 1992: 54).

There is likely to be a complex *interdependent* causal structure, according to which cognitive processes, entrepreneurial actions and cultural and insti-tutional factors interact to produce changes in a bidirectional manner.[4] These phenomena are linked in causal sequences of mutual interaction and interdependence. '[H]uman influence, whether individual or collective, is a two-way process rather than one that flows unidirectionally' (Bandura 1995a: 38).

For example, the institutional and regulatory framework in a democratic society is at least partly the outcome of a political process that is responsive, among other things, to the personal agency beliefs of individuals and organ-ised interest groups whose political support is sought. Easton's (1965) systems-theoretic analysis of political processes can be adapted to this context. The prevalent personal agency beliefs of potential coalitions, in combination with their motivations, interests and ideologies, comprise the aggregate back-ground of *wants* which shape *demands* for public policy. Demands refer to those wants that the members of organised interest groups would wish to see imple-mented through public policy outputs of some sort (e.g. tax reform, tariffs and trade restrictions, and wealth transfers). The result of this complication is that in explaining the supply of entrepreneurship and the determinants of entrepreneurial alertness, we run into problems of identification: that is, difficulties in sorting out the potential simultaneous and lagged relationships which often characterise economic phenomena.

As a starting point for analysing the complex social and economic issues associated with entrepreneurship, the mostly unidirectional account of causation adopted in this book is not unreasonable.[5] As a *methodological* matter, a piecemeal approach that provisionally treats some variables as relatively constant and free of the effects of feedback disturbances is an appropriate way to promote the growth of our knowledge in this area. '[I]t is the only method by which science has ever made any great progress in dealing with complex and changeful matter, whether in the physical or moral world' (Marshall 1920: 380). In the language of Knight's (1999: 239) philosophical study of values, the strategy in this book treats some variables as 'relatively absolute absolutes'. That is, the approach tentatively takes some institutions to be given for the purpose of current analysis, while at the same time acknowledging that at another level of analysis (or over a longer time frame), those assumed absolutes may well undergo endogenous changes. '[I]n the fullness of time, the system is fully interconnected' (Williamson 2000: 596).

As an *empirical* matter, there is also good reason to suppose that culture and informal institutions have relatively enduring and self-reinforcing elements that persist from generation to generation. Cultural norms and customs can change very slowly, perhaps in the order of hundreds of years.[6]

Empirical evidence of the persistence of cultural values is provided by the cross-cultural study of McGrath *et al.* (1992b) which was referred to in Chapter 6. They found that the basic group-oriented values and attitudes among entrepreneurs in Taiwan and the People's Republic of China were strikingly similar and enduring, in spite of decades of different ideological and economic pressures for change.

Similarly, Feldman and Rosenthal (1990) provided evidence that cultural conceptions of the self, in particular, seem to change very slowly. They examined expectations for autonomy across two generations of Chinese immigrants from Hong Kong in Australia and the USA. They found that first- and even second-generation Chinese high-schoolers residing in these two Western nations held autonomy expectations that were closer to those of Hong Kong Chinese than to Anglo-Australian or US high-schoolers.

> Although Chinese family patterns undergo modest changes when Chinese families live in the West, they nonetheless remain different from their Western counterparts, in terms of the amount of structure they provide and the extent to which they use child-rearing practices which promote autonomy.
>
> (p. 277)

Whitman's (1998) critical defence of Hayek's theory of cultural evolution provides an explanation of why cultural norms (beliefs, practices and rules) have a tendency to persist once they are absorbed into the cultural corpus and why they might therefore have an enduring impact upon how economies operate in the long run. According to Whitman, the process of cultural evolution entails a *dual* selective mechanism. The first prong is a *psychological* selective process that involves a process by which various cultural practices and beliefs are screened by human minds for their reasonability, usefulness, appeal or ease of imitation and then adopted by them. The second prong is *environmental* selection, which involves the process by which cultural norms may contribute to the survival or downfall of the group of people that adopts them. Only after cultural norms have withstood psychological selection – that is, satisfied the preferences and subjective desires of human minds acting as filters – are they subject to environmental selection. Once selected by both sets of selective forces, cultural traits might thereafter display a great deal of inertia because of such factors as path dependence and trend persistence. Thus, treating culture and informal institutions as undisturbed by feedback effects in the relatively short to medium term is not to do too great violence to the facts.

There is indirect empirical evidence to support the claim that differences in timing differentiate how culture, institutional structure and personal agency beliefs affect each other. Reciprocal causation does not imply that the different causal elements must occur simultaneously (both from the point of view of the economic actors themselves and the outside observer). Indeed, with time lags, some causal factors take a while to kick in and to trigger reciprocal forces so that we do not have to consider every type of interaction all at once. '[I]n economics the full effects of a cause seldom come at once, but often spread themselves out after it has ceased to exist' (Marshall 1920: 109).

In particular, there are tentative indications that culture and institutional structures appear to be less readily influenced by people's psychological functioning than is individual psychological functioning affected by culture and institutions. In a series of studies, Kohn and his associates have examined the relationship between a person's location in a social (specifically occupational) structure and the individual's perceptions of personal agency, or what they refer to as 'self-directedness of orientation' (Kohn and Schoenbach 1983; Kohn and Slomczynski 1990; Naoi and Schooler 1985). Summarising the results of their previous research, they report that:

> People of higher [stratification] position enjoy greater opportunity to be self-directed in their work; the experience of occupational self-direction, in turn, has a profound effect on people's values, orientations, and cognitive functioning. ...
>
> [O]n the basis of our analyses of job conditions and psychological functioning (Kohn and Schooler 1983), we believe that what is psycho-

logically crucial about control in the workplace is not control over others, but *control over the conditions of one's own life – occupational self-direction.*

(Kohn *et al.* 1990: 967; emphasis added)

Moreover, using statistical methods on survey data from the USA, Poland and Japan, Kohn and Schooler (1983) found that occupational conditions (such as the extent of opportunities for self-direction at work) generally have *contemporaneous* effects on psychological functioning (including people's sense of agency on and off the job), whereas psychological functioning generally has *lagged* effects on occupational conditions. Their empirical results suggest that, although there is a reciprocal relationship between these two phenomena, people's cognitive functioning is more readily amenable to change and is more quickly affected by occupational conditions (itself an aspect of economic institutions and organisational culture) than are occupational conditions affected by cognitive functioning.

As Bowles (1998: 98–99) points out, these findings do not result solely or primarily because people with a strong sense of personal agency select or are recruited into jobs that afford greater scope for self-direction. Kohn and Schoenbach (1983) specifically investigate the issue of causal directionality between psychological orientation and occupational conditions. Although they found evidence of reciprocal influence, the causal effects of job position on psychological factors are powerful and robust. (See too Kohn *et al.* 1990: 995–1001.)

On the issue of the direction of causation, we should also remember Gwartney *et al.*'s (1999) econometric study of the effect of changes in economic freedom on economic growth. They found a strongly positive and robust correlation between changes in economic freedom and economic growth. More importantly for present purposes, they also found that causation was unidirectional – increases in economic freedom in a country generate higher rates of economic growth, but not vice versa. They rejected the hypothesis that economic freedom is strongly correlated with growth because countries that grow faster tend to become freer. In their revised regression model with the annual economic growth rate from 1975 to 1985 as the dependent variable, they found that neither of the two additional independent variables representing future changes in economic freedom from 1985 to 1990 and 1990 to 1995, respectively, was statistically significant. (Other independent variables measured such things as levels and changes in human capital.)

Because higher growth from 1975 to 1985 is not correlated with more economic freedom after 1985, the evidence suggests that higher economic growth does not cause an increase in future economic freedom. … There is a plausible argument that faster economic growth could lead to increases in economic freedom, but we find no evidence that this is so.

(Gwartney *et al.* 1999: 654)

## Further work on public policy analysis

Chapter 7 spelt out some general market-process principles that can be used as a basis for developing public policy in general and policy towards entrepreneurship in particular. Further work in this area must proceed in a number of directions: at the level of analysis, application and appraisal. As a first step, the analysis so far has focused upon enhancing successful entrepreneurial alertness in isolation of other objectives. The policy goal of increasing entrepreneurship is taken as given, and it is implicitly assumed that enhancing the degree of entrepreneurship in a society is in general worthwhile. Although this is an acceptable limitation for developing a line of analysis, it is clearly a simplification. In practice, policy analysts invariably have to give advice on the implications of different ends, the tradeoffs between them and the effects of shifting means (resources) from one end to others.

Thus, the next step would be to analyse the relationship between the goal of increasing the level of entrepreneurship in a society and other objectives of public policy (such as social cohesion).[7] Such an analysis would need to address a number of questions. To what extent is the objective of enhancing successful entrepreneurial alertness an intermediate goal for the achievement of other policy objectives? To what extent do other proximate goals contribute to increasing the level of entrepreneurship? To what extent does the pursuit of the goal of enhancing successful entrepreneurial alertness leave other goals unaffected? To what extent does it conflict with or completely exclude the attainment of other policy objectives?

Further work also needs to be done at the level of practical application. This could include illustrating the application of the market-process policy programme (MPP) to solving real-world policy problems. The aim would be to generate concrete exemplars of outstanding policy analysis from the perspective of the market-process approach. The sorts of policy problems contemplated include competition policy issues (e.g. the regulation of access to network industries) and business law issues (e.g. insolvency) that clearly have implications for entrepreneurship. In addition, application can also proceed in the direction of evaluating the generic public policy framework in a country (see, for example, Harper (1994b) for an application of the MPP to assessing economic liberalisation and the policy environment in New Zealand). Intellectual resources could also be devoted to explaining why some real-world economies have been sluggish to respond to changes in their institutional and policy frameworks, especially major reforms brought about by comprehensive programmes of economic deregulation.

Another direction is to tease out the implications of the market-process approach for the mix, design and sequencing of public policies. What advice can a market-process economist give on rules about the sequencing of policy changes, such as industry deregulation and privatisation? Should the domestic house be put in order first before external liberalisation? Should product markets be liberalised before financial markets? What are the relative merits of gradualism in reform versus sharp breaks from established policies (i.e. a 'cold turkey' strategy)? What are the effects of different initial conditions in determining sequencing tactics? How is the reform process affected by the situational context and the character of events that present an opportunity to effect broad reform (e.g. financial crisis as in New Zealand, military coup as in Chile, collapse as in the former Soviet Union)?

Another important item on the agenda for future research is to evaluate the MPP relative to other policy programmes in terms of its internal consistency, theoretical progressiveness (does it produce bold new policy recipes?) or empirical progressiveness (how successful are policies developed according to its requirements?). Consequently, it is necessary to undertake a retrospective comparative appraisal of the MPP and to form a judgement about whether the MPP is up to the challenges of the decades ahead.

# 9 Concluding remarks

Competitive market processes are essential for long-run development. 'The way to permit long-run entrepreneurial growth processes to take off is to recognize and encourage the kinds of entrepreneurial discoveries that make up the short-run processes' (Kirzner 1985: 41). If we wish to explain the growing capacity of market economies to coordinate increasingly complex arrays of economic decisions and capital structures, and if we wish to explain how markets are better than any other feasible system at increasing the economic means available to people to satisfy their disparate and manifold ends, we need a theory of entrepreneurial-discovery processes and an analysis of the institutions and policies that engender these processes.

The disequilibrium, process-oriented framework adopted in this book provides a foundation to analyse the growth potential of market economies. It expands on, and applies, Kirzner's contribution to pure economic theory in important directions. The focus of Kirzner's theory of entrepreneurship is upon generating universal propositions about the *pure* entrepreneurial function within markets, propositions that *transcend* history, culture and the specifics of human psychology. By abstracting from the cultural and institutional considerations relevant to the entrepreneurial role, Kirzner's pure notion of entrepreneurial alertness reflects the usual preference of economists for 'thin description' and parsimonious explanations of social phenomena. Economists usually consider social and cultural factors and institutional arrangements to be intractable determinants and typically treat them (if they mention them at all) as exogenously given constraints in economic analysis.[1] The upshot is that Kirzner, in line with mainstream economics, has tended to ignore the impact of culture and socialising forces on entrepreneurial behaviour and economic development.[2]

In contrast, this book injects a more broadly based social-scientific approach to the study of entrepreneurship. Unlike Kirzner's approach which is at the pure level of economic enquiry, this book is an *applied* study of entrepreneurship and market processes. It delves further into the rich institutional and social complexity in which human behaviour (and especially entrepreneurial decision making) is embedded. It investigates and combines the economic, psychological, cultural, political and legal antecedents of entrepreneurship into a single theoretical framework. With the guidance of Kirzner's theory and other approaches, the book provides a 'thicker description' of entrepreneurship that identifies the complex of shared meanings (such as culturally established conceptions of the self) that orients entrepreneurial alertness in group-oriented as well as individualist cultures.[3] The analysis thereby advances beyond the culturally limited perspective of Western individualism that pervades most economics scholarship on entrepreneurship. In addition, the approach avoids treating the internal structure of economic actors as static and exogenous. It explores the conceptual models in terms of which people perceive and interpret entrepreneurial opportunities and economic events. It investigates how cause–effect relations are represented in the entrepreneur's mind and how these cognitive representations are translated into a propensity to discover opportunities for mutually gainful exchange. 'Profit opportunities are not so much like road signs to which we assign an automatic meaning as they are like difficult texts in need of a sustained effort of interpretation' (Lavoie 1991: 46). Paying closer attention to the psychological and cultural contexts of entrepreneurial discovery helps us to explain significant variables affecting the realisation of entrepreneurial talent (rather than just its allocation) that have usually been treated as exogenous and not amenable to economic analysis.

Expanding on Gilad's work (1982a; 1982b), the approach in this book predicts that people's expectations of the contingency of economic outcomes on certain actions and their expectations of their competence to perform the relevant actions are major determinants of entrepreneurial alertness. More specifically, the prediction is that a heightened belief in internal locus of control and a robust sense of personal efficacy in the economic sphere generate more acute and sustained alertness to profit opportunities. People who perceive that economic events are contingent on their behaviour and who see themselves as competent in business pursuits are more alert to opportunities than people who locate the source of control over events in external powers.

A more 'thickly' articulated conception of entrepreneurial alertness is required if we are to make more precise predictions about market processes and to offer a fuller account of the discovery of new ends–means relationships. This book helps us to go beyond explaining the mere existence of entrepreneurial opportunities at a highly abstract level and to begin to explain why, when and how some people and not others discover and exploit profit opportunities in particular contexts and situations. It yields insights about the different forms that entrepreneurship and innovation can take in different cultural and institutional settings (for instance, see Table 6.3). It explains the impact that culture can have on the background knowledge that frames entrepreneurs' discoveries, and it identifies the most significant situational influences that affect the alertness of people from different cultures.

In addition, the 'thicker' description of entrepreneurship provided in this work rejects aggregated notions of national culture, and it shows that the real world is far more complicated than the received view that individualist cultures are necessarily more entrepreneurial than group-oriented ones. It predicts that a subset of group-oriented cultures will be highly entrepreneurial. Moreover, and again in contrast to conventional wisdom, it suggests why the process of economic development may well give rise to greater heterogeneity in cultural values rather than cultural uniformity across nations (such as convergence on individualist values).

Furthermore, the approach in this book explains how the cognitive drivers of entrepreneurial alertness (i.e. personal agency beliefs) are determined in part by cultural and institutional factors. In particular, the institutional analysis predicts that entrepreneurial alertness is most likely to be stimulated under institutional arrangements that promote a maximum realisation of the principle of economic freedom. It is argued, among others, that the rule of law, institutions of private property and contract, market coordination of resources, and self-enforcing constraints on state power are the best means for achieving economic freedom and enhancing personal agency perceptions and alertness to opportunities. The general thrust of the argument is that entrepreneurship will be most vigorous in those societies that rely heavily upon the self-regulating capacity of markets to generate spontaneous order.

Because almost all government actions affect entrepreneurial discovery, public policy-makers cannot afford to take entrepreneurship for granted and neglect its role in both short-run and long-run economic processes. A deeper understanding of the institutional framework within which entrepreneurial processes can thrive is central to designing institutions and policies that are more conducive to economic growth and development.

# Notes

## 1 Introduction

1 Compare Baumol (1993: 4–5):

> If we seek to explain the success of those economies that have managed to grow significantly, compared with those that have remained relatively stagnant, we find it difficult to do so without taking into consideration differences in the availability of entrepreneurial talent and in the motivational mechanisms that drive them on.

2 Rothbard urges us to be cautious in our use of the term 'economic growth':

> What, in point of fact, *is* economic 'growth'? Any proper definition must surely encompass an increase of economic means available for the satisfaction of people's ends – in short, increased satisfaction of people's wants, or as P. T. Bauer has put it, 'an increase in the range of effective alternatives open to people'.
>
> Finally, the very term 'growth' is an illegitimate import of a metaphor from biology into human action. 'Growth' and 'rate of growth' connote some sort of automatic necessity or inevitability and have for many people a value-loaded connotation of something self-evidently desirable.
>
> (Rothbard 1993: 837–838)

3 For example, see Barreto (1989), Baumol (1968), Casson (1982), Harper (1996), Kirzner (1962; 1973; 1979), Latsis (1972; 1976b) and Loasby (1989). See too Hébert and Link (1982; 1989).

4 See Kirzner (1984a: 52–54) and Lachmann (1986: 125–127). From Kirzner's perspective, all three kinds of entrepreneurship express alertness and are cut from the same cloth:

> The entrepreneurial alertness which notices pure arbitrage possibilities today is fundamentally similar to that which presciently envisages the profit possibilities to be obtained through intertemporal arbitrage. And it is analytically parallel, at least, to that alertness to the possibilities that can be opened up through innovation that inspires the creativity and inventiveness of entrepreneurial producers.
>
> (Kirzner 1992: 50)

5 For his recent reconsideration of the differences between his and Schumpeter's conception of the entrepreneurial role, see Kirzner (2000: 239–257). In this chapter, Kirzner argues that his notion of alertness to opportunities prompted by externally generated change is 'not necessarily inconsistent' with Schumpeter's conception of entrepreneurs as the agents who creatively initiate economic change (p. 6). For an alternative view on the distinction between Kirznerian and Schumpeterian entrepreneurs, see Choi (1995).

6 The individual entrepreneur is the unit of analysis in the theories developed by Casson (1982), Harper (1996) and Kirzner (1973; 1979; 1982c). According to Casson (1982), the entrepreneur is a person, not a team, committee or organisation. Casson's later work (1990), however, emphasises the nature and role of social groups in entrepreneurship.

7 Cantillon (1931) was the first scholar to emphasise the general economic function rather than the personality, occupation or social status of the entrepreneur.

## 2 The theory of entrepreneurial discovery

1 Kirzner's theory of entrepreneurial discovery has been subject to extensive scrutiny. For one of the more insightful and comprehensive critiques, see Ricketts (1992).

2 See, for instance, Dulbecco and Garrouste (1999), Ioannides (1999), Lewin and Phelan (2000) and Sautet (2000).

3 For further discussion of competition as a type of discovery procedure, see Hayek (1948: Ch. 5; 1978: Ch. 12; 1979: Ch. 15). See too Kirzner (1979: Ch. 2) and O'Driscoll and Rizzo (1996: Ch. 6). For a highly critical appraisal from a Marxian perspective, see Ioannides (1992: Chs 3, 4).

4 Not all present-day Austrian economists would subscribe to this view. See, for example, Salerno (1993) who strongly disapproves of attempts to 'homogenise' Mises and Hayek and who argues that on the contrary their approaches constitute two distinct and conflicting paradigms for explaining how markets work.

5 Jevon's law of indifference or law of one price asserts that there cannot be two prices for the same good in the same open market at any given point in time. The law of indifference can be extended to situations in which the sum of input prices is equal to the price of the output that those inputs generate.

6 Even though it has a different physical form, the bundle of inputs is regarded as the 'same' as the end product into which the bundle is transformed, because the bundle of inputs 'contains all that is technologically required (and no more than is required)' to make the end product (Kirzner 1973: 85, 222).

7 Thus, Kirzner's position differs markedly from that of Casson (1982: 333–338). Casson attempts to apply the equilibrium method to analyse entrepreneurship. His supply curve relates the number of 'active' entrepreneurs (who are willing to supply their coordination services) to the 'expected reward per entrepreneur'. The position of the supply curve for entrepreneurship depends on the number of able entrepreneurs in the economic system (i.e. the stock and distribution of entrepreneurial ability among the population) and the proportion of able entrepreneurs who are 'qualified' (i.e. who have access to resources for backing their judgements). The supply curve will shift with changes in any of these parameters. The other schedule in his analysis of the market for entrepreneurs is not a demand curve in the conventional sense but rather shows how, conditional upon the expected rate of change in the economy, the expected reward per entrepreneur varies with the number of entrepreneurs. See too Hamilton and Harper (1994: 8–9).

8 Because of the methodological limitations of case studies in testing theory, Shane also conducted two further studies involving two separate experiments – one randomised, the other non-randomised – on MIT students, the results of which are also consistent with those of the field study.

9 For further discussion of Kirzner's conception of the market process and criticisms of it, see Buchanan and Vanberg (1991), High (1986), Littlechild (1979), Rizzo (1996), Thomsen (1992: Ch. 2) and Vaughn (1994: Ch. 7).

10 See Kirzner (1992: 42–43) for his interpretation of Lachmann's system. According to Kirzner, Lachmann (1986) sees the market process as the *actual* movement of the IVs over time. The actual sequence of IV values reflects the *joint effect* of the two sets of forces for change that Kirzner identifies: that is, both exogenous changes in UVs and endogenous adjustment in IVs. Lachmann considers the two sets of forces for change to be inextri-

cably linked to such an extent that they are not amenable to separate analysis (Kirzner 1992: 42–43). As Lachmann (1976: 60) says: 'What emerges from our reflections is an image of the market as a particular kind of process, a continuous process without beginning or end, propelled by the interaction between the forces of equilibrium and the forces of change'.

## 3 Psychological determinants of entrepreneurial alertness

1   In referring here to the 'differences' between people, Venkataraman (1997: 123) is referring not so much to psychological or sociological traits but rather to knowledge (and information) differences, cognitive differences and behavioural differences.

2   Thus, the term 'agency' is not being used here in the sense of the function of a person who is appointed by other persons to undertake stipulated duties on their behalf, as it is employed in the principal–agent literature in economics.

3   Consequently, contingency expectations might be a more precise term than locus of control beliefs to describe these expectations (Flammer 1995; Weisz and Stipek 1982). However, the term 'locus of control beliefs' is so well established in entrepreneurship research that I will stick with current usage. For similar typologies distinguishing between control beliefs (or contingency judgements or outcome expectations) and efficacy beliefs (or competence expectations), see too Bandura (1997), Earl (1987), Ford and Thompson (1985), Gurin and Brim (1984), Skinner *et al.* (1988) and Weisz (1990).

4   Indeed, Shaver and Scott suggest that the search for 'personological' differences between entrepreneurs and non-entrepreneurs should be abandoned in favour of a 'truly psychological perspective on new venture creation' that considers 'person, process, and choice' (1991: 39). Such an approach would focus on the individual (the *person* rather than the personality) in his or her situational context as the unit of analysis and would also consider how the external world becomes represented in the entrepreneur's mind (via social cognitive *processes*) and how the entrepreneur's cognitive representations of the world are translated into action (the exercise of *choice*).

5   For extensive surveys of the literature on the psychology of the entrepreneur, see Brockhaus (1982), Brockhaus and Horwitz (1986), Gilad (1982a; 1982b; 1986), Ginsberg and Bucholtz (1989), Kets de Vries (1977) and Maital (1988: Vol. II, Part 9).

6   For a review of the psychological literature on locus of control, see Lefcourt (1982), Phares (1976) and Strickland (1977; 1989). For a review of the literature on locus of control as it relates to entrepreneurship, see Brockhaus (1982), Gilad (1982a; 1982b), Jennings and Zeithaml (1983), and Venkatapathy (1984).

7   For a brief review of the literature on the self-efficacy concept, with an emphasis upon its implications for managerial decision-making and organisational behaviour, see Gist (1987), Gist and Mitchell (1992) and Wood and Bandura (1989).

8   In the mediating-effects model, organisational conditions (the antecedent variable) have a direct effect on self-efficacy (the mediating variable), and self-efficacy has a direct effect on personal initiative (the outcome variable). It is hypothesised that organisational conditions provide for direct mastery experiences that lead to a higher degree of generalised self-efficacy that in turn leads to higher personal initiative. In the moderating-effects model, the relationship between organisational conditions and personal initiative varies as a function of the level of self-efficacy. The model implies that organisational conditions should have a stronger impact on the personal initiative of people who have low self-efficacy than for highly self-efficacious individuals (Speier and Frese 1997: 175–176).

    For a brief review of other research into how occupational hierarchies and working conditions affect people's sense of self-directedness, see Bowles (1998: 97–99).

9   What follows is a development of a simpler model by Gilad (1982b: 149–153) that was examined in Harper (1998: 248–251). His model focuses exclusively upon the impact of

LOC beliefs upon alertness and, consequently, it does not take account of the role of individual self-efficacy in the process of entrepreneurial discovery. This omission is a significant drawback: 'In any given instance behavior would be best predicted by considering *both* self-efficacy and outcome [i.e. control] beliefs' (Bandura 1982: 140; emphasis added). Gilad's model is incomplete because believing that actions determine valued outcomes (positive contingency expectations, internal LOC beliefs) does not generate a high, stable level of alertness if one does not also believe that one is capable of producing the actions that bring about those very outcomes (high sense of self-efficacy).

10  For a survey of research into how different types of educational practices and different aspects of school organisation influence students' perceived efficacy, see Schunk (1989) and Bandura (1997: 174–176, 244–249).

# 4  Institutions I: Rule of law, property and contract

1  In using this terminology, I do not wish to imply that a market exists for the hire of entrepreneurial services. Nor do I wish to imply that it is possible to treat entrepreneurship in terms of demand and supply curves. The market does not demand (in the ordinary sense) the services of entrepreneurs. See chapter 2.

2  For penetrating critiques of Hayek's conception of the rule of law, see Hamowy (1971) and Leoni (1972).

3  Weingast's argument emphasises the need for citizens to share similar views on what constitutes a transgression by the state and about how to respond to it. In contrast, Voigt argues that the rule of law will only survive if there is a sufficiently large number of groups that represent *diverse interests* and that possess a credible threat of retaliation. 'If interest groups are successful in preventing government and other groups from agreeing on exemptions from universalizable rules, they can become the unintended watchdogs of the rule of law' (Voigt 1998: 204). This point of view also contrasts markedly with that of Olson (1982) who suggests that organised interest groups are detrimental to the rule of law.

4  Hayek (1960: 157–158) makes a related point:

> The rules [under which citizens act] may have come to exist merely because, in a certain type of situation, friction is likely to arise among individuals about what each is entitled to do, which can be prevented only if there is a rule to tell each clearly what his rights are. Here it is necessary merely that some known rule cover the type of situation, and it may not matter greatly what its contents are.

5  However, Hayek (1960: 154) would admit the possibility of some legislation aimed at specific groups of entrepreneurs, but only provided that particular requirements were satisfied. In order to be legitimate and consistent with the rule of law, such legislation would have to be favoured by the majority of both those within and those outside that group. Hamowy (1971: 286) suggests that this criterion is subject to majoritarian bias which would give law-makers a great deal of leeway in developing legislation inconsistent with freedom.

6  The concept of the alienability of property is thus at odds with the idea that one's property becomes an inseparable extension of one's self. William James, for example, suggests that the things that properly belong to us 'become, with different degrees of intimacy, parts of our empirical selves' and that whenever they are lost or interfered with, we undergo 'a sense of the shrinkage of our personality, a partial conversion of ourselves to nothingness' (James 1890: 291–293, quoted in Pipes 1999: 72).

7  De Soto (2000: 161–187) suggests that rectifying lacunae in the property rights framework requires creating an integrated and formal legal property system that recognises and codifies existing local conventions on property. De Soto's solution, however, is by no

means a straightforward exercise. In particular, trying to integrate and centralise apparently contradictory property regimes – different informal norms dispersed throughout various regions as well as any existing, though unenforced, formal law – may generate numerous counterclaims over property that can overload the courts and frustrate the process of assigning formal private titles to those who can put assets to better use. (Certainly, litigation has been a major problem in the transfer of property rights in Eastern Europe during the privatisation process (Pistor 1998: 607).) In addition, informal property norms may have an important tacit component, which frustrates attempts to articulate them in legislation. Furthermore, codifying existing customary rights in formal statute laws could, in the longer term, create legal uncertainty for entrepreneurs if these very laws become prone to arbitrary and radical changes, such as those motivated by reconfigurations in political coalitions of special interests.

It should be noted that the problem that de Soto identifies – the absence of well-defined, generally recognised and freely transferable property rights – is not the necessary consequence of customary law per se. Some customary legal systems, such as the medieval Law Merchant and modern private commercial law, are capable of producing precisely specified and uniform legal rules that are recognised and enforced across regions and nations. The norms of medieval customary mercantile law, for instance, were recorded in the form of written commercial instruments and contracts. '[T]he objectivity of mercantile law, the specificity of its norms, and the precision of its concepts increased over time; its universality and generality, its uniformity, increasingly prevailed over local differences ... and the degree of integration of commercial law increased' (Berman 1983: 354–355).

8 Property rules are just one of the means by which entitlements in complex modern societies are protected. When transaction costs are high, liability rules may also emerge (Calabresi and Melamed 1972). Under liability rules, economic actors are permitted to take or use other people's entitlements without prior permission if they are willing to compensate them afterwards by an amount of money to be determined by a third party, such as a court. For example, in the case of a car accident that destroys a farmer's fence, it would be impossible for the negligent driver causing the damage to negotiate a voluntary sale with the farmer beforehand, presuming that the driver does not know the victim or anticipate the accident. The potential transaction costs of arranging a prior sale of the fence to the driver are unbounded and prohibit a voluntary exchange between both parties before the accident. A major drawback of liability rules, however, is that they permit one party to take the assets of others without their consent.

9 In light of Rickett's (1987) definition of rent seeking discussed in Chapter 1, any economic actors who try to capture, through uncompensated transfer, attributes of an asset that have hitherto been a communal resource (and therefore not unowned) are rent seeking rather than being entrepreneurial because they are challenging the communal property rights of others: 'A successful challenge will result in a loss to those now excluded of the value of their communal rights, in which case an unwilling transfer is involved' (p. 461).

10 For a recent collection of essays on the historical evolution of the concept of contractual freedom, with an emphasis upon Anglo-American legal history, see Scheiber (1998).

11 Doctrinal developments in both common and statute law may be making inroads into contractual autonomy and may fail to satisfy the rule of law's requirement that the enforceability of contracts should depend only on general rules. For example, the freedom of contract is curtailed by the modern notion of *substantive unconscionability*, according to which a court may, under special circumstances, set aside a contract if it perceives the bargaining outcome (e.g. the price negotiated) to be so grossly unfair that enforcing the contract would shock the conscience of the court. The economic effect of the courts intervening in an ad hoc manner on the grounds of substantive unconscionability is to undermine the security of entrepreneurial transactions and to increase legal uncertainty in contractual relationships. See Eisenberg (1982) and Epstein (1975).

## 5 Institutions II: Money, political and legal decentralisation and economic freedom

1   In addition, the infusion of money into a market system has an effect on the behaviour of market participants because money is always more than just a medium of exchange. 'In particular, people may seek to hold money as a particularly desirable form of asset under conditions of uncertainty' (Kirzner 1963: 50). Austrian monetary theory examines the non-neutrality of money. See Garrison (2001) and Horwitz (2000).

2   For an examination of Mises's discussion of 'appraisement', see the series of papers by Salerno (1990a; 1990b; 1993; 1994) and Rothbard (1991).

3   According to Marshall, because money is generalised purchasing power, people can afford to keep large holdings of money. In addition, there are also likely to be many arbitraging dealers who can readily receive or supply large amounts of money. Thus, the stock available of one of the things being offered in all market exchanges is therefore likely to be very large and in the hands of many participants, so that there is generally no change in their willingness to part with money (in neoclassical terms, its marginal utility to them is more or less constant).

These steadying influences are generally absent under barter.

In barter a person's stock of either commodity exchanged needs to be adjusted closely to his individual wants. If his stock is too large he may have no good use for it. If his stock is too small he may have some difficulty in finding any one who can conveniently give him what he wants and is also in need of the particular things of which he himself has a superfluity.

(Marshall 1920: 336)

Under barter, the marginal utilities to buyers and sellers of all commodities exchanged will thus change as their stocks of these commodities change, requiring further adjustments in their allocation and holdings of different items.

4   Elsewhere Menger (1996) claimed that the institution of money can also be brought about by express agreement and legislation, though in many cases legislation did not create money as such but merely officially recognised an item that was already being used as a general medium of exchange. Consider too the more extreme perspective of the 'new monetary economics' (NME) that views money as merely an artefact of a specific set of legal restrictions: 'money is exactly a creation of [inefficient] regulation' (Hall 1982: 1554). According to the NME, a laissez-faire economy could operate without money. 'Money in the usual sense would not exist' (Black 1970: 9). In an unregulated economy with monetary competition, so the argument goes, the two traditional monetary functions – medium of exchange and medium of account – would not be combined in a single class of assets called money but would be separated. In addition, there might be multiple media of account as well as of exchange. For an Austrian-inflected approach to NME that draws upon Mengerian and Hayekian insights, see Cowen and Kroszner (1993). See too Cowen and Kroszner (1994) for a brief treatment.

5   There is some debate about whether the spontaneous emergence of a generally accepted medium of exchange (i.e. money) does itself rely upon entrepreneurial alertness and discovery. According to High, 'the opportunity to use indirect exchange will be present in the early stages of the division of labor, but in the beginning at least, *the adoption of the practice will be an entrepreneurial discovery*' (1990: 63; emphasis added). Other things being equal, the most successful traders will be those who not only are the first to discover the opportunity to use indirect exchange (by acquiring an intermediate good to exchange later for what they ultimately want) but also correctly perceive which are the most marketable intermediate goods.

In contrast, Kirzner sees the transition from a barter to a monetary economy as definitely not driven by market entrepreneurship. 'No entrepreneur could, by himself, discover opportunities for pure profit by attempting to move the barter society towards the use of money' (Kirzner 1992: 178). The spontaneous emergence of money, as captured by Menger's invisible-hand explanation, does not involve any creative, entrepreneurial adjustment to correct market errors. Rather, the Mengerian process is the gradual result of a snowballing effect that simply occurs because each act of using a particular commodity as a means for indirect exchange unintentionally makes it more worthwhile for other market participants to take similar steps.

> The alertness which market participants display in the course of the Mengerian process regarding the steadily increasing liquidity of the commodity in question is never alertness to prospects of *further* increasing that liquidity; what is involved is strictly alertness to the personal efficiencies to be achieved by taking advantage of that commodity's *already increased* liquidity.
>
> (Kirzner 1992: 178; original emphasis)

6  This also suggests that psychological research on 'token economies' in clinical populations is of limited relevance to an analysis of the effects of money on entrepreneurial alertness in a market setting. 'A token economy is a self-contained economic system where clients/patients are paid (reinforced) for behaving appropriately (socialising, working), and in which many desirable commodities (food, entertainment, cigarettes) must be purchased' (Furnham and Lewis 1986: 48). The token in such a system does not evolve spontaneously into a medium of exchange but is specified *ex ante* by those in control and outside the 'economy'. In addition, the target behaviours that are rewarded and the token price of each good or service are also specified centrally beforehand (see Ayllon and Azrin 1968). Moreover, the behavioural gains from these programmes seem not to generalise to situations in which the token-economy reinforcement schedule is absent (Kazdin and Bootzin 1973; Kazdin 1977).

7  There is another respect in which money may actually *increase* the discretionary impact of 'powerful others' in entrepreneurs' affairs and therefore *weaken* their internal locus of control:

> Money is an *instrument that can lower the ruler's transaction cost of wielding his power.* For example, the payment of taxes in money rather than in kind enlarges the opportunity set of the ruler and his cohorts, and money is an efficient unit of account that lowers the cost of measuring the tax base and the subjects' taxes.
>
> (Eggertsson 1990: 242; emphasis added)

8  For works on the theory of 'free banking' and historical experience with free banking systems, see Dowd (1996; 2001), Hayek (1990), Selgin (1988; 1996), White (1984) and Selgin and White (1994).

9  Tiebout (1956) was the first to highlight how the free mobility of people or assets between local government jurisdictions improves the economic coordination of resources. The economic theory of fiscal federalism that emerged following his seminal contribution focuses upon the preferences of the *owners of mobile resources*. From a market-process perspective, however, the mobility of entrepreneurs is also crucial, and it must be remembered that entrepreneurship is neither a factor of production nor does it involve prior ownership of resources (see Chapter 2).

10  Furthermore, the regulatory power of subnational governments is further constrained by any general restraining powers that the national government might have. The purpose of these powers is to prevent lower-level governments from interfering with market processes in ways that compromise the economic unity of the whole federal structure. An

example is the set of clauses in the US Constitution protecting freedom of contract (Article I, Section 10) and the rights to property (the Fifth and Fourteenth Amendments) (Hayek 1948: 267). However, a general restraining power is a purely negative power. It does not give the federal government any positive powers to regulate in place of the separate states or provinces.

11 An important qualification, however, is that the existence of a coercive authority backing the court to induce compliance has been a feature of the common law since its inception: 'The first notable characteristic of the embryonic common law is that it is royal law, backed by royal power, and administered by royal officials' (Simpson 1998: 58). Common law judges derive their power and elevated status from their position as agents of the state. (Indeed, judges originally acted as deputies for the monarch.) Furthermore, the process of making common law is not just based on custom but recognises other sources of law, especially statute. Although much of the early common law was a codification of customary practices, medieval common law judges sometimes rejected particular customary rules, and they also relied upon royal legislation as a source of law. Modern-day common law judges are less likely to acknowledge custom explicitly as a source of law (Benson 1998: 89).

12 For example, Leoni (1972: 91) argues that legislation in private affairs is incompatible with individual economic freedom and the free market:

> [I]f one seeks historical confirmation of the strict connection between the free market and the free law-making process, it is sufficient to consider that the free market was at its height in the English-speaking countries when the common law was practically the only law of the land relating to private life and business.

13 Empirical studies of the impact of government spending on economic growth tend to find that the size of government is negatively related to growth. For instance, Scully (1989) found that the size of the state and its growth have had significant negative consequences for economic growth and the efficiency of resource allocation for 115 market economies for the period 1960–1980. More recently, Gwartney *et al.* (1998) found a persistent robust negative relationship between the level and the expansion of government expenditures and the growth of GDP. 'Our findings indicate that a 10 percent increase in government expenditures as a share of GDP results in approximately a 1 percentage point reduction in GDP growth' (p. 165). See Przeworski and Limongi (1993: 65) and Gwartney *et al.* (1998: 165) for references to other studies on the impact of government spending on economic growth.

14 According to Przeworski and Limongi (1993), the empirical studies in their survey suffer from serious limitations in their research design. The crux of the statistical difficulties is that political regimes might be selected endogenously – democratic regimes might be more likely to emerge at a higher level of economic development, and democracies and authoritarian regimes might have different probabilities of survival in different economic situations, such as crises. Przeworski and Limongi (1997) investigate whether the close relationship between levels of economic development and the incidence of democratic systems arises because democracies are more likely to emerge or only more likely to survive in more developed countries. They found that 'the level of economic development does not affect the probability of transitions to democracy but that affluence does make democratic regimes more stable' (p. 155). See too Przeworski (2000).

15 Gwartney *et al.* (2001) provide a more comprehensive index of economic freedom that more adequately registers cross-country differences in the regulation of labour markets, the freedom to operate and compete in business, and the quality of the legal system (especially security of property rights). The index comprises forty-five components and is only available for a small set of countries (fifty-eight nations). It uses survey data to supplement the more objective components of the regular EFW index.

## 6 Culture and alertness

1 Modernisation is a complex process of economic, technological, political and socio-cultural changes in a society. As such, it includes but extends beyond economic development (Morse 1969).

2 Calvinism emphasises intense commitment to an occupational calling, rationality in the allocation of means to ends and a 'this-worldly' asceticism (which is nevertheless combined with a drive to the accumulation of assets). Taken together, these imperatives comprise the Protestant ethic.

3 In many cases, the link between individualism and entrepreneurship might be an artefact of the research design. Definitions of the entrepreneur typically exclude at the outset economic actors who might tend to exhibit more group-oriented values, such as corporate entrepreneurs who start up new ventures within the boundaries of existing firms. In addition, samples are often biased in favour of Western industrial countries, which tend towards individualism. Furthermore, the studies investigate correlation not causation. They do not examine whether people become entrepreneurs because they hold individualist values, or whether the experience of starting and running their own business promotes or accentuates an individualist mindset.

4 See, for example, Bendix (1967), Gusfield (1967), Lauterbach (1974), Abraham (1980), Greenfield and Strickon (1981) and Lal (1998; 2000). Yang (1988) criticises a strong version of the convergence hypothesis and its corollaries. However, in a weaker, revised hypothesis, he predicts convergence in those values that support adaptation by most members of the society to some aspects of social life that are specific to societies of that type (e.g. agrarian, pastoral, industrial, etc.) (pp. 83–85).

5 I am grateful to Don Lavoie for articulating this point.

6 See Spinosa *et al.* (1997: 58–62) for a critique of Lavoie's emphasis on the intense embeddedness of entrepreneurs in their culture's dominant practices.

7 Triandis (1989) captures this notion in his analysis of how people 'sample' different aspects of the self, such as their 'private' (i.e. independent) self and their 'collective' (i.e. interdependent) self. He suggests that the more individualist the culture, the more often people sample the private self and the less frequently they sample the collective self. Group-oriented cultures, by way of contrast, increase the frequency of sampling of the collective self.

8 The quotation was translated by Minoura (1979) and taken from Price-Williams (1985: 1007). It should be noted that there is no single dominant conception of the self in the Japanese language. My thanks to Tsutomu Hashimoto for pointing this out.

9 In any case, empirical evidence supports focusing upon individual-level variables when individualists operate within groups requiring a low degree of plan coordination (Earley 1994; Earley *et al.* 1999). With minimal interdependence of action in the group, the aggregation of individualists' personal efficacy beliefs is a better predictor of group performance than is the sum of their beliefs in their group's efficacy (cf. Bandura 1997: 480).

10 Rothbaum *et al.* (1982) use the term 'control-related' beliefs to refer to what I call agency beliefs. I have chosen to cast their model using my terminology so as to maintain consistency of exposition.

11 There has been a flurry of research into differences in LOC beliefs across cultures. However, a detailed review of seventy or so cross-cultural studies found that they had not produced consistent and conclusive results (Hui 1982). The conceptual and methodological pitfalls that have contributed to these mixed findings include issues to do with cross-cultural equivalence and multi-dimensionality of the traditional LOC construct, and the poor reliability and validity of measuring instruments. With progress made on rectifying these shortcomings, however, Hui still regards cross-cultural research on LOC to be fruitful.

12 Chia *et al.*'s distinction between direct and indirect control is similar to Wong and Sproule's (1984) dual-dimensional view of LOC. They identify a group of individuals whom they term 'bilocals' – people who consider control as emanating from *both* internal and external sources. Bilocal people emphasise dual control or shared responsibility, and they recognise that a potential for external control exists in 'powerful others' rather than just chance. They observe a balance between personal responsibility (internal LOC) and trust in relevant outside resources (external LOC).

13 Bandura's analysis (1997: 477–482) tends to focus upon 'shared' beliefs of group efficacy. He downplays the significance of intragroup variation in people's beliefs about the group's efficacy. He actually defines perceived collective efficacy as 'a group's *shared* belief in its conjoint capabilities to organize and execute the courses of action required to produce given levels of attainments' (1997: 477; emphasis added). In more precise terms, however, this shared belief is only a representative *index* of a group's sense of its efficacy. It is characterised by a measure of the central tendency of the group efficacy beliefs of its individual members and the degree of dispersion around that central belief (p. 479). Whenever the variation in efficacy beliefs within groups is as wide as the variation between groups, there is no identifiable shared belief in group efficacy. The 'major criterion of a shared belief is agreement within groups' (p. 480).

14 Indeed, differences in cultural conceptions of the self might lead to differences in the ways that people process multi-dimensional information from various sources on contingency (LOC) and competence (efficacy) in order to form their *overall* sense of agency. Across cultures, contingency and competence expectations might vary in the structure of their relations to agency beliefs. For example, in forming their judgements of agency, do people integrate contingency and competence information by using an additive rule, a relative-weighting rule or a multiplicative rule?

# 7 The market-process approach to public policy

1 My concerns are two-fold: First, because Hayek (and his followers) failed to develop formal models of the market process, it is not possible to assess claims concerning the efficiency of that process, and second (and relatedly), in the absence of such modeling, it is not possible to address the central issues of concern here, the *mix* and *design* of public and private activities, including alternative forms of regulations (alternative 'rules of the game' that the government might establish) and the advantages of alternative policies toward decentralization–centralization.

(Stiglitz 1994: 24–25; original emphasis)

2 For surveys of the notion of value freedom in Austrian economic analysis, see Kirzner (1976; 1994). This notion has been subject to extensive criticism. See, for example, Boettke (1995b).

3 Littlechild goes on to say that 'The lack of focus on political processes means they have relatively little to say about the problem of transition from a mixed economy to a market economy, which is of particular relevance in Britain today' (1986: 89). I do not agree with this judgement. There have been several works in the Austrian tradition which address these very issues, especially as it relates to the transitional economies of Eastern Europe and the former Soviet Union (e.g. Boettke 1993; 2001).

Indeed, Austrians, including Schumpeter, Hayek and Mises, have made seminal contributions to the economic analysis of politics. In *Human Action*, Mises provided a political–economic critique of interventionism and a theory of the instability of the mixed economy. In *The Road to Serfdom*, Hayek explored the limits of representative democracy and investigated the pernicious consequences of substituting the market process with socialist planning even when it is legitimated by democratic forms of government (Boettke 1995a). As a more recent contribution in Austrian political economy, Ikeda (1997) provides an analysis of the public sector inefficiencies that arise from dispersed knowledge and the radical ignorance of public decision-makers, even when it is assumed that they are benevolent and intent on promoting the general welfare.

4   Structural uncertainty means that the structure that the future can take is not known beforehand, so that people do not know the probabilities of various outcomes or even the outcomes and actions that are possible. Structural uncertainty is to be contrasted with parametric uncertainty. In a world of parametric uncertainty, the structure of the future is known in advance: although decision-makers do not know the outcome of every available action, they do have a full listing of all possible courses of action, together with an exhaustive listing of the set of all possible outcomes and the probability of each outcome occurring. On these two conceptions of uncertainty, see Harper (1996: 93–103).

5   Path dependence and irreversibility were emphasised by Schumpeter:

> Creative response changes social and economic situations for good, or, to put it differently, it creates situations from which there is no bridge to those situations that might have emerged in its absence. This is why creative response is an essential element in the historical process.
>
> (1947: 150)

6   I would like to thank Roger Garrison and Steven Horwitz for their comments on macroeconomic and monetary heuristics within the market-process programme.

7   In this context, 'well corroborated' does not just mean that a hypothesis (or premise) has withstood empirical testing. It may also mean that it has withstood severe (a priori, non-empirical) criticism of its logical consistency.

8   According to Lakatos, refutations (i.e. the falsification of specific hypotheses) are not important to the direction of the growth of scientific knowledge (Lakatos 1970: 121–123, 135–137). It is the 'positive heuristic' (a set of rules) of a scientific research programme and not empirical anomalies, which determine the evolution of a science. The 'heuristic power' of a research programme is expected to preserve its relative autonomy from the verdict of experiment, including policy experiments. However, Musgrave (1976; 1978) argues that Lakatos overestimates the heuristic power of scientific research programmes so that these programmes are not as autonomous as Lakatos proposes.

9   Even though it is in the hard core of the Austrian scientific research programme, it is fair to say that the spontaneous-ordering postulate (*H1*, *R1*) is not accorded the supreme status of the maximisation postulate in the simple neoclassical hard core. There are degrees of hardness in a hard core.

10  The protective belt of a research programme comprises a buffer of auxiliary hypotheses, which bears the brunt of experience – it contains the flexible, dispensable parts of a research programme.

11  For a comparison of Austrian and neoclassical economics, see McKenzie (1980). For a comparison of the Austrian and Chicago schools of economic thought, see Paqué (1985).

12  It should be noted that the perfect-markets approach does not encompass Coase's contributions on externalities and property rights or extensions of his work by other scholars, such as Demsetz, even though both Coase and Demsetz were economists at the University of Chicago. Neither of these authors is a perfect-market theorist since they both focus upon the effects of market frictions (e.g. transaction costs) and repudiate 'nirvana' analysis: that is, a tendency to compare the real world with an unattainable ideal.

13  A scale of values ranks various ends in the order of their importance to the particular actor.

> It is customary to say that acting man has a scale of wants or values in his mind when he arranges his actions. ... However, one must not forget that the *scale of*

*values or wants manifests itself only in the reality of action.* These scales have no independent existence apart from the actual behavior of individuals. The only source from which our knowledge concerning these scales is derived is the observation of a man's actions.

(Mises 1966: 94–95; emphasis added)

For further discussion on individual preference scales as revealed through choice and concrete action, see too Mises (1966: 102, 221) and Rothbard (1993: 14–15, 224, 266).

14 Not all neoclassical models take technology as given. Endogenous growth models assume an exogenously given technical change function. The technology production function generates blueprints from time $t_0$ to $t_\infty$.

# 8 Empirical testing and conceptual development

1 Gilad (1982a: 205–209) also provides some suggestions for using laboratory experimentation to test hypotheses about the relationship between institutional arrangements and locus of control beliefs.

For a pilot laboratory experiment that specifically seeks to examine entrepreneurial discovery directly, see Demmert and Klein (2001). They set up an outdoor laboratory experiment to test the conjecture that the availability of profit opportunities stimulates entrepreneurial discovery. Their experiment involved subjects transferring water from one bucket to another. Built into the experiment was an opportunity for subjects to discover another, far superior method for transferring water. Although their experiment was not successful, it is instructive:

Our failure is useful for what it teaches about the difficulty of working empirically with the idea of entrepreneurial discovery. Not only it is very difficult to control the motivation for entrepreneurial discovery, it is difficult merely to identify discovery as *entrepreneurial* discovery [rather than the discovery obtained from deliberate problem-solving], even when it happens right in front of the investigator.

(p. 3)

In addition, they recommend that future experiments be designed in such a way that the opportunities for gain are discoverable but not obvious.

2 For an introduction to ANCOVA, see Wildt and Ahtola (1978). For an introduction to logistic regression, see Kleinbaum (1994), Rice (1994) and Tabachnick and Fidell (2001). The papers by Chen *et al.* (1998) and Mueller and Thomas (2000) could serve as helpful exemplars on the application of these techniques to entrepreneurship research.

3 As discussed in Chapter 6, the definition of personhood and the boundaries of the self are determined by culture and not by the law. I thus disagree with the statement that 'the delineation of property rights is, in effect, the instrument or means through which a "person" is initially defined' (Buchanan 1975: 10). Property rights might define the characteristics of a person (e.g. citizenship) or group of persons (lobster-fishing communities of Maine) that might own property, enter contracts and so on, but they do not in themselves define personhood.

4 Schooler (1990) provides historical case studies of England between 1300 and 1840 and sixteenth-century Japan that explore the reciprocal causal structure among cultural, institutional and economic factors and personal agency beliefs and innovation.

5 The following discussion underscores the crucial importance of the phenomenon of time in economic problems.

The element of time is a chief cause of those difficulties in economic investigations which make it necessary for man with his limited powers to go step by step;

breaking up a complex question, studying one bit at a time, and at last combining his partial solutions into a more or less complete solution of the whole riddle.

(Marshall 1920: 366)

6 On the persistent quality of cultures, see too Fischer (1989), Hodgson (1998), Nisbett and Cohen (1996), Putnam (1993) and Schooler (1976).

7 See Streit (1991: 240–244) for a taxonomy of potential relationships between policy goals. According to Streit, these relationships can be either of a vertical or horizontal nature. Two goals stand in a vertical relationship to one another when the achievement of one goal is a means to the pursuit of the other. Horizontal relationships are of two types: logical and empirical. Logical relationships include identity (goals are indistinguishable) and inconsistency (pursuit of one goal completely rules out another goal). Empirical relationships arise whenever the application of means to achieve a goal has side effects on other goals. These effects can be either positive (so that goals are complementary), nil (independent goals) or negative (conflicting goals).

# 9 Concluding remarks

1 Mayhew (1987) argues that an emphasis upon standard microeconomic reasoning and its rationality assumptions eliminates culture as a core concept from social-scientific analysis of human behaviour. The methodology and techniques of neoclassical economics can transform cultural norms of behaviour into 'irrelevancies' or at best 'mere constraints' that limit certain types of behaviour (p. 602). This perspective renders institutions to be 'relatively trivial' as well (p. 588). In a similar vein, Ruttan notes the lack of attention that economists give to the role of culture and institutions in economic development:

[A]lmost no attention has been devoted by economists to the role of cultural endowments. To the extent that cultural endowments are considered at all by economists, they tend to be subsumed under the concept of tastes. And tastes, even more so than technology and institutions, are traditionally regarded as not subject to economic analysis.

(Ruttan 1988: S250)

2 However, Kirzner's approach does accept that cultural factors play a role backstage in influencing the extra-market moral and institutional foundations that must be in place before spontaneous, entrepreneurially driven, market processes can emerge and operate (Kirzner 2000: 77, 85).

3 Borrowing the idea of 'thick description' from Ryle (1971), Geertz (1973; 1975) makes a case for 'thick description' in anthropology and ethnography in particular: 'Culture is not a power, something to which social events, behaviors, institutions, or processes can be causally attributed; it is *a context, something within which they can be intelligibly – that is, thickly – described*' (Geertz 1975: 14; emphasis added). Boettke correctly points out that coherent and empirically relevant social science requires both 'thick' and 'thin' descriptions:

[E]conomic theory is a necessary (though not sufficient) component of a social analysis which hopes to make sense of ... human diversity and the particularities of the human experience. ... The justification of the 'thin description' of economic theory is that it affords us more compelling 'thick descriptions' of the social experience of particular times and places.

(Boettke 2001: 253)

# Bibliography

Abraham, M.F. (1980) *Perspectives on Modernization: Toward a General Theory of Third World Development*, Washington, DC: University Press of America.

Ackerman, B.A. (1984) *Reconstructing American Law*, Cambridge, MA: Harvard University Press.

Aitken, H.G.J. (1965a) 'Entrepreneurial Research: The History of an Intellectual Innovation', in H.G.J. Aitken (ed.), *Explorations in Enterprise*, Cambridge, MA: Harvard University Press, 3–19.

Aitken, H.G.J. (ed.) (1965b) *Explorations in Enterprise*, Cambridge, MA: Harvard University Press.

Allan, T.R.S. (1998) 'Rule of Law', in P. Newman (ed.), *The New Palgrave Dictionary of Economics and the Law*, Volume Three, 369–381, New York: Stockton Press.

Anderson, C.R. (1977) 'Locus of Control, Coping Behaviors and Performance in a Stress Setting: A Longitudinal Study', *Journal of Applied Psychology* 62, 446–451.

Anderson, T.L. and Hill, P.J. (1988) 'Constitutional Constraints, Entrepreneurship, and the Evolution of Property Rights', in J.D. Gwartney and R.E. Wagner, *Public Choice and Constitutional Economics*, Greenwich, CT: JAI Press, 207–228.

Angleitner, A. and Wiggins, J.S. (eds) (1986) *Personality Assessment via Questionnaires*, Berlin: Springer-Verlag.

Aoki, M. (1986) 'Horizontal vs. Vertical Information Structure of the Firm', *American Economic Review* 76(5), 971–983.

Aoki, M. (1990) 'Toward an Economic Model of the Japanese Firm', *Journal of Economic Literature* 28(1), 1–27.

Armentano, D.T. (1990) 'Time to Repeal Antitrust Regulation?', *The Antitrust Bulletin* Summer, 311–328.

Arnold, F.S. (1995) 'An Evaluation of Environmental Life Cycle Assessment', *Advances in Austrian Economics* 2(Part B), 241–276.

Ashcraft, M.H. (1992) 'Cognitive Arithmetic: A Review of Data and Theory', *Cognition* 44(1–2), 75–106.

Atkinson, J.W. (1957) 'Motivational Determinants of Risk Taking Behavior', *Psychological Review* 64(6), 359–372.

Ayllon, T. and Azrin, N. (1968) *The Token Economy: A Motivational System for Therapy and Rehabilitation*, New York: Appleton-Century-Crofts.

Bailey, M.J. (1998) 'Property Rights in Aboriginal Societies', in P. Newman (ed.), *The New Palgrave Dictionary of Economics and the Law*, Volume Three, 155–157, New York: Stockton Press.

Bajt, A. (1968) 'Property in Capital and in the Means of Production in Socialist Economies', *Journal of Law and Economics* 11(April), 1–4.

Bandura, A. (1977a) 'Self-Efficacy: Toward a Unifying Theory of Behavioral Change', *Psychological Review* 84(2), 191–215.

Bandura, A. (1977b) *Social Learning Theory*, Englewood Cliffs, NJ: Prentice Hall.

Bandura, A. (1982) 'Self-Efficacy Mechanism in Human Agency', *American Psychologist* 37, 122–147.

Bandura, A. (1986) *Social Foundations of Thought and Action: A Social Cognitive Theory*, Englewood Cliffs, NJ: Prentice Hall.

Bandura, A. (1995a) 'Exercise of Personal and Collective Efficacy in Changing Societies', in A. Bandura (ed.), *Self-Efficacy in Changing Societies*, New York: Cambridge University Press, 1–45.

Bandura, A. (ed.) (1995b) *Self-Efficacy in Changing Societies*, New York: Cambridge University Press.

Bandura, A. (1997) *Self-Efficacy: The Exercise of Control*, New York: W.H. Freeman.

Bandura, A. and Cervone, D. (1986) 'Differential Engagement of Self-Reactive Influences in Cognitive Motivation', *Organizational Behavior and Human Decision Processes* 38(1), 92–113.

Bandura, A. and Wood, R.E. (1989) 'Effect of Perceived Controllability and Performance Standards on Self-Regulation of Complex Decision-Making', *Journal of Personality and Social Psychology* 56, 805–814.

Barnlund, D.C. (1975) *Public and Private Self in Japan and the United States: Communicative Styles of Two Cultures*, Tokyo: Simul Press.

Barreto, H. (1989) *The Entrepreneur in Microeconomic Theory: Disappearance and Explanation*, London: Routledge.

Barro, R.J. (1996) 'Democracy and Growth', *Journal of Economic Growth* 1(1), 1–27.

Barzel, Y. (1997) *Economic Analysis of Property Rights*, Second Edition, Cambridge: Cambridge University Press.

Bauer, P.T. (1987) 'The Disregard of Reality', *Cato Journal* 7(1), 29–42.

Baumol, W.J. (1968) 'Entrepreneurship in Economic Theory', *American Economic Review, Papers and Proceedings* 58, 64–71.

Baumol, W.J. (1983) 'Towards Operational Models of Entrepreneurship', in J. Ronen (ed.), *Entrepreneurship*, Lexington, MA: D.C. Heath, 29–48.

Baumol, W.J. (1990) 'Entrepreneurship: Productive, Unproductive, and Destructive', *Journal of Political Economy* 98(5), Part 1, October, 893–921.

Baumol, W.J. (1993) *Entrepreneurship, Management, and the Structure of Payoffs*, Cambridge, MA: MIT Press.

Baumol, W.J. (2002) *The Free-Market Innovation Machine: Analyzing the Growth Miracle of Capitalism*, Princeton, NJ: Princeton University Press.

Beattie, J. (1980) 'Representations of the Self in Traditional Africa', *Africa* 50(3), 313–320.

Begley, T.M. and Boyd, D.P. (1987) 'Psychological Characteristics Associated with Performance in Entrepreneurial Firms and Smaller Businesses', *Journal of Business Venturing* 2, 79–93.

Bellah, R.N., Madsen, R., Sullivan, W.M., Swidler, A. and Tipton, S.M. (1996) *Habits of the Heart: Individualism and Commitment in American Life*, Updated Edition, Berkeley, CA: University of California Press.

Bendix, R. (1967) 'Tradition and Modernity Reconsidered', *Comparative Studies in Society and History* 9, 292–346.

Benson, B.L. (1990) *The Enterprise of Law: Justice without the State*, San Francisco: Pacific Research Institute for Public Policy.

Benson, B.L. (1998) 'Evolution of Commercial Law', in P. Newman (ed.), *The New Palgrave Dictionary of Economics and the Law*, Volume Two, 88–93, New York: Stockton Press.

Berger, B. (ed.) (1991a) *The Culture of Entrepreneurship*, San Francisco: Institute for Contemporary Studies.

Berger, B. (1991b) 'The Culture of Modern Entrepreneurship', in B. Berger, *The Culture of Entrepreneurship*, San Francisco: Institute for Contemporary Studies, 13–32.

Berger, P.L. (1988) 'An East Asian Development Model?' in P.L. Berger and H.M. Hsiao (eds), *In Search of an East Asian Development Model*, New Brunswick, NJ: Transaction Books, 3–11.

Berger, P.L. and Hsiao, H.M. (eds) (1988) *In Search of an East Asian Development Model*, New Brunswick, NJ: Transaction Books.

Berman, H.J. (1983) *Law and Revolution: The Formation of Western Legal Tradition*, Cambridge, MA: Harvard University Press.

Bernstein, L. (1992) 'Opting Out of the Legal System: Extralegal Contractual Relations in the Diamond Industry', *Journal of Legal Studies* 21(1), 115–157.

Bernstein, L. (1998) 'Private Commercial Law', in P. Newman (ed.), *The New Palgrave Dictionary of Economics and the Law*, Volume Three, 108–114, New York: Stockton Press.

Bernstein, L. (2001) 'Private Commercial Law in the Cotton Industry: Creating Cooperation through Rules, Norms and Institutions', *Michigan Law Review* 99, 1724–1788.

Berry, J.W. and Bennett, J.A. (1992) 'Cree Conceptions of Cognitive Competence', *International Journal of Psychology* 27(1), 73–88.

Berry, J.W., Dasen, P.R. and Saraswathi, T.S. (eds) (1997a) *Handbook of Cross-Cultural Psychology*, Second Edition, Volume Two, *Basic Processes and Human Development*, Boston: Allyn and Bacon.

Berry, J.W., Poortinga, Y.H. and Pandey, J. (eds) (1997b) *Handbook of Cross-Cultural Psychology*, Second Edition, Volume One, *Theory and Method*, Boston: Allyn and Bacon.

Berry, J.W., Segall, M.H. and Kagitçibasi, C. (eds) (1997c) *Handbook of Cross-Cultural Psychology*, Second Edition, Volume Three, *Social Behavior and Applications*, Boston: Allyn and Bacon.

Beudant, L. Charles A. (1891) *Le Droit Individuel et l'Etat: Introduction à L'Etude du Droit*, 2e éd., Paris.

Black, F. (1970) 'Banking and Interest Rates in a World without Money: The Effects of Uncontrolled Banking', *Journal of Banking Research* 1(3), 9–20.

Boettke, P.J. (1993) *Why Perestroika Failed: The Politics and Economics of Socialist Transformation*, London: Routledge.

Boettke, P.J. (ed.) (1994) *The Elgar Companion to Austrian Economics*, Aldershot: Edward Elgar.

Boettke, P.J. (1995a) 'Hayek's *Serfdom* Revisited: Government Failure in the Argument against Socialism', *Eastern Economic Journal* 21(1), 7–26.

Boettke, P.J. (1995b) 'Why Are There No Austrian Socialists? Ideology, Science and the Austrian School', *Journal of the History of Economic Thought* 17(Spring), 35–56.

Boettke, P.J. (2001) *Calculation and Coordination: Essays on Socialism and Transitional Political Economy*, New York and London: Routledge.

Boettke, P.J. and Rizzo, M.J. (1995) 'Preface', *Advances in Austrian Economics* 2(Part A), xiii–xv.

Böhm, F. (1980) *Freiheit und Ordnung in der Marktwirtschaft*, Baden-Baden: Nomos.

Böhm, F. (1989) 'The Rule of Law in a Market Economy', in A. Peacock and H. Willgerodt (eds), *Germany's Social Market Economy: Origins and Evolution*, London: Macmillan, 46–67.

Bonnett, C. and Furnham, A. (1991) 'Who Wants to Be an Entrepreneur? A Study of Adolescents in a Young Enterprise Scheme', *Journal of Economic Psychology* 12(3), 465–478.

Borland, G. (1974) 'Locus of Control, Need for Achievement and Entrepreneurship', Doctoral Dissertation, The University of Texas at Austin.

Bowles, S. (1998) 'Endogenous Preferences: The Cultural Consequences of Markets and Economic Institutions', *Journal of Economic Literature* 36(1), 75–111.

Boyd, N.G. and Vozikis, G.S. (1994) 'The Influence of Self-Efficacy on the Development of Entrepreneurial Intentions and Actions', *Entrepreneurship Theory and Practice* 18(4), 63–77.

Brenner, R. (1994) *Labyrinths of Prosperity: Economic Follies, Democratic Remedies*, Ann Arbor, MI: University of Michigan Press.

Brockhaus, R.H. (1975) 'I–E Locus of Control Scores as Predictors of Entrepreneurial Intentions', *Proceedings*, New Orleans: Academy of Management.

Brockhaus, R.H. (1980) 'Risk Taking Propensity of Entrepreneurs', *Academy of Management Journal* 23(3), 509–520.

Brockhaus, R.H. (1982) 'The Psychology of the Entrepreneur', in C.A. Kent., D.L. Sexton and K.H. Vesper (eds), *Encyclopedia of Entrepreneurship*, Englewood Cliffs, NJ: Prentice Hall, 39–57.

Brockhaus, R.H. and Horwitz, P.S. (1986) 'The Psychology of the Entrepreneur', in D.L. Sexton and R.W. Smilor (eds), *The Art and Science of Entrepreneurship*, Cambridge, MA: Ballinger, 25–48.

Brockhaus, R.H. and Nord, W.R. (1979) 'An Exploration of Factors Affecting the Entrepreneurial Decision: Personal Characteristics vs. Environmental Conditions', *Proceedings of the Thirty-Ninth Annual Meeting of the Academy of Management*, 364–368.

Brozen, Y. (1971) 'Bain's Concentration and Rates of Return Revisited', *Journal of Law and Economics* 14(October), 351–369.

Brunner, K. and Meltzer, A.H. (1971) 'The Uses of Money: Money in the Theory of an Exchange Economy', *American Economic Review* 61(5), 784–805.

Buchanan, J.M. (1965) 'An Economic Theory of Clubs', *Economica* (New Series), 32(125), 1–14.

Buchanan, J.M. (1973) 'Introduction: L.S.E. Cost Theory in Retrospect', in J.M. Buchanan and G.F. Thirlby (eds), *L.S.E. Essays on Cost*, London: Weidenfeld and Nicolson, 1–18.

Buchanan, J.M. (1975) *The Limits of Liberty: Between Anarchy and Leviathan*, Chicago: University of Chicago Press.

Buchanan, J.M. (1986) *Liberty, Market and State: Political Economy in the 1980s*, New York: New York University Press.

Buchanan, J.M. (1995) 'Federalism as an Ideal Political Order and an Objective for Constitutional Reform', *Publius – The Journal of Federalism* 25(2), 19–27.

Buchanan, J.M. (1995/96) 'Federalism and Individual Sovereignty', *Cato Journal* 15(2–3), 259–268.

Buchanan, J.M. and Vanberg, V.J. (1991) 'The Market as a Creative Process', *Economics and Philosophy* 7(2), 167–186.

Busenitz, L.W. (1996) 'Research on Entrepreneurial Alertness: Sampling, Measurement, and Theoretical Issues', *Journal of Small Business Management* 34(4), 35–44.

Butos, W.N. and Koppl, R. (1999) 'Hayek and Kirzner at the Keynesian Beauty Contest', *Journal des Economistes et des Etudes Humaines* 9(2–3), 257–275.

Calabresi, G. and Melamed, A.D. (1972) 'Property Rules, Liability Rules, and Inalienability: One View of the Cathedral', *Harvard Law Review* 85(6), 1089–1128.

Caldwell, B.J. and Boehm, S. (eds) (1992) *Austrian Economics: Tensions and New Directions*, Boston, MA: Kluwer Academic Publishers.

Cantillon, R. (1931) *Essai sur la Nature du Commerce en Général*, London: Macmillan. First Published 1755.

Casson, M.C. (1982) *The Entrepreneur*, Oxford: Martin Robertson.

Casson, M.C. (1990) *Enterprise and Competitiveness: A Systems View of International Business*, Oxford: Clarendon Press.

Caudill, S.B., Zanella, F.C. and Mixon, F.G., Jr (2000) 'Is Economic Freedom One Dimensional? A Factor Analysis of Some Common Measures of Economic Freedom', *Journal of Economic Development* 25(1), 17–39.

Cha, J. (1994) 'Aspects of Individualism and Collectivism in Korea', in U. Kim *et al.* (eds), *Individualism and Collectivism: Theory, Method, and Applications*, Thousand Oaks, CA: Sage, 157–174.

Chambliss, C. and Murray, E.J. (1979) 'Cognitive Procedures for Smoking Reduction: Symptom Attribution versus Efficacy Attribution', *Cognitive Therapy and Research* 3, 91–95.

Chen, C.C., Greene, P.G. and Crick, A. (1998) 'Does Entrepreneurial Self-Efficacy Distinguish Entrepreneurs from Managers?', *Journal of Business Venturing* 13(4), 295–316.

Chia, R.C., Cheng, B.S. and Chuang, C.J. (1998) 'Differentiation in the Source of Internal Control for Chinese', *Journal of Social Behavior and Personality* 13(4), 565–578.

Chinese Culture Connection (1987) 'Chinese Values and the Search for Culture-Free Dimensions of Culture', *Journal of Cross-Cultural Psychology* 18(2), 143–164.

Choi, Y.B. (1995) 'The Entrepreneur: Schumpeter versus Kirzner', *Advances in Austrian Economics* 2(Part A), 55–65.

Cole, D.L. and Cole, S. (1977) 'Counternormative Behavior and Locus of Control', *Journal of Social Psychology* 101(February), 21–28.

Converse, P.E. (1964) 'The Nature of Belief Systems in Mass Publics', in D.E. Apter (ed.), *Ideology and Discontent*, New York: Free Press, 206–261.

Cooter, R.D. (1993) 'Against Legal Centrism', *California Law Review* 81, 417–429.

Cooter, R.D. (1994) 'Structural Adjudication and the New Law Merchant: A Model of Decentralized Law', *International Review of Law and Economics* 14, 215–231.

Cooter, R.D. (1996) 'Decentralized Law for a Complex Economy: The Structural Approach to Adjudicating the New Law Merchant', *University of Pennsylvania Law Review* 144, 1643–1696.

Cordato, R.E. (1992) *Welfare Economics and Externalities in an Open Ended Universe: A Modern Austrian Perspective*, Boston: Kluwer Academic.

Cowan, R. (1995) 'Path Dependence, Causation and Economic Policy', Unpublished mimeo.

Cowen, T. and Kroszner, R.S. (1993) *Explorations in the New Monetary Economics*, Cambridge, MA: Blackwell.

Cowen, T. and Kroszner, R.S. (1994) 'The New Monetary Economics', in P.J. Boettke (ed.), *The Elgar Companion to Austrian Economics*, Aldershot: Edward Elgar, 593–598.

Cromie, S. and Johns, S. (1983) 'Irish Entrepreneurs: Some Personal Characteristics', *Journal of Occupational Behaviour* 4(4), 317–324.

Davis, J.B. (2001) ' Agent Identity in Economics', in U. Mäki (ed.), *The Economic World View: Studies in the Ontology of Economics*, Cambridge: Cambridge University Press, 114–131.

Davis, K. (1948) *Human Society*, New York: Macmillan.

De Haan, J. and Sierman, C.L.J. (1998) 'Further Evidence on the Relationship between Economic Freedom and Economic Growth', *Public Choice* 95 (3–4), 363–380.

Dehaene, S. (1992) 'Varieties of Numerical Abilities', *Cognition* 44(1–2), 1–42.

Demmert, H. and Klein, D.B. (2001) 'Experiment on Entrepreneurial Discovery: An Attempt to Demonstrate the Conjecture of Hayek and Kirzner', Leavey School of Business, Santa Clara University, Faculty Working Papers, 01/02–28–WP.

Demsetz, H. (1967) 'Toward a Theory of Property Rights', *American Economic Review* 57(2), 347–359.

Demsetz, H. (1983) 'The Neglect of the Entrepreneur', in J. Ronen, *Entrepreneurship*, Lexington, MA: D.C. Heath, 271–280.

Demsetz, H. (1998) 'Property Rights', in P. Newman (ed.), *The New Palgrave Dictionary of Economics and the Law*, Volume Three, 144–155, New York: Stockton Press.

Dietze, G. (1976) 'Hayek on the Rule of Law', in F. Machlup (ed.), *Essays on Hayek*, New York: New York University Press, 107–146.

Dolan, E.G. (ed.) (1976) *The Foundations of Modern Austrian Economics*, Kansas City: Sheed and Ward.

Dowd, K. (1996) *Laissez-Faire Banking*, London and New York: Routledge.

Dowd, K. (2001) *Money and the Market: Essays on Free Banking*, London and New York: Routledge.

DuCette, J.P. and Wolk, S. (1973) 'Cognitive and Motivational Correlates of Generalized Expectancies for Control', *Journal of Personality and Social Psychology* 26, 420–426.

Dulbecco, P. and Garrouste, P. (1999) 'Towards an Austrian Theory of the Firm', *Review of Austrian Economics* 12(1), 43–64.

Dyal, J.A. (1984) 'Cross-cultural Research with the Locus of Control Construct', in H.M. Lefcourt (ed.), *Research with the Locus of Control Construct*, Volume 3, 209–306, New York: Academic Press.

Earl, W.L. (1987) 'Creativity and Self-Trust: A Field Study', *Adolescence* 22, 419–432.

Earley, P.C. (1993) 'East Meets West Meets Mideast: Further Explorations of Collectivistic and Individualistic Work Groups', *Academy of Management Journal* 36(2), 319–348.

Earley, P.C. (1994) 'Self or Group? Cultural Effects of Training on Self-Efficacy and Performance', *Administrative Science Quarterly* 39(1), 89–117.

Earley, P.C. and Gibson, C.B. (1998) 'Taking Stock in Our Progress on Individualism–Collectivism: 100 Years of Solidarity and Community', *Journal of Management* 24(3), 265–304.

Earley, P.C., Gibson, C.B. and Chen, C.C. (1999) '"How Did I Do?" Versus "How Did We Do?": Cultural Contrasts of Performance Feedback Use and Self-Efficacy', *Journal of Cross-Cultural Psychology* 30(5), 594–619.

Easterbrook, W.T. (1965) 'The Climate of Enterprise', in H.G.J. Aitken (ed.), *Explorations in Enterprise*, Cambridge, MA: Harvard University Press, 65–79.

Easton, D. (1965) *A Systems Analysis of Political Life*, New York: John Wiley & Sons.

Eggertsson, T. (1990) *Economic Behavior and Institutions*, Cambridge: Cambridge University Press.

Eisenberg, M.A. (1982) 'The Bargain Principle and its Limits', *Harvard Law Review* 95(4), 741–801.

Eisenberg, M.A. (1998) 'Contracts and Relationships', in P. Newman (ed.), *The New Palgrave Dictionary of Economics and the Law*, Volume One, 445–449, New York: Stockton Press.

Ellickson, R.C. (1991) *Order without Law: How Neighbors Settle Disputes*, Cambridge, MA: Harvard University Press.

Epstein, R.A. (1975) 'Unconscionability: A Critical Reappraisal', *Journal of Law and Economics* 18(2), 293–315.

Epstein, R.A. (1995) *Simple Rules for a Complex World*, Cambridge, MA: Harvard University Press.

Feldman, S.S. and Rosenthal, D.A. (1990) 'The Acculturation of Autonomy Expectations in Chinese High-Schoolers Residing in Two Western Nations', *International Journal of Psychology* 25(3), 259–281.

Ferguson, E. (1993) 'Rotter's Locus of Control Scale: A Ten-Time Two-Factor Model', *Psychological Reports* 73, 1267–1278.

Fischer, D.H. (1989) *Albion's Seed: Four British Folkways in America*, New York: Oxford University Press.

Fisher, F.M. (1983) *Disequilibrium Foundations of Equilibrium Economics*, Econometric Society Publication No. 6, Cambridge: Cambridge University Press.

Fisher, F.M. (1987) 'Adjustment Processes and Stability', in J. Eatwell *et al.* (eds), *The New Palgrave: A Dictionary of Economics*, Volume One, 26–29, London: Macmillan.

Flammer, A. (1995) 'Developmental Analysis of Control Beliefs', in A. Bandura (ed.), *Self-Efficacy in Changing Societies*, New York: Cambridge University Press, 69–113.

Fong, Pang Eng (1988) 'The Distinctive Features of Two City-States' Development: Hong Kong and Singapore', in P.L. Berger and H.M. Hsiao (eds), *In Search of an East Asian Development Model*, New Brunswick, NJ: Transaction Books, 220–238.

Ford, M.E. and Thompson, R.A. (1985) 'Perceptions of Personal Agency and Infant Attachment: Toward a Life-Span Perspective on Competence Development', *International Journal of Behavioral Development* 8, 377–406.

Foss, N.J. (1997) 'Austrian Insights and the Theory of the Firm', *Advances in Austrian Economics* 4, 175–198.

Freeman, R.B. (2000) 'Single Peaked vs. Diversified Capitalism: The Relation between Economic Institutions and Outcomes', NBER Working Paper 7556.

Frese, M., Fay, D., Hilburger, T., Leng, K. and Tag, A. (1997) 'The Concept of Personal Initiative: Operationalization, Reliability and Validity in Two German Samples', *Journal of Occupational and Organizational Psychology* 70, Part 2, 139–161.

Friedman, D. (1979) 'Private Creation and Enforcement of Law: A Historical Case', *Journal of Legal Studies* 8, 399–415.

Friedman, M. (1982) *Capitalism and Freedom*, Chicago: University of Chicago Press.

Fukuyama, F. (1995) *Trust: Social Virtues and the Creation of Prosperity*, New York: Free Press.

Fuller, L.L. (1964) *The Morality of Law*, New Haven, CT: Yale University Press.

Furby, L. (1979) 'Individualistic Bias in Studies of Locus of Control', in A.R. Buss (ed.), *Psychology in Social Context*, New York: Irvington.

Furby, L. (1980) 'The Origins and Early Development of Possessive Behavior', *Political Psychology* 2(1), 30–42.

Furnham, A. and Lewis, A. (1986) *The Economic Mind: The Social Psychology of Economic Behavior*, New York: St Martin's Press.

Galanter, M. (1981) 'Justice in Many Rooms: Courts, Private Ordering, and Indigenous Law', *Journal of Legal Pluralism* 19, 1–47.

Garrison, R.W. (1982) 'Austrian Economics as the Middle Ground: Comment on Loasby', in I.M. Kirzner (ed.), *Method, Process, and Austrian Economics. Essays in Honour of Ludwig von Mises*, Lexington, MA: Lexington Books, 131–138.

Garrison, R.W. (2001) *Time and Money: The Macroeconomics of Capital Structure*, London and New York: Routledge.

Gartner, W.B. (1989) 'Some Suggestions for Research on Entrepreneurial Traits and Characteristics', *Entrepreneurship Theory and Practice* 14(1), 27–37.

Gastil, R.D. (1984) *Freedom in the World: Political Rights and Civil Liberties, 1983–1984*, Westport, CN: Greenwood Press.

Gastil, R.D. and Wright, L.M. (1988) 'The State of the World: Political and Economic Freedom', in M.A. Walker (ed.), *Freedom, Democracy and Economic Welfare: Proceedings of an International Symposium*, Vancouver, BC: Fraser Institute, 85–125.

Geertz, C. (1973) *The Interpretation of Cultures: Selected Essays By Clifford Geertz*, New York: Basic Books.

Geertz, C. (1975) 'On the Nature of Anthropological Understanding', *American Scientist* 63(1), 47–53.

Gesell, A.L. and Ilg, F.I. (1949) *Child Development: An Introduction to the Study of Human Growth*, New York: Harper.

Gifford, A., Jr (1999) 'Being and Time: On the Nature and the Evolution of Institutions', *Journal of Bioeconomics* 1(2), 127–149.

Gilad, B. (1982a) 'An Interdisciplinary Approach to Entrepreneurship: Locus of Control and Alertness', PhD Thesis, New York University.

Gilad, B. (1982b) 'On Encouraging Entrepreneurship: An Interdisciplinary Approach', *Journal of Behavioral Economics* 11(1), Summer, 132–163.

Gilad, B. (1984) 'The Case of the "Partnership Approach" to Public Regulation', *Journal of Economic Psychology* 5, 265–280.

Gilad, B. (1986) 'Entrepreneurial Decision Making: Some Behavioral Considerations', in B. Gilad and S. Kaish (eds), *Handbook of Behavioral Economics*, Volume A, 189–208, *Behavioral Microeconomics*, Greenwich, CT: JAI Press.

Gilad, B. and Kaish, S. (eds) (1986) *Handbook of Behavioral Economics*, Volume A, *Behavioral Microeconomics*, and Volume B, *Behavioral Macroeconomics*, Greenwich, CT: JAI Press.

Ginsberg, A. and Buchholtz, A. (1989) 'Are Entrepreneurs a Breed Apart? A Look at the Future', *Journal of General Management* 15(2), 32–40.

Gist, M.E. (1987) 'Self-Efficacy: Implications for Organizational Behavior and Human Resource Management', *Academy of Management Review* 12(3), 472–485.

Gist, M.E. and Mitchell, T.R. (1992) 'Self-Efficacy: A Theoretical Analysis of its Determinants and Malleability', *Academy of Management Review* 17(2), 183–211.

Goldberg, V.P. (1998) 'Relational Contract', in P. Newman (ed.), *The New Palgrave Dictionary of Economics and the Law*, Volume Three, 289–293, New York: Stockton Press.

Gould, S.J. and Lewontin, R.C. (1994) 'The Spandrels of San Marco and the Panglossian Paradigm: A Critique of the Adaptionist Programme', in E. Sober (ed.), *Conceptual Issues in Evolutionary Biology*, Second Edition, Cambridge, MA: MIT Press, 73–90.

Gray, J. (1989) 'Hayek on the Market Economy and the Limits of State Action', in D. Helm (ed.), *The Economic Borders of the State*, Oxford: Oxford University Press, 127–143.

Greenfield, S.M. and Strickon, A. (1981) 'A New Paradigm for the Study of Entrepreneurship and Social Change', *Economic Development and Cultural Change* 29(3), 467–500.

Greenwald, A.G. and Pratkanis, A.R. (1984) 'The Self', in R.S. Wyer and T.K. Srull (eds), *Handbook of Social Cognition*, Volume Three, Hillsdale, NJ: L. Erlbaum Associates, 129–178.

Greenwald, B. and Stiglitz, J.E. (1993) 'New and Old Keynesians', *Journal of Economic Perspectives* 7(1), 23–44.

Greif, A. (1994) 'Cultural Beliefs and the Organization of Society: A Historical and Theoretical Reflection on Collectivist and Individualist Societies', *Journal of Political Economy* 102(5), 912–950.

Grossman, G. (1981) 'The "Second Economy" of the USSR', in M. Bornstein (ed.), *The Soviet Economy: Continuity and Change*, Boulder, CO: Westview Press.

Grossman, S.J. and Stiglitz, J.E. (1976) 'Information and Competitive Price Systems', *American Economic Review (Papers and Proceedings)* 66(2), 246–253.

Gudykunst, W.B., Yoon, Y.C. and Nishida, T. (1987) 'The Influence of Individualism–Collectivism on Perceptions of Communication in Ingroup and Outgroup Relationships', *Communication Monographs* 54(3), 295–306.

Gudykunst, W.B., Gao, G., Schmidt, K.L., Nishida, T., Bond, M.H., Leung, K., Wang, G. and Barraclough, R.A. (1992) 'The Influence of Individualism–Collectivism, Self-Monitoring, and Predicted-Outcome Value on Communication in Ingroup and Outgroup Relationships', *Journal of Cross-Cultural Psychology* 23(2), 196–213.

Gurin, P. and Brim, O.G., Jr (1984) 'Change in Self in Adulthood: The Example of Sense of Control', in P.B. Baltes and O.G. Brim, Jr (eds), *Life-Span Development and Behavior*, Volume 6, 282–334, New York: Academic Press.

Gusfield, J.R. (1967) 'Tradition and Modernity: Misplaced Polarities in the Study of Social Change', *American Journal of Sociology* 73, 351–362.

Gwartney, J.D. and Lawson, R.A. (2001) *Economic Freedom of the World: Annual Report 2001*, Vancouver, BC: Fraser Institute.

Gwartney, J.D., Holcombe, R. and Lawson, R. (1998) 'The Scope of Government and the Wealth of Nations', *Cato Journal* 18(2), 163–190.

Gwartney, J.D., Lawson, R.A. and Holcombe, R.G. (1999) 'Economic Freedom and the Environment for Economic Growth', *Journal of Institutional and Theoretical Economics* 155(4), 643–663.

Gwartney, J.D., Skipton, C. and Lawson, R.A. (2001) 'A More Comprehensive Index of Economic Freedom for 58 Countries', in J.D. Gwartney and R.A. Lawson, *Economic Freedom of the World: Annual Report 2001*, Chapter 2, 23–69, Vancouver, BC: Fraser Institute.

Hall, R. (1982) 'Monetary Trends in the United States and the United Kingdom: A Review from the Perspective of New Developments in Monetary Economics', *Journal of Economic Literature* 20(4), 1552–1556.

Hamilton, R.T. and Harper, D.A. (1994) 'The Entrepreneur in Theory and Practice', *Journal of Economic Studies* 21(6), 3–18.

Hamowy, R. (1971) 'Freedom and the Rule of Law in F.A. Hayek', *Il Politico* 36(2), 349–377.

Hanke, S.H. and Walters, J.K. (1997) 'Economic Freedom, Prosperity, and Equality: A Survey', *Cato Journal* 17(2), 117–146.

Hardin, R. (1989) 'Why a Constitution?', in B. Grofman and D. Wittman (eds), *The Federalist Papers and the New Institutionalism*, New York: Agathon Press, 100–120.

Harper, D.A. (1994a) *Teaming Up: A Study of Japanese-Affiliated Firms in New Zealand*, NZIER Research Monograph 62.

Harper, D.A. (1994b) *Wellsprings of Enterprise: An Analysis of Entrepreneurship and Public Policy in New Zealand*, NZIER Research Monograph 64.

Harper, D.A. (1996) *Entrepreneurship and the Market Process: An Enquiry into the Growth of Knowledge*, London and New York: Routledge.

Harper, D.A. (1998) 'Institutional Conditions for Entrepreneurship', *Advances in Austrian Economics* 5, 241–275.

Harper, D.A. (2002) 'Money and Alertness', *Journal des Economistes et des Etudes Humaines* 12(2/3), 283–297.

Harrison, L.E. (1992) *Who Prospers? How Cultural Values Shape Economic and Political Success*, New York: Basic Books.

Harrison, L.E. and Huntington, S.P. (eds) (2000) *Culture Matters: How Values Shape Human Progress*, New York: Basic Books.

Hayek, F.A. (1935) *Prices and Production*, Second Revised and Enlarged Edition, New Jersey: Augustus M. Kelley.

Hayek, F.A. (1944) *The Road to Serfdom*, Chicago: University of Chicago Press.

Hayek, F.A. (1948) *Individualism and the Economic Order*, Chicago: University of Chicago Press.

Hayek, F.A. (1955) *The Political Ideal of the Rule of Law*, Cairo: National Bank of Egypt.

Hayek, F.A. (1960) *The Constitution of Liberty*, London: Routledge & Kegan Paul.

Hayek, F.A. (1967) *Studies in Philosophy, Politics and Economics*, London: Routledge & Kegan Paul.

Hayek, F.A. (1973) *Law, Legislation and Liberty. A New Statement of the Liberal Principles of Justice and Political Economy*, Volume One, *Rules and Order*, London: Routledge & Kegan Paul.

Hayek, F.A. (1976) *Law, Legislation and Liberty. A New Statement of the Liberal Principles of Justice and Political Economy*, Volume Two, *The Mirage of Social Justice*, Chicago: University of Chicago Press.

Hayek, F.A. (1978) *New Studies in Philosophy, Politics, Economics and the History of Ideas*, London: Routledge & Kegan Paul.

Hayek, F.A. (1979) *Law, Legislation and Liberty. A New Statement of the Liberal Principles of Justice and Political Economy*, Volume Three, *The Political Order of a Free People*, London: Routledge & Kegan Paul.

Hayek, F.A. (1988) *The Fatal Conceit: The Errors of Socialism*, Chicago: University of Chicago Press.

Hayek, F.A. (1990) *Denationalisation of Money – The Argument Refined: An Analysis of the Theory and Practice of Concurrent Currencies*, Third Edition, London: Institute of Economic Affairs.

Hébert, R.F. and Link, A.N. (1982) *The Entrepreneur: Mainstream Views and Radical Critiques*, New York: Praeger.

Hébert, R.F. and Link, A.N. (1989) 'In Search of Entrepreneurship', *Small Business Economics* 1(1), 39–49.

Hewett, E. (1988) *Reforming the Soviet Economy*, Washington, DC: Brookings Institution.

Higgs, R. (1987) *Crisis and Leviathan: Critical Episodes in the Growth of American Government*, New York: Oxford University Press.

High, J. (1986) 'Equilibration and Disequilibration in the Market Process', in I.M. Kirzner (ed.), *Subjectivism, Intelligibility and Economic Understanding*, New York: New York University Press, 111–121.

High, J. (1990) *Maximizing, Action, and Market Adjustment: An Inquiry into the Theory of Economic Disequilibrium*, Munich: Philosophia-Verlag.

Hirschman, A.O. (1970) *Exit, Voice and Loyalty: Responses to Decline in Firms, Organizations, and States*, Cambridge, MA: Harvard University Press.

Ho, D.Y. and Chiu, C. (1994) 'Component Ideas of Individualism, Collectivism, and Social Organization: An Application in the Study of Chinese Culture', in U. Kim *et al.* (eds), *Individualism and Collectivism: Theory, Method, and Applications*, Thousand Oaks, CA: Sage, 137–156.

Hodgson, G.M. (1998) 'The Approach of Institutional Economics', *Journal of Economic Literature* 36(1), 166–192.

Hofstede, G.H. (1980) *Culture's Consequences: International Differences in Work-Related Values*, Beverly Hills, CA: Sage.

Hofstede, G.H. (1983) 'Dimensions of National Cultures in Fifty Countries and Three Regions', in J.B. Deregowski *et al.* (eds), *Explications in Cross-Cultural Psychology*, Lisse, NL: Swets and Zeitlinger, 335–355.

Hofstede, G.H. (1991) *Cultures and Organizations: Software of the Mind*, London: McGraw-Hill.

Holderness, C.G. (1985) 'A Legal Foundation for Exchange', *Journal of Legal Studies* 14, 321–344.

Holt, D.H. (1997) 'A Comparative Study of Values Among Chinese and U.S. Entrepreneurs: Pragmatic Convergence between Contrasting Cultures', *Journal of Business Venturing* 12(6), 483–505.

Hoover, K.D. (1988) *The New Classical Macroeconomics: A Sceptical Inquiry*, Oxford: Basil Blackwell.

Horwitz, S. (1998) 'Monetary Calculation and Mises's Critique of Planning', *History of Political Economy* 30(3), 427–450.

Horwitz, S. (2000) *Microfoundations and Macroeconomics: An Austrian Perspective*, London and New York: Routledge.

Hui, C.H. (1982) 'Locus of Control: A Review of Cross-Cultural Research', *International Journal of Intercultural Relations* 6, 301–323.

Hull, D.L., Bosley, J.J. and Udell, G.G. (1980) 'Renewing the Search for the Heffalump: Identifying Potential Entrepreneurs by Personality Characteristics', *Journal of Small Business Management* 18(1), 11–18.

Hume, D. (1969) *A Treatise of Human Nature*, London: Penguin. First Published 1739 and 1740.

Ichheiser, G. (1970) *Appearances and Realities*, San Francisco: Jossey-Bass.

Ikeda, S. (1997) *Dynamics of the Mixed Economy: Toward a Theory of Interventionism*, London: Routledge.

Inman, R.P. (2001) 'Transfers and Bailouts: Institutions for Enforcing Local Fiscal Discipline', *Constitutional Political Economy* 12(2), 141–160.

Ioannides, S. (1992) *The Market, Competition, and Democracy: A Critique of Neo-Austrian Economics*, Aldershot: Edward Elgar.

Ioannides, S. (1999) 'Towards an Austrian Perspective on the Firm', *Review of Austrian Economics* 11(1/2), 77–97.

Irigoin, A.M. (1990) 'Economic Development: A Market Process Perspective', PhD Thesis, New York University.

Iwawaki, S. (1986) 'Achievement Motivation and Socialization', in S.E. Newstead *et al.* (eds), *Human Assessment: Cognition and Motivation*, Boston: Nijhoff.

Jacobsson, R. (1992) 'The Austrian Theory of Strategy', *Academy of Management Review* 17(4), 782–807.

James, W. (1890) *The Principles of Psychology*, New York: Macmillan.

Jessor, R., Graves, T.D., Hanson, R.C. and Jessor, S. (1968) *Society, Personality and Deviant Behavior*, New York: Holt, Rinehart and Winston.

Jennings, D.F. and Zeithaml, C.P. (1983) 'Locus of Control: A Review and Directions for Entrepreneurial Research', *Academy of Management Proceedings*, 417–421.

Jensen, M.C., Meckling, W.H. and Holderness, C.G. (1986) 'Analysis of Alternative Standing Doctrines', *International Review of Law and Economics* 6, 205–216.

Kagitçibasi, C. (1990) 'Family and Socialization in Cross-Cultural Perspective: A Model of Change', in J.J. Berman and G. Jahoda (eds), *Cross-Cultural Perspectives: Nebraska Symposium on Motivation 1989*, Lincoln, NE: University of Nebraska Press, 135–200.

Kagitçibasi, C. (1994) 'A Critical Appraisal of Individualism and Collectivism: Toward a New Formulation', in U. Kim *et al.* (eds), *Individualism and Collectivism: Theory, Method, and Applications*, Thousand Oaks, CA: Sage, 41–51.

Kagitçibasi, C. (1996) *Family and Human Development across Cultures: A View from the Other Side*, Mahwah, NJ: L. Erlbaum Associates.

Kagitçibasi, C. (1997) 'Individualism and Collectivism', in J.W. Berry *et al.* (eds), *Handbook of Cross-Cultural Psychology*, Second Edition, Volume Three, 1–49, *Social Behavior and Applications*, Boston: Allyn and Bacon.

Kaish, S. and Gilad, B. (1991) 'Characteristics of Opportunities Search of Entrepreneurs versus Executives: Sources, Interests, General Alertness', *Journal of Business Venturing* 6 (1), 5–61.

Karatnycky, A. (1996) *Freedom in the World: The Annual Survey of Political Rights and Civil Liberties, 1995–1996*, New York: Freedom House.

Kashima, Y. and Callan, V.J. (1994) 'The Japanese Workgroup', in M.D. Dunnette *et al.* (eds), *Handbook of Industrial and Organizational Psychology*, Second Edition, Volume Four, 609–646, Palo Alto, CA: Consulting Psychologists Press.

Kasper, W. and Streit, M.E. (1998) *Institutional Economics: Social Order and Public Policy*, Cheltenham: Edward Elgar.

Kaufmann, P.J., Welsh, D.H. and Bushmarin, N.V. (1996) 'Locus of Control and Entrepreneurship in the Russian Republic', *Entrepreneurship Theory and Practice* 20(1), 43–56.

Katz, A.W. (1998) 'Contract Formation and Interpretation', in P. Newman (ed.), *The New Palgrave Dictionary of Economics and the Law*, Volume One, 425–432, New York: Stockton Press.

Kazdin, A.E. (1977) *The Token Economy: A Review and Evaluation*, New York: Plenum Press.

Kazdin, A.E. and Bootzin, R.R. (1973) 'The Token Economy: An Evaluative Review', *Journal of Applied Behavior Analysis* 5(3), 343–372.

Keenan, S. (1994) 'The New Keynesian Economics', in P.J. Boettke (ed.), *The Elgar Companion to Austrian Economics*, Aldershot: Edward Elgar, 582–587.

Kelly, K. (1996) 'The Economics of Ideas', *Wired* 4(6), 148.

Kent, C.A. (ed.) (1984) *The Environment for Entrepreneurship*, Lexington, MA: Lexington Books.

Kent, C.A., Sexton, D.L. and Vesper, K.H. (eds) (1982) *Encyclopedia of Entrepreneurship*, Englewood Cliffs, NJ: Prentice Hall.

Kets de Vries, M.F.R. (1977) 'The Entrepreneurial Personality: A Person at the Crossroads', *Journal of Management Studies* February, 34–57.

Keynes, J.M. (1936) *The General Theory of Employment, Interest and Money*, New York: Harcourt Brace Jovanovich.

Kim, U., Triandis, H.C., Kagitçibasi, C., Choi, S. and Yoon, G. (eds) (1994a) *Individualism and Collectivism: Theory, Method, and Applications*, Thousand Oaks, CA: Sage.

Kim, U., Triandis, H.C., Kagitçibasi, C., Choi, S. and Yoon, G. (1994b) 'Introduction', in U. Kim *et al.* (eds), *Individualism and Collectivism: Theory, Method, and Applications*, Thousand Oaks, CA: Sage, 1–16.

Kimura, B. (1973) *Hito To Hito No Aida* [In-Between Persons], Tokyo: Baifukan.

Kirton, M.J. (1976) 'Adaptors and Innovators: A Description and Measure', *Journal of Applied Psychology* 61(5), 622–629.

Kirzner, I.M. (1962) 'Rational Action and Economic Theory', *Journal of Political Economy* 70, 380–385.

Kirzner, I.M. (1963) *Market Theory and the Price System*, Princeton, NJ: Van Nostrand.

Kirzner, I.M. (1973) *Competition and Entrepreneurship*, Chicago: University of Chicago Press.

Kirzner, I.M. (1976) 'Philosophical and Ethical Implications of Austrian Economics', in E.G. Dolan (ed.), *The Foundations of Modern Austrian Economics*, Kansas City: Sheed and Ward, 75–88.

Kirzner, I.M. (1979) *Perception, Opportunity, and Profit*, Chicago: University of Chicago Press.

Kirzner, I.M. (ed.) (1982a) *Method, Process, and Austrian Economics. Essays in Honor of Ludwig von Mises*, Lexington, MA: Lexington Books.

Kirzner, I.M. (1982b) 'The Theory of Entrepreneurship in Economic Growth', in C.A. Kent *et al.* (eds), *Encyclopedia of Entrepreneurship*, Englewood Cliffs, NJ: Prentice Hall, 272–277.

Kirzner, I.M. (1982c) 'Uncertainty, Discovery, and Human Action: A Study of the Entrepreneurial Profile in the Misesian System', in I.M. Kirzner (ed.), *Method, Process, and Austrian Economics. Essays in Honor of Ludwig von Mises*, Lexington, MA: Lexington Books, 139–160.

Kirzner, I.M. (1983a) 'Entrepreneurs and the Entrepreneurial Function: A Commentary', in J. Ronen (ed.), *Entrepreneurship*, Lexington, MA: D.C. Heath, 281–290.

Kirzner, I.M. (1983b) 'The Primacy of Entrepreneurial Discovery', in *The Entrepreneur in Society*, CIS Policy Forums, St Leornards, New South Wales: Centre for Independent Studies, 57–79. Reprinted in I.M. Kirzner (1985) *Discovery and the Capitalist Process*, Chicago: Chicago University Press, 15–39.

Kirzner, I.M. (1984a) 'The Entrepreneurial Process', in C.A. Kent (ed.), *The Environment for Entrepreneurship*, Lexington, MA: Lexington Books, 41–58.

Kirzner, I.M. (1984b) *The Role of the Entrepreneur in the Economic System*, CIS Occasional Papers 10, St Leornards, New South Wales: Centre for Independent Studies.

Kirzner, I.M. (1985) *Discovery and the Capitalist Process*, Chicago: Chicago University Press.

Kirzner, I.M. (ed.) (1986) *Subjectivism, Intelligibility and Economic Understanding*, New York: New York University Press.

Kirzner, I.M. (1989) *Discovery, Capitalism and Distributive Justice*, Oxford: Basil Blackwell.

Kirzner, I.M. (1992) *The Meaning of Market Process: Essays in the Development of Modern Austrian Economics*, London and New York: Routledge.

Kirzner, I.M. (1994) 'Value Freedom', in P.J. Boettke (ed.), *The Elgar Companion to Austrian Economics*, Aldershot: Edward Elgar, 313–319.

Kirzner, I.M. (1997a) 'Entrepreneurial Discovery and the Competitive Market Process: An Austrian Approach', *Journal of Economic Literature* 35(1), 60–85.

Kirzner, I.M. (1997b) *How Markets Work: Disequilibrium, Entrepreneurship and Discovery*, IEA Hobart Paper No. 133, London: Institute of Economic Affairs.

Kirzner, I.M. (2000) *The Driving Force of the Market: Essays in Austrian Economics*, London and New York: Routledge.

Klein, D.B. (1999) 'Discovery and the Deepself', *Review of Austrian Economics* 11, 47–76.

Kleinbaum, D.G. (1994) *Logistic Regression: A Self-Learning Text*, New York: Springer-Verlag.

Knight, F.H. (1921) *Risk, Uncertainty and Profit*, Boston: Houghton Mifflin.

Knight, F.H. (1999) *Selected Essays by Frank H. Knight*, ed. R.B. Emmett, Two Volumes, Chicago: University of Chicago Press.

Kohn, M.L. (1969) *Class and Conformity: A Study in Values*, Homewood, IL: Dorsey Press.

Kohn, M.L. and Schoenbach, C. (1983) 'Class, Stratification, and Psychological Functioning' in M.L. Kohn and C. Schooler, *Work and Personality: An Inquiry into the Impact of Social Stratification*, Norwood, NJ: Ablex, 154–189.

Kohn, M.L. and Schooler, C. (1983) *Work and Personality: An Inquiry into the Impact of Social Stratification*, Norwood, NJ: Ablex.

Kohn, M.L., and Slomczynski, K.M. (1990) *Social Structure and Self-Direction: A Comparative Analysis of the United States and Poland*, Cambridge, MA: Basil Blackwell.

Kohn, M.L., Naoi, A., Schoenbach, C. and Schooler, C. (1990) 'Position in the Class Structure and Psychological Functioning in the United States, Japan, and Poland', *American Journal of Sociology* 95(4), 964–1008.

Koppl, R. and Yeager, L. (1996) 'Big Players and Herding in Asset Markets: The Case of the Russian Ruble', *Explorations in Economic History* 33(3), 367–383.

Kronman, A.T. (1978) 'Mistake, Disclosure, Information, and the Law of Contracts', *Journal of Legal Studies* 7(1), 1–34.

Krueger, N.F., Jr (1994) 'Strategic Optimism: Antecedents of Perceived Success Probabilities of New Ventures', Paper presented at the Academy of Management, Dallas, Texas.

Krueger, N.F., Jr and Brazeal, D.V. (1994) 'Entrepreneurial Potential and Potential Entrepreneurs', *Entrepreneurship Theory and Practice* 18(3), 91–104.

Krueger, N.F., Jr and Dickson, P.R. (1993) 'Perceived Self-Efficacy and Perceptions of Opportunity and Threat', *Psychological Reports* 72: 1235–1240.

Krueger, N.F., Jr and Dickson, P.R. (1994) 'How Believing in Ourselves Increases Risk Taking: Perceived Self-Efficacy and Opportunity Recognition', *Decision Sciences* 25(3), 385–400.

Lachmann, L.M. (1971) *The Legacy of Max Weber*, Berkeley, CA: The Glendessary Press.

Lachmann, L.M. (1976) 'From Mises to Shackle: An Essay on Austrian Economics and the Kaleidic Society', *Journal of Economic Literature* 14(1), 54–62.

Lachmann, L.M. (1979) 'The Flow of Legislation and the Permanence of the Legal Order', *Ordo: Jahrbuch für die Ordnung von Wirtschaft und Gesellschaft* 30, 69–77.

Lachmann, L.M. (1986) *The Market as an Economic Process*, Oxford: Basil Blackwell.

Lachmann, L.M. (1994) *Expectations and the Meaning of Institutions: Essays in Economics by Ludwig Lachmann*, ed. Don Lavoie, London and New York: Routledge.

Lakatos, I. (1970) 'Falsification and the Methodology of Scientific Research Programmes', in I. Lakatos and A. Musgrave (eds), *Criticism and the Growth of Knowledge*, Cambridge: Cambridge University Press, 91–196.

Lakatos, I. (1978) *Philosophical Papers*, Volume One, 'The Methodology of Scientific Research Programmes', ed. J. Worrall and G. Currie, Cambridge: Cambridge University Press.

Lal, D. (1998) *Unintended Consequences: The Impact of Factor Endowments, Culture, and Politics on Long-Run Economic Performance*, Cambridge, MA: MIT Press.

Lal, D. (2000) 'Does Modernization Require Westernization?', *The Independent Review* 5(1), 5–24.

Lane, R.E. (1991) *The Market Experience*, Cambridge, Cambridge University Press.

Langlois, R.N. (1982) 'Austrian Economics as Affirmative Science: Comment on Rizzo', in I.M. Kirzner (ed.), *Method, Process, and Austrian Economics. Essays in Honor of Ludwig von Mises*, Lexington, MA: Lexington Books, 75–84.

Latsis, S.J. (1972) 'Situational Determinism in Economics', *British Journal for the Philosophy of Science* 23, 207–245.

Latsis, S.J. (ed.) (1976a) *Method and Appraisal in Economics*, Cambridge: Cambridge University Press.

Latsis, S.J. (1976b) 'A Research Programme in Economics', in S.J. Latsis (ed.), *Method and Appraisal in Economics*, Cambridge: Cambridge University Press, 1–42.

Lauterbach, A. (1974) *Psychological Challenges to Modernization*, Amsterdam: Elsevier Scientific.

Lavoie, D. (1985a) *Rivalry and Central Planning: The Socialist Calculation Debate Reconsidered*, Cambridge: Cambridge University Press.

Lavoie, D. (1985b) *National Economic Planning: What is Left?*, Cambridge, MA: Ballinger.

Lavoie, D. (1991) 'The Discovery and Interpretation of Profit Opportunities: Culture and the Kirznerian Entrepreneur', in B. Berger (ed.), *The Culture of Entrepreneurship*, San Francisco: Institute for Contemporary Studies, 33–51.

Lavoie, D. and Chamlee-Wright, E. (2000) *Culture and Enterprise: The Development, Representation and Morality of Business*, London and New York: Routledge.

Lefcourt, H.M. (1967) 'Effects of Cue Explication Upon Persons Maintaining External Control Expectancies', *Journal of Personality and Social Psychology* 5(3), 372–378.

Lefcourt, H.M. (1982) *Locus of Control: Current Trends in Theory and Research*, Second Edition, Hillsdale, NJ: Lawrence Erlbaum Associates.

Lefcourt, H.M. and Wine, J. (1969) 'Internal versus External Control of Reinforcement and the Deployment of Attention in Experimental Situations', *Canadian Journal of Behavioral Science* 1, 167–181.

Lefcourt, H.M., Gronnerud, P. and McDonald, P. (1973) 'Cognitive Activity and Hypothesis Formation During a Double Entendre Word Association Test as a Function of Locus of Control and Field Dependence', *Canadian Journal of Behavioral Science* 5, 161–173.

Leibenstein, H. (1968) 'Entrepreneurship and Development', *American Economic Review* 58, 72–83.

Leoni, B. (1972) *Freedom and the Law*, Los Angeles: Nash.

Leung, K. (1997) 'Negotiation and Reward Allocations Across Cultures', in P.C. Earley and M. Erez (eds), *New Perspectives on International Industrial/Organizational Psychology*, San Francisco: New Lexington Press.

Levenson, H. (1973) 'Multidimensional Locus of Control in Psychiatric Patients', *Journal of Consulting and Clinical Psychology* 41, 397–404.

Lewin, P. (1998) 'The Firm, Money and Economic Calculation', *American Journal of Economics and Sociology* 57(4), 499–512.

Lewin, P. and Phelan, S.E. (2000) 'An Austrian Theory of the Firm', *Review of Austrian Economics* 13(1), 59–79.

Libecap, G.D. (1989) *Contracting for Property Rights*, Cambridge: Cambridge University Press.

Littlechild, S.C. (1979) 'Comment: Radical Subjectivism or Radical Subversion', in M.J. Rizzo (ed.), *Time, Uncertainty and Disequilibrium: Exploration of Austrian Themes*, Lexington, MA: Lexington Books, 32–50.

Littlechild, S.C. (1981) 'Misleading Calculations of the Social Costs of Monopoly Power', *Economic Journal* 91, June, 348–363.

Littlechild, S.C. (1986) *The Fallacy of the Mixed Economy: An 'Austrian' Critique of Recent Economic Thinking and Policy*, Second Edition, Hobart Paper No. 80, London: Institute of Economic Affairs.

Liu, I. (1986) 'Chinese Cognition', in M.H. Bond (ed.), *The Psychology of the Chinese People*, New York: Oxford University Press, 73–105.

Loasby, B.J. (1976) *Choice, Complexity and Ignorance: An Enquiry into Economic Theory and the Practice of Decision-Making*, Cambridge: Cambridge University Press.

Loasby, B.J. (1982a) 'Economics of Dispersed and Incomplete Information', in I.M. Kirzner (ed.), *Method, Process, and Austrian Economics. Essays in Honor of Ludwig von Mises*, Lexington, MA: Lexington Books, 111–130.

Loasby, B.J. (1982b) 'The Entrepreneur in Economic Theory', *Scottish Journal of Political Economy* 29(3), 235–245.

Loasby, B.J. (1989) *The Mind and Method of the Economist: A Critical Appraisal of Major Economists in the 20th Century*, Aldershot: Edward Elgar.

Lonner, W.J. and Adamopoulos, J. (1997) 'Culture as Antecedent to Behavior', in J.W. Berry *et al.* (eds), *Handbook of Cross-Cultural Psychology*, Second Edition, Volume One, 43–83, *Theory and Method*, Boston: Allyn and Bacon.

Louw, D.J. (2002) '*Ubuntu* and the Challenges of Multiculturalism in Post-Apartheid South Africa', Unpublished manuscript.

Macfarlane, A. (1978) *The Origins of English Individualism: The Family, Property and Social Transition*, New York: Cambridge University Press.

Machlup, F. (1969) 'Liberalism and the Choice of Freedoms', in E. Streissler (ed.), *Roads to Freedom: Essays in Honour of Friedrich A. von Hayek*, London: Routledge & Kegan Paul, 117–146.

MacIntyre, A. (1990) 'Individual and Social Morality in Japan and the United States: Rival Conceptions of the Self', *Philosophy East and West* 40(4), 489–497.

Mackaay, E. (1997) 'On Property Rights and Their Modification', Unpublished manuscript.

Magee, S.P., Brock, W.A. and Young, L. (1989) *Black Hole Tariffs and Endogenous Policy Theory*, New York: Cambridge University Press.

Maital, S. (ed.) (1988) *Applied Behavioral Economics*, Volumes One and Two, Brighton: Wheatsheaf.

Mäki, U. (ed.) (2001) *The Economic World View: Studies in the Ontology of Economics*, Cambridge: Cambridge University Press.

Markus, H.R. and Kitayama, S. (1991) 'Culture and the Self: Implications for Cognition, Emotion, and Motivation', *Psychological Review* 98(2), 224–253.

Markus, H.R. and Kitayama, S. (1998) 'The Cultural Psychology of Personality', *Journal of Cross-Cultural Psychology* 29(1), 63–87.

Marsella, A.J. and Choi, S.C. (1993) 'Psychosocial Aspects of Modernization and Economic Development in East Asian Nations', *Psychologia* 36(4), 201–213.

Marsella, A.J., De Vos, G. and Hsu, F.L.K. (1985) *Culture and Self: Asian and Western Perspectives*, New York: Tavistock.

Marshall, A. (1920) *Principles of Economics: An Introductory Volume*, Eighth Edition, London: Macmillan.

Mayhew, A. (1987) 'Culture: Core Concept under Attack', *Journal of Economic Issues* 21(2), 587–603.

McChesney, F.S. (1987) 'Rent Extraction and Rent Creation in the Economic Theory of Regulation', *Journal of Legal Studies* 16(January), 67–100.

McChesney, F.S. (1991) 'Rent Extraction and Interest-Group Organization in a Coasean Model of Regulation', *Journal of Legal Studies* 20, 73–90.

McClelland, D.C. (1961) *The Achieving Society*, Princeton: D. Van Nostrand.

McClelland, D.C. (1962) 'Business Drive and National Achievement', *Harvard Business Review* 40(4), 99–112.

McCline, R.L., Bhat, S. and Baj, P. (2000) 'Opportunity Recognition: An Exploratory Investigation of a Component of the Entrepreneurial Process in the Context of the Health Care Industry', *Entrepreneurship Theory and Practice* 25(2), 81–94.

McGavin, P.A. (1993) 'Review of Casson's *The Economics of Business Culture: Game Theory, Transaction Costs, and Economic Performance*', *Economic Record* 69(204), 96–98.

McGinnies, E., Nordholm, L.A., Ward, C.D. and Bhanthumnavin, D.L. (1974) 'Sex and Cultural Differences in Perceived Locus of Control Among Students in Five Countries', *Journal of Consulting and Clinical Psychology* 42, 451–455.

McGrath, R.G. and MacMillan, I.C. (1992) 'More Like Each Other than Anyone Else? A Cross-Cultural Study of Entrepreneurial Perceptions', *Journal of Business Venturing* 7(5), 419–429.

McGrath, R.G., MacMillan, I.C. and Scheinberg, S. (1992a) 'Elitists, Risk-Takers, and Rugged Individualists? An Exploratory Analysis of Cultural Differences between Entrepreneurs and Non-Entrepreneurs', *Journal of Business Venturing* 7(2), 115–135.

McGrath, R.G., MacMillan, I.C., Yang, E.A. and Tsai, W. (1992b) 'Does Culture Endure, or Is It Malleable? Issues For Entrepreneurial Economic Development', *Journal of Business Venturing* 7(6), 441–458.

McKenzie, R.B. (1980) 'The Neoclassicalists vs. the Austrians: A Partial Reconciliation of Competing Worldviews', *Southern Economic Journal* 47(1), 1–13.

Menger, C. (1892) 'On the Origins of Money', *Economic Journal* 2, 239–255.

Menger, C. (1994) *Principles of Economics*, Grove City, PA: Libertarian Press. First German edition 1871.

Menger, C. (1996) *Investigations into the Method of the Social Sciences*, Grove City, PA: Libertarian Press. First German edition 1883.

Mescon, T.S. and Montanari, J.R. (1981) 'The Personalities of Independent and Franchise Entrepreneurs: An Empirical Analysis of Concepts', *Academy of Management Proceedings*, 413–417.

Messick, R.E. and Kimura, K. (1996) *World Survey of Economic Freedom 1995–1996: A Freedom House Study*, New Brunswick, NJ: Transaction Books.

Miller, J.G. (1984) 'Culture and the Development of Everyday Social Explanation', *Journal of Personality and Social Psychology* 46(5), 961–978.

Minoura, Y. (1979) 'Life In-Between: The Acquisition of Cultural Identity Among Japanese Children Living in the United States', PhD Dissertation (Anthropology), University of California at Los Angeles (*Dissertation Abstracts International* 40, 5922A, UCLA).

Mises, L. von (1966) *Human Action. A Treatise on Economics*, Third Revised Edition (Paperback), San Francisco: Fox & Wilkes.

Mises, L. von (1971) *The Theory of Money and Credit*, New Enlarged Edition, Irvington-on-Hudson, NY: Foundation for Economic Education. First German Edition 1912.

Mises, L. von (1981) *Socialism: An Economic and Sociological Analysis*, Indianapolis: Liberty Classics. First German Edition 1922.

Mishra, R.C. (1994) 'Individualist and Collectivist Orientations Across Generations', in U. Kim *et al.* (eds), *Individualism and Collectivism: Theory, Method, and Applications*, Thousand Oaks, CA: Sage, 225–238.

Mitchell, W.C. (1937) *The Backward Art of Spending Money and Other Essays*, New York and London: McGraw-Hill.

Morse, C. (1969) 'Becoming Versus Being Modern: An Essay on Institutional Change and Economic Development', in C. Morse *et al.* (eds), *Modernization by Design: Social Change in the Twentieth Century*, Ithaca, NY: Cornell University Press, 238–382.

Mueller, S.L. and Thomas, A.S. (2000) 'Culture and Entrepreneurial Potential: A Nine Country Study of Locus of Control and Innovativeness', *Journal of Business Venturing* 16(1), 51–75.

Murphy, K.M., Shleifer, A. and Vishny, R.W. (1991) 'The Allocation of Talent: Implications for Growth', *Quarterly Journal of Economics* 106(2), May, 503–530.

Murray, H.A. (1938) *Explorations in Personality*, New York: Oxford University Press.

Musgrave, A.E. (1976) 'Method or Madness? Can the Methodology of Research Programmes be Rescued from Epistemological Anarchism', in R.S. Cohen *et al.* (eds), *Essays in Memory of Imre Lakatos*, Dordrecht: D. Reidel, 457–491.

Musgrave, A.E. (1978) 'Evidential Support, Falsification, Heuristics, and Anarchism', in G. Radnitzky and G. Andersson (eds), *Progress and Rationality in Science*, Boston Studies in the Philosophy of Science 58, Dordrecht: D. Reidel, 181–201.

Naoi, A. and Schooler, C. (1985) 'Occupational Conditions and Psychological Functioning in Japan', *American Journal of Sociology* 90(4), 729–752.

Newman, P. (ed.) (1998) *The New Palgrave Dictionary of Economics and the Law*, Volumes One, Two and Three, New York: Stockton Press.

New Zealand Business Roundtable and New Zealand Employers Federation (1992) *The Labour/Employment Court: An Analysis of the Labour/Employment Court's Approach to the Interpretation and Application of Employment Legislation*, Wellington: NZ Business Roundtable and NZ Employers Federation.

Nisbett, R.E. and Cohen, D. (1996) *Culture of Honor: The Psychology of Violence in the South*, Boulder, CO: Westview Press.

Noll, R. (1977) 'Government Policy and Technological Innovation: Where Do We Stand and Where Should We Go?', in K.Stroetmann (ed.), *Innovation, Economic Change and Technology Policies*, Stuttgart: Birkhauser-Verlag.

North, D.C. (1981) *Structure and Change in Economic History*, New York: W.W. Norton.

North, D.C. (1990) *Institutions, Institutional Change and Economic Performance*, Cambridge: Cambridge University Press.

O'Driscoll, G.P., Jr (1978) 'Spontaneous Order and the Coordination of Economic Activities', in L.M. Spadaro (ed.), *New Directions in Austrian Economics*, Kansas City: Sheed, Andrews & McMeel, 111–142.

O'Driscoll, G.P., Jr and Rizzo, M.J. (1996). *The Economics of Time and Ignorance*, London and New York: Routledge.

O'Driscoll, G.P., Jr, Holmes, K.R. and Kirkpatrick, M. (2001) *2001 Index of Economic Freedom*, Washington, DC: Heritage Foundation and New York: Wall Street Journal.

Oettingen, G. (1995) 'Cross-Cultural Perspectives on Self-Efficacy', in A. Bandura, A. (ed.), *Self-Efficacy in Changing Societies*, New York: Cambridge University Press, 149–176.

Oettingen, G., Little, T.D., Lindenberger, U. and Baltes, P.B. (1994) 'Causality, Agency, and Control Beliefs in East versus West Berlin Children: A Natural Experiment on the Role of Context', *Journal of Personality and Social Psychology* 66(3), 579–595.

Olson, M., Jr (1982) *The Rise and Decline of Nations*, New Haven, CT: Yale University Press.

Olson, M., Jr (1996) 'Big Bills Left on the Sidewalk: Why Some Nations Are Rich, and Others Poor', *Journal of Economic Perspectives* 10(2), 3–24.

Ordeshook, P. (1992) 'Constitutional Stability', *Constitutional Political Economy* 3(2), 137–175.

Pandey, J. and Tewary, N.B. (1979) 'Locus of Control and Achievement Values of Entrepreneurs', *Journal of Occupational Psychology* 52, 107–111.

Paqué, K. (1985) 'How Far is Vienna from Chicago? An Essay on the Methodology of Two Schools of Dogmatic Liberalism', *Kyklos* 38(3), 412–434.

Parisi, F. (2000) 'Sources of Law and the Institutional Design of Lawmaking', George Mason University, School of Law, Law and Economics Working Paper Series, 00–42.

Parisi, F. (2001) 'The Formation of Customary Law', George Mason University, School of Law, Law and Economics Working Paper Series, 01–06.

Paulhus, D.L. (1983) 'Sphere-Specific Measures of Perceived Control', *Journal of Personality and Social Psychology* 44(6), 1253–1265.

Perry, C., Macarthur, R., Meredith, G. and Cunnington, B. (1986) 'Need for Achievement and Locus of Control of Australian Small Business Owner-Managers and Super-Entrepreneurs', *International Small Business Journal* 4(4), 55–64.

Phares, E.J. (1976) *Locus of Control in Personality*, Morristown, NJ: General Learning Press.

Pipes, R. (1999) *Property and Freedom*, New York: Alfred A. Knopf.

Pistor, K. (1998) 'Transfer of Property Rights in Eastern Europe', in P. Newman (ed.), *The New Palgrave Dictionary of Economics and the Law*, Volume Three, 607–612, New York: Stockton Press.

Platteau, J.-P. (1994a) 'Behind the Market Stage Where Real Societies Exist – Part I: The Role of Public and Private Order Institutions', *Journal of Development Studies* 30(3), 533–577.

Platteau, J.-P. (1994b) 'Behind the Market Stage Where Real Societies Exist – Part II: The Role of Moral Norms', *Journal of Development Studies* 30(4), 753–817.

Plosser, C.I. (1989) 'Understanding Real Business Cycles', *Journal of Economic Perspectives* 3(3), 51–77.

Popper, K.R. (1959) *The Logic of Scientific Discovery*, London: Hutchinson.

Popper, K.R. (1961) *The Poverty of Historicism*, Third Edition, London: Routledge & Kegan Paul.

Popper, K.R. (1963) *Conjectures and Refutations. The Growth of Scientific Knowledge*, London: Routledge & Kegan Paul.

Pospisil, L.J. (1971) *Anthropology of Law: A Comparative Theory*, New York: Harper & Row.

Price-Williams, D.R. (1985) 'Cultural Psychology', in G. Lindzey and E. Aronson, *Handbook of Social Psychology*, Volume Two, *Special Fields and Applications*, 993–1042, New York: Random House.

Przeworski, A. (2000) *Democracy and Development: Political Institutions and Material Well-Being in the World, 1950–1990*, Cambridge: Cambridge University Press.

Przeworski, A. and Limongi, F. (1993) 'Political Regimes and Economic Growth', *Journal of Economic Perspectives* 7(3), 51–69.

Przeworski, A. and Limongi, F. (1997) 'Modernization: Theories and Facts', *World Politics* 49(2), 155–183.

Putnam, R.D. (1993) *Making Democracy Work: Civic Traditions in Modern Italy*, Princeton, NJ: Princeton University Press.

Pye, L.W. (2000) ' "Asian Values": From Dynamoes to Dominoes?', in L.E. Harrison and S.P. Huntington (eds), *Culture Matters: How Values Shape Human Progress*, New York: Basic Books, 244–255.

Raaij, W.F. van (1985) 'Attribution of Causality to Economic Actions and Events', *Kyklos* 38(1), 3–19.

Raico, R. (1992) 'Prolegomena to a History of Liberalism', *Journal des Economistes et des Etudes Humaines* 3(2/3), 259–272.

Ramose, M.B. (1999) *African Philosophy through Ubuntu*, Harare: Mond Books.

Rapaczynski, A. (1996) 'The Roles of the State and the Market in Establishing Property Rights', *Journal of Economic Perspectives* 10(2), 87–103.

Reder, M.W. (1982) 'Chicago Economics: Permanence and Change', *Journal of Economic Literature* 20(1), 1–38.

Reekie, W.D. (1984) *Markets, Entrepreneurs and Liberty: An Austrian View of Capitalism*, Brighton: Wheatsheaf.

Remenyi, J.V. (1979) 'Core Demi-Core Interaction: Toward a General Theory of Disciplinary and Subdisciplinary Growth', *History of Political Economy* 11(1), 30–63.

Rice, J.C. (1994) 'Logistic Regression: An Introduction', *Advances in Social Science Methodology* 3, 191–245.

Richardson, G.B. (1960) *Information and Investment: A Study in the Working of the Competitive Economy*, Oxford: Oxford University Press.

Ricketts, M. (1987) 'Rent Seeking, Entrepreneurship, Subjectivism, and Property Rights', *Journal of Institutional and Theoretical Economics* 143, 457–466.

Ricketts, M. (1992) 'Kirzner's Theory of Entrepreneurship – A Critique', in S. Boehm and B. Caldwell (eds), *Austrian Economics: Tensions and New Directions,* Boston: Kluwer Academic Publishers, 67–84.

Riesman, D. (1950) *The Lonely Crowd: A Study of the Changing American Character*, New Haven, CT: Yale University Press.

Riker, W.H. (1964) *Federalism: Origin, Operation, and Significance*, Boston: Little Brown.

Rizzo, M.J. (1978) 'Praxeology and Econometrics: A Critique of Positivist Economics', in L.M. Spadaro (ed.), *New Directions in Austrian Economics*, Kansas City: Sheed, Andrews & McMeel, 40–56.

Rizzo, M.J. (ed.) (1979) *Time, Uncertainty and Disequilibrium: Exploration of Austrian Themes*, Lexington, MA: Lexington Books.

Rizzo, M.J. (1982) 'Mises and Lakatos: A Reformulation of Austrian Methodology', in I.M. Kirzner (ed.), *Method, Process, and Austrian Economics. Essays in Honor of Ludwig von Mises*, Lexington, MA: Lexington Books, 53–74.

Rizzo, M.J. (1985) 'Rules Versus Cost–Benefit Analysis in the Common Law', *Cato Journal* 4(3), 865–884.

Rizzo, M.J. (1992a) 'Austrian Economics for the Twenty-First Century', in B.J. Caldwell and S. Boehm (eds), *Austrian Economics: Tensions and New Directions*, Boston, MA: Kluwer Academic Publishers, 245–255.

Rizzo, M.J. (1992b) 'The Morality of Profits, and the Struggle for Existence', C.V. Starr Center for Applied Economics, New York University, Economic Research Report 92–17.

Rizzo, M.J. (1994) 'Cost', in P.J. Boettke (ed.), *The Elgar Companion to Austrian Economics*, Aldershot: Edward Elgar, 92–95.

Rizzo, M.J. (1996) 'Introduction: Time and Ignorance After Ten Years', in G.P. O'Driscoll, Jr and M.J. Rizzo, *The Economics of Time and Ignorance*, London and New York: Routledge, xiii–xxxiii.

Rizzo, M.J. (2002) 'Introduction', Manuscript prepared for two special issues of the *Journal des Economistes et des Etudes Humaines* in honour of Israel M. Kirzner.

Robbins, L. (1932) *An Essay on the Nature and Significance of Economic Science*, London: Macmillan.

Rodin, J., Schooler, C. and Schaie, K.W. (1990) *Self-Directedness: Cause and Effects Throughout the Life Course*, Hillsdale, NJ: Lawrence Erlbaum Associates.

Rodrik, D. (2000) 'Institutions for High-Quality Growth: What They Are and How to Acquire Them', NBER Working Paper 7540.

Romer, P.M. (1993) 'Economic Growth', in D.R. Henderson (ed.), *The Fortune Encyclopedia of Economics*, New York: Time Warner Books, 183–189.

Ronen, J. (ed.) (1983) *Entrepreneurship*, Lexington, MA: D.C. Heath.

Rosen, S. (1983) 'Economics and Entrepreneurs' in J. Ronen (ed.), *Entrepreneurship*, Lexington, MA: D.C. Heath, 201–310.

Rosen, S. (1997) 'Austrian and Neoclassical Economics: Any Gains from Trade?', *Journal of Economic Perspectives* 11(4), 139–152.

Rothbard, M.N. (1963) *America's Great Depression*, Princeton: Van Nostrand.

Rothbard, M.N. (1981) 'The Myth of Neutral Taxation', *Cato Journal* 1(2), 519–564.

Rothbard, M.N. (1991) 'The End of Socialism and the Calculation Debate Revisited', *Review of Austrian Economics* 5(2), 51–76.

Rothbard, M.N. (1993) *Man, Economy, and State*, Auburn, AL: Ludwig von Mises Institute. First published 1962.

Rothbaum, F.M., Weisz, J.R. and Snyder, S. (1982) 'Changing the World and Changing the Self: A Two-Process Model of Perceived Control', *Journal of Personality and Social Psychology* 42(1), 5–37.

Rotter, J.B. (1954) *Social Learning and Clinical Psychology*, Englewood Cliffs, NJ: Prentice Hall.

Rotter, J.B. (1966) 'Generalised Expectancies for Internal versus External Control of Reinforcement', *Psychological Monographs* 80(1), 1–28.

Rotter, J.B. (1990) 'Internal versus External Control of Reinforcement: A Case History of a Variable', *American Psychologist* 45(4), 489–493.

Ruttan, V.W. (1988) 'Cultural Endowments and Economic Development: What Can We Learn from Anthropology?', *Economic Development and Cultural Change* 36(3) Supplement, S247–S271.

Ryle, G. (1971) 'The Thinking of Thoughts: What is "Le Penseur" Doing?', in *Collected Papers*, Volume 2, 465–96, *Collected Essays 1929–1968*, New York: Barnes and Noble.

Salerno, J.T. (1990a) 'Postscript: Why a Socialist Economy is "Impossible"', in L. von Mises, *Economic Calculation in a Socialist Commonwealth*, Auburn, AL: Praxeology Press of the Ludwig von Mises Institute, 51–71.

Salerno, J.T. (1990b) 'Ludwig von Mises as Social Rationalist', *Review of Austrian Economics* 4, 26–54.

Salerno, J.T. (1993) 'Mises and Hayek Dehomogenized', *Review of Austrian Economics* 6(2), 113–146.

Salerno, J.T. (1994) 'Reply to Leland B. Yeager on "Mises and Hayek on Calculation and Knowledge"', *Review of Austrian Economics* 7(2), 111–125.

Sargent, T.J. and Wallace, N. (1975) 'Rational Expectations, the Optimal Monetary Instrument and the Optimal Money Supply Rule', *Journal of Political Economy* 83(2), 241–254.

Sautet, F.E. (2000) *An Entrepreneurial Theory of the Firm*, London: Routledge.

Schama, S. (1988) *The Embarrassment of Riches: An Interpretation of Dutch Culture in the Golden Age*, Berkeley, CA: University of California Press.

Scheiber, H.N. (ed.) (1998) *The State and Freedom of Contract*, Stanford, CA: Stanford University Press.

Scherer, R.F., Maddux, J.E., Mercandante, B., Prentice-Dunn, S., Jacobs, E. and Rogers, R.W. (1982) 'The Self-Efficacy Scale: Construction and Validation', *Psychological Reports* 51, 663–671.

Scherer, R.F., Adams, J.S. and Wiebe, F.A. (1988) 'Social Learning Theory as a Conceptual Framework for Entrepreneurship Research: The Role of Observational Learning', in G.B. Roberts *et al.* (eds), *Entrepreneurship: New Direction for a Global Economy. Proceedings of the International Council for Small Business*, 243–249.

Scherer, R.F., Adams, J.S., Carley, S.S. and Wiebe, F.A. (1989) 'Role Model Performance Effects on Development of Entrepreneurial Career Preference', *Entrepreneurship Theory and Practice* 13(3), 53–71.

Scherer, R.F., Adams, J.S. and Wiebe, F.A. (1990) 'Developing Entrepreneurial Behaviors: A Social Learning Theory Perspective', *Journal of Organizational Change Management* 2, 16–27.

Schneewind, K.A. (1995) 'Impact of Family Processes on Control Beliefs', in A. Bandura (ed.), *Self-Efficacy in Changing Societies*, New York: Cambridge University Press, 114–148.

Schooler, C. (1976) 'Serfdom's Legacy: An Ethnic Continuum', *American Journal of Sociology* 81(6), 1265–1286.

Schooler, C. (1990) 'Individualism and the Historical and Social-Structural Determinants of People's Concerns over Self-Directedness and Effficacy', in J. Rodin *et al.* (eds), *Self-Directedness: Cause and Effects Throughout the Life Course*, Hillsdale, NJ: Lawrence Erlbaum Associates, 19–49.

Schultz, T.W. (1975) 'The Value of the Ability to Deal with Disequilibria', *Journal of Economic Literature* 13, 827–846.

Schumpeter, J.A. (1934) *The Theory of Economic Development: An Inquiry into Profits, Capital, Credit, Interest and the Business Cycle*, Cambridge, MA: Harvard University Press.

Schumpeter, J.A. (1947) 'The Creative Response in Economic History', *Journal of Economic History* 7(2), 149–159.

Schumpeter, J.A. (1954) *History of Economic Analysis*, London: George Allen & Unwin.

Schunk, D.H. (1989) 'Self-Efficacy and Cognitive Skill Learning', in C. Ames and R. Ames (eds), *Research on Motivation in Education*, Volume 3, 13–44, *Goals and Cognitions*, San Diego: Academic Press.

Schwartz, S.H. (1992) 'Universals in the Content and Structure of Values: Theoretical Advances and Empirical Tests in 20 Countries', *Advances in Experimental Social Psychology* 25, 1–65.

Schwartz, S.H. (1994) 'Beyond Individualism/Collectivism: New Cultural Dimensions of Values', in U. Kim *et al.* (eds), *Individualism and Collectivism: Theory, Method, and Applications*, Thousand Oaks, CA: Sage, 85–119.

Scott, G. (1992) 'Reflections on Managing the Treasury', Mimeo.

Scully, G.W. (1989) 'The Size of the State, Economic Growth and the Efficient Utilization of National Resources', *Public Choice* 63(2), 149–164.

Scully, G.W., (1992) *Constitutional Environments and Economic Growth*, Princeton, NJ: Princeton University Press.

Scully, G.W. and Slottje, D.J. (1991) 'Ranking Economic Liberty across Countries', *Public Choice* 69(2), 121–152.

Seabright, P. (1998) 'Local Common Property', in P. Newman (ed.), *The New Palgrave Dictionary of Economics and the Law*, Volume Two, 591–594, New York: Stockton Press.

Selgin, G.A. (1988) *The Theory of Free Banking: Money Supply Under Competitive Note Issue*, Totowa, NJ: Rowman and Littlefield.

Selgin, G.A. (1995) 'The "Productivity Norm" versus Zero Inflation in the History of Economic Thought', *History of Political Economy* 27(4), 705–735.

Selgin, G.A. (1996) *Bank Deregulation and Monetary Order*, London and New York: Routledge.

Selgin, G.A. (1997) *Less than Zero: The Case for a Falling Price Level in a Growing Economy*, Hobart Paper 132, London: Institute of Economic Affairs.

Selgin, G.A. and White, L.H. (1994) 'How Would the Invisible Hand Handle Money?', *Journal of Economic Literature* 32(4), 1718–1749.

Sexton, D.L. and Smilor, R.W. (eds) (1986) *The Art and Science of Entrepreneurship*, Cambridge, MA: Ballinger.

Shackle, G.L.S. (1969) *Decision, Order and Time in Human Affairs*, Second Edition, Cambridge: Cambridge University Press.

Shackle, G.L.S. (1972) *Epistemics and Economics: A Critique of Economic Doctrines*, Cambridge: Cambridge University Press.

Shane, S.A. (1993) 'Cultural Influences on National Rates of Innovation', *Journal of Business Venturing* 8(1), 59–73.

Shane, S.A. (1994) 'Cultural Values and the Championing Process', *Entrepreneurship Theory and Practice* 18(4), 25–41.

Shane, S.A. (2000) 'Prior Knowledge and the Discovery of Entrepreneurial Opportunities', *Organization Science* 11(4), 448–469.

Shane, S.A. and Venkataraman, S. (1996) 'Renegade and Rational Championing Strategies', *Organization Studies* 17(5), 751–771.

Shane, S.A. and Venkataraman, S. (2000) 'The Promise of Entrepreneurship as a Field of Research', *Academy of Management Review* 25(1), 217–226.

Shane, S.A., Venkataraman, S. and MacMillan, I.C. (1994) 'The Effects of Cultural Differences on New Technology Championing Behavior within Firms', *Journal of High Technology Management Research* 5, 163–181.

Shane, S.A., Venkataraman, S. and MacMillan, I.C. (1995) 'Cultural Differences in Innovation Championing Strategies', *Journal of Management* 21(5), 931–952.

Shapero, A. (1975) 'The Displaced, Uncomfortable Entrepreneur', *Psychology Today* November, 83–133.

Shaver, K.G. and Scott, L.R. (1991) 'Person, Process, Choice: The Psychology of New Venture Creation', *Entrepreneurship Theory and Practice* 16(2), 23–45.

Shweder, R.A. (1990) 'Cultural Psychology: What Is It?', in J.W. Stigler *et al.* (eds), *Cultural Psychology: Essays on Comparative Human Development*, Cambridge and New York: Cambridge University Press, 1–46.

Simpson, A.W.B. (1998) 'English Common Law', in P. Newman (ed.), *The New Palgrave Dictionary of Economics and the Law*, Volume Two, 57–70, New York: Stockton Press.

Sinha, D. and Tripathi, R.C. (1994) 'Individualism in a Collectivist Culture: A Case of Coexistence of Opposites', in U. Kim *et al.* (eds), *Individualism and Collectivism: Theory, Method, and Applications*, Thousand Oaks, CA: Sage, 123–136.

Skinner, E.A., Chapman, M. and Baltes, P.B. (1988) 'Control, Means-Ends, and Agency Beliefs: A New Conceptualization and Its Measurement During Childhood', *Journal of Personality and Social Psychology* 54(1), 117–133.

Smith, P.B. and Bond, M.H. (1993) *Social Psychology Across Cultures: Analysis and Perspectives*, New York: Harvester Wheatsheaf.

Smith, P.B. and Schwartz, S.H. (1997) 'Values', in J.W. Berry *et al.* (eds), *Handbook of Cross-Cultural Psychology*, Second Edition, Volume Three, 77–118, *Social Behavior and Applications*, Boston: Allyn and Bacon.

Smith, R.J. (1985) 'A Pattern of Japanese Society – I.E. Society or Acknowledgment of Interdependence?', *Journal of Japanese Studies* 11, 29–45.

Soto, H. de (1989) *The Other Path: The Invisible Revolution in the Third World*, New York: Harper & Row.

Soto, H. de (2000) *The Mystery of Capital: Why Capitalism Triumphs in the West and Fails Everywhere Else*, New York: Basic Books.

Spadaro, L.M. (ed.) (1978) *New Directions in Austrian Economics*, Kansas City: Sheed, Andrews & McMeel.

Speier, C. and Frese, M. (1997) 'Generalized Self-Efficacy as a Mediator and Moderator Between Control and Complexity at Work and Personal Initiative: A Longitudinal Field Study in East Germany', *Human Performance* 10(2), 171–192.

Spence, J.T. (1985) 'Achievement American Style: The Rewards and Costs of Individualism', *American Psychologist* 40(12), 1285–1295.

Spinosa, C., Flores, F. and Dreyfus, H.L. (1997) *Disclosing New Worlds: Entrepreneurship, Democratic Action, and the Cultivation of Solidarity*, Cambridge, MA: MIT Press.

Spiro, M.E. (1975) *Children of the Kibbutz*, Revised Edition, Cambridge, MA: Harvard University Press.

Stam, H.J. (1987) 'The Psychology of Control: A Textual Critique', in H.J. Stam *et al.* (eds), *The Analysis of Psychological Theory: Metaphysical Perspectives*, Washington, D.C.: Hemisphere, 131–156.

Steele, C.N. (1998) 'Entrepreneurship and the Economics of Growth', *Advances in Austrian Economics* 5, 51–84.

Stiglitz, J.E. (1987) 'The Causes and Consequences of the Dependence of Quality on Price', *Journal of Economic Literature* 25(1), 1–48.

Stiglitz, J. E. (1994) *Whither Socialism?*, Cambridge, MA: MIT Press.

Streit, M.E. (1991) *Theorie der Wirtschaftspolitik*, Fouth Edition, Düsseldorf: Werner-Verlag.

Streit, M.E. (1996) 'Competition among Systems as a Defence of Liberty', in H. Bouillon (ed.), *Libertarians and Liberalism: Essays in Honour of Gerard Radnitzky*, Aldershot: Avebury, 236–252.

Strickland, B.R. (1977) 'Internal versus External Control of Reinforcement', in T. Blass (ed.), *Personality Variables in Social Behavior*, Hillsdale, NJ: Erlbaum, 219–280.

Strickland, B.R. (1989) 'Internal–External Control Expectancies: From Contingency to Creativity', *American Psychologist* 44(1), 1–12.

Sugden, R. (1998) 'Spontaneous Order', in P. Newman (ed.), *The New Palgrave Dictionary of Economics and the Law*, Volume Three, 485–495, New York: Stockton Press.

Tabachnick, B.G. and Fidell, L.S. (2001) *Using Multivariate Statistics*, Fourth Edition, Boston, MA: Allyn and Bacon.

Thomsen, E.F. (1992) *Prices and Knowledge: A Market-Process Perspective*, London: Routledge.

Tiebout, C.M. (1956) 'A Pure Theory of Local Expenditures', *Journal of Political Economy* 64(5), 416–424.

Tiessen, J.H. (1997) 'Individualism, Collectivism, and Entrepreneurship: A Framework for International Comparative Research', *Journal of Business Venturing* 12(5), 367–384.

Tocqueville, A. de (1990a) *Democracy in America*, Volume One, New York: Vintage Books. First published 1835.

Tocqueville, A. de (1990b) *Democracy in America*, Volume Two, New York: Vintage Books. First published 1840.

Toumanoff, P.G. (1984) 'A Positive Analysis of the Theory of Market Failure', *Kyklos* 37(4), 529–541.

Trebilcock, M.J. (1997) *The Limits of Freedom of Contract*, Cambridge, MA: Harvard University Press.

Triandis, H.C. (1972) *The Analysis of Subjective Culture*, New York: Wiley-Interscience.

Triandis, H.C. (1989) 'The Self and Social Behavior in Differing Cultural Contexts', *Psychological Review* 96(3), 506–520.

Triandis, H.C. (1994a) *Culture and Social Behavior*, New York: McGraw-Hill.

Triandis, H.C. (1994b) 'Theoretical and Methodological Approaches to the Study of Collectivism and Individualism', in U. Kim *et al.* (eds), *Individualism and Collectivism: Theory, Method, and Applications*, Thousand Oaks, CA: Sage, 41–51.

Triandis, H.C. (1995) *Individualism and Collectivism*, Boulder, CO: Westview Press.

Trommsdorff, G. (1989) 'Sozialisation und Werthaltungen im Kulturvergleich [Socialisation and Values in a Cross-Cultural Perspective]', in G. Trommsdorff (ed.), *Sozialisation im Kulturvergleich*, Stuttgart: Enke, 97–121.

Tullock, G. (1987) *The Politics of Bureaucracy*, Lanham, MD: University Press of America.

Vanberg, V.J. (1994) *Rules and Choice in Economics*, London and New York: Routledge.

Vanberg, V.J. (1998) 'Freiburg School of Economics' in P. Newman (ed.), *The New Palgrave Dictionary of Economics and the Law*, Volume Two, 172–179, New York: Stockton Press.

Vanberg, V.J. (2001) *The Constitution of Markets: Essays in Political Economy*, London and New York: Routledge.

Vanberg, V.J. and Kerber, W. (1994) 'Institutional Competition among Jurisdictions: An Evolutionary Approach', *Constitutional Political Economy* 5(2), 192–219.

Vaughn, K.I. (1984) 'The Constitution of Liberty from an Evolutionary Perspective', in *Hayek's 'Serfdom' Revisited: Essays by Economists, Philosophers and Political Scientists on 'The Road to Serfdom' After 40 years*, Hobart Paperback No. 18, Institute of Economic Affairs, 119–142.

Vaughn, K.I. (1994) *Austrian Economics in America: The Migration of a Tradition*, Cambridge: Cambridge University Press.

Vaughn, K.I. (1998) 'Does Austrian Economics Have a Useful Future?', *Advances in Austrian Economics* 5, 3–14.

Veblen, T. (1899) *The Theory of the Leisure Class*, New York: Macmillan.

Venkatapathy, R. (1984) 'Locus of Control among Entrepreneurs: A Review', *Psychological Studies* 29(1), 97–100.

Venkataraman, S. (1997) 'The Distinctive Domain of Entrepreneurship Research', *Advances in Entrepreneurship, Firm Emergence and Growth* 3, 119–138.

Vihanto, M. (1992) 'Competition Between Local Governments as a Discovery Procedure', *Journal of Institutional and Theoretical Economics* 148(3), 411–436.

Voigt, S. (1993) 'Values, Norms, Institutions and the Prospects for Economic Growth in Central and Eastern Europe', *Journal des Economistes et des Etudes Humaines* 4(4), 495–529.

Voigt, S. (1998) 'Making Constitutions Work: Conditions for Maintaining the Rule of Law', *Cato Journal* 18(2), 191–208.

Voigt, S. (1999) *Explaining Constitutional Change: A Positive Economics Approach*, Cheltenham: Edward Elgar.

Wagner, R.E. (1980) 'Boom and Bust: The Political Economy of Economic Disorder', *Journal of Libertarian Studies* 4(1), 1–37.

Wagner, R.E. (1989a) 'Politics, Central Banking and Economic Order', *Critical Review* 3(3–4), 11–22.

Wagner, R.E. (1989b) *To Promote the General Welfare: Market Processes vs. Political Transfers*, San Francisco: Pacific Research Institute for Public Policy.

Wagner, R.E. (1998) 'Common Law, Statute Law and Economic Efficiency' in P. Newman (ed.), *The New Palgrave Dictionary of Economics and the Law*, Volume One, 313–317, New York: Stockton Press.

Weber, M. (1930) *The Protestant Ethic and the Spirit of Capitalism*, trans. Talcott Parsons, London: G. Allen & Unwin.

Weingast, B.R. (1995) 'The Economic Role of Political Institutions: Market-Preserving Federalism and Economic Development', *Journal of Law, Economics, & Organization* 11(1), 1–31.

Weingast, B.R. (1997) 'Political Foundations of Democracy and the Rule of Law', *American Political Science Review* 91(2), 245–263.

Weisz, J.R. (1990) 'Development of Control-Related Beliefs, Goals, Styles in Childhood and Adolescence: A Clinical Perspective', in J. Rodin *et al.* (eds), *Self-Directedness: Cause and Effects Throughout the Life Course*, Hillsdale, NJ: Lawrence Erlbaum Associates, 103–145.

Weisz, J.R. and Stipek, D.J. (1982) 'Competence, Contingency, and the Development of Perceived Control', *Human Development* 25, 250–281.

Weisz, J.R., Rothbaum, F.M. and Blackburn, T.C. (1984) 'Standing Out and Standing In: The Psychology of Control in America', *American Psychologist* 39(9), 955–969.

Wellmer, A. (1991) 'Models of Freedom in the Modern World', in M. Kelly (ed.), *Hermeneutics and Critical Theory in Ethics and Politics*, Cambridge, MA: MIT Press.

White, L.H. (1976) 'Entrepreneurship, Imagination, and the Question of Equilibrium', Unpublished paper.

White, L.H. (1978) 'Entrepreneurial Price Adjustment', Paper presented at the session on Entrepreneurship and Economic Activity at the Southern Economic Association meetings, Washington, DC, November.

White, L.H. (1984) *Free Banking in Britain: Theory, Experience, and Debate, 1800–1845*, Cambridge: Cambridge University Press.

Whiting, B.B. (1976) 'The Problem of the Packaged Variable', in K.F. Riegel and J.A. Meacham (eds), *The Developing Individual in a Changing World*, Hawthorne, NY: Aldine.

Whitman, D.G. (1998) 'Hayek contra Pangloss on Evolutionary Systems', *Constitutional Political Economy* 9(1), 45–66.

Wildt, A.R. and Ahtola, O.T. (1978) *Analysis of Covariance*, Beverly Hills, CA: Sage.

Williamson, O.E. (1979) 'Transaction Cost Economics: The Governance of Contractual Relations', *Journal of Law and Economics* 22(October), 233–261.

Williamson, O.E. (1985) *The Economic Institutions of Capitalism: Firms, Markets, Relational Contracting*, New York: The Free Press.

Williamson, O.E. (2000) 'The New Institutional Economics: Taking Stock, Looking Ahead', *Journal of Economic Literature* 38(3), 595–613.

Wolk, S. and DuCette, J. (1974) 'International Performance of Incidental Learning as a Function of Personality and Task Dimensions', *Journal of Personality and Social Psychology* 29(1), 90–101.

Wong, P.T.P. and Sproule, C.F. (1984) 'Attributional Analysis of Locus of Control and the Trent Attribution Profile (TAP)', in H.M. Lefcourt (ed.), *Research with the Locus of Control Construct*, Volume Three, 309–360, *Limitations and Extensions*, New York: Academic Press.

Wong, S. (1985) 'The Chinese Family Firm: A Model', *The British Journal of Sociology* 36(1), 58–72.

Wood, R. and Bandura, A. (1989) 'Social Cognitive Theory of Organizational Management', *Academy of Management Review* 14(3), 361–384.

Wright, L.M. (1982) 'A Comparative Survey of Economic Freedoms', in R.D. Gastil and C.R. Beitz, *Freedom in the World: Political Rights and Civil Liberties 1982*, Westport, CT: Greenwood Press, 51–90.

Yamaguchi, S. (1994) 'Collectivism Among the Japanese: A Perspective from the Self', in U. Kim *et al.* (eds), *Individualism and Collectivism: Theory, Method, and Applications*, Thousand Oaks, CA: Sage, 175–188.

Yang, K. (1988) 'Will Societal Modernization Eventually Eliminate Cross-Cultural Psychological Differences?', in M.H. Bond (ed.), *The Cross-Cultural Challenge to Social Psychology*, Newbury Park, CA: Sage, 67–85.

Yeager, L.B. (1997a) 'Austrian Economics, Neoclassicism, and the Market Test', *Journal of Economic Perspectives* 11(4), 153–165.

Yeager, L.B. (1997b) *The Fluttering Veil: Essays on Monetary Disequilibrium*, ed. G. Selgin, Indianapolis: Liberty Fund.

# Index